DIMENSIONS OF JAPAN

DIMENSIONS OF JAPAN A COLLECTION OF REPORTS WRITTEN FOR THE AMERICAN UNIVERSITIES FIELD STAFF ❁ ❁ ❁ ❁

by Lawrence Olson

AMERICAN UNIVERSITIES FIELD STAFF, INC.
366 MADISON AVENUE   NEW YORK 17, N.Y.

To Theodor Jaeckel
formerly of Kokura
for his help and example during the early years

CONTENTS

Preface   ix

1. Introduction   1

Part One LOCAL STUDIES

2. A Japanese Small Industry   13
3. The Kyoto Superintendent of Schools   34
4. In a Country Temple   44
5. Takehara: A Good Place to Be From   54
6. Mrs. Masuda and the *Buraku* People   64
7. "Mizuchō" in His District   78

Part Two NATIONAL ISSUES AND PROBLEMS

8. Four Family Budgets   91
9. Birth Control in Japan   112
10. Ethics, Yes, But Which Ethics?   123
11. How the Japanese Divorce   138
12. Pages From a Political Notebook   151
13. The Japanese Elections of 1958: Preview   167
14. The Japanese Elections of 1958: Outcome   178
15. The Police Bill Controversy   189
16. The Prince and the Politicians   199

17. A Japanese Marxist   203
18. Six Months After the Storm:
     The Japanese Elections of 1960   225
19. Atomic Crosscurrents in Japan   239
20. The Utopia of the Conservatives   249
21. Japan's Search for an Oil Policy   262

Part Three   JAPAN IN ASIA AND THE WORLD

22. On the "Orphan Japan"   283
23. The Japanese in India Today   290
24. Japanese Activities in Burma   312
25. The Politics of Flower Arrangement   325
26. "In Ten Years, in Fifty Years":
     Comments on China Trade   335
27. Japan and Korea: The Bitter Legacy   347
28. Okinawan Perspectives   361
29. Berlin from Japan   373

Part Four   THE NEW JAPAN

30. A Note on Japan   385

PREFACE

In a decade when, bemused by robot devices for processing and delivering data, we may forget the personal relationship between a sentient writer and his reader, Lawrence Olson, an author whose work is as felicitous in style as it is informative in detail, helps remind us that the sharing of intellectual experience goes beyond the collection and analysis of facts.

Mr. Olson, in this book of essays, proves himself to be one of the more sensitive and acute observers writing about Japan today. Without becoming an expatriate, he has shown it possible to communicate effectively despite cultural differences that make it difficult for most Westerners to understand the Japanese people and their nation.

His interpretation of the Japanese scene has been welcomed by readers whose interest in Japan is general rather than specific, as well as by those who themselves are specialists in Japanese studies or in one of the subjects Mr. Olson has chosen to investigate—whether it be industrial policy, politics, foreign affairs or population problems.

Dimensions of Japan does not set out to tell all there is to know about Japan; it has its own reason for deserving to be recognized as an important book about Japanese society in this postwar world. A genuinely creative work written out of firsthand experience by a thoughtful, informed observer, it is illuminating for the specialist, the person who is just starting to learn about Japan or the scholar who has given years to the study of that country and its people.

Readers familiar with Mr. Olson's Reports from Japan issued under the imprint of the American Universities Field Staff will be pleased to have them in book form for rereading and reference. Others will have the pleasure of discovering an author whose knowledge of his subject is equaled by his ability to give expression to it in the tradition of the essay form.

Teg C. Grondahl
Executive Director
American Universities Field Staff

New York, March 1963

CHAPTER *1*

INTRODUCTION

I went to Japan to live and work in January 1955. The American Occupation had been over for nearly three years and the main themes and patterns of the post-Occupation period were already well established. The productive economy, which lay smashed in 1945, had fully revived; the race to "catch up with the West" was on again, at least in the economic sense, and Japanese industry was on the verge of a prodigious new stage of growth. The conservative government ruled with a quasi-permanent majority and faced a humorless, heavily Marxist opposition, which had gone about as far as it could go without some internal change, but which seemed unable to change. Most leaders on both sides were bosses: conservatives had close connections in industry and government bureaus, while old Socialists and Communists were bureaucrats of the labor movement or intellectuals who had been enshrined in opposition for years, even decades.

Neither side trusted the other, and neither felt entirely comfortable in the new era of popular sovereignty, equality of the sexes, and other innovations introduced by foreigners and guaranteed by the foreign-sponsored Constitution. But although the tone of politics was harsh, it was not revolutionary. The new military had little power; labor was badly split; farmers were better off than ever, organizations of the far right and left disunited and ineffectual. For the foreseeable future the government would be dependent on America for economic and military support. These ties were accepted by most people as a more or less disagreeable necessity; but to many they were a positive danger, and the Socialists gained votes by attacking Japan's alignment with the West and pointing to the risk of annihilation in such a policy. They said less of the danger to Japan from the Communist bloc.

In the phoenixlike cities the new mood was reminiscent of Japan in the 1920's, except that more people had money and freedom of choice in more ways than they had then. They could not cease to be Japanese simply by losing a war, but what was "Japanese" to mean? Race, language, and a resilient ethic based on centuries of indoctrination helped to keep them different from other people; but two generations of increasingly repressive government controls had brought them and their nation to ruin, and symbols or men associated with the discredited past could not soon serve to rally the people to new national goals. Great chasms had opened in Japanese society during and after the war. On the role of the individual, as on the kind of government or Japan's role in world affairs, there was little consensus. National power and expansion had been replaced by an unreasoning desire for peace. Peace was the name of the most popular cigarette, of a sewing machine, and of other products; as one Japanese put it, peace had become the "mainstream of the national soul." In the long afterglow of Hiroshima and Nagasaki most Japanese were more concerned with making money and spending it for new things than with national problems or international struggles for which they denied responsibility. The age of mass communications had finally arrived: television went into mass production in the mid-1950's; bookstores were piled high with Japanese books and magazines as well as translations of Western works. In music, painting, the theater, sports, and other amusements the people could take their pick of their own traditional genres or Western imported forms. City life was jagged and uncomfortable; only the ability of people to close their ears to noise and their eyes to dazzling ugliness seemed somehow to preserve them.

In such an atmosphere of economic progress but political and social uncertainty I arrived to observe and report on developments. I was thirty-six, married, with two children. Behind me was a lifelong love for writing and an interest in Japan that dated from 1942. I had grown up in Mississippi, had taught in universities and worked in government agencies, played piano in a dance orchestra on ships between New York and Liverpool, studied literature at Harvard and Wisconsin, been a stack boy in the Library of Congress, published a volume of poems, spent three years as a Japanese Language Officer in the Navy, and earned a Ph.D. in Asian History and Languages at Harvard. Except for a weekend in 1952, I had never been in Japan and knew few Japanese.

My assignment in Japan was very broad. As an Associate of the American Universities Field Staff I was to settle in, read and study, talk with people, look, listen, and write reports on what I thought was important. I had no connection with any government agency, university, or other organization, Japanese or American, lived as a private foreigner dependent on the local economy, was identified in my passport as a writer. My audience consisted of subscribers to the AUFS Reports Service—at first mainly a few universities but later including American newspapers, magazines, government agencies, business firms, and public affairs groups as well as an increased number of educational institutions. Like my colleagues in other "non-Western" parts of the world, I was stationed in Japan to provide an independent flow of information and interpretation of the contemporary scene.

The present book is a selection of published AUFS Reports written during the first seven years of this continuing assignment. As the title indicates, the reader will find here some "dimensions" of present-day Japan, but he will not find a complete account of Japanese life and culture. For example, nothing bearing directly on literature, art, or music is included, nor have farming or fishing been described. These omissions are not necessarily due to my lack of interest but to a belief that economic, political, and social developments in the cities were of overriding importance and took first priority in my work. I hope in future visits to write about a variety of other topics.

Since many different subjects are covered, it may be well to give some idea of how I proceeded. From the first I conceived of my work in long-range terms. I did not have in mind becoming an expatriate—I expected to return to the United States periodically to give lectures—but saw the opportunity to write about Japan as a more or less permanent challenge. I was not sent to Japan to report the ebb and flow of short-term news. What interested me was process, how things operated, who put them together, and how they affected people individually and collectively. My aim was to select subjects which (a) were susceptible to accurate treatment in an article within a reasonably short time, say a month to six weeks, and (b) would lead to a greater understanding by the reader of areas of Japanese life considered important by the Japanese themselves. Often I tried to combine a historical training and interest in the evolution of modern Japan with a writer's natural desire to write about specific people. Much, of course, depended on what was available, especially in the early stages; when I knew my way around better I could be more selective.

I began in Kyoto, where we spent our first year in a Japanese house that served as home and office. (During my entire time in Japan I kept neither office nor staff.) There I experienced the cycle of enthusiasm and withdrawal common to foreigners in Japan. Like many Americans I wanted to know quickly about everything, was convinced everything had an answer and that some Japanese should take the time to give it to me. My initial meetings with Japanese professors, from whom I had expected so much, were stiff and disappointing. Partly this was because I chose to start at Kyoto University, a cold, difficult place even to other Japanese. Partly it was because I saw the wrong professors. My spoken Japanese left much to be desired. But some of my difficulties arose from deeper problems of identity. Businessmen, missionaries, diplomats, soldiers, newspapermen, Fulbright professors, all fit into separate niches in the Japanese mind; as long as each keeps to his niche he may find a considerable measure of ready-made acceptance. Things are different for the foreigner with a general interest in the country, who goes without invitation, works nowhere in particular, and may not wish to bind himself to any one professor, university, or other agency, but to keep free from cliques and range widely across the society, seeking answers and friends where he will. Such friends and answers can be found, of course; one should not push the difficulties of the generalist too far. Nevertheless, he is likely to be suspect. His horizontal mode of action in a vertical society is eccentric. How often he may be envious of those who can identify themselves without ambiguity!

In any case, instead of trying to force information from older professors who were uninterested in my empirical aims and who would not, in any event, be forced, I soon managed to meet enough younger scholars with whom I could communicate and who were ready to help me in my first research ventures. Through one of them I met the president of a small company and almost before I realized it was at work on my first substantial piece, a case study of a small industry. Here was a vital area of Japanese life which could be illuminated by placing one small group of people—the Motono establishment—in its own historical setting and reporting its current problems. To do this I had to rely like everybody else on Japanese co-operation and assistance; because of my ignorance this in turn led to some awkward situations, which I have described in an appendix to Chapter Two and included as an admonition to those pursuing similar projects.

Not all of the pieces would fall into such a clear-cut pattern, but especially in the grouping I have called "Local Studies" my method tended to be to look through an individual or a set of individuals to find the essence of some current issue of significance to the larger society. Thus, in "The Kyoto Superintendent of Schools" I tried to dramatize the problem of communism among schoolteachers by reporting how one official dealt with an uprising in his school system. "In a Country Temple" reported a week's stay in a Shin sect temple in Ishikawa prefecture, made possible by another young Japanese scholar, where my aim was to explore the role of a Buddhist priest in the economic and social life of his village community. In "Takehara: A Good Place to Be From" I took advantage of my friendship with a high-school principal—begun years before in the home of a missionary —to describe the process of mobility through the schools from the provinces upward to the center, a nationwide phenomenon. In the next piece, "Mrs. Masuda and the *Buraku* People," I merely let one survivor of the Hiroshima disaster speak for herself and relate her lifelong concern for a serious social problem that most Japanese have sought to conceal even from one another. In " 'Mizuchō' in His District" I tried to describe some of the methods of a local political boss while hoping at the same time not to lose the flavor of his own personal humor and humanity, which I had experienced during a rare weekend in Kyoto. In each of the above pieces I attempted to collect and use as much written material as I could, especially Japanese material, which I could read fairly easily from the beginning. But what made each subject really meaningful to me was the people I talked with, who provided whatever element of originality I was able to achieve.

After a year in Kyoto we moved to Tokyo. There I continued to work on local subjects from time to time (note that the table of contents is not arranged chronologically), but in the wider world of the capital I sought to move on to more explicitly national problems. By 1958 about two-thirds of my Reports had a national rather than a local focus; later the balance shifted even more markedly toward national or international subjects.

The largest category of pieces I have grouped together under the heading "National Issues and Problems." Here I sometimes clung to the personal approach, as in "Four Family Budgets," where instead of using questionnaires (I never used them) to gather a data sample I worked through friends to gain access to persons willing to co-operate with my research in their own homes. The results may have lacked the breadth of a "survey," but they had a more convincing immediacy. Many other topics, e.g., birth control, "moral education," or divorce, needed a broader expository treatment if all the essential facts were to get across to the reader; but all such subjects, no matter how they were finally written, required me to read and interview, to travel the railroads, go into offices, homes, and workplaces, take notes and gather materials and then retreat into my own part of whatever house we were living in at the time to bring order to the material and produce (one hoped) a reliable, readable essay. Nothing in this book was written off the top of my head. Like anybody else I fell into a work routine. Mine had four parts: the decision to work on a subject, collection, production and collapse, followed by a certain period of fermentation (perhaps sourness would be a better word) before the next decision was reached. Some choices, of course, proved abortive; but the great majority of projects embarked upon eventually were completed and printed as AUFS Reports.

In Tokyo in the late 1950's most foreign observers, like most Japanese, were absorbed with national politics, and I was no exception. The standoff of the two sides, conservatives and Socialists, was so fierce and had so many repercussions throughout the society that many thoughtful persons, Japanese and aliens alike, despaired of parliamentary government. The democratic optimism of the early postwar period was seen to have been naïve, left and right stood at each other's throats over domestic issues—proposed changes in the Constitution, wider powers for the police, authoritarian trends in education—while Japan's foreign alignments were used constantly to inflame the public, and negative radicalism of right and left was substituted for any more constructive national objectives. This period culminated in two crises, one domestic (the Miike strike), the other foreign (revision of the Japan-U.S. Mutual Security Treaty).

The central portion of this collection is a series of essays on political themes, approached from a number of angles. In "Pages From a Political Notebook" I reproduced entries from a journal kept early in my second period of residence in Tokyo, following a year in America. Here the sharp clash in politics was foreshadowed in a sequence of informal conversations with friends and others. This piece also throws a good deal of light on the way I went about settling in and taking hold again after an extended absence from the Japanese scene. Three other Reports in 1958 analyzed the general elections of that year and described in detail Prime Minister Kishi's bold but unsuccessful attempt to change the police laws. Early in 1959 I reported briefly on the Crown Prince's marriage to a commoner, a glamorous event that momentarily diverted the public from the grim realities of politics. The next two pieces were written after returning a third time from the United States. In the meantime the crisis had come in mid-1960, and I felt the necessity of exploring and recapitulating some of the elements within it. "A Japanese Marxist" describes the life and political activities of a famous professor of economics, now retired, who played a key role in the Miike coal-mine strike and in Socialist politics generally. In "Six Months After the Storm" I analyzed the general elections following the resignation of the Kishi government in the summer of 1960 and described the political mood as a new conservative regime took office under Prime Minister Ikeda.

With Ikeda Japan entered a new period of economic achievement. Political hostilities were not ended, but the left had been exhausted by the Miike strike and feelings of crisis had worked themselves out of the national blood for a time. The new government shrewdly sought to make the most of its own natural talents in the economic sphere. It encouraged a great new wave of investment to expand productive facilities and modernize the structure of the economy. In my last Reports in this section I discussed some major problems in the realm of energy supply and described the Ikeda cabinet's blueprint for economic progress in the decade ahead.

By this time my range of acquaintances was much broader than it had been in the early days in Kyoto and included journalists, commentators, businessmen, professional economists, Diet members and their secretaries, party headquarters staff workers, judges, government officials, and many others besides university professors. Though most of my relationships were with Japanese I also knew many Americans, British, Europeans, and Asians, some of them long-time residents of Japan and far more knowledgeable than I was about certain aspects of the life there. To a number of these I gave printed copies of my Reports and they came to understand what I was doing; as their trust in me increased they were more willing to pass me on to other sources of information.

As I wrote more and gained confidence in describing issues of national scope I began to turn to wider problems relating to Japan's role in Asia. Since the mid-1950's Japan had been paying war-damage reparations to Burma, Indonesia, South Viet Nam, and the Philippines. In 1958 Japanese interest in assisting India's economic plans had grown. Japan and Communist China were in a standoff; with no diplomatic ties and little trade their future relations were a mystery to Japanese and foreigners alike. In 1957–58 I did a study of Japanese-Indian relations as seen from Tokyo and wrote several pieces on the Philippines. None of these are included in the present volume. However, in the third section I have grouped together nine Reports on foreign relations.

The first of these, "On the 'Orphan Japan,'" is an abridged version of a young Japanese anthropologist's article on her own countrymen's ignorance of Asia, which appeared in a national magazine. This Report illustrates another tool, translation, which I used constantly in my work. The next three pieces were the product of a trip through South and Southeast Asia in the autumn of 1961. In six weeks in India I concentrated on the Japanese and their contribution in as many fields as I could cover; in shorter periods in Burma and the Philippines I collected materials, interviewed Japanese and local leaders, and summarized Japanese activities. "In Ten Years, in Fifty Years" gives a sample of Japanese attitudes toward Communist China as of the end of 1958. "Japan and Korea: The Bitter Legacy" describes the main obstacles to reconciliation between two countries that are close neighbors whether they like it or not. In "Okinawan Perspectives" I tried to present as much factual data as possible and interpret the Japanese-Okinawan-American triangle as I saw it during a two-week visit to the islands. The two pieces on Berlin at the end of this section represent an attempt to distill out some attitudes of a parochial, isolated people toward a world they fancy they never made but in which they must live and find a way. At the end of the book I have placed a general essay on Japan written in the spring of 1962. This was done in preparation for my return to the United States for a lecture tour; it may be read by itself but will be more meaningful if set against the other writings of the previous seven years.

* * *

Except for some small editorial changes and chronological rearrangements the material in this book has not been tampered with but appears exactly as printed in separate Report form. I owe a debt to literally hundreds of people who gave me help, but my obligation is particularly heavy to the following: Mr. and Mrs. Thomas L. Blakemore and the staff of Mr. Blakemore's law offices; Mr. and Mrs. Hidezō Inaba and the staff of the Research Institute for the People's Economy; Mr. and Mrs. Shigeharu Matsumoto and the staff of International House of Japan; Mr. and Mrs. Carl F. Bartz, Mr. Shimpei Fujimaki, Miss Naomi Fukuda, Mr. Robert Grant and the late Mrs. Jean Grant, Miss Haruko Hosono, Miss Mary Jones (formerly of Hiroshima), Mr. and Mrs. Yoshirō Kawashima, Mr. Kenkichi Konishi, Prof. and Mrs. Kiyomi Morioka, Miss Kimiko Okamura, Mr. Saburō Ōkita, Prof. and Mrs. Shōzō Ōmori, Mr. Ichirō Oshikawa, Mr. Sol Sanders, Judge and Mrs. Kōji Tanabe, Mr. Motohiko Toyama, Mr. Matsutarō Ueki, Prof. Shumpei Ueyama, Mr. Hiroshi Wagatsuma, and Miss Matsuyo Yamamoto (of the Asia Foundation).

I should like to thank Messrs. Phillips Talbot and Teg C. Grondahl for their constant support and encouragement, and Misses Jan Perlstin and Alice Shiller for their editorial forbearance and skill. Finally, I am grateful to my wife, Jeane, and our daughters, Alix and Sally, for the joy they brought to the adventure that we found in Japan.

L. O.

Manchester, Massachusetts
March 12, 1963

PART ONE ❀ ❀ ❀

LOCAL STUDIES

CHAPTER *2*

A JAPANESE SMALL INDUSTRY

October 10, 1955

Readers of the Japanese press lately have noticed a number of news stories and articles concerning the problems of "small and medium enterprise" (*chūshō kigyō*). Many figures have been quoted to show the significant position of small-scale industry in the economy and the distress recently felt by small entrepreneurs because of high costs, tight credit, export restrictions, heavy interest rates, and other difficulties.

Such reports, in themselves often fragmentary, touch on Japan's economic situation at a vital spot. They are witness to the fact that, despite government neglect and a drift to bigness in industrial enterprise, small concerns still display marked powers of survival. They also are symptomatic of a growing awareness, not only among businessmen, but among scholars and officials as well, of the importance of small industry to this country's total well-being and growth.

In the manufacturing field today, factories of fewer than 200 employees (the usual statistical dividing line) account for over 65 per cent of all workers and comprise over 95 per cent of all manufacturing plants, producing some 45 per cent of Japan's industrial output by value. There are, of course, many different types of small plants, but for the most part they fall into two categories. Most of the traditional Japanese home requirements and fancy items for the domestic market have always been made in small shops, which often were mere family enterprises. Foodstuffs, floor mats, sake, footwear, pottery, lacquer ware, special silks come under this head. Demand for these and many

13

similar products has tended to remain strong even in the face of foreign imports. For example, the family next door to my house in Kyoto is locally famous for the manufacture of *chimaki*, a kind of rice dumpling wrapped in bamboo leaf. Demand also has continued local and distinctive; one area wants only one type of pottery, special food, or other product. Tastes have remained peculiar, perpetuating small shops which deal in specialized goods.

Alongside these old trades, with which anyone living in Japan soon becomes familiar, new enterprises grew up in the Meiji period, producing bicycle parts, electric light bulbs, Western-type toys, metal machine parts, woven and knit textiles, and innumerable other products introduced under Western influence. Many of these establishments soon were exporting a substantial percentage of their output. Before World War II, "Japan's principal exports of manufactures, except for raw silk, cotton yarn, and sugar, were the products of medium and small factories." [1] Today such export items as toys, pigments, umbrellas, fishing rods, imitation pearls, silk and rayon fabrics, pencils, binoculars, and telescopes are manufactured almost exclusively in small- and medium-sized shops. Furthermore, as will be seen below, many products of large enterprises are made in part or in entirety by smaller shops.

Small industry thus persisted and for various reasons remained small. Capital was scarce, and small entrepreneurs could get started without large capital investment. Japan was never a colony, and as national security grew in the Meiji period the incentive to go into business grew also. Business investment acquired social prestige, just as land ownership did in countries like the Philippines. Mass education produced near-universal literacy, facilitating the rapid diffusion of new mechanical and technical skills throughout the country. In small, mountainous Japan, hydroelectric output rapidly expanded. Factories could be located cheaply near power supply, and a serviceable rail network provided distribution facilities. Thus an important segment of Japanese industry today still operates with small increments of capital and uses family or quasi-family labor to produce not only for the domestic market but also for export around the world.

[1] Lockwood, W. W., *The Economic Development of Japan.* (Princeton, N.J., 1954), p. 206. A basic source on the subject of small industries is still the late Teijirō Uyeda's *The Small Industries of Japan* (New York, 1938). See also *The Smaller Industry of Japan*, Society for Economic Cooperation in Asia (Tokyo, 1954).

In this Report I have attempted to describe a small Kyoto manufacturing enterprise insofar as I have been able to observe and understand it. My objective has been not to write an exhaustive economic treatise but (1) to see the enterprise in terms of its own past, (2) to suggest the management's outlook in human terms, and (3) to bring out, if possible, some of the qualities which strike me as most impressive among small businessmen, and all Japanese businessmen, today.

Material on the enterprise was gathered in interviews with its owners and operators and in visits to its workshops over a period of three months. However, the total number of visits was not large. Although voluble enough where past history is concerned, small management is, on the whole, reticent in replies to outside inquiry about the present. This is due partly to a tight family organization which is diffident toward outside scrutiny, and partly to worries over business problems and a consequent reluctance to spend much time answering questions. Visits to numerous similar enterprises in Osaka, Sakai, and neighboring towns filled some gaps. Interviews with neighbors, friends of the management, and professors who teach in universities in Kyoto, Tokyo, and Osaka also provided helpful data.

* * *

In the early years of the Meiji era, around 1880, a rice merchant named Teiyu Motono moved to Kyoto from a town on the shores of nearby Lake Biwa. Motono set up his house and shop among other small merchants on Muromachi in the northwestern quarter of this city, and for some years his son, Tōjirō, assisted him in the business. However, to young men like Tōjirō, the period presented many opportunities more challenging than selling rice. Wholesale borrowing from the West was changing Japanese life in many fields, and being of inquisitive mind, Tōjirō decided to learn a trade with a future. He became interested in iron forging, and in 1894, during the industrial expansion that came out of the war with China, he traveled to Osaka against the wishes of his parents to learn the ironworking business. As soon as his objective had been accomplished he returned to Kyoto, where he remained for the rest of his long life.

For a time Tōjirō hired himself out, working in firms making medical and scientific instruments, and finally in a textile machinery plant. This last may have been a deliberate choice, because the Japanese textile industry was undergoing a great expansion in the late 1890's, and machines for both spinning and weaving were in great demand. After some years of working for other people, Tōjirō had saved a few hundred yen, and in 1905, during the Russo-Japanese War, he founded his own shop for the "repair and manufacture of French-style thread-

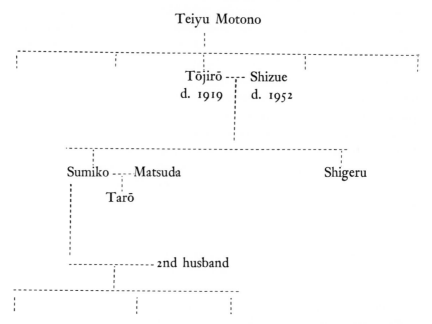

GENEALOGY OF MOTONO FAMILY

Teiyu Motono

Tōjirō --,-- Shizue
d. 1919 ¦ d. 1952

Sumiko --,--Matsuda   Shigeru
Tarō

-----------2nd husband

twisting machines" on Marutamachi in the central part of Kyoto. At first there were three hired workers and no electricity: all the tools were man-driven. To become an entrepreneur Tōjirō exhausted his savings and went 200 yen in debt.

The preserved record of Tōjirō's career is little more than a bare chronicle, but fortunately he was joined in the shop in 1908 by Junnosuke Hara, at that time a young man of twenty-odd years. Hara became Tōjirō's close business associate and long-time survivor, and through conversations with him I have been able to reconstruct something of the personality of Tōjirō Motono.

Although he got no farther than elementary school, Tōjirō had a fertile imagination. He seems always to have been interested in inventing things, and as he grew older he accumulated a half-dozen or more patents. However, he had little money sense. In 1907, on order of a Chinese merchant, he invented a firecracker machine and made firecrackers for three or four years as a side line. But in the end he was swindled by the Japanese middleman and lost everything he had put into the venture. Later he became worried by the shortage of electric power and the high power rates in Kyoto and attempted to invent a perpetual-motion machine, drawings of which still are in existence.

Tōjirō never invested in other enterprises or in real estate but freely used the money he made in business to develop his numerous inventions. As a result he never accumulated much wealth. He did live, however, long enough to see his textile-machine business prosper during World War I. During that war "the dazzling world demand for Japanese goods and services had effects within the country which might be expected. Money incomes rose, note issue and bank credit expanded. Industry and trade embarked on a period of unprecedented prosperity." [2] With Japanese textiles winning new markets in India and Southeast Asia, Tōjirō found himself swamped with orders for machines, and now for the first time he also made other equipment for the textile trade. Even his notorious improvidence was insufficient to prevent profits from piling up.

Tōjirō's career illustrates certain features of the industrialization process in modern Japan. To begin with, he came from a *Kansai* small-merchant family with a history reaching far back into the Tokugawa era. Like other small merchants, his father had little capital. But Tōjirō was vigorous and diligent, and he loved machinery. "Technical know-how" came easily to him, as it did to hundreds of other young men scattered over the Japanese islands. After he had learned his trade in an Osaka iron mill, he was forced to become a wageworker for a while. But at the earliest possible moment he set up as a small entrepreneur. Characteristically, he supplied a nearby demand: for years his best customer was the Japan Twisted Thread Company of Kyoto. While the Meiji government was giving aid and comfort to large heavy industries and encouraging the formation of great trading combines, Tōjirō and his fellows, with cheap help, mechanical dexterity, and shoestring capital, were founding innumerable small establishments, the *chūshō kigyō* of modern Japan. By World War I, 94.9 per cent of all privately

[2] Lockwood, *op. cit.*, p. 39.

owned factories in Japan were establishments of fewer than 100 employees; 45.8 cent had fewer than ten employees.[3]

On July 3, 1919, before the war boom had collapsed, Tōjirō died. He left his widow, Shizue; a daughter, Sumiko, of perhaps twenty; and a son, Shigeru, of about ten. Over the years since Junnosuke Hara had joined the firm, Tōjirō had come to repose confidence in him, and on the latter's death the firm continued (as it were, in trust) under Hara's actual direction, although Tōjirō's widow continued to have a financial interest until her death at an extreme age in 1952. Someone had to take charge until Shigeru should come of age, and Hara was the logical choice.

Tōjirō's death had little immediate effect on the business of the shop. By that time he had developed the trust of a small group of customers in the Kyoto-Osaka-Kobe area. With these textile-mill owners, and with others in Nagoya, Hara was able to continue orders as before. However, within a year of Tōjirō's death the world-wide boom began to collapse; business turned bad, and Japan entered a long period of financial instability. The normal troubles of this period of deflation and readjustment were deepened by the great Tokyo earthquake of 1923.

Hara still remembers this event and recalls bitterly the depression it brought. Machinery orders ceased for a time, but Hara responded to this crisis in a manner Tōjirō would have approved. Instead of closing down the shop, he set about improving the twisting machine. After a number of unsuccessful experiments, he perfected a counting device which, when attached to the machine, would regulate the thickness and evenness of the thread. As soon as this was offered to the market, orders rapidly picked up. Many orders now came from the area of Kanazawa on the Japan Sea, an important center of high-grade export silk fabrics. According to Hara's account, up to this time twisted thread had not been used in the manufacture of *habutae*, or glossy silk, but now Hara's new standardized machines found a ready market, and through his contacts with Kanazawa merchants he was able to expand the shop's operations. Customers in Kanazawa urged him to move there, but like Tōjirō, he was attached to Kyoto. "To go elsewhere would have been bad for the business."

From this point the record of the Motono Company proceeds with-

[3] Lockwood, *op. cit.*, p. 202.

out notable event until a few months after the Japanese invasion of North China and the outbreak of the "China Incident" in July 1937. In October of that year an entry in the company history reveals that Hara became a subcontractor of Kyoto's Shimazu Manufacturing Company "under orders of the government to manufacture mining machinery." Thereafter the drift to militarization of the economy gathered speed. In January 1940 the company switched production from mining machinery to airplane dismantling gear. During the Pacific War it made a variety of military items, including shell casings. In March 1945 it was placed directly under the Munitions Bureau. Hara freely expressed to me his pride in the shop's record of loyalty to Japan's cause during World War II. Thus even after Tōjirō's death the company's fortunes followed the ups and downs of the Japanese economy through peace and war.

When he reached maturity Shigeru Motono did not take over his father's business. Tōjirō's eldest child, the girl Sumiko, married a man named Matsuda soon after her father's death. They had a son, Tarō Matsuda, who is now about thirty-five; and it is this Tarō, Tōjirō's grandson, who went into the business and is today the president of the Motono Company. Tarō, however, labors under a considerable cloud, because his mother had the misfortune to be deserted by her husband. She eventually divorced him and remarried, but the stigma of the divorce still plagues the family, and Tarō more or less stays in the background. Naturally he is overshadowed by the patriarchal figure of Hara, who, although he is not a tyrant, nevertheless wields the real power in the shop. As a close friend of the family smilingly told me, "Hara is Hatoyama [the Prime Minister] and Tarō is the Emperor."

The Motono Company now operates on a back street in the Nishijin silk-weaving district in northern Kyoto. Its full name is Motono Machine Manufacturing Co., Limited (*Yūgengaisha Motono Kikai Seisakujo*). It employs 15 workers and has been in its present location since shortly after Tōjirō's death. The shop still produces a variant of the original thread-twisting machine, but Hara has long since adapted it to the Osaka market for elastic core thread—rayon thread wound around a rubber center for use in stockings, underwear, and elastic materials of many sorts.

Organization of the company is simple. Tarō Matsuda keeps his own books, and Hara directly oversees production. There are no de-

partments and a minimum of bureaucracy. All raw materials are supplied by Kyoto firms, and the machines are fabricated on order from
long-established customers and personal contacts. Since the war the
company has performed no subcontract work. However, when orders
lag Hara makes parts for Shigeru's business (see below).

Working conditions in this shop are as poor as any I have seen in
Japan. There are only two rooms, a production room about 25' x 40'
and a smaller machine-testing room. In the production room workers
stand on the damp littered dirt floor beside their lathes, drills, etc.,
most of which are prewar Japanese-made models. The only light available comes from a few weak drop bulbs and one small hole in the
ceiling. The room has no windows, and there is no place to sit down
in the whole establishment. The wooden slab walls are adorned with
a few old "safety first" posters. The shop office is in a small house
nearby where one tiny Japanese-style room is used for reception of
visitors. Here one sees faded photographs of the Shōwa Emperor and
Empress and of Tōjirō and his wife, he in formal Western dress, she
in kimono.

Although the Motono shop has a longer history and undoubtedly
rests on a firmer foundation than many such concerns, to the eye it is
indistinguishable from literally thousands of small enterprises concentrated in the Kyoto-Osaka area. Hara presides over the establishment, as a distinctly paternalistic figure who looks rather like a character in a Hiroshige color print. At sixty-two he is bald, with a grizzled
beard, a cast in one eye, and two front teeth full of gold and silver.
He greets visitors in a filthy BVD undershirt, blue serge trousers, and
a grimy brown coat, and chain-smokes *Hikari* cigarettes while rem-
iniscing about Tōjirō and their early days together in the shop. Hara
is a likable figure, but one cannot fail to realize that he insists on being
the only channel of information about the company; he discourages
direct contact with the employees and frowns on the taking of photographs.

All 15 employees—13 men and 2 women—live in Kyoto or its
environs, but except for Hara and Tarō Matsuda there are no lodging
facilities in the shop itself. One-half of workers' transportation costs
are paid as a commuting allowance, a practice common in Japanese
industry. The legal work week is 48 hours, with Sundays off, but overtime is common. Time-and-a-fifth is paid for overtime until 10 P.M.,

time-and-a-half after 10 P.M. On one occasion when I left the premises at about 10:30 P.M. two men were still operating lathes. There is no shift work. The basic daily wage, exclusive of allowances, ranges from Y200 (US $.55) a day for "beginners learning the trade" to Y500 (US $1.38) a day for "top skills." There is no incentive pay, but fractional pay increases are granted each year. Bonuses of approximately one month's pay are paid at *O-Bon*, the Buddhist festival of the dead in August, and at the New Year.

Like most such small concerns, the shop has no labor union. As Hara explained to me, "We work as a family here." This concept naturally carries with it job security so long as the business itself goes on. Within Hara's memory only one person has ever been fired, and he was a thief. Length of service ranges from 25 years (one man) to one year (one man). But the average length of service is only three or four years. Most of the men workers are second or third sons, who are part of the stream of migrant labor moving from farm to city. Some of them find jobs in shops like Motono's on their arrival from the country, but after a few years they often move on to larger factories, where salaries are higher and working conditions better.

On the whole, Hara's attitude toward his employees is paternalistic and old-fashioned. Newfangled terms like "human relations" and "personnel management" mean nothing to him. He is sure of the rightness of his own "human relations" and incurious about any other system. Just as the visible appearance of the shop cannot have changed much over the years, so Hara's relationship to his men has remained essentially undisturbed. New labor-standards laws and such modern innovations have not made much difference in the operation of the shop. As he confessed frankly to me, "The only way to make a living is to work long hours. Everybody knows that." Workers are likely to realize that their own future is tied up with the future of the business, regardless of the abstract desirability of some law or other.

Of course, some invisible changes have occurred and are slowly occurring today. Most new workers still are recruited through personal contacts or kin, but the public employment office (*shokugyō anteisho*) is assuming more importance. During the present deflationary phase, one often sees crowds of young people, many of them in students' uniforms, examining the want ads posted at the neighborhood employment office. Resistance of employers to unknown applicants is high among tiny establishments like Motono's; yet even here, though Hara gives no figures, he is using the public employment system to replace labor. At the moment turnover is slight, but if it increases in the future he will probably turn to the public office for help.

Another sign of slow change is Hara's admission that educational level is beginning to have some relationship to the wage scale. Before the war workers customarily were primary-school graduates. Now 11 of his 15 employees have had only a primary-school education (prewar system), but two are graduates of middle school (prewar), one graduated from a postwar high school, and one is going to night school at a local university, much to the admiration of his fellows. The arrival on the job last year of the high-school graduate disturbed Hara's thinking about wages; since then he claims that he and Matsuda "have been giving thought to educational qualifications." No concrete wage differential has yet resulted, but with more high-school graduates seeking jobs, level of education may become a criterion for wage determination in the Motono shop.

Readers of this Report probably are wondering what the employees themselves think of the shop in which they work, what their attitudes are toward labor unions, toward their own future and that of their children. Due to the reluctance of Hara and Matsuda to permit direct questioning of workers and the impossibility of using a questionnaire approach, I have been unable to collect much systematic material on their workers' attitudes. Answers to the few questions I asked were perfunctory and clearly indicated fear of the employee to express himself freely.

However, I have been able to use results of recent research by the Osaka Prefectural Economic Research Bureau, a government-subsidized agency where teams of Japanese observers for several years have been conducting opinion surveys. Methods used in these surveys do not measure up to the objective standards used in the United States and are unsatisfactory in other respects. However, workers interviewed closely resemble Hara's own employees, and it may be useful in understanding the small factory to translate a few recent findings. In the publication, *Actual Living Conditions of Workers in Medium and Small Industry* (*Chūshō Kōgyō Rōdōsha no Seikatsu Jittai*), published in July 1955, results are presented of interviews with 193 workers in 14 workshops manufacturing four different kinds of products: textile machinery, glass, cotton piece goods, and bicycle parts. I quote from the section entitled "Job Consciousness":

First we asked, "With your present skills do you think you will be able to maintain yourself in the future?" Yes: 40%. No: 17%. Don't know: 43%. The percentage of those who said "Yes" was highest in the field of textile machinery.

"Do you wish to continue working in your present job?" "For the time being": 38%. "As long as the business lasts": 32%. "If there were a good place to move to I would move": 23%. 7% had other assorted answers. The percentage of workers who wish to sink or swim with the enterprise was unexpectedly large. . . . They were mostly found in paternalistic establishments and were mostly men of rural origin over 25 years old.

In cases where there were labor unions we inquired about present attitudes toward the union. "Are you satisfied with the present activities of the union?" Yes: 51%. No: 23%. Don't know: 26%. Most of those who showed little interest had less than nine years of schooling, were single men of rural origin, and either had not worked in a shop before or had worked in only one sort of shop.

In shops where there was no union, we asked, "Do you think a union is necessary?" Yes: 57.5%. No: 22.2%. Don't know: 20.3%.

From the above we can see that skilled workers have a fair amount of confidence in their own skill, but taking them all together, they show little confidence in their job, and merely stay in it because they have little choice. While some have no interest in unions, the general level of consciousness on this subject is rather high.

"Do you want your children to continue in your same work?" Yes: 2.5%. No: 60%. Don't know: 37.5%.

* * *

In order to complete my description of the Motono establishment, it is now necessary to return and pick up the career of Shigeru Motono, Tōjirō's only son. As mentioned above, he did not go into his father's business. Shigeru's early life is obscure, and he is not free with details. He went through higher school (*kōtōgakkō*) in Kyoto, and his relationship with Hara during this time must have been close, for he told me that he regards Hara as his own father. For a time Shigeru worked at various jobs, and in the early 1930's he was employed as a cameraman in a local movie studio. However, he did not stay at this for long. Like his father he was interested in mechanical things and had an inventive streak, and just before the war he opened his own textile-machinery manufacturing business in buildings adjacent to the original Motono factory.

For a description of a single small industry it would be sufficient to stop with Hara's workshop. But Shigeru's business is closely connected with Hara's in a web of family relationships and obligations. Neither is complete without the other, and the relationship between the two needs to be clearly explained.

Expressed in Japanese terms, Shigeru feels *on* toward Hara, i.e., he is placed under an endless obligation to Hara for the latter's role in helping to bring him up and take care of his widowed mother after Tōjirō died. It is important to realize that Shigeru feels this obligation very strongly. He himself told me that he owes everything he is to Hara, that Hara has taught him everything he knows.

In Japanese terms, then, Hara's shop, the original Motono company, is the parent organization and Shigeru's business is the child. In actual fact the two businesses are separate financial entities; however, Shigeru's requirements tide Hara's men over slack periods, and Shigeru has an obligation to see that this is done, that Hara does not go under, even though he might buy parts more cheaply elsewhere. His relationship to Hara thus has a direct bearing on the efficiency of his own operation.

Shigeru's business is somewhat larger than Hara's, with a different organization and different problems. Shigeru employs 85 men. He manufactures loom accessories and one type of preparatory textile machine called a "reaching-in" machine. This is an electrically driven, man-operated machine which prepares yarn for placing on the weaving loom. Shigeru holds a patent on one variant of this machine as well as on a "yard meter" which measures loom production and a "pick counter" which calculates the number of "picks" or weft threads in woven fabric.

Production capacity of the small counting machines is over 1,000 each per month, but ordinary production is well under this figure. Shigeru produces anywhere from 30 to 100 reaching-in machines each month, about 40 per cent of which are exported to Pakistan, India, and Indonesia. His export business is mainly handled through a large trading company, *Dai Ichi Bussan* (now part of *Shin Mitsui Bussan*); however, Shigeru himself made a trip to Pakistan three years ago to look over market prospects. He is mum about what orders he receives, but today he is actively seeking to expand his export business wherever he can find customers.

Shigeru's factory has five departments: Construction (Production), 64 men; Accounting, 6; Sales, 5; Design, 7; Warehousing, 3. Except for a girl or two in the office, all employees are male. Unlike Hara's shop, which serves an old, established clientele, Shigeru maintains a five-man sales force, including two men in Tokyo, one in Nagoya, and two in the Osaka area. His raw materials—mainly cast iron, bar steel, brass, and aluminum—he gets in Kyoto and Osaka and transports to the shop in his own little three-wheeled truck. Actually the Design Department is engaged much of the time in buying. One group buys iron and steel, another buys bolts, nuts, wood, mortar, and such miscellaneous small parts, for which Shigeru sometimes subcontracts with smaller Kyoto firms and sometimes uses Hara's shop.

Shigeru's men work in five rambling wooden sheds which are connected by tin-roofed galleries. His forge and large machines are housed in one fairly large building. Working conditions are no better than in the smaller shop. Lighting is very poor, and aside from a few Japanese and American pin-ups and a bit more space, there is nothing to distinguish this from Hara's workroom. Here the basic parts are fabricated and shaped. Next door are plating and painting rooms, where Shigeru proudly displays his gas-fueled paint-baking oven, about six feet long and the "largest of its kind in Kyoto." In the polishing room workers wear dirty towels around their mouths and hair. Their clothing is often inadequate, and one or two men still wear their old black school uniforms. Parts of the finished machines are brought to one end of the main building and placed on rice-straw mats awaiting assembly. Upstairs above the painting room, five or six workers under a section chief are engaged in making the carriage mechanism for the reaching-in machine. Here there is light and a quieter atmosphere, but for the most part conditions seem unhealthy, machinery and buildings antiquated.

If you ask Shigeru and his fellows how business is, they will tell you that times are bad. Costs are high, equipment old, and competition ruthless. Shigeru is waging a terrific fight to keep his head above water. Since early 1954 credit has been tight, and interest rates on loans to small business are higher than on loans to larger firms or big-name concerns like Mitsubishi, Mitsui, or Sumitomo. In recent months many small businesses have defaulted on their obligations and gone bankrupt. Among small enterprises there is a widespread feeling that the big companies run few risks and get the lion's share of the profits. As one small import-exporter told me, "If a new line becomes popular, either at home or overseas, the big companies move in on it. They wine and dine visiting buyers. We little fellows have to take the crumbs. We even have gone to Nagoya to grab visitors off the Osaka-bound train because we can't afford to give them big geisha parties in Kyoto and Nara. The big companies are merging with government encouragement, and they are tied in with the politicians as always."

Shigeru himself has many complaints, but he also realizes that there are certain advantages in selling through a large trading company which has representatives overseas and a widespread organization skilled in locating the market. Furthermore, Shigeru knows that he is much luckier than many small operators in not being bound to a subcontracting relationship with larger firms.

Under the subcontracting (*shitauke*) system, larger parent companies (*oyagaisha*) take advantage of cheap labor in small shops to obtain many parts or processes which they require. In slack times subcontract unit prices fall, and large plants may withhold orders to their subcontractors and sometimes delay payment for deliveries for as long as six months or more. An example is the auto-parts industry. Mostly concentrated in the *Kantō* area, more than 300 small workshops are engaged in the manufacture of auto parts. About 16 per cent of them are capitalized at $14,000 or more, 40 per cent at less than $3,000. Eighty per cent employ fewer than 200 workers and 35 per cent fewer than 30 workers. They produce parts to fit Japanese-made cars as well as some foreign cars, e.g., Ford, Chevrolet, or Dodge. Each of the six leading Japanese chassis manufacturers has many, perhaps more than a hundred, subcontractors associated with him. Some of these small plants, particularly those making high-precision parts like piston rings, spark plugs, and generators, are as well established as the chassis makers. But suppliers of parts like horns, fuel tanks, and door handles are often very precariously based. Even when they are organized, as they usually are, into co-operative societies, they must turn in bad times to making other products to keep alive. For example, auto-parts factories may also make textile-machine accessories, sewing-machine parts, household utensils, or office appliances.

Shigeru has remained relatively independent, but his business problems have made him touchy, suspicious of questions from outsiders. In name his company, Motono Manufacturing Co., is a joint-stock company (*Kabushikikaisha Motono Seisakujo*); actually he owns all the stock. The company is capitalized at three million yen (about US $10,000). Monthly sales average six to seven million yen. Raw materials cost about three million yen a month. Monthly wages total about 850,000 yen to factory workers, 500,000 to office staff, including sales force and designers. Monthly overhead costs reach nearly one and one-half million yen. Additional costs include advertising: printing of brochures, ads in trade journals, exhibits at trade fairs, catalogues. Unknown sums go for business entertainment, including geisha parties for important customers or prospects, and company parties and outings. As Shigeru says, the only way he can keep ahead of his creditors is by driving his employees harder. "Unless profits reach ten per cent, I cannot improve the conditions of the workers." Overtime in his shop averages 13 hours per worker per week.

Shigeru Motono is a proud, sensitive man who inherited his father's mechanical inventiveness but not his financial ineptitude. Shigeru is a shrewd business operator with strong views about how to run his business. He is well assisted by his wife, a women's college graduate with a strong, almost a harsh, character. The two of them are openly against the idea of a labor union in their factory. "Everybody here should go in the same direction," says Shigeru, echoing Hara's paternalistic sentiments.

Shigeru's vigor, ingenuity, and the comfortable way he fits into the familylike hierarchy of the factory all are clear when one watches him stroll through the place. As he walks from room to room, asking a question here and there, agreeably smiling, stepping in to lend a hand with a part that is not operating smoothly or bending over to look at a blueprint, Shigeru presents a striking image of "know-how" and definite purpose. One cannot help contrasting his positive sureness on his own ground with the indecision, vagueness, introversion or bluff of many Japanese intellectuals—the writers of autobiographical novels, professors, students, and the like. Shigeru's strength is the strength and canniness of the small entrepreneur, and the traditions of the *chōnin* merchant class of Tokugawa times survive in him. Despite war and occupation, to a remarkable degree he carries within him the attitudes and qualities of his father, of Hara, of Teiyu, his rice-merchant grand-father, and earlier merchant forebears. One recognizes in him a high survival value for an important stream of traditional Japanese culture.

Such attempts as this to describe the operation of one small industry in Japan always impress me anew with the great diversity of the subject, the multiplicity of organizational forms, and the variety of productive enterprises. There is no question that many small businesses go under; neither is there any doubt that working conditions are bad and paternalism still a prevalent state of mind among employers and employees alike. But when I visit small businessmen around Kyoto or Osaka today and talk with them or look over their establishments, I am most impressed with their enduring vitality and ingenuity in spite of their fierce problems. A small concern may fail, but often it starts again under another name. It does not occur to the bankrupt to move to the country to try farming or even to leave their home areas. Often they just stay put and draw unemployment insurance for a while (six months' worth is available) or borrow a little capital from relatives to start another business.

Many of them are full of complaints, but when it comes to action they have ideas, and they go to some lengths to get business, e.g., diverting buyers in Nagoya before they can reach their destination in Osaka. They are very actively seeking to increase exports, and recent figures indicate they are having at least temporary success. Almost without exception, those with whom I have talked want to open trade with Red China. As one shop manager told me, the China market would be a "godsend" to little fellows like himself. They are so convinced that China trade would solve all their problems that they often do not stop to consider seriously how the composition of such trade might have changed from the prewar situation.

This, then, is the present situation of Shigeru Motono and his fellows, who occupy a vital position in the Japanese economy. Before the war Japanese business performed prodigious feats of modernization:

Combining as they did the factory, the railway, and the battleship, power machinery and modern chemistry, the joint-stock principle and the world-wide market, they opened up revolutionary opportunities to expand national power and to reap personal rewards . . . the opportunities at hand were reinforced and made effective by a new framework of national security, political ambition, and credit expansion. In this climate of incentives, innovation and imitation worked with cumulative effect to enlarge the country's capital stock and improve its efficiency—albeit very unevenly in various sectors of economic life. . . .[4]

This was the prewar picture, now of course greatly changed. The battleship and much else are gone; but of one quality, I am convinced plenty remains. This is compounded of personal ambition, energy, and ingenuity and is found nowhere more than on the level of small entrepreneurs like Shigeru Motono. Politically and socially conservative, Shigeru wants the Western standard of living, but he wants it on Japanese terms. It would be incorrect to say that he and his fellows have become "democratized." But, given a period of international peace and expanding economic and political trust, the drive behind the Motonos of Kyoto, Osaka, and the rest of Japan may find realization without danger of distortion. Equal education, more objective employment methods, rationalization, wider credit, increased exports—all these may combine, in a period of peace, to produce positive, though Japanese, results. But change in the small workshops is a slow process, and the loyalties engendered there, like the distrusts, will not be quick to dissolve.

September 28, 1958

Several years ago, when I was living in Kyoto, I met through an intermediary the owner of a small textile-machinery manufacturing plant, a man of about fifty. Our first conversation took place in his office, but after he accepted my suggestion that I return we met three more times in the evening at his home next door to the factory.

These meetings were stiff, awkward affairs. I had not been in Japan very long or established relationships with very many Japanese. Kyoto people had a reputation even among Japanese for their arrogant attitudes; with foreigners they were polite so long as one was admiring something about Japan or about themselves, but often ungenerous where dispensing useful information was concerned. At Kyoto University I had found a cold intellectual and social climate. I had just come from studying Japanese history for several years at an American university and was baffled by the indifference to this fact among my

[4] Lockwood, *op. cit.*, p. 268.

imagined peers in Japanese universities. Most of them couldn't have cared less.

Several other people always were present in my meetings with the businessman: on his side his wife and nephew, and on mine (or, rather, between us) the person who had introduced us, a friend of a friend, who gave me some sense of support. The room was uncomfortable. We sat in low, heavy chairs placed in a rigid square around a table, which was too low to get my legs under and too far away to push my knees against, a setup I was to discover infinitely repeated in homes and offices throughout this country.

Seeing a chance to learn rapidly about a portion of Japanese life that I knew few foreigners understood, I pushed forward my questions into every aspect of the business that I could think of. By myself or through the go-between I asked about raw-materials supply, production problems, wages and employee welfare, and other phases of the history and management of the enterprise. These questions came pouring from me without much understanding of what their effect might be, but in my host's cautious replies, and in the eyes of the other people around the table, I could sense the precariousness of the situation. His suspicions increased as my questions became more detailed and their significance to him grew vaguer. We had met through proper introductions, but he seemed unable to understand who I was or what I represented. The American Universities Field Staff meant nothing to him, nor could it be explained in any meaningful way. The phrase "field staff" itself was untranslatable in Japanese except as a military term, and universities do not behave in such a manner in this country. I thought that I convinced him that I was not connected with the U.S. government, but I couldn't be sure. The Occupation had recently ended, and many Americans were apt to be regarded by strangers as soldiers in civilian clothes. I had not yet learned how to explain myself to a society that expected me to be one of a few things and nothing else.

My host's manner was restrained but polite, and toward the close of an interview he would sometimes relax a bit so that the tension in the ugly little room would subside. This was generally the sign that the interview was ending; but on the third night my need to know pushed me past this signal and I innocently asked a question about taxes. He smiled but did not reply; somebody changed the subject, and in a few minutes I excused myself and left. He went to the door with me and spoke the usual words; there was, of course, no open break, but a few days later when I asked for another appointment he sent back word that he was busy. The frail relationship seemed to have been abandoned by all concerned, and I did not see him or the go-between again. Later I wrote a Report based on the data I had gathered which now comprises the first part of this chapter in which I certainly did not mention taxes and in which all the names were carefully faked. The article was sympathetic to the businessman and his problems, but because the experience had been embarrassing and I had not known how to resolve it, I did not send him a copy. Soon I became absorbed in other matters and the interrupted relationship was left up in the air.

Recently, thinking that I might renew my acquaintance with the businessman, I wrote to the former go-between and suggested a meeting during a forthcoming trip to western Japan. A few days ago I received his reply, which, translated, is as follows:

"I have received your letter. I am busy on the——and can't go with you, but I will inquire about what is convenient for M. However, before I do that, there is something I want you to understand.

"If you wrote anything—an article, or a book—from the material of your earlier interviews, please give copies of them to him on your next visit. In Japan it is customary, when someone has done you a favor such as M. did, to send a gift in return. Then, when you returned from America the second time, you should have sent him a letter immediately, informing him of that fact. On these points I feel a great spiritual obligation toward M. and his younger brother (who at that time was living in my house) for having introduced him to you. I think you know very well that the time is past and gone when Americans were welcomed gladly without any conditions. Students and academic people may get some profit from having relationships with you, but this is not the case with M., who is engaged in productive activities and must consume his precious time. Whatever you do, you must use discretion in asking questions about taxes, because this caused him great anguish (he was afraid his replies would be used in your writing). After you left he sent word over and over through his nephew, saying that he wanted a copy of your article, and asking if there was any news of you, etc.

"Therefore, if you go to his house again you must take whatever you wrote from the interview material as well as some suitable gift.

After I have received your agreement to this, I will ask about a convenient time for an interview.

"You may feel after reading these unpleasantnesses that you don't want to meet M. again. But these are things I have wanted to say for a long time. Please let me know how you feel about what I have suggested."

Though it is written in careful language, this is an unusually frank letter, containing bald statements of a very un-Japanese sort. Why did he write such a letter and say such unsayable things? Because long ago he had been put by me in an intolerable social position. Out of ignorance I had created an awkward situation and then walked out of it, leaving others dangling. M. was left worried about what I might write about his taxes and had turned to the only person he could, the go-between, to get satisfaction. But the latter could not provide it, because I had thought my part in the affair ended when M. refused to see me, and the go-between could not bring himself to come to me directly to talk the thing out then and show me what I had to do. The pressure was on him; he was the fulcrum of the situation, and when I gave him a new opportunity to make contact he exploded. He was not satisfied to spell out in explicit terms what it is "customary" to do in such a case in Japan and what I have long since learned to do; his lecture on manners spilled over to include Americans generally, who once lorded it over the Japanese and had to be "welcomed gladly without conditions."

What is to be done? Obviously only one course is indicated: to follow the suggestions of the go-between and get him off the hook of his "spiritual obligations," to reassure M. that I have not speculated in public about his taxes, and to produce the suspect document which I wrote long ago, wrapped around a bottle of good Scotch.

All these things can be done. And yet, reading the carefully polite, yet offended, words of this letter brings back to me all the cold formalism and the sense of alienation that I felt in that first bleak season in Kyoto. Travelers to this country are fond of remarking how modern Japan seems, especially after passage through the other countries of Asia; and of course there are good reasons for feeling in this way. But the social distance between Japan and the West is greater than the technological distance. This little episode exposes the fundamental remoteness of a society like the one I live in in America, where an individual person moves among other individual persons more or less freely, meeting people and leaving them, changing the Christmas-card list from year to year, from a society like Kyoto, where social ties turn into entangling alliances, a gift received requires a gift of nicely calculated equivalent value, and there may be no cutoff date for the complications arising from an occasional meeting.

With these thoughts, I am off next week for Kyoto.

CHAPTER *3*

THE KYOTO SUPERINTENDENT
OF SCHOOLS

August 1, 1955

On December 15, 1953, parents of some of the children in the Asahi-gaoka Junior High School on Kyoto's northern outskirts sent a delegation to wait on the superintendent of schools. The delegation complained that students were receiving Communist-slanted teaching, and it listed some specific grievances. Mathematics and science teachers were lecturing against Japanese rearmament and United States military bases. They openly attacked the San Francisco Peace Treaty and condemned the Mutual Security program as well as the government of Premier Shigeru Yoshida. Teachers were reading aloud long passages from *Akahata* (*Red Flag*), the Communist party newspaper. Propaganda movies were being shown at the school, especially films concerning Hiroshima and Nagasaki. Passers-by heard the children inside the school singing the "Internationale." Although many parents had protested such indoctrination, the school authorities, they said, showed only indifference. Worst of all, teachers were telling children that their parents were stupid and should be defied and that filial piety should be transferred from parents to student "leaders." As the parents' petition put it: ". . . it was plainly shown that the techniques beloved and used by a certain foreign country had been adopted." The parents, moved to action by the growing estrangement and insubordination of their children, demanded that the school board and the superintendent either clean house or transfer them to other schools.

34

Thus began the notorious Asahigaoka case, which filled the Japanese press in the spring and early summer of 1954 and which even now has not been finally settled. I have recently had access to Kyoto city records on this case, as well as to documentary materials issued by the Kyoto Teachers Union.

The Asahigaoka school is located on the northwestern edge of Kyoto, at the foot of the mountains that surround this city on three sides. Here the city streets quickly play out into gravel lanes that run among truck gardens and bamboo groves, rising toward the mountains. The long, barrackslike concrete buildings of the school lie along the flank of a hill just at the point where the solid blocks of city houses stop and the scattered dwellings of the countryside begin. From this hilltop on the periphery of urban settlement one can see all the way across the bowl in which Kyoto sits to the great mass of Mount Hiei over the Kamo River to the east. Immediately below the school grounds, lane after lane of row houses and small shops stand crowded together, with an occasional firebreak street among them. People here are somewhat poorer than the Kyoto average, and nearby are districts known euphemistically as *tokushu* or "special," where live the *eta* or outcast people, workers in leather and other despised trades.

In contrast with the crowded quarters below the school are a number of suburban "villas" in the area just above it, where vegetable fields predominate and the landscape quickly turns to countryside. There are not so many of these better-class homes, each behind its high hedge, each with its small pine-tree garden. But these houses represent a movement out of the city which has been going on very slowly since before the war. Being on somewhat higher ground, this area offers especially fine views of the nearby mountains, and it is slightly cooler in summer. Consequently over the years a number of white-collar workers, college professors, and other intellectuals have moved into the Asahigaoka area, from which they commute daily by bus, streetcar, or bicycle. (It is not an area of real wealth, and only wealthy Kyoto people own automobiles.)

Thus the Asahigaoka school serves an area which is transitional geographically and mixed socially. Living there are a small number of well-educated doctors, contractors, professors and other *interi*, some of them with "progressive" political views, and a large number of craftsmen, shopkeepers, and tradesmen. This small but significant migration has had some effect on the political situation in the neighborhood. One of the present Kyoto city assemblymen in this ward was elected on the Communist ticket. Many children of *interi* attend the Asahigaoka school along with children of poorer parents, and *interi* are active in the local P.T.A. and other organizations. The North Kyoto Citizens Council (*Rakuhoku Minsei Kyōgikai*) was formed largely by *interi* before the school began to attract attention. This organization had a strong anti-American orientation and was propagating the Communist line in public meetings. Some of its most vocal leaders were teachers, including eight or ten of the school's 45 faculty members, and many parents of its 1,400 students were active in council meetings.

In addition to this small elite and its neighborhood following, there was another important player in the Asahigaoka drama. This was the Kyoto branch of the Japan Teachers Union (*Nikkyōso*). With over half a million members, the heavily leftist Teachers Union is now one of the main pillars of *Sōhyō*, the General Council of Trade Unions, Japan's largest and most powerful labor federation. In the Asahigaoka case the schoolteachers, the *Rakuhoku* organization, the Teachers Union, and the local P.T.A. all joined together to make the school a center for Communist-slanted "peace education." One of the three teachers who became ringleaders in the affair wrote a pamphlet called "The Fight to Protect Peace Education in the Asahigaoka School," which spelled out the teachers' views in detail and called for a movement of teachers and students to make the school principal "powerless" and force him to resign. This pamphlet was published under the auspices of the Teachers Union and bore its imprint.

The man the parents met at City Hall, Osamu Fuwa, has been superintendent of Kyoto city schools since 1947. In coming to Fuwa, the aggrieved parents had, whether they knew it or not, found a resourceful official who already had sized up the situation and knew what kind of fight he was in for.

Fuwa is about fifty. A small, wiry man with a fixed half-smile, he is dignified, but not cold, and very verbal. At our first interview he was quick to tell me that he is a Christian and that he has twice visited the United States, once before and once after the war. He graduated from Kyoto's Dai San Kōtōgakkō, one of prewar Japan's best higher schools, and finished Kyoto University. Since the 1930's he has been in the Japanese school system, first as a classroom teacher, later as supervisor and superintendent.

Fuwa is a complicated figure about whom one hears mixed reports. According to some he is primarily an opportunist who pushed himself with the Occupation and continues to push himself with Americans. As the mayor's old friend and unofficial interpreter, he has many chances to impress foreign visitors. Others regard him as a high-minded official with a genuine feeling for the democratic reforms of the Occupation. Certainly he survived the changes of the last 20 years, the stifling thought control of the 1930's, the war, and the Occupation. Certainly he is a conservative bureaucrat devoted to educating children, thoroughly competent and strong in defense of his own authority. But certainly also he is not the sinister autocrat that some would make him. Perhaps his actions in the Asahigaoka case will at least serve to illumine his complexities, which are also in a sense Japan's.

Fuwa and his staff at City Hall had long been aware of the problem at the Asahigaoka school and several others in the city. But they were moving slowly. The radical teachers had gathered considerable support. They had, as their own propaganda declared, worked hard to "democratize" the P.T.A., with some success. A variety of newspapers and magazines here and in Tokyo, always on the alert for real or fancied evidence of bureaucratic arrogance, would support them in any disturbance. The Teachers Union was solidly behind the nucleus of pro-Communist teachers in the school; indeed, the issue was drawn most clearly between the city on one hand and the union on the other.

That this was true is shown by the situation on the city school board. The board is composed of five members. Four are publicly elected, while the fifth is chosen on the floor of the city assembly. At the time the case broke, four members of the board were in Kyoto. Two of these, Fukuhara and Kitamura, were conservatives linked with the Yoshida wing of the Liberal party. Two, Ichikawa and Yoshikawa, were Socialists of the left-wing variety. They had been hand-picked by the Teachers Union and were under union control. The fifth member, Mrs. Kanzaki, a prominent women's leader, was in the United States on a government grant. She was a conservative of the Hatoyama-Liberal persuasion. Fuwa, as superintendent of schools, executed the board's policies and had no voting rights. Therefore, in the early stages of the dispute the board was split two-two and could reach no decision.

Under growing pressure from parents' groups, Fuwa saw the necessity of disciplining the Asahigaoka teachers and cleaning out what he described as a "warm bed" of radical activities there. But he did not choose to draw the issue of slanted education (*henkō kyōiku*) openly, since, as he told me, "it is extremely difficult to get evidence in this sort of case, and without evidence it is impossible to go to court. We knew the teachers would take it to court." Instead, he decided to call the teachers to account for their insubordinate remarks in the pamphlet already mentioned, "The Fight to Protect Peace Education . . ." On April 1, 1954, he issued an order transferring the three ringleaders—Yamamoto, Terashima, and Kitaoji—to three other schools in the city. Their transfer was buried in a long list of routine personnel changes. At the same time Fuwa accepted the resignation of the principal at Asahigaoka, who had clearly shown his inability to curb the trend to crisis in his administration.

On April 11 the three teachers mailed back their transfer orders to the superintendent and remained where they were, teaching as before. Their insubordination now was clearly in the open.

Dismissal of the teachers was the next step, but in order to dismiss them Fuwa had to have the approval of the school board, and this he could not get. Therefore he moved to summon Mrs. Kanzaki from the United States as rapidly as possible. This little episode illustrates how a foreign travel grant can sometimes affect local politics. Fortunately for Fuwa, Mrs. Kanzaki was already in California, her trip nearly completed. She returned immediately, arriving in Kyoto on April 28, seventeen days after the teachers refused transfer.

In the interval before her arrival Fuwa worked with a deft hand to move public opinion. In fact, throughout the case his strategy was to go slowly and consolidate support in press and public, rather than to move police in and alienate the people. He was sure that if the public got the facts it would support him. Therefore, he arranged a number of open meetings and forums. One was held at the auditorium of the Kyoto Press, where representatives of the Teachers Union, the superintendent's office, and neutrals debated the case. This forum was re-broadcast several times by the largest local radio station. The Kyoto central P.T.A. organization, unlike the local Asahigaoka branch, was on the superintendent's side; and on April 23, just before Mrs. Kanzaki was to arrive, it issued a public statement warning the Teachers Union not to resort to violence. Meanwhile the Tokyo press was playing up the case, and the Ministry of Education sent a delegation to investigate and report.

During this period in late April, while Fuwa worked to bring the behavior of the teachers into the open, he committed his first and most serious error. Delegations from both sides were coming to his office nearly every day to make demands. *Nikkyōso* sent one of its top officials from Tokyo to support the teachers' position (April 4). The two Socialist school-board members put out a declaration accusing the superintendent of "unfair treatment of personnel" (April 15). The two conservative members countered with a declaration supporting Fuwa (April 19). In the confusion of opposing declarations and conflicting press reports Fuwa suddenly slammed the door shut. On April 19 he announced he would grant no more interviews on the Asahigaoka case. In effect, he had frozen into opposition to the Teachers Union. He refused to admit the union's right to negotiate in a case involving three of its own members. He claimed that disciplining the teachers was a matter to be decided within his own and the school board's authority. Like most officials, his opinion of unions was dim. But he was to regret his action later, when it became the basis for the teachers' successful court appeal.

One week after Mrs. Kanzaki returned, on May 5, the school board voted three to two to dismiss the three teachers and so notified them by official mail. At this point real trouble threatened, because the teachers refused to accept dismissal and continued to teach in the school. They were joined in their stand by about eight of their colleagues.

Fuwa again hesitated to use force. Instead he declared the school officially closed. The teachers responded by raising red flags over the school and continuing to teach. (The official account says red flags "bristled" over the school buildings.) Two days later, on May 7, they held a kind of kangaroo court at the school and forced the newly appointed principal to resign in front of his students. A photograph of this occasion shows the students taunting the principal as he signs his resignation. It does not show any policemen; but when I questioned Fuwa about this episode he volunteered the information that plainclothes men had attended the meeting. They had, in fact, managed to make a tape recording of the proceedings which was broadcast later to discredit the teachers involved. During the meeting "progressive" teachers cruised the neighborhood in sound trucks to urge public support and denounce the superintendent. To Fuwa "it was a revolution."

After consulting the school board, he announced that, during the official closing of the Asahigaoka school, classes would be held in another location and free public transportation provided to all children who wished to attend. At the same time he warned all teachers not to continue teaching at Asahigaoka, on pain of certain dismissal.

Three days later, on May 11, temporary classes began at Okazaki Public Hall, four miles away from Asahigaoka. Although the spring tourist season was at its height and transportation difficult to find, Fuwa was able to charter 30 sight-seeing buses to move the students in the morning and afternoon. On the morning of May 11, partisans of both sides patrolled the Asahigaoka area, exhorting parents to choose one school or the other. Parents who wished their children to go to Okazaki formed a double line to protect them as they walked toward the buses.

Luckily there was no violence; and in the end it was Fuwa who won, because when heads were counted the first day at Okazaki, 800 children showed up, while only about 250 attended Asahigaoka. The remainder stayed home altogether. As the days passed, more and more children deserted the old school and switched to Okazaki. By not forcing the issue and by playing his cards carefully, Fuwa had won over most of the parents. The denouement was swift, for when the Teachers Union saw that most students were attending the new school and that the "progressive" teachers had lost their local support, it notified the superintendent that Asahigaoka was closing (May 16).

Shortly thereafter Asahigaoka reopened with an entirely new faculty. The three offending teachers were removed from their jobs, but the Teachers Union was able to appeal to the local court on the ground that the superintendent had shut his office and refused to give the teachers a full hearing. This appeal was upheld (May 5, 1955), and the teachers were ordered reinstated. The school board appealed the case immediately to the Osaka district court, where a decision is pending. Thus, although the case was a victory for Fuwa in public opinion, its aftermath continues to harass him.

In a crisis a majority of the parents at Asahigaoka voted to send their children to the authorized city schools. But in normal times they tend to sit by while the Teachers Union controls the school boards. This baffles Fuwa and leads him to criticize the Occupation for the "suddenness" of the change-over to a school-board system—just as conservative businessmen have told me SCAP was at fault for encouraging labor unions in the early years of the Occupation. Brought up in one system, but administering another, Fuwa is encountering the usual difficulty of making the Occupation's reforms work in spirit as well as in letter. In the United States, he says, candidates seek election to the school board for a chance to serve the community. But the Japanese are "professionalizing" their school boards. Members of the Kyoto board get exactly the same salary as the superintendent.

According to Fuwa, 80 per cent of all school-board members in the nation are handpicked by the Teachers Union. This is probably too high an estimate; but he insists that the union has assumed the control over education that once was exercised by the all-powerful Ministry of Education. This has happened, he says, not because the school-board system is itself bad, but because "you can't get desirable people to run for election." "Right-minded" people usually despise the taint of politics. Controlling elements seek to remain in the background. They do not want to get up and make speeches and jounce around in sound trucks, showing themselves off. Respect for politicians of any sort is low, but school-board elections especially are meaningless to many citizens. In the last Kyoto election only 20 per cent of the qualified voters voted. This contrasts with 70 to 75 per cent in the February 1955 national Diet elections. The idea of electing people to run the schools has not caught on in this city.

Given this situation and his own background, it is not surprising that Fuwa favors changes in the school-board system. Specifically he backs a plan now under consideration in Tokyo which would eliminate elected school boards. Instead, boards would be appointed by mayors or governors, as the case might be, and approved by city or prefectural assemblies. In this way, says Fuwa, "you could get the right kind of people into the school boards instead of the Communists or pro-Communists who are there now." To him, reaching this objective seems more important than preserving the elective principle.

Should this plan fail, Fuwa would redistrict the city to control the Teachers Union. At present all Kyoto is one district in school-board elections, and the union has welded the teachers into a city-wide organization. "You are workers, not professional people," it tells them, "and you deserve workers' rights." If the election districts could be reduced in size, union organization could be fragmented and union candidates defeated.

Deeper than Fuwa's vexation with school boards is his concern, which is shared by many conservative Japanese of his generation, over the lack of "moral education" in the schools. It is all very well, he says, for the Americans to have abolished chauvinistic indoctrination and Emperor-worship; but the democratic give-and-take philosophy of the American school as introduced here is unfamiliar to Japanese children and teachers alike, even ten years after the war. The Emperor has lost his prestige as a binding force in national life, especially among young people. But what exists to take his place? To the young, the country is drifting, no one knows whither. *Kokutai*, the *mystique* of Japan's nationhood, evaporated in the vast loss of self-confidence at war's end. Americans have Christian values taught them from childhood, but Buddhism is of importance mainly to the old, who seek to preserve orthodoxy. Buddhism, thinks Fuwa, has no real moral force for young people. Tokyo politicians do not impress the youth. Real leaders are few and hard to identify. Communists have tried to move into this vacuum and work their discipline among students to alienate them from parents and principals, as at Asahigaoka. Their violent methods have in turn alienated many Japanese, but the problem of belief, a sense of direction, and a firm allegiance remain important to most Japanese in a period of economic stringency and uncertainty about the future. To Fuwa the natural answer is to provide some sort of "moral education." He is vague about how this would be done, but he would not scrap the whole American-modeled system. He would "adapt, not adopt." He is the man on the spot, and the practical problems he faces have made him want to change the system here and there. No doubt more changes will be made.

His own future as superintendent of schools is by no means assured, because since the Asahigaoka affair the balance on the school board has been upset. Mrs. Kanzaki resigned last winter to campaign (unsuccessfully) for the national Diet, while Fukuhara, the former board chairman, quit for personal reasons. When the city assembly met to choose his successor, it unexpectedly elected a Socialist. As a result, the board now contains three Socialists, one conservative (Kita-mura, now elevated to chairman), and one vacancy (the one created by Mrs. Kanzaki's resignation). With the balance against him, Fuwa realizes that, if the Osaka district court upholds the three teachers, the board will not appeal to the Supreme Court in Tokyo. For this reason, he says, "I am keeping my resignation in my pocket."

Fuwa is easy to like but hard to judge. He fits no clear-cut pattern. In his excellent training and experience, his government has assets which it would do well not to squander. Likewise, he has at least two qualities that endear him to USIS personnel and other Americans who may have daily business on his level: he is staunchly anti-Communist and he speaks fluent English. It may be argued that in the Asahigaoka case he should have kept the door open to all comers and been more willing to negotiate with the union. But of course he was sorely pro-voked and, even so, acted with considerable restraint. He naturally wishes now that he had been more patient, since in the end he was reversed by the court. This may teach him a new lesson in democracy —may even cost him his job. On the deeper issue of the future of Japan's children he may be vague about the means of enforcing "moral education"; but his mind is running toward youth organizations like the Boy Scouts and the YMCA rather than toward a resumption of the hated indoctrination of earlier times. In any event, he and officials like him will continue to "adapt, not adopt," to shape foreign borrowings more nearly to the Japanese mold.

CHAPTER *4*

IN A COUNTRY TEMPLE

August 30, 1958

The village of Kanakura lies 15 kilometers beyond Wajima, an old lacquer-making town on the Japan Sea at the northern end of the Noto Peninsula, in Ishikawa prefecture. From Tokyo it takes 18 hours to reach Kanakura: overnight by trunk line across the central mountains, four hours on a grimy local train to Wajima, bus to Kawanishi village, where the new steel bridge is a landmark known all over the peninsula, and from there on foot or in a hired car up a narrow, rocky track into the hills. Trains and buses all are packed to their doors with standing people, but the Noto country is some of the poorest and most isolated in Japan, largely without industry, shut in by heavy snows in winter and with an average of less than 100 days of clear weather in the year.

In Kanakura there are 104 households settled in three communities —mainly dispersed farmsteads lying within shouting distance of each other near the top of the inside slope of a range of hills that runs along the north shore of the peninsula bordering the Japan Sea. Ninety-two of the households are farmers, and they cultivate 152 acres of land, two-thirds of it in irrigated rice that has been kept diked in level paddies through constant human labor for hundreds of years. The rest is in dry fields that grow corn, millet, sesame, cabbages, and other vegetables. The largest farm in the village is two and one-half acres. In addition the village owns 20 acres of forest land that is used communally for firewood or forage for animals—a few black work cattle, horses, and goats. There are no milch cows in Kanakura.

44

Besides the farm households, there are 12 households that are without land for crops: a few schoolteachers and several families of day laborers at the bottom of the local society. Kanakura has no commercial center and no full-time merchant, but two farm stores stock hand tools and threshing machines, plus an assortment of candy, dried seaweed, iron kettles, and cigarettes. There also are a post office, a young people's hall where the village assembly meets, and a public primary school where one of the village's three telephones is located.

Although the Noto Peninsula is only a poor portion of one prefecture out of 46 prefectures in Japan, it supports 622 temples of established Buddhist sects, as well as 36 temples of assorted "new religions," some of which have sprung up since the war and have some relation to Buddhism or Shintō or both. (There also are two Christian churches.[1]) To an extent unrealized by the foreign visitor to Tokyo, the Japanese countryside is densely studded with Buddhist temples, from the most remote local establishments, such as this Report describes, to the great headquarters edifices in the Kyoto-Nara district to the southwest.

In Kanakura there are three Buddhist temples. With their soaring tile roofs and great hand-hewn timbers, set in groves of cedars and pines, some of them a thousand years old, and surrounded by subordinate buildings and gardens, they completely dominate the other structures in the landscape—the thatched-roofed farmhouses and modest wood-and-tile buildings of school and stores. The temples give an impression of desolate stability. Two of them, the Shōganji and the Kyōganji, are Shin sect temples dating from the sixteenth century. The third, the Konzōji, is a Shingon sect temple and is much older. Recently I had an opportunity to spend a week at the Shōganji, where I was received with warmth by the head priest and his family. The description which follows sums up what I was able to learn about the people who keep a temple going, live in it, and represent it in a rural community.

Minoru Matsubara, head priest of the Shōganji, is the nineteenth generation of his family to preside over this temple since it was founded in 1526. Like the Japanese Emperor, he is the continuity of history

[1] Ikegami, Hiromasa; Morioka, Kiyomi; Tsuchiya, Terumichi. "Shūkyō Seikatsu" ("Religious Life"), in *Noto: Shizen, Bunka, Shakai (Noto: Nature, Culture, Society)*. (Tokyo, 1955). I am greatly indebted to Professor Morioka for his help in collecting materials for this Report.

made visible to his followers. Matsubara was born in the Shōganji in 1909, the second son in a family of eight children. He attended primary school in Kanakura and middle school in Kanazawa, the old castle town which now has become the metropolis of the Hokuriku district. Since as a second son he had no prospect of inheriting the priest's office and the village offered no other opportunity, after graduation from middle school he was given for adoption to the Kamata family, took the name of that family, and was sent to Tokyo to prepare for university entrance examinations. However, he was unhappy in his preparatory school and soon left it to return to Kanakura. With this the Kamata family rejected him—apparently it wanted only a university graduate for an adopted son—and the adoption was terminated. Matsubara reassumed his original name; and since his parents felt that he should learn more about the religious life, he was sent to live with his uncle, a teacher of Buddhism in Kyoto. There the young Matsubara spent several important years studying with his uncle and attending classes at the Higashi Honganji, the headquarters temple of that branch of the Shin sect to which the Shōganji belongs. During this period his faith in the teachings of Shinran, the sect's founder, grew strong. However, Matsubara decided not to remain in Kyoto. Instead, in 1933 he left the Japanese islands entirely and spent four years as a farmer in Manchuria where, he says, he would have been glad to stay permanently. But in 1937 his father and his elder brother both unexpectedly died, and he was called back to Kanakura to take over the leadership of the temple. This ended his wanderings. Shortly after returning home he married and settled down to the life of a country priest in the hills where he was born.

Today Matsubara, his wife, and four children live in the temple rectory, which is connected by a roofed passageway to the main hall, or *hondō*, of the Shōganji. Building rectory and temple under one roof serves the same practical purpose as joining barn and house in snowy New England and elsewhere. It also symbolizes the fusion of Matsubara's two roles as a spiritual and a secular leader of the village.

His day reflects these roles. Up every morning at six, he puts on his robes and walks to the *hondō*. There he meets the subordinate priest of the Shōrakuji, the "child temple" of the Shōganji (see below), which occupies a building at the opposite side of the temple grounds from the rectory. Together the two priests chant the sutras of the morning

service, then each retires again to his separate quarters. Of the 104
households in Kanakura, 55 are followers of the Shōganji; since the
Shōganji's congregation totals 270 households, this represents only a
small percentage, but most of the rest live in the neighboring village
of Kawanishi, and only a handful live outside the immediate area. On
some days Matsubara may be busy with many special observances
which take him to the homes of his congregation or bring them to the
temple. But other days he spends until sunset sitting beside his iron
teapot in the rectory, surrounded by a litter of canisters, odd vases,
ink sticks, and calligraphy scrolls. There he dispenses tea and informal
advice and holds court for his followers. And although he is somehow more prepossessing there than when he stands among the gilded
images of the *hondō*, he and his followers are relaxed and comfortable
in the teacher-disciple relationship with which they are familiar.

The men slip in silently, bow low, and sit around drinking tea,
smoking, and talking with Matsubara. He himself smokes *Shinsei*
cigarettes cut into very short lengths and stuck straight up, Tito-
fashion, in a curved silver holder. Because it is the time of *O-Bon*, when
families traditionally gather for special services commemorating the
dead who have gone before, several members of Matsubara's own family
are present. There is the younger brother of his dead father, "Osaka-
san," so called because many years ago he left Kanakura to establish a
branch family in the Osaka area, where he has lived ever since. There
also is Mrs. Matsubara's mother's brother, "Taiwan-san," who spent 50
years as a farmer and small-time businessman in Formosa. Both of these
men are in their eighties, and naturally this is a time for retelling many
stories of the old days: the murder of Kinsuke, for example, which
happened forty years ago and is the only real crime of violence any of
them can remember having happened in the village. Poor man, he was
given poison by somebody, perhaps his wife, and though he was able
to vomit some of it, he died an unpleasant death in the end. This is good
for half an hour of elaboration, with side themes interrupting the plot
from time to time. Broader subjects may also be discussed. When some
of the hearthside group take up the theme of peace, Matsubara declares
that if a man finds peace within himself and makes his own life peaceful,
then nations will eventually find a way to live in peace with each other.
But one grizzled farmer disagrees: "What good is it," he asks, "to be
peaceful if others are not peaceful, too? What is the meaning of peace-

ful coexistence in such a situation?" A third man seems to suggest that the rationale of Buddhism is found in its peacemaking role, whereupon Matsubara closes off that subject with a short lecture on Shinran's views of peace.

In his exchanges with his followers Matsubara is solicitous: you are not looking well today; have you been taking penicillin for what ails you? It is plain that his congregation respects him the more because his own nature is regarded as innocent. There is, for instance, the well-known story of how he was defrauded by a supposedly faithful follower. For a long time the temple has been unable to invite the chief priest of the sect from Kyoto for a visit because no suitably splendid room is available in the rectory. A year ago a follower of the temple, who is known to be a leading merchant in a nearby village, suggested to Matsubara that the temple should buy a certain new house in that village as quarters for distinguished guests. He advised the priest to contract for an advance payment of 100,000 yen, to which Matsubara enthusiastically agreed. He did not know that the merchant had already arranged with the house owner to make a neat profit from the deal; but when the council of temple elders met they disapproved the entire transaction. With the priest's children now being supported by the congregation in schools in Kanazawa city, they argued that the temple could get along without more expenses until Hiroshi, the priest's son and heir, is ready to marry five or six years from now. Matsubara did not get his wish, but according to local sources, his guilelessness has strengthened his value as a spiritual leader.

No doubt there is much that is admirable in this. But what struck me more than anything else was the archaic, hierarchical quality of personal relations. My own visit there, though not of the same order of distinction as the Honganji chief priest's, nevertheless was a "passage" and had its own less splendid material result: they had just managed to finish the new tile bathtub before my arrival. However, a sewage system still is for the future; and what with the stench of the pit-privies, the mosquitoes swarming up from the lotus pond in the evening, and the monotonous chanting of sutras in the *hondō*, the whole place seemed to me stagnant at its core. At any rate, I was too busy slapping mosquitoes and trying to navigate the *zu-zu-zu* of the local dialect to engage in any more exalted speculations or to receive any intimations of the extinguishment of the self.

While the men talked, the women callers stayed in the kitchen with Matsubara's wife. Nearly everybody brought some contribution to the family larder—a pumpkin, three or four cucumbers, some eggplants, or a sack full of rice which was emptied into a large wooden tub in one corner of the sitting room within sight of the priest. Some of these things were brought on my account; before my arrival the priest's wife had gone the rounds of nearby households and asked them to bring any specially good things to eat for my visit. But the process of tribute goes on constantly under Mrs. Matsubara's care.

The congregation is responsible for temple upkeep and maintenance of the priest and his family. Without direct help from its congregation the Shōganji could not exist or could exist only in some different form. At the time of the postwar land reforms it had almost no land to lose, and what it had was kept by transferring title from the temple corporation to the head priest personally. But this land, though valuable, supplies only a part of the food the temple requires; the rest, and all other expenses, must be furnished by the families of the congregation. Some of the congregation's temple allotments have been converted into cash, but to a considerable degree they still contribute food, clothing, and services in kind. (Each household also contributes 670 yen a year to the headquarters temple, for a total annual contribution from the Shōganji of about $500.) When the temple was reconstructed 40 years ago all the labor was contributed by its followers. They had all the skills necessary to cut and dress the enormous timbers, decorate the beams with ornate carvings, and erect the whole structure along classic lines of temple architecture. Some of these skills may have been lost since then, but during my visit one member of the congregation was busy repairing the roof tiles at the very crest of the great temple roof, a job requiring considerable skill, or at least nerve.

Relationships between the temple and its congregation tend to remain stable as long as economic conditions do not change very much. In such a remote area as Kanakura the number of households has not fluctuated much in recent years. Village records indicate that in the 1890's there were about 80 households in the village. One reason for the relatively stable situation is shortage of land needed to establish branch families. Holdings in the Noto Peninsula are notoriously fragmented. One narrow valley, all of which may be seen at a glance from a bus window, contains more than 2,000 parcels of paddy, some of them no larger than a card table. Another reason for stability is the social requirement that new households purchase the right to use the communal forest lands before they can be established successfully. Legally there is no need for this, but since as a matter of social custom the profits from this land are used for village projects and each household must contribute its share, a household without such communal rights is in an unfavorable position. New rights become available when a family dies out or leaves the area; but few families leave Kanakura permanently for the cities. Jobs are scarce there and the demand for local skills low. Some who have left have become bathhouse operators in Tokyo, possibly because early migrants from Noto succeeded in that occupation. But most families stay where they are, and the temple congregations of Kanakura remain steadier than those in regions closer to factories or large cities where there is greater mobility.

If the temple depends on its congregation out of economic need, why are its followers willing to give it support? The hereditary character of the congregations helps explain the hold which Japanese temples exert over their followers. Casual observers who conclude from the emptiness of temples that they are dying institutions are liable to misjudge their function. The followers of the Shōganji do not primarily support the temple or go there in order to be assured of personal salvation. While doctrinal ties undoubtedly exist between temples and followers in Shin sect Buddhism, the essential article of faith is repetition of a simple oral formula which does not require a trip to the temple. But the temple remains necessary to its congregation precisely because the priest of that particular temple, and no other, must conduct each dead member of each follower's family into his new state of being in the Buddhist paradise. The priest's presence is mandatory at funerals, and only one's own priest can, in theory, conduct the periodic observances connected with the veneration of ancestors. Temple and family thus are intimately linked; but here again the integrity of the relationship depends on maintaining stationary social and economic conditions. Some temples, driven by the scattering of their congregations to seek other sources of income, have resorted to nursery schools or "consultation centers," and a few have even held jazz concerts to lure more people into the temple grounds. So far the Shōganji has scorned such stratagems; yet mobility is undermining the relationship of temple and congregation. With more and more people dying far away from home, how can the priest's vital functions be maintained?

The tie between Matsubara and his congregation is paternalistic in essence and rests on reciprocal needs which still are felt nearly in their pure form. This parent-child relationship also is expressed in the institution of the *kodera*, or "child temple." In feudal times the *kodera* was regarded as a member of the congregation of its parent temple in a special sense. In return for assistance in performing religious rites and other duties, the *kodera* priest and his family were supported directly out of the contributions levied on the congregation of the parent temple, a portion of which was set aside for the *kodera*'s use. The *kodera* thus had no congregation of its own but lived as a kind of welcome parasite on the largess of its host temple. It formed the bottom layer of a hierarchy extending through its local parent temple to the regional headquarters temple and the national headquarters temple in Kyoto.

These subordinate relationships were legally abolished at the time of the Meiji Restoration, and the tie between local temple and regional headquarters temple broke down rather quickly because of the distance usually separating them. However, in many instances the parent temple-child temple relationship remained very much as it was in the Tokugawa period, because the two temples continued to occupy the same grounds and have complementary functions, one assisting the other and being supported in return. *Kodera* may of course break off from parent temples if they care to take the risk. They may migrate to Hokkaidō and begin again as independent temples with congregations of their own—a trend encouraged by Kyoto authorities who fear a shortage of temples in the northern island. Or they may enlist the support of some powerful followers of the parent temple or of some other temple in the vicinity and set up independently. However, this appears to happen only rarely in a community as stable as Kanakura.

Although the relationship between the Shōganji and its *kodera* is apparently calm, underneath there are serious tensions. Such situations, which are common, illustrate how the force of group opinion in an isolated village can overrule and distort the fulfillment of individual preferences. Ten years ago the then priest of the *kodera* had an illicit affair with a widow of the village. Against the wishes of the temple's followers, he eventually brought the widow's grown daughter to be the wife of his own son. This marriage has never been sanctioned by the temple's council of elders. As a result, the wife of the subordinate priest has never been accepted by the community, and the two families sharing the same temple enclosure have become permanently estranged. The association of the two priests is limited to performing their religious duties, and the two wives ordinarily do not meet each other; even the children have been taught to avoid playing together as much as possible. Matsubara will not openly cross his elders' council, even though he knows that a minority would like to resolve the situation in some peaceable way. He insists that the *kodera* priest must make the first move, but the latter has accepted the situation and, perhaps out of fear for his security, has made no effort to improve it.

The religious role of the priest in remote Noto still has not lost its vitality. At the same time, as I have suggested, he plays a significant part in the secular life of the community. Five years ago a serious stomach operation forced Matsubara to cut down his schedule somewhat, but he continues to carry influence behind the scenes. He is consulted on all important civic matters, such as road construction, improvement of the elementary-school curriculum, or the assignment of new teachers. Occasionally he is invited to attend meetings of the *sōkai*, or village assembly, and at such times he sits in front near the village mayor and is regarded as a high-ranking adviser. At election times, he told me, everybody asks, "How is Matsubara voting?" He recognizes candidly that his influence stems from the authority of the church. "I sometimes wonder what I would be without the church. The people confuse me with the temple in their minds. I am like the president of a political party. Without the organization I would be nothing." But because he has the organization and in addition is a wise and kind man, he has been able to keep the position of the temple strong in the community.

Matsubara is one of a company of local opinion-formers, arbiters of local affairs, about whom I have written at various times during the past several years. In his political and social judgments he is unfailingly conservative, reflecting the intense conservatism of an institution which is built on family stability and the *status quo*. He hates labor unions, whether of rail workers or schoolteachers, as incarnations of evil and disturbers of the public peace. He adores order and hierarchy. His political ideal is Hideji Masutani, conservative Diet representative whose district includes the Noto Peninsula and who, incidentally, served as speaker of the Lower House in the recent Diet. Conservative politicians occasionally have used the temple as a public hall during election campaigns.

Matsubara's opinions are shared by his congregation, who for the most part are farmers at the periphery, or beyond the periphery, of the mass media of communication. Television has not yet penetrated the Noto hills, though it is everywhere in Kanazawa, 75 miles away, and radio reception is poor except for a couple of hours at night. Most people in the villages do not even read the mass-circulation weekly magazines that flood the towns and cities. The power of city intellectuals and journalists to move them is still limited, while the power of men like Matsubara remains strong.

New roads, railroads, the penetration of new ideas are slowly changing the Noto area. Before the war the village was controlled by local bosses, called *kumioya*, descendants of families selected by the feudal lord and made responsible for tax collections and other duties. Twenty of these landlords controlled five-sixths of the farm land of the village. With land reform these families lost most of their land and were replaced as formal power-holders by elected officials, some of whom were former tenants. In the first village assembly election in 1949, seven former landowners, three former tenants, and two former combinations of the two were elected. The first village mayor to be elected was himself a former tenant, but since 1954 the mayor has been a prewar independent farmer, though not a *kumioya*.

Obviously some new local leaders have emerged since the land reform. The village assembly is responsible to the whole village in a way the *kumioya* bosses never were before the war. But new forms of land tenure have not changed a whole way of life, at least not in one decade. The framework of personal relations, the structure of social etiquette, the language with its niceties of obeisance, all change more slowly than laws change. Status, rather than individual personality, is what is respected in the Noto Peninsula, as in most of this country. They still breathe hierarchy, not equality, the Matsubaras of Japan.

CHAPTER 5 ❁ ❁ ❁

TAKEHARA: A GOOD PLACE TO BE FROM

May 7, 1961

East of Hiroshima the rough, scrub-covered hills come down at right angles to the Inland Sea, forming a broken coast line of capes and coves, protected by offshore islands but offering few large harbors. Here, on the rail line along the shore, pinched in by hills on three sides, the town of Takehara follows the narrow valley of the Kamo River and spreads out over the tiny delta where the river flows into the sea.

With just under 40,000 people, Takehara two years ago qualified to be called a city, but it still looks like a hundred other Japanese market towns that spread their tile roofs wherever patches of suitable land exist, in every upland basin or sea-level cove. Like the others, in the plaza in front of the railway station it presents the traveler with a map of its noted sights and nearby attractions, painted in garish colors with a design resembling the arterial system of a dragon. Beyond lies the usual wilderness: the shopping "Ginza," a neon-bedazzled copy of others all over Japan; the town offices in their two-story wooden building with empty bell tower, that might be in the freight yards at Carbondale, Illinois; the branch banks and insurance companies of stone and glass; the streets clogged with wholesalers' merchandise, through which messenger boys in black leather jackets race the engines of their motorbikes and blare their horns; other streets of small manufacturing, full of sparks and smells; and above all these, the smokestacks of the town's

54

one large factory. One gets an impression of jagged vitality; but a little farther from the station the modern town peters out suddenly, the narrow streets grow narrower and turn into lanes lined with wood and stucco houses pressed down under black tile roofs, with doorways that open into dark interiors where merchants offer tea, tea utensils, sweet cakes, or traditional clothing, or where craftsmen and their apprentices work at matmaking and other trades. Still farther out stands the high school in its stark compound of beaten yellow earth, and not far away the town's oldest Buddhist temples and Shintō shrines cling, intermingled with each other, to the worn slopes of the hills.

Like the rest of Japan, Takehara is an ancient place that has carried its antiquity with it into the churned-up present. Until recently the town was remote and lived on the credit of history, preoccupied with itself. According to local tradition, the place has been inhabited since the second century; after the Taika reforms in the seventh century the area was occasionally mentioned in the chronicles that passed for history. Though no castle was built there in medieval times, the river mouth was a point of arrival and departure for seafarers and a local market center. In the seventeenth and eighteenth centuries, when salt was produced near the shore, the town became more important, and Takehara salt was transported to various parts of the country. In this period, too, the town reached the peak of its cultural fame as the home of Rai Sanyō and his family, Confucian scholars of historical importance. The old homestead of this family is preserved today.

After the Meiji Restoration salt continued to be the special product of the region, but grapes were also introduced, and Takehara became known for its grape culture as well as for the brewing of fine rice wine. The town was not regarded with favor as an industrial site by the new Meiji leaders: its hinterland was too rugged to support a large urban center, and the harbor was too small. The main line of the railroad passed Takehara to the north, and not until 1932, when a branch line was opened through the naval base at Kure, did Takehara secure a rail connection with the outside, making possible rapid east-west communication through the coastal hills.

With the railroad came the first important industry, a copper smelter, built in 1934 by a Tokyo-financed concern on coastal land between the railroad and the sea. Electric smelting of ore from a nearby island was begun, and as Japanese industry turned more and more to military production the Takehara smelter grew to national importance. Later it shifted to processing lead ore and produced materials for submarine batteries, among other things. In 1943 the factory was bought by the Mitsui family interests and soon after was placed under national control for wartime purposes.

After World War II the special products for which Takehara had been noted went into decline. The town still was a marketing center for a rich rice-producing area, but the Occupation's land reform forced landlords to sell their salt fields to small holders, while technical advances were made in salt production abroad and the cost of imported salt fell below that of the domestic product. At the same time the soil in which grapes had grown for many years was thin and depleted; the fruit turned sour, and wine producers began to look to other territories. Thus some of the links with a distinctive past, the *meibutsu* or special products of the area that set it apart from other areas, were disappearing.

Of course, Takehara's people could not let go of the past simply because the local economy was changing. A few families bearing names of hierarchical resonance continued to dominate the genteel tradition in the town and to maintain their influence over local affairs, sometimes even after the basis of their wealth had disappeared. When one asks who are the local *yūryokusha*, or persons of power, the same old names recur, some of them going back to rice-merchant forebears in the Tokugawa era. But to others, including some of the postwar new-rich, the past was acquiring a merely antiquarian interest. They encouraged the collection of old books and genealogical records in the town's historical library and led tourists to picturesque sites, such as a Zen monastery sometimes visited by baseball players to "strengthen their spirit" before important games. What the town had been was still a reason for pride or arrogance to some, and the old, stagnant tyrannies and scandals of this "little Kyoto" were the familiar raw material of local gossip. But Takehara was losing its identity in an economic sense and coming to resemble any modern commercial or industrial city.

At war's end the smelter of the Mitsui Metals Mining Company never closed down entirely, and after several bad years it was rejuvenated by the Korean War. Today it is thriving, with sources of ore established abroad and orders from the booming electronics industry. The factory employs 700 men and provides Takehara with 20 per cent of its local tax revenues. It has helped the town to expand its harbor facilities, and when the salt industry finally was closed down last year, Mitsui Metals acquired some of the fields for its own future construction needs.

Apart from the Mitsui plant and a food cannery on the edge of town, Takehara has been designated one of the new "sea-front industrial zones" by the central government in its latest economic plans; and at the town hall or the chamber of commerce one has only to show the most casual interest to be furnished with elaborate maps and blueprints of the industrial future. Local officials are full of dreams. They talk of digging a tunnel ten kilometers long through the mountains to bring adequate industrial water supplies to the town. Their plans call for a further expansion of the harbor and its docking facilities, new cement and iron works, and a small shipyard, all to be built on or near the former salt beds. Their biggest project, not yet begun, involves filling in large areas of sea front for a refining and manufacturing center under the auspices of the Japanese-owned Arabian Oil Company, which is now busily exploiting new oil concessions in the Persian Gulf. Huge tankers could anchor offshore in deep, protected waters, unloading their crude for refineries and chemical plants that would put Takehara on the map in an unprecedented way.

Thus the future jostles the past and present in Takehara, and this telescoping of the time dimension, so characteristic of Japan, is seen in all the town's institutions—the factory with its modern products and less modern personnel relations, the declining old commercial and agricultural pursuits and the new industrial ones coming to birth on the planning boards. Everywhere the past drags its slow weight; but the compulsion to move ahead also is clear. Perhaps it is clearest of all in the school, which furnishes people to the rest and is the channel through which all, or almost all, must pass if they are to move upward through this changing society.

*   *   *

Nearly 800 children attend the Takehara Senior High School, a cluster of long, weather-beaten wooden buildings on the northern edge of town. The only public high school in the district, it was created by the Occupation's educational reforms in 1948 as a three-year school on the American pattern.

Most of the students live in Takehara city. (Children must attend the public high school in the district in which they live, though they may go wherever they like to private schools. Takehara has one private high school.) Most of them are accustomed to walking to and from school; only if home is more than two kilometers away are they permitted to ride bicycles. Before 8:00 A.M. and after 3:30 P.M. the streets and roads of Takehara are choked with children walking or cycling, boys in their black caps and black uniforms, girls in navy-blue middy suits, with their hair cut straight across their foreheads. Many children come by train from nearby smaller towns; a few use ferries that cross from islands in the Inland Sea.

Before reaching Takehara High these young Japanese, like hundreds of thousands of others, finished nine years of compulsory education in primary and junior-high schools. Since the school district takes in a sizable tract of back-country agricultural territory as well as several islands, many students come from farming families. Brought up in traditional households, some began their education in small, isolated schools, called in Japanese *hekichi gakkō*, many of them one-teacher schools. Takehara teachers complain that these children arrive at the high school relatively inarticulate, with somewhat poorer equipment for further education than their town-bred classmates. Nevertheless, many come: more than half of all Japanese junior-high graduates last year entered high school. About half of Takehara High's students come from families of tradespeople in the town or wage employees of companies, including the Mitsui Company. These and the remainder of the students—children of local officials and miscellaneous other professional people—have gone through urban lower schools. At Takehara all these children of different backgrounds and levels of achievement are brought together for the first time.

Public high schools in Japan are coeducational, but girls are particularly numerous in this one, because before the war a private girls school on the same site established a reputation as the best in the prefecture. During the war a commercial high school, later offering industrial courses, also was opened there, and today Takehara High offers separate courses in homemaking (145 students) and commercial subjects (311 students). However, the core of the school is the general college-preparatory course (326 students), with curriculum and graduation requirements modeled on those of American high schools of the early postwar era. Principal subjects are Japanese language, "social studies" (something resembling civics, plus Japanese history and world history), mathematics, science, physical education, arts (music, painting, and calligraphy), and English. To this is added a compulsory period called "home room," which meets once a week for an hour, plus ten-minute periods every morning, during which students are supposed to "socialize" and discuss their common problems together. This has not worked well, because most teachers and students do not know how to communicate easily with each other. The curriculum has been revised once since 1948 and will be revised again in 1963 on a nationwide basis to increase its moralistic tone and nationalistic content. However, at Takehara it still resembles its foreign model; although the school may be deficient in some respects, it is not yet dedicated to producing little chauvinists.

For the great majority of students, high school is the end of their formal education. A few girls in the homemaking course at Takehara go on to two-year colleges, where they study domestic subjects. Most girls soon marry and either return to the place from which they came or settle in Hiroshima, Osaka, or Tokyo.

Few graduates of the commercial course go on to a university. A majority of them, including many girls, take clerkships or other low-level positions in a large variety of businesses, which mirror Japanese society at this stage of its development. Last year's commercial graduates went to 91 different job destinations: shipping and shipbuilding firms, textile companies, bank and insurance companies, public offices, agricultural or commercial co-operative organizations, electrical and other machinery manufacturing concerns, book publishers, gas companies, department stores, pharmaceutical firms, nursery schools, rolling-stock manufacturers, and so on. Not a single graduate of the school last year desired to return to farming, and according to school records, none has yet done so. Most of the above job destinations were located within Hiroshima prefecture, including the city of Hiroshima or the larger towns along the coast, of which Takehara is of course one. But many of last year's graduates took jobs in other areas, principally in and around Osaka, the nearest real metropolis, and a few made the jump directly to Tokyo or its industrial environs.

Each year at Takehara a certain number of graduates of the general course pass university entrance examinations. (About 15 per cent of all Japanese high-school graduates advance to junior colleges or universities, although the percentage finishing the latter is much smaller.) A few enter the best universities in the country and eventually take positions in the ranks of management in good companies or enter government or the professions. For a tiny number there may even be the possibility of reaching positions of national prominence. For although the students laugh at such a suggestion, they all know that the present Prime Minister of Japan, Hayato Ikeda, was born and brought up at the next little town down the coast and received his early education in local schools before going on to Kyoto University and the Finance Ministry. The possibility of such a career may seem remote to most children, but the school is geared to push its best students upward and outward, beyond Takehara, into the larger society. This is what most interests the principal and the teachers; the success or failure of this venture determines the school's true worth in their minds more than anything else. Their thoughts are bent to the cruel competitiveness of the university entrance examinations, a life crisis that has been magnified until it often literally defines the future itself.

The principal of Takehara High, Matsutarō Ueki, confirms this. He also deplores the fact that Takehara is not getting many of the best students in the district. With education largely determining the way up, parents are preoccupied with the problem of proper schools from the time their children are born or even before. If possible, they will send them to private schools or to schools attached to one of the universities, where they are eventually assured of a good chance to receive higher education. For those who must go to Takehara, their fate in the examinations affects not only the morale of the school but its very operation. Though the school is "public" and run by the prefecture, parents pay tuition of 650 yen a month (about $1.75). In addition they are called upon for an assortment of other contributions, including a 4,000 yen registration fee and regular monthly assessments for P.T.A. meetings, the "school support association," construction fees (for a new auditorium), equipment fees, and fees for health, athletics, library, and student associations. These levies may seem small to Americans, but out of an annual school budget of 25 million yen parents provide nearly 12 million through tuition and monthly contributions. The best way to encourage cheerful giving, in the principal's view, is to get a good percentage of children successfully into the universities.

Last year 101 students graduated from the general course. Of these,

36 (34 boys, two girls) took entrance examinations for four-year universities. Thirty (28 boys, two girls) passed. This was not a bad average by national standards. But most succeeded in entering private universities; only seven students (six boys, one girl) even tried to enter national universities, where standards and prestige are highest and examinations normally must be passed in seven or eight different subjects. Three boys and one girl passed into national universities, but none reached Tokyo; one entered Hiroshima University, and the rest went into lesser-known government institutions in the western Japan region. This illustrates the difficulty of reaching the top government schools—considered by far the most desirable ones by most children—from such outlying public schools

The high-school teachers, especially those in the general course, are caught up in this process of priming students for the university examinations. Although at first sight the teachers may appear to be indefatigable, a closer look will discover much strain and fatigue. Not only must they teach an average of 19 hours of classes each week, but they must also meet students at home in the morning before school commences or in the evening after supper for special coaching. For those students who are not going to a university the teachers have a peculiar responsibility, hardly encountered in American schools, to help find jobs. This is not quite so difficult nowadays, when times are good; indeed, last year for the first time in history a couple of company representatives turned up at the school looking for prospective employees. But teachers still must often travel as far as Osaka or Tokyo to make the rounds of offices where they have connections and recommend students to possible employers.

Their heaviest responsibility, however, is toward those who want to go on to a university. To these they must give mock examinations and advise them as best they can. The "examination complex" causes teachers much concern. Two young teachers at Takehara appealed to me for help. They asked: What should we do about truancy? Should we be severe or lenient? When students cut music to study math, and then pass the examinations, have they done wrong? Nothing in the books answers this question for them, or the deeper, more perplexing question of how to communicate with students, whose inarticulateness baffles them. Nowhere is the stratification of loneliness, the isolation of different age groups in a rapidly changing society more touching than in such a school. The principal, at fifty, takes an uneasy view of the "weakness of spirit" of some of his younger teachers, who reached maturity during or just after World War II. Six years ago, when I first met him, I found the principal pro-Socialist and highly critical of government policies. Today, a loyal member of the establishment, he is disturbed by his teachers' lack of interest in the values of a re-emergent nationalism, their indifference toward national flag and national anthem. To him, some of them spend far too much time playing *pachinko* and drinking sake in local inns, though he, too, is required to do a lot of the latter in the course of his official duties. He declares that some of the students, who never experienced the war, are more patriotic than their teachers, though they persist in their own characteristic delinquencies. The principal led in organizing a society to study Takehara's local history. But some of his younger assistants are bothered by more immediate problems. "How," one of them asked, "can I break down the impenetrable wall of my students' reserve? The Teachers Union is no help; all it wants us to do is demonstrate and struggle. None of the older teachers is able to help very much, either. We can play softball with other teachers and be friends in that way, but we can't really get to know their problems."

The boys from Takehara who go on to universities go mainly into economics or engineering, especially mechanical or electrical engineering. Some enter the standard course in government and administration, called "jurisprudence," which often leads into the bureaucracy, and a small number study literature, history, art, or some other branch of the humanities. By this standard of measurement, as by some others, what is being produced here is a technical civilization without much concern for problems of the human heart or spirit, or much interest in the past, except as a kind of incongruous prop, as the baseball players use Zen. The most evident intention of the smarter students is to better their condition, to go up the line. To achieve this the university is the indispensable path.

At Takehara I talked with four boys who now are seniors and who plan to take university entrance examinations next year. All are residents of the town. The first is the son of a tailor, who wants to go to Hiroshima University to study electrical engineering. Two others, children of a drugstore owner and high-school teacher, want to go to government universities and become journalists, often a way into politics. The fourth, son of a noodle-shop proprietor, intends to study education at Hiroshima University and become a junior-high-school teacher. His ambition is nicely circumscribed: "I don't think I am good enough to teach in high school."

Although children are pointed relentlessly toward the examination barrier from earliest childhood, some parents complain of one obvious consequence: the best students leave Takehara and never come back. Of unskilled labor there is no shortage. More and more people are moving down out of the hills and settling along the coast, and the planners in Takehara expect to use many of them to run the new factories now in the blueprint stage. Trade schools will train others in special skills. New industries could also afford more good managerial opportunities for university graduates and eventually bring them back to the area in larger numbers. But for the best educated and most venturesome, the real leaders of the future, Takehara is still a good place to be from, a through station on the life line. Their destinations are elsewhere.

CHAPTER *6*   ✿

MRS. MASUDA AND THE
BURAKU PEOPLE

May 28, 1958

A few months ago *Shūkan Asahi*, a mass-circulation weekly magazine published in Tokyo, carried a 15-page lead article on the eta, Japan's three million social outcasts who live in 6,000 segregated "special communities" (*tokushu buraku*). The illustrated article reported that these Japanese, identical with their fellows and legally free to live where they please, still follow a few restricted occupations and suffer discrimination at school, government office, and workplace. Numerous instances were cited to show how companies screen and reject job applicants with eta backgrounds; how prejudice leads to regular suicides of eta; how marriage within the group still is the rule; how eta have hardened in their attitudes toward the "outside" and strengthened social solidarity within their segregated areas. After describing poverty, poor housing and sanitation, unemployment, and apathy within the *buraku*, the article observed that neither of Japan's two major political parties has any effective policy for removing the eta from segregation and assimilating them into the larger society.

Two weeks ago at a Christian social center in the heart of Fukushima-chō, an eta community in Hiroshima, I interviewed a group of people, eta and non-eta, who are working with this problem at close range. The narrative which follows is a translation of a tape-recorded interview with one of these remarkable people, who herself is not an eta. Following her account I have summarized the historical background of this social problem and added some other current opinions concerning it.

* * *

Mrs. Etsuko Masuda, a gray-haired midwife in her fifties, speaks rapidly and profusely in the Hiroshima idiom:

"I was born on the twenty-eighth of November, 1905, in the town of Kōchi, in southern Shikoku. I was the fourth of six children; one brother and two sisters came before me, one brother and one sister after.

"My memory goes back only to about 1910, but I remember some of the things my mother told me about my father's youth. Our family came originally from Hiroshima, where my ancestors had been samurai of the lord of Asano. Father was born in 1860, and until he was seventeen he wore his hair in the old-fashioned topknot (*chommage*). Then he was forced by the new laws to have it cut. When he went to the barber he had his hair done up very beautifully in the formal fashion; his mother went along with him, and after the barber had done his work she held the cut hair in her hand and cried for a long time.

"As a very young man Father left Hiroshima and went to Tokyo to school. He finished his school days there (I never knew the name of the school) and taught for a while, but when his own father died he was called back to Hiroshima to take his place as a village headman in Yamagata-gun, up in the mountains behind the city of Hiroshima. Father was in his twenties at the time, very young for a village headman. But for some reason he soon left this and went to Kōchi to work in the local forestry bureau there. And there I was born.

"After the Meiji Restoration (1868) the position of the samurai and their families became very poor. They were dispossessed as a privileged military class and fell into bad times. Because of their immense pride many of them refused to go into trade. Father was no exception: he was conservative and old-fashioned and had his pride to consider; keeping up appearances meant everything to him, and he thought nothing was lower than a businessman. So like many of his old friends, he lost out in the new business era and the family gradually went downhill. Still, no matter how difficult things became, he never lost his spirit; he was always stiff and straightforward about what he believed.

"I got some of my own stubbornness from Father. I remember well when I was in the third grade in the primary school in Kōchi, one day

Father and I were in the sitting room, and I saw what I thought was a black bean on the surface of the floor mat. I pointed it out to Father. 'There's a black bean,' I said. Father retorted, 'That's not a bean. That's a fly.' I said nothing for a moment, and after a while I noticed that the bean began to move across the floor. Father noticed it, too, and said, 'See, what did I tell you, it's a fly. See it crawling.' But I would not admit that I was wrong. I insisted it was a black bean even though it was somehow moving. After that my nickname in the family was always *kuromame*, or black bean. Years later whenever anybody called me *kuromame* I would remember how mad Father had been at me for my stubbornness. We quarreled a good deal at that time; I think it was caused by Father's financial worries and the decline of the family's fortunes. He seemed to be inept at everything, but he never admitted it.

"When I was five, in the second grade, my younger brother was born. I remember that it was during the night. I woke up and smelled smoke and thought that something strange must be happening in the house. Then I heard the baby's crying. An old lady of the neighborhood was the midwife. This brother was a favorite of my mother. When he was three or four years old I remember how he would keep us laughing by imitating the fishmonger who peddled fish in the neighborhood. He carried a long bamboo pole balanced across his shoulders with a metal can at each end, and he would come round calling '*Aji*' or some such fish name in a loud voice. Little Brother's imitation of this was wonderful. I think this was when he was four.

"The next year he died. It was in February, and we were to celebrate Founding Day at the school. I was not a shy girl; I did well in school and took part in all the exercises. Mother was helping me to put on my *hakama* in the bedroom, and Little Brother was sitting on the bedclothes beside us. He was coughing a little, and as I walked out of the house I remember thinking he must have caught a cold. When the ceremony at school was done I came back home, but Mother and Father were both gone, and Little Brother, too. I asked the old lady who lived next door what had happened, where was Suteo? She told me they had taken him to the hospital. She said for us to wait in the house, and my two sisters and I stayed there until nightfall. Then the news came that Little Brother had died. We went quickly to the hospital and learned that he had died after just one day's illness. It was diphtheria. They had operated, but without success. We began to cry, and Mother was wild with grief. She spent many days at the memorial tablet for Suteo, and she would pour milk for him before the tablet just as though he were alive to drink it.

"Things were very unhappy at home after this. The next year my elder brother died at the age of eighteen. At about this time Father quit his job at the office and opened a store selling tobacco and handicrafts from Miyajima. But he had never been in trade—he had such pride— he would display all his goods for sale, but when customers came he didn't know how to get them to buy. It wasn't his nature to be a store- keeper, so he didn't prosper. He hated having to demean himself in such a way. After that he took to fishing all the time. He would go every day to the river or even sometimes to the sea, and he brought back so many fish that we would distribute them to the people of our neighbor- hood. I remember this very well. We had more fish than we could possibly eat, because Father was so fond of fishing. But he couldn't make a living. We moved from place to place. Father liked to change houses. After two or three years in a place he would rent a new house —it was never our own house that we lived in—and we went here and there looking for a less crowded place to live.

"Father and Mother were Buddhists, but they were not very strict about it. They taught me to put my hands together before the altar, but Buddhism never was something about which I personally had any feel- ing. When I was in the fifth grade we moved next door to a temple, and I used to take the short cut through the back gate of the temple to get through to the next street. Sometimes I would go to hear the priest give a sermon from his high platform. I remember once when the priest told a story that must have dated from Tokugawa times. A priest met a samurai on a bridge, and somehow the priest's cloak was blown by the wind so that it touched the sword of the samurai. At this the samurai got very angry and drew his sword to kill the priest, but the priest tucked up his cloak and, putting his hands together, intoned his *Namu Amida Butsu*. The samurai became frightened and ran away. I thought it was a foolish story, and going to the temple seemed a foolish thing to do. Yet I sometimes went and did my best to listen. At about this time I first went to the Christian Sunday School in Kōchi. One of my friends was going there, and she took me with her; she was a

Christian, and soon I began going to church on Sunday and to prayer meetings on Tuesday. God was inviting me, and so I became interested in Christianity. I had no interest in Buddhism, really.

"A few years later, when I was about fourteen, I met an evangelical missionary who had come to Kōchi from America many years before. This must have been in 1919 or 1920. The missionary's name was Miss Annie Doud, and she had come from Aberdeen, Mississippi. She was twenty-five when she arrived in Japan in 1892, so that she was already in her fifties when I met her. She is still alive, I believe, somewhere in America. Here is her picture. [Square face with sad, determined eyes, high-pompadoured sandy hair, black silk high-necked dress, white ruffles and a cameo at the throat.]

"This woman came all the way from a foreign country to work for the poor people of Kōchi, a country district far from the center of Japan. In the beginning she went out to remote and mountainous places, where most Japanese would not go. She traveled in a palanquin carried by two men, or sometimes she would go on horseback into distant parts where even the palanquin couldn't go. From the first she went alone, without an interpreter; although she may have known a little Japanese before she arrived, it couldn't have been much.

"On her travels she soon became interested in poor children and orphans, and she brought two small children back to Kōchi from one trip and adopted them and raised them as her own children. Where she got them and how she arranged it I never knew. Gradually she gathered together a whole collection of girl orphans, without any help from others, and gave them some education at her home. Then as the group got bigger and bigger she found it impossible to do everything by herself, and she communicated with a friend in America. Soon individual Americans began to support individual Japanese girls at Miss Doud's school in Kōchi. When I entered the school somebody in America paid my fees, too; but Miss Doud never told us the names of our benefactors. We called them *mama-san*, these Americans who sent us money for so long.

"At first Miss Doud had the school at her house, but later some money came from America and she was able to build a small school. I have a picture of the school at home. All the girls boarded at the school. Half the day we studied, and the other half we did embroidery. The produce of our labor was sent to America, and each student had a

monthly allotment of work. People in America would write to Miss
Doud what they wanted embroidered and we would do the work. For
every three yen worth of work we would get 25 sen pocket money
from America. Miss Doud tried to discourage us from asking our families for money, but we were all getting some help from our parents.

"In the morning every day we had an hour of English, then music
lessons, piano and songs sung together. There were about 100 girls in
the school when I arrived, and they took turns leading the church
services. During Miss Doud's early days in Kōchi she was helped by a
British couple named Ellis. Mr. Ellis was supposed to be of noble birth.
Mrs. Ellis had been sick, and the Japanese climate was supposed to be
good for her health. They came first to Yokohama, but then they were
told the climate in Kōchi was better, and Mr. Ellis sent his wife there
while he remained in his office in Yokohama. Mrs. Ellis gave some
financial help to Miss Doud. Mr. Ellis would come to see his wife from
time to time in his own motor launch from Yokohama.

"Miss Doud taught with her whole body, not just with her mouth. If
there is anything good in me, it is because of her. Although I had an
unknown benefactor in America and received four or five years of
education at the school, I had no formal obligation whatever to fulfill
after graduation. Nor did any of us. If we wanted to go to mission
school we could; or we could go back home if we wished. All that she
told us was that we should try to do as she did, to follow her example
and interest ourselves in poor people or people who had troubles. She
told us to welcome anyone who came to us; whether they were beggars
or wealthy people made no difference, she said. She was friendly to
everyone; I liked this best about her. It was through her concern for
the *tokushu buraku* people that I first became interested in their problems and decided to do what work I could among them.

"Of course, I had known about the *buraku* people since childhood.
From the time I was in the third grade many of the eta children who
lived in the *buraku* went to the same public school with me. In those
days discrimination against the *buraku* people was general and quite
overt. They lived in segregated areas as they do today; they were
treated like animals and had a fierce inferiority complex. Like everyone
else, Father said they were very different from other people and used
all the old terms of prejudice toward them. The *buraku* people themselves would say that since they were of the *buraku* there was nothing

they could do about it, no matter how much prejudice they felt. If discrimination was openly showed toward them, they would merely remain wrapped in silence. I remember feeling sorry for them, but as a child I had nothing to do with them and the problem did not concern me. Only after I met Miss Doud did the *buraku* begin to mean more to me.

"Today there is less prejudice against Christians in Japan, but when I was in Miss Doud's school things were different. While we were all leading the same group life at school we felt safe, but we knew that we could expect prejudice to show itself after we graduated. So before I left school Miss Doud told me that I must be ready for this, I must continue to go to church and otherwise to keep my faith strong. I graduated in 1924 and the same year returned to Hiroshima. I remember it was just after Grandmother died at the age of 92. Father and the family remained in Kōchi, but I had heard of an opportunity in Hiroshima. The city government had established a sort of neighborhood social center in Fukushima-chō, where *buraku* people lived; mostly they were shoemakers or people who slaughtered or sold meat. I decided to try for a job as a nursery worker and general helper at this center, or *Rimpokan*, as it is still called.

"This was a terribly hard decision for me to make. When my mother's brother, who was living in Hiroshima, heard about it, he declared that he would cut me off completely from my mother's side of the family. He was, I remember, a very old-fashioned person. Up until the end of the Second World War (he was killed by the atom bomb in 1945) he kept a full suit of armor standing in the front entrance of the house at night; and a samurai's spear and shield always hung from the crossbeam in his bedroom. He told me that the work I contemplated was unclean, that it would ruin the family name; he warned me he would disinherit me. He made me so mad by his stubbornness that my own stubbornness was aroused, and I told him that since he refused to understand, I would no longer recognize him as my uncle. We had a bad scene, and I left the house. I got the job at the *Rimpokan*, but soon I had trouble there, too. The head of the *Rimpokan* was a Buddhist, and he told me that, since Buddhism had a very strong hold in Fukushima-chō, if the city officials found out there was a Christian working there, it would mean trouble for him and for me. He urged me to hide the fact that I was a Christian and not to say anything about it.

"This may have been my testing time. I thought that if I hid my Christianity and then failed to do a good job, it would be worse than if a Buddhist had failed, and I would be in trouble with myself. After all, I had gone to the *Rimpokan* in the first place *because* I was a Christian, and I thought I could not stay there if I had to conceal my faith. So I told everyone clearly from the beginning that I was a Christian. It was my *kuromame* nature, I guess; anyhow, everybody recognized that I was stubborn, and they didn't bother to try to change my mind. As soon as I declared openly that I was a Christian I had no trouble, nobody asked me anything; apparently they thought it couldn't be helped. Some of my friends at Miss Doud's school failed to state their faith clearly and openly, and they ran into difficulties along the way. But since that time I have never had any real difficulty from being identified as a Christian.

"Not long after that I was married. This was in 1925. I met my husband at the *Rimpokan*, where he was on the staff. He was not a *buraku* person, but neither did his family have the pretensions that mine had; and since he was working among the *buraku* people I knew there would be difficulties with my family over the match. When I made up my mind to marry him, my father's older brother went to consult my maternal uncle, the proud one. But he said that since I no longer had any connection with the family I could do as I liked. He refused to become involved in any way in the marriage transaction. So I was married after this one consultation only, without the sanction of my mother's side of the family. For several years we worked side by side at the *Rimpokan*, and then my husband became its head, replacing the devout Buddhist who had been there when I first came. My husband held that position for more than ten years. Later he was transferred to the social welfare department of the city of Hiroshima. For more than a decade after my marriage I never set foot in my mother's brother's house. But later on my uncle softened somewhat. By this time the *buraku* and the people who lived in them were becoming more generally talked about, and I think he understood a little what my motives had been. Finally I went to see him, and he received me; he really was delighted to see me, and he even came to call on us in our new home.

"After my husband left the *Rimpokan* to work downtown I began to work as a midwife in the *buraku* neighborhood where we lived. Before the war nearly all babies were delivered at home by midwives.

Only abnormal cases would enter clinics or hospitals. But just after the war an American came here and gave training to midwives in American maternity-clinic procedures. This person said that in the United States nearly all expectant mothers went to maternity clinics or hospitals. After that the midwives in Hiroshima began to turn their homes into "clinics." Now 70 per cent to 80 per cent of all babies are born in these "clinics," and only 20 per cent to 30 per cent in private homes. Of course, there are many qualified doctors, but licensed midwives still do much of the work. The kind of house-to-house practice I was doing when I began has almost disappeared.

"However, I was kept busy with my practice during the war; and on the morning the atom bomb fell I was on my way to give nursing care to nine new babies I had delivered in the western outskirts of Hiroshima. I was in a hurry, and since I had trouble getting a streetcar I started out on foot in the direction of Koi. I was wearing *mompei* [coarse cotton trousers] and carrying my satchel and a silk umbrella. When I had got about halfway across the big bridge between Fukushima and Koi I heard the sound of an airplane. I had just opened my umbrella, and swinging it around, I looked back over my shoulder but saw nothing. I turned back to go on over the bridge, and in the instant of turning I saw the flash. At the same moment I realized that my umbrella was on fire, and I sensed that everything behind me was burning. In my astonishment I was thrown completely off the bridge onto the riverbank below. For a few moments the air became very dark, but then I got up and the sky lightened again. I saw a plane disappearing in the distance, its sound growing more and more faint.

"I thought I had better get home quickly, and then I remembered that I was the head of a rescue unit. Since I had some responsibility I hurried back toward the nearest streetcar stop. But there I met a mob of people, many of them burned, rushing out of the city. From then on I was busy trying to give first aid. A crowd of children came, and I took them to an open field not far away. The next thing I remember was trying to put many of these children to sleep in that field. Finally toward night I got back to my house. It was then that I first realized that the whole back of my *mompei* had been burned off. My neighbor, Mrs. Nogi, saw me come in and she told me in such an embarrassed way that I had on absolutely nothing behind. All day I had been treating and waiting on people and I hadn't even noticed it. I was amazed. Our house had been knocked over, but I went inside the mess and took off the *mompei* and put on some others I found. That night I became sick. I had been burned on my back, on the backs of my legs and hands. I hurt so that I could barely move, but during the night someone came to ask me to deliver a baby. It was a girl of nineteen who was having her first baby, and she had been pulled out of a knocked-down house. Her leg was broken, and we couldn't make a fire to boil water, so I just cleaned the baby with a cloth and borrowed a shirt from somebody to wrap it in. On my way back I fainted and had to be carried home. From then on I stayed in bed. My burns healed in about eight months. Last year I had some fainting spells and my blood count was low, but I had an examination at the hospital, and I'm all right now.

"As far as the *buraku* is concerned, on the surface there have been some improvements, but underneath the problem still remains. Only the forms of prejudice are changing. When I was a girl people refused to eat with eta, to go into their houses or allow them to cross the threshold. But today there is fairly free access both ways. My five children are, of course, not eta, but they were brought up here in the *buraku* and have lived here all their lives. Naturally they have become aware of the problem. I know that when someone asks one of them, 'Don't you live in Fukushima-chō?' the child is well aware of the implications of the question. They have made a conscious effort not to develop feelings of inferiority simply because they lived in this district, but of course this is difficult for them to avoid.

"Discrimination is worst when marriage is the issue. There still is a feeling that the *buraku* people have dirty blood, that they are in some way more closely akin to animals than ordinary people are—although such prejudice may be hidden. Young people nowadays are marrying into the *buraku*, or *buraku* people are marrying out of it, more than before, but this is still the most serious point of prejudice. On the whole, *buraku* people want to stay where they are, because there they are relatively safe. Limited in occupation and living area, apathetic and resigned, they have become hardened in their isolation. Since the war they have been somewhat more receptive toward Christianity, but Buddhism, especially Shin sect Buddhism, maintains a tight hold. My second and fourth sons have been baptized as Christians. The first and third sons have been to church with me since they were small children, and although they have not been baptized, they know the hymn book very well . . ."

* * *

Discrimination against the eta is ancient, predating the arrival of Buddhism in the sixth century A.D., when Japanese society was divided roughly into the free and the base. After Buddhism became popular, a stigma attached to those who killed meat and worked with leather, and this Buddhist feeling fused with Shintō emphasis on ritual purification and an abhorrence of defilement, e.g., by blood or death. Certain groups from the lower levels of society became specialized in hereditary occupations as butchers, shoemakers, and workers in other despised trades. Later, during the civil wars of the fifteenth and sixteenth centuries, leather workers were needed to supply weapons and articles of armor, and for a time their status rose somewhat; but during the Tokugawa era (1615–1868) strict regulations kept the eta in place at the bottom of society. They were rigidly segregated by dwelling area on the banks of rivers or in other unproductive fringe districts. There they were forbidden to marry "ordinary" Japanese, and eventually the mere fact of living in a segregated community led to discrimination from outsiders, who regarded, and still regard, the eta with fear, disgust, and loathing.

In 1871, after the Meiji Restoration, the eta were legally emancipated and allowed to live where they wished; however, social and economic discrimination against them continued. In the early 1920's, when liberal ideas spread in educated circles, the eta became an object of concern. A movement called the *Suiheisha* developed, which adopted for its flag a crown of thorns and encouraged the eta to confront and accuse those who showed prejudice against them. These radical tactics shocked most Japanese, and the *Suiheisha* failed to achieve its goals through confrontation. However, its descendants survived and have reappeared, in weakened and transformed condition, in the post-World War II period. Along with a general radicalization of the "social movement" the eta have found themselves championed by new leagues and committees ostensibly devoted to their "liberation" and unquestionably eager for their votes. Ever since 1922 the "liberation" movement has been led by Jiichirō Matsumoto, Diet member from Fukuoka prefecture, himself a *buraku* person and leader of an extreme left-wing faction of the Social-ist party. On the testimony of persons interviewed in Hiroshima, Matsumoto's Liberation Committee (*Kaihō Iinkai*) and later Liberation League (*Kaihō Dōmei*) were and are penetrated by Communists.

The Japanese government has not yet made any concerted effort to break up the eta communities or to provide more than remedial meas-ures inside their boundaries. Some say this is because the eta are concen-trated in western Japan, remote from Tokyo and out of the focus of national interest. A more likely cause for neglect is that, with new millions annually seeking jobs, the government can scarcely be eager to enlarge the variety of opportunities for eta. Some slow steps are being taken in the public-school system, where a program of "equality education" is under way; but it cannot be said that anything tangible has yet resulted from this.

One member of the Hiroshima City Assembly, a *buraku* person who is prominent in local efforts to improve the situation, insisted that neither conservatives nor Socialists have much real interest in solving the problem. "The conservatives try to exploit the *buraku* people," he said, "and to organize cliques of followers among them for personal gain. Socialists and Communists are emphasizing control through loy-alty to party organizations; but in either case control, not freedom from prejudice, is the main objective. The prefectural government has built some public toilets, a few wells and water systems, and two new apartments accommodating 48 families. The *Rimpokan* provides a day nursery for 100 children whose parents are working and some treat-ment for trachoma and other ailments common in the *buraku*. Gen-erally, though, prejudice persists and the real problem of assimilation remains unsolved. Most Japanese simply avoid talking about the subject and pretend it doesn't exist. But as long as it is unsolved we Japanese cannot afford to laugh at you Americans in Little Rock."

Other opinions reflect the spread of leftist propaganda in the *buraku*. In Kyoto the Buraku Problems Research Institute, closely associated with the Liberation League, has published a number of books on the subject. In 1955, for example, Tatsuya Naramoto, executive director of the Institute and a professor at Ritsumeikan University, wrote a book in which he blamed the whole problem on the "feudalism" which continues to characterize Japanese social relationships. According to Naramoto, this "feudalism" is encouraged by American policy toward

Japan. "The thing that intensifies discrimination and nourishes the *buraku* today is American imperialism combined with reactionary forces in our own country. The great road to liberation lies in resisting this by the power of democracy." [1] In Hiroshima the head of the local branch of the Liberation League, an eta shoemaker, took a similar line: "Strikes in the *buraku* or other direct action will not succeed, because the big capitalists would bring in machines to make the shoes, and where would we be then? Already our business is declining in the face of machine-made products. The U.S. and the big capitalists in Tokyo are putting us out of business. Our league constantly is talking about what sort of action to take, but we have shifted from direct action to training young leaders who will not have an inferiority complex. Political consciousness is low, and the *buraku* people feel strongly only about local or sensational issues, such as suicides caused by discrimination. Labor union people think they are better than we are and won't bring in unions. Nobody will spend any of his own time or money in the *buraku* if he can help it."

The magazine article with which I began and a number of similar articles in other magazines and newspapers have done more than anything else to bring the eta to widespread public attention in recent months. What the Japanese call *masu komi*, mass communications, undoubtedly are playing an important part in spreading awareness of all sorts of problems, social and otherwise. Government officials confirm this judgment: prefectural authorities in Hiroshima showed me two scrapbooks of news clippings, many of them concerning the eta, compiled within the last four or five years.

Today many of the old proscriptions against meat eating and the like have declined or vanished. Not all butchers or shoemakers are eta, by any means. But the segregated communities remain, and antagonism against those who live within them is still harsh. Animal characteristics often are imputed to eta: for example, there is a superstition that every eta contains one dog bone in his skeleton. Commonly they are identified with *yotsu*, the number four, which implies close association

[1] Naramoto, Tatsuya. *Buraku Mondai* (*The Buraku Problem*). (Kyoto, 1955), p. 12. For recent work in English see John D. Donoghue, "An Eta Community in Japan: The Social Persistence of Outcaste Groups," *American Anthropologist*. Vol. 59, No. 6 (December 1957), pp. 1000–1017. Also Shigeaki Ninomiya, "An Inquiry Concerning the Origin, Development, and Present Situation of the Eta, etc.," *Transactions of the Asiatic Society of Japan*, Second Series, Vol. 10 (December 1933), pp. 47–154.

with four-legged animals. (The meaning of this term may be communicated silently by extending four fingers of one hand; sometimes two fingers of each hand, or three of one and one of the other, are used.) In recent years more and more eta have been able to "pass" on the outside, in the swarms of Tokyo, Osaka, and elsewhere. Since no color difference is involved the problem is not the same as that faced by an American Negro. However, "passing" means cutting off completely from the *buraku;* even a postmark on a letter might give away one's origins, and the consequences of failure to "pass" are catastrophic. On the whole, however, centuries of discrimination have created reactions among the eta which tend to keep them together within the *buraku.*

CHAPTER *7*

"MIZUCHŌ" IN HIS DISTRICT

January 20, 1958

The expectation that the Japanese Diet will be dissolved and a general election called in the near future has greatly raised the pitch of excitement in this normally political season. Commuters packed by the hundreds of thousands into the clammy subways or crowded at bus stops on these frosty January mornings read of pre-election maneuverings among the many cliques and factions of government officials, party politicians, and the businessmen who help to support them; in the remarkably free press the inner workings of Japan's parliamentary system are daily exposed for all to see. Guessing the dissolution date has become the main pastime of newspaper, radio, and television commentators, and *kaisan* (dissolution) shares the Tokyo headlines with *jinkō eisei* (man-made satellite) and *uchū jidai* (space age).

As the pace of politics quickens, Diet members return frequently from the capital to their home districts to tend to their *jiban*, or base of support in their constituencies. Incumbents as well as new competitors for the nomination may go directly to the people. They may charter buses to take constituents to hot spring resorts or pay taxi drivers to advertise their abilities to their fares. Some will send gifts of various sorts to children or to old people. One recent novelty is the showing of color slides by candidates who have traveled abroad—which may help to explain why every Japanese tourist carries a camera! Those who feel more secure will concentrate on many meetings with key power holders on the local scene: labor bosses, heads of farm organizations, town assemblymen and bureaucrats, or representatives of women's and youth groups who are in a position to influence voting when the election comes. All alike are preoccupied with their *jiban*, and with how to strengthen it for the test ahead.

Among the politicians who returned from Tokyo to their home districts during the recent New Year holidays was one who is well-known all over Japan. His name is Chōzaburō Mizutani, and his district is the Kyoto First, which includes nearly the whole of the city of Kyoto.

Mizutani, or "Mizuchō," as he is familiarly called, was born in 1897, the son of an innkeeper in Fushimi, now a part of Kyoto city. His father died early, but his mother promised to keep him in school if he was diligent, and he finished Dai San Kō, the old "Third High School," and graduated from the Law Department of Kyoto Imperial University in 1921. At this time popular interest in *demokurashii*, Marxism and the "social movement" was sweeping over Japan; the Allied victory over the Central Powers, the apparent efficacy of democracy and the League of Nations, and especially the success of the Russian Revolution impressed educated people in the old city of Kyoto. At Kyoto University Mizutani studied economics under the famous Hajime Kawakami, the leading Marxist scholar of his time in Japan. Moved by Kawakami's interest in problems of the poor, Mizutani absorbed Marxist theory and turned naturally to the labor movement, then in its infancy and destined to lead a persecuted existence until the end of World War II. For a time he did research and lectured at the Ōhara Institute of Social Problems in Osaka and taught at Ritsumeikan University, a school with a long radical tradition and close ties with Kyoto University. Many members of the Kyoto University faculty also taught at Ritsumeikan. During this early period Mizutani wrote several tracts, including one called *Kaikyū Ishiki Ron* (*Class Consciousness*). Also during this period he was associated with the Christian Socialist leader, Toyohiko Kagawa, who already was well-known for his work among the laborers in the Kobe slums. On the evidence of a contemporary of those days, Mizutani was baptized as a Christian by Kagawa. Mizutani himself kept a voluminous diary, but he says that he later destroyed it for fear it would incriminate too many people if found by the police.

In 1928, in the first general election after the granting of universal manhood suffrage, Mizutani was elected to the Lower House of the Diet. He has remained there ever since, successfully weathering nearly a dozen general elections. At one time he was secretary-general of the Labor-Farmer party (*Rōdō-Nōmintō*), which was to the left of the Socialists and practically indistinguishable in policies from the Communists. Later he joined the Social Masses party (*Shakai Taishūtō*), a merger of left-wing groups, which was taken over by the conservative forces and absorbed into the Imperial Rule Assistance Association just before the war. Shortly before the party disappeared Mizutani was one of a group of eight Socialist leaders who were expelled for "radical" views in a party controversy.

Although, like many other young Japanese of his generation and later, Mizutani was deeply impressed by Marxism, he did not become a Communist. Rather, as he grew older, he became known as a shrewd politician and an advocate of gradual parliamentary progress toward socialism. In 1947–48 he served as Minister of Commerce and Industry in the coalition government of the right-wing Socialist, Tetsu Katayama; and he retained this post when Katayama was succeeded as Premier (early in 1948) by the conservative ex-diplomat, Hitoshi Ashida. In 1951, when the Socialist party split wide open over the San Francisco Peace Treaty, Mizutani was found in the right wing, where he served up until 1955 as chief of the Policy Research Board (*Seisaku Shingikai*). Since reunification of the party in 1955 he has moved up into the role of official party "councilor," a position reserved for a small number of elder statesmen in the party.

Mizutani lives today in a rambling old house a few doors back of the Minamiza, the *kabuki* theater in Gion, across the river from downtown Kyoto. A vigorous man of sixty-one, he holds forth on any and all subjects, full of zest and humor ("America must be very rich to send so many scholars to study Japan"), and loves rich food and drink more than is good for his high blood pressure. Watching him restrain himself to a few swallows of beer while going through a five-course *fugu* dinner can be a fairly painful experience. His temperament is humane without being vulgar, and no doubt his qualities of conscientiousness and sincerity, coupled with a proper restraint, have helped to make him popular among the Japanese. Women are said to be fond of his manner of speaking, and university students regard him as a kind of model, full of uncorrupted humor and humanity, and genuinely concerned with improving the lot of the poor.

Mizutani's concern for social problems has taken a number of forms during his career, but he has taken the deepest interest in one question which grows directly out of the needs of the district he represents: how to improve the economic position of those who spend their lives working at low wages in small shops, the so-called *chūshō kigyō* of Japan.

In an earlier Report (see Chapter 2, "A Japanese Small Industry") I discussed the role of small-scale industry in the Japanese economy and reported in some detail on the operation of a small factory in the northern section of the city of Kyoto. I mentioned the tenacious survival of small shops, both of producers and merchandisers, alongside more modern large-scale enterprises, and suggested some of the reasons for this phenomenon: the persistence of Japanese taste for traditional consumer goods, the weakness of capital resources, the diffused character of power resources and technology throughout the country, and so on. I also stressed that many, perhaps most small industries were forced to accept subcontract relationships with larger concerns in order to stay afloat, and this meant they often remain at the mercy of large operators for supplies of raw materials and for access to the market, both domestic and foreign. Other problems such as high taxes and deteriorating equipment also have forced small entrepreneurs into debt and made their position generally precarious.

Japanese conservative politicians, oriented toward and supported by large *zaibatsu*-type corporations and business combinations, have been very slow to do anything effective to improve the position of small enterprise in the economy.

The problem is a serious one for the Socialists. The conclusion is generally accepted in Japan that the Socialists have got about all the votes they can expect to get from the organized labor movement. The heavily leftist General Council of Trade Unions (*Sōhyō*) with 3,500,000 members has up to now been the main financial support of the Socialists and an important core of their strength at election time. Many moderate Socialists, including Mizutani, have felt that the party was in danger of being swallowed by *Sōhyō*, with its strong emphasis on class struggle and its virtual identification with Communist party policies. As Mizutani put it, "The left wing of the party insists on breaking off Japan's dependence on the U.S. But first the Socialist party should break off its own dependence on *Sōhyō*. Of 80 Socialists in the Upper House of the Diet, 43 are candidates put up by *Sōhyō*."

As a cabinet minister Mizutani pressed unsuccessfully for remedial legislation in the field of small business and industry. No doubt the desire for personal political gain and the improvement of society were nicely balanced in his mind. He came from a city famous for its ancient handicrafts and composed very largely of small shops, where the line between proprietors and laborers was often vague or even nonexistent. It was among these people that his *jiban* lay, rather than among the more highly unionized workers in large factories under *Sōhyō* control.

Finally, in 1949, shortly after Premier Yoshida returned to office, a bill was passed providing for the widespread organization of producers and retailers co-operatives of several types among small establishments. Although the Small Enterprise Co-operatives Law has been amended several times by the conservatives to increase government control and inspection, it still is on the books and the co-operative movement has developed a close relationship to Mizutani's political career.

Article One of the law states that it is intended "to provide corporate organizational structure by which smaller enterprises, workers or other persons may engage in lawful business on the co-operative plan and, by mutual aid, achieve fair and equal business opportunity in the field of commerce, industry, mining, transportation, marketing and related services. . . ." Co-operatives have been formed steadily among small enterprises since the law passed. By the end of 1956 there were more than 24,000 so-called common-facility co-operatives (*jigyō kyōdō kumiai*) and about 11,000 joint-enterprise co-operatives (*kigyō kyōdō kumiai*), as well as several hundred credit co-operatives. Common-facility co-ops are groups of independent businessmen who organize to improve productivity in various ways but retain their separate identities as private operators. In joint-enterprise co-ops enterprises to some extent pool their capital and labor resources, and the *kumiai* headquarters operates all the businesses which belong to the co-op. Councils of individual proprietors retain voting rights, but managerial authority is centralized in the hands of a *kumiai* manager with a full-time staff, which receives earnings, enforces bookkeeping procedures, sets wages and hours and production quotas, fixes prices, and distributes profits. *Kumiai* members also receive some income-tax advantages from joining the co-operative. In the city of Kyoto today there are at least 200 such co-operatives, comprising about half of all small enterprises engaged in retailing and service functions, as well as many small producers.

Co-operatives attracted a variety of leaders with a great assortment of backgrounds. The great majority of co-operatives, in Kyoto and elsewhere, have remained under the control of conservative politicians: the naturally conservative inclinations of the members have kept loyalty to the government party strong. On the other hand, at least a half-dozen of the joint-enterprise-type co-ops in Kyoto are reported to have come under the control of the Communist party, and a number of others are subject to varying degrees of Communist penetration, which is probably impossible to chart with much accuracy.

One outstanding person connected with co-operatives in Kyoto is Saburō Okazaki, managing director of the *Daiwa Kigyō Kumiai*, a joint-enterprise co-operative, which has just opened its new building, erected out of profits of the *kumiai*, in the center of the city. Mizutani is an "adviser" to this *kumiai*, and the relationship between Mizutani and Okazaki may help to explain how local politics works.

Okazaki is about fifty, an intense, loquacious man, one of those Japanese one immediately recognizes as important in his own field, surer of himself than most and ready to give opinions on his subject. Mizutani, introducing him to me, called him the "boss" of the co-operative he directs. But Okazaki wears two hats: he is director of a *kumiai*, but he also serves as chief of the education and propaganda section and a member of the executive committee of the Kyoto branch of the Japan Socialist party. Thus he combines in an interesting way the roles of businessman and politician. His hostility toward *Sōhyō* is clear, and he is aligned with Mizutani against the *Sōhyō* faction in the local party hierarchy.

Okazaki grew up before the war as the son of a small embroidery merchant in Kyoto. However, his father's business went under during the 1930's ("on account of the discriminatory policies of the government") and Okazaki went to Manchuria, where for a time he was employed in a government corporation building houses for factory workers. During the war he joined the Japanese Army and remained in Manchuria, where he was captured when the Russians occupied the territory. According to one source (not Okazaki), he remained a prisoner for a year, received political indoctrination, and became a Communist. On repatriation to Japan, however, Okazaki was repelled by the violent tactics of the local Communists and refused to join the party. Instead, he joined the Socialist party. For a time he engaged in organizing farmers unions, but when the Small Enterprise Co-operative Law went into effect, Okazaki returned to the area in which he had grown up and soon came to Mizutani's notice as an able and experienced organizer. Okazaki had wide connections which could be useful to Mizutani, while if the Socialists came to power Mizutani would be in a position to help Okazaki. Naturally, their relationship soon become close.

In describing the operation of the *kumiai* Okazaki is careful to point out that the law prohibits the co-operative from any political activity; especially it prohibits contributions to any party in the name of the *kumiai*. By this he does not mean that there are no contributions, but merely that they are accepted from *kumiai* members as individuals and that it will be quite impossible to secure specific figures. He readily admits that the *kumiai* have great political significance to the local Socialists. As he explains it, there is absolutely no use trying to get small businessmen to become party members, nor is there any need for this; ideology has little or no appeal to those who work in the myriads of small shops. Most of them are not politics-conscious, but they are acutely profit-conscious and tax-conscious and money-conscious generally. If the *kumiai* can do something for them, if it can rationalize their production methods and raise their purchasing power even a little, they will incur that much obligation to the *kumiai*, and the *kumiai* chief and his circle of politically alert assistants will be able to exert some degree of influence over them when elections come. They will be able to deliver the votes of a certain proportion of the 1,200 members of the *kumiai* and the 1,800 wives and children of voting age who depend upon them. Moreover, Mizutani will be glad to add their contributions to his campaign fund, to which the party can contribute only some 20 per cent of what he needs for reelection.

In Okazaki's *kumiai* there are 195 establishments, including such enterprises as fabric-dyeing shops, beauty parlors, bookstores, and stores selling Western-style clothes or traditional foods. Among the 1,200 members (employers and employees together) probably not more than a handful are members of the Socialist party. Nationwide dues-paying membership is estimated at around 50,000. The story is different, however, in the office of the *kumiai*. There, out of 200 employees 50 are dues-paying members of the party. These headquarters personnel are making a considerable effort to spread "education" among the member enterprises; regular weekly lecture meetings are being held at headquarters to discuss (mainly) economic issues Japan faces, such as raw-materials shortage, marketing problems, trade difficulties with the U.S., and so on. Mizutani himself gives an occasional lecture at the *kumiai*, and often uses the time to explain some new legislation which is pending in the Diet and which may pertain to the world of small enterprises. Such occasions also give him an opportunity to pass decisions of the central authorities in Tokyo down to local power circles, and such channels may be more important than formally established ones. Just as the left-wing labor unions have set up "labor schools" to utilize the services of noted Marxist professors, so there is some effort to spread Socialist ideas among the workers in small industries.

Mizutani is a good example of the prewar variety of "old Socialist" in Japan. To many of the more radical theoreticians in the party, who have come to prominence since the war, it seems he has compromised too often and too long with "monopoly capitalism." Though his early training in Marxist economics has never quite relinquished its grip on his mind, the experience of several decades in the labor movement under very unfavorable conditions did not make him a Communist. In his social life, far from espousing violence, he has fit into his place and accepted his obligations in the "hierarchy of statuses" which still to some extent describes Japanese society. The fact that he never was put in jail, as so many of his colleagues were before the war, indicates that his views could not have been considered very dangerous by the government.

His personal popularity increased with time; he had the combination of humor and decorum which is so much admired, and he returned again and again to the national Diet. In seven of the last ten elections he received the highest number of votes cast in his district, a rather rare feat for a Socialist candidate. Slowly building his *jiban*, he became almost unassailable in his district and in the process developed into a political boss, a benevolent ruler but nonetheless a ruler of a local hierarchy based first on personal ties and only secondarily on any ideological program.

Although the Socialists are glad to have him, those young men who would like to strengthen local party organization and reduce the party's dependence on personalities regard Mizutani with somewhat mixed feelings. They speak proudly of him as the "Emperor" of Kyoto, but in the same breath they admit that "unfortunately Mizutani *is* the party" in that city.

Such feelings are shared, though only partly expressed, by Mizutani's protégé, Eiichi Nagasue, who is slated to run with Mizutani's blessing when the latter retires. Nagasue is not quite sure when this will be; in the meantime he is engaged in building up his own *jiban* by serving in the city and prefectural assemblies, lecturing at Dōshisha University, and conducting public opinion polls at the "Nagasue Public Opinion Research Institute" in the best-approved manner.

Nagasue, like Okazaki, is a keen and energetic person, but he is not a businessman, but rather an intellectual with an interest in Socialist theory who has got into politics. He wants to attract more people into the party and wonders how to do this. As he says, "If a person joins the party and pays 50 yen a month dues, he has a right to expect more in return than two issues of the party newspaper." Unlike Mizutani, who has no international interests, Nagasue has traveled abroad, has been much impressed by labor and farm organizations in Israel, and maintains some ties with Asian Socialist youth groups and elsewhere. Possibly Mizutani had similar interests when he was younger, but Nagasue strikes me as less of a practical politician, at least at this stage of his career.

One of Nagasue's most perplexing problems is determining when Mizutani will retire and perhaps discreetly stimulating him to make the decision to do so. Nagasue is now around forty and anxious to get into the national arena. But although he has established himself locally, and has an eventual mandate to run, Mizutani has not shown any signs of withdrawing from his seat, and he thus controls Nagasue's future in a very literal way.

The nominating process is now going on all over the country, in anticipation of the coming general election. Candidates are chosen on the local level by party committees, which submit names to local party plenary bodies. Here the choices are rubber-stamped and forwarded to Tokyo, where central party authorities make most of the real decisions. The conservatives, who have been in power almost continuously since the end of the war, now have a majority of 291 seats out of 467 in the Lower House of the Diet. The coming election will be the first since the conservatives merged into a single party in November 1955. In the last election, in February 1955, the two then-existing conservative parties put up a total of 537 candidates. Since only 291 of these were elected, there exists a pool of more than 200 defeated candidates, many of whom seek to run again. In addition to these, many brand-new candidates have appeared. On the other hand, party leaders wish to limit candidates to 400 in the coming election and concentrate on electing as many of them as possible. This means only some 110 openings are available for several times that many aspiring candidates.

This is the sort of problem that plagues the conservatives under the present medium-sized electoral district system (three to five seats per district). They are eager to push through a single member district system in which they could elect by securing a simple majority of the votes. Such a system could hurt the Socialists, most of whose candidates, unlike Mizutani, squeeze in near the end of the list and would not be able to win a majority in many districts.

The Socialists also are busy choosing candidates, and Mizutani attended meetings for this purpose during his recent visit to Kyoto. The Socialists have 157 seats, a bare one-third of the Lower House. The party wants to put up around 300 candidates and hopes to win 25 to 30 seats. Thus they need about 140 new candidates, in addition to incumbents. However, qualified candidates are scarce and are found mainly in the large cities, whereas party leaders are turning more and more to rural areas to find candidates who can overthrow conservative strongholds in back-country prefectures.

Nagasue recently attempted to get his name approved as a candidate from Kyoto's First District. He argued that with Mizutani's strength so secure the district would be certain to elect another Socialist, if given the chance (actually there are two Socialist incumbents in the district, and Nagasue wants to make it three). However, Mizutani did not agree with this reasoning. As a result the nominating committee voted against Nagasue. They told him he was young enough to wait awhile; for the time being he could continue to cultivate his *jiban* in local elective positions (he now serves in the prefectural assembly). As Nagasue himself explained it, Mizutani feared that another candidate in the field would endanger his own chances. He was inclined to put his own safety ahead of the opportunity, as Nagasue saw it, to pick up another seat for the party—his own.

Nagasue was disgruntled over his setback and a bit dubious about how much longer he would have to wait for his day. But whatever the reason for his rejection, his case was far from unique. Such questions of nomination and support are the stuff of which Japanese politics is made. As the time for the election grows nearer every Diet member will have to face and solve his own special problems. These will differ greatly depending on the area, its pressure groups, and its other peculiarities. Many older politicians are as secure in their districts as Mizutani, with their reputations made, their *jiban* intact, their lieutenants at the ready, their successors chosen and waiting. The rest—the one-timers, would-be new candidates and former also-rans—all would like to be.

PART TWO   ❁   ❁   ❁

NATIONAL ISSUES AND PROBLEMS

CHAPTER *8* ❀   ❀   ❀

FOUR FAMILY BUDGETS

February 15, 1959

Down in Kasumigaseki, the Japanese government center in Tokyo, two banners flap in the wind from buildings on opposite sides of the street. One, atop the Ministry of Finance, proclaims in bold, black characters that "Savings are the power of tomorrow!" The other, suspended from a window of the Ministry of Agriculture and Forestry, advises the people to "Protect your health with milk!"

These slogans, with their solemn, modern ring, embody two of the most central concerns of those who govern this country. For on proper consumption and proper restraint from it depend the strength of the people, the expansion of exports, and the health of Japan's whole island economy.

For nearly a decade now the government's formidable statistical machinery has produced white paper after white paper to inform the world that the Japanese standard of living is unquestionably rising; that in most categories, average consumer spending by household passed the prewar level in 1954 and continued to climb, until by 1957 it had reached about 117 per cent of 1934–36; and that the ratio of savings to disposable income now exceeds the prewar average and is higher than the savings rate of any other country in the world. Nearly every economic summary emphasizes postwar urban wage increases, higher levels of rural living, and improvements in the people's diet, as well as increases in consumer purchases of household durables and other items.

While economic statistics can tell a great deal about the changing

91

level of Japanese living standards, they are somewhat less helpful in conveying a sense of the scale of actual living conditions. But what are some of the everyday dimensions within which Japanese families earn and buy and achieve different levels of livelihood? What do consumers take for granted, and for what do they mainly yearn? How, short of writing 92 million biographies, can the context of consumer living be made more meaningful to those distant from the scene?

In the hope of suggesting partial answers to these questions I shall present material on the income and household living expenditures of four urban Japanese families. Two are white-collar, two blue-collar. The youngest of the husbands is thirty-four, the oldest forty-six. No claim is made that these are "average" families; in general, however, they represent a cut across urban Japanese society from the lower-middle toward the upper-middle levels, and their living conditions are more or less similar to those of millions of other Japanese. The upper levels of society, about which most is known in the West, are not represented here. None of the families was known to me previously, but access to them was arranged through personal contacts without resort to opinion-polling agencies or questionnaires. Most of the information was collected during interviews in the home of each family, with husbands, wives, and some of the children participating. Most of the figures quoted were taken from written budget records kept by each housewife. Obviously there is room for error here; however, in most cases data was given readily, and I have no reason to believe that any of it was deliberately falsified.

I: A YOUNG "SALARY MAN"

Akira Kondō, a graduate of Tokyo University Literature Department, works in the foreign news section of a large Tokyo newspaper. He is thirty-four, his wife twenty-nine. They have two children, a boy, five, and a girl, two and a half. The family lives in Kokubunji, a town on the western fringes of Tokyo, about an hour from downtown by train. To reach work by 8:30, Akira gets up at 6:00, rides a bus two miles to the station, then stands up in a commuters' train as far as Shinjuku. From there he takes another bus to his office farther downtown. Returning, he leaves work about 7:30 in the evening and reaches home about 8:30. Sometimes he works afternoon or night shifts, and he customarily earns two or three hours' overtime daily.

Akira and his wife, a women's college graduate, are part of a great army of young married people living by themselves in Japan's jam-packed cities. They have moved eight times in Tokyo in the last six years. Usually they lived in rented rooms, but Akira's wife disliked the noise and personal frictions engendered by rooming-house living. She wanted to escape from the pressures of membership in group organizations, and he, too, though weaker by nature, felt no particular obligation to those among whom he lived. One landlord especially offended him by telling of how he had been in the "thought police" and arrested professors living in the vicinity during the war. After Akira rejected his landlord's advice to vote for an ultraconservative candidate in the 1958 Diet elections, he and his family moved to the Kokubunji suburb.

There they live in a rented cottage in a newly developed area of suburban homes for "salary men." It is a raw environment. Running water and electricity are installed, but the streets are unpaved, muddy tracks and the area, like most of Tokyo, has no sewage system, no sidewalks, no gardens, and no trees. The one-story house is tiny, and like most Japanese houses it is made of the simplest materials—uninsulated wood frame and roof, straw mats for floors, and a few panes of glass and lath for walls. There are two small rooms, one of six mats, one of four and a half, plus a three-mat kitchen. (One mat measures 6' x 3', or 18 sq. ft.) The house has no entryway; visitors must leave their shoes in the dirt and step up in stockinged feet onto the narrow wooden veranda and through the sliding glass doors into the larger of the two rooms. An inside toilet of the nonflushing type is available, but for a bath Akira and his family must walk to the local public sentō, ten minutes away. Garbage is left to decompose in a trench in an open field nearby. All around the house are other houses with similar facilities, but the Kondō family has not lived in the vicinity long enough to get to know their neighbors. In fact, they do not especially want to know them, and Akira was annoyed to discover that the householder next door is a policeman. They are not running away from the law; they just want to be left alone.

The house inside hardly conforms to the foreign image of the conventional Japanese home. There is no elegant lacquer table, no flower arrangement, no hanging scroll painting. Instead, a cheap Van Gogh reproduction is stuck on one wall. The floor mats are badly worn and encrusted with dirt and spilled bits of food. The Kondōs are experiencing some of the universal grievances of tenancy. According to Akira, their landlord is a miser who insists that they must share the cost of new floor mats, although when they agreed to rent the house he vowed to supply them himself.

In the kitchen Mrs. Kondō cooks on a propane-gas-fueled hot plate, while heat in the other rooms is provided by a cheap, blue ceramic charcoal brazier (*hibachi*) set beside a low wooden table. Above a small desk in one corner are a couple of shelves of books: odd works of Goncharov, Pushkin, and other writers in Russian-language editions, a copy of the memoirs of the Marquis de Sade in French, a book on how to play tennis in English, and several back numbers of the literary magazine *Bungakkai*. Also in evidence, stored on the floor at various points in the cold, cramped little house, are an electric toaster, electric foot warmer, small electric washing machine (29.2 per cent of all households have one [1]) table radio (91.7 per cent), electric razor in a leather case, electric clock, nonelectric sewing machine (66.3 per cent), and an old 78-RPM turntable for attachment to the radio. Most of these things, like most of their clothing, were bought and paid for on the installment plan. All of the gadgets must be hooked up by extension cords to one of the two drop-bulb outlets which the house possesses. They have no refrigerator or TV set—the latter, "not yet, but soon, we hope."

Akira has worked at his present job for six years, and his basic monthly salary is Y20,000 (US$55.56 at the official rate of 360 to 1). However, when overtime and other allowances are added, he earns Y34,000 ($94.44). Besides this he earns irregular amounts by writing book reviews for newspapers and magazines. Total monthly income averages Y40,000 ($111.11). To this must be added his annual bonus, which in 1958 was Y70,000 ($194.44), paid in two equal installments in January and August. Akira's wife earns nothing inside or outside the home.

Outgo of the Kondō family in a typical month (based on figures supplied by Mrs. Kondō, who handles all family accounts) totals Y37,000 ($102.77), including approximately Y20,000 ($55.56) for food. This is 54 per cent of the family's total outgo and is higher than the

[1] Source for all statistical abstract data: Bureau of Statistics, Office of Prime Minister, *Monthly Bulletin of Statistics*, November 1958.

average 42 per cent spent by Tokyo households for food in 1957. The reason for this becomes clear when their food costs are broken down. Staple foods (rice, bread, noodles) cost them Y3,000 ($8.33).[2] Condiments and seasonings (including butter, soy sauce, sugar, salt, bean paste, etc.) cost another Y3,000. The bulk of the Kondōs' food expenses are for so-called "subsidiary foods" (including meat, fish, eggs, vegetables, fruits, and milk), which cost them Y14,000 ($38.88). Unlike most Japanese, they eat meat three or four times a week, "because we like it and don't want to economize on it." Fish they usually eat only twice a week, since Mrs. Kondō believes the fish at the local market are not very fresh. She uses five or six eggs a day. Neither of them drinks alcohol, but the children consume a total of one pint of milk and a half pint of yogurt every day. Vegetables are plentiful and inexpensive, and the Kondōs eat them daily.

After food their most important expense is for rent. With 13½ mats at their disposal (including the kitchen), their living space is nearly equal to the national average of 3.5 mats per person (63 sq. ft.) in 1955. For this they pay Y6,000 ($16.67) a month, a very high price in Japanese terms for what they are getting. In rented rooms they were paying from Y3,000 to Y4,000, and Akira is bitter about his pinch-penny landlord. He would like to qualify for tenancy in a new 19-flat apartment house which his newspaper is building much nearer the office, where rents will range from Y2,000 to Y5,000 a month, but he fears that older staff men will be given first priority. Clique allegiances at the office also are involved; the staff is split into the so-called "mainstream" faction, grouped around one powerful official, and the "outcasts," who support another. Since Akira belongs to the "outcasts," he says he has little hope of any important preferment in the near future, including a chance at cheaper company housing.

For heat and electricity the Kondō family pays about Y2,000 ($5.56) a month. This includes Y500 ($1.39) for electricity, Y500 for charcoal, and Y1,000 ($2.78) for propane gas. Furnishings and kitchen equipment are negligible expenditures. Family clothing is not budgeted monthly but is paid for out of the bonus and replenished seasonally. They have few clothes. He wears an old blue suit to work and has

---

[2] If all Y3,000 were spent for rice, the amount purchased at current prices would be approximately 62 lbs. For prices of food and other household commodities see Appendix I.

one "Sunday best" woolen suit, three or four white shirts, and a couple of corduroy sport shirts. She wears slacks and a sweater around the house and owns a couple of "one-piece" dresses, a skirt and blouse or two, and one or two Japanese kimono outfits which she seldom wears. Like everyone else, the whole family wears wooden clogs around the neighborhood.

For education they pay Y1,000 a month to the nursery school where their five-year-old is attending the second-year class. In winter they must also pay Y400 ($1.11) a month to help heat the schoolroom. Health insurance (Y300), unemployment insurance (Y350), and income taxes (Y1,500) are withheld from his pay each month. They spend Y3,000 a month on books, magazine subscriptions, and movies. She is especially fond of Marlon Brando, while he enjoys live concerts and plays and recently splurged to see two separate performances of the touring Moscow Art Theater. They take the daily *Asahi Shimbun,* which costs them Y300 a month. Akira has taken out an endowment policy on his younger child, payable when she becomes twenty. Premiums are Y12,000 ($33.33) a year. He has no life insurance. (During my visit to their home we were interrupted by an insurance saleslady who was working the neighborhood from door to door.) Up until last year they were Y100,000 ($277.77) in debt because of Mrs. Kondō's past illnesses, but all of this has been paid off and they now owe nothing except a small portion of the money Akira borrowed for college expenses nearly ten years ago. He is putting aside small, irregular amounts but up to now has accumulated only Y14,000 ($38.88) in savings-bank deposits.

Kondō comes from a well-educated family, and he considers himself an intellectual. He says that he usually votes for the Socialists, but "once or twice" he has voted for Communist party candidates. "If I were only a high-school graduate and worked in a small company I would vote conservative," he says. His father was a Tokyo Imperial University graduate, who became a minor official in the old South Manchuria Railway Company and was stationed in Dairen, where Akira was born in 1925. Earlier, just after the Russian Revolution, his father had been sent to Germany to study; while there he bought and read the works of Lenin, Kropotkin, and others and developed Socialist sympathies. Akira recalls seeing these books in his father's library as a child. He grew up in Manchuria and learned to speak Mandarin, and from an early age he was interested in literature. At the time of Pearl Harbor the family had returned to Japan and Akira was attending high school. During the war he was mobilized along with other students to work in war plants, and his education was interrupted. In May 1945 his father's house was destroyed in an incendiary-bomb raid, and on August 20, 1945, two weeks after Hiroshima, Akira finally was ordered to active service in the Army. However, the war ended before he could be put into uniform.

After the war Akira was forced to work at odd jobs to help support his parents, and he did not enter Tokyo University until 1948, when he was twenty-three. According to him, the entrance examinations for the Literature Department were more difficult than those for the more popular jurisprudence course, but he went into literature "because I didn't want to be a bureaucrat." He passed the exams on the first try and graduated in 1952 with a major in Russian literature. Deciding to enter journalism, he took the competitive job exams at three newspapers but failed all three. However, in 1954 he finally passed both oral and written exams and was hired by the paper where he now works. Because of his familiarity with Chinese and Russian he was assigned to the foreign news department, where he translates incoming press dispatches into Japanese.

In some ways Akira is like commuters everywhere; he is one of the commuting herd. During his off hours he claims he feels relatively independent of his workplace. Although he belongs to the newspaper union, he appears to take no interest in its activities. At the same time he denies that the people in the neighborhood where he lives have much influence over his opinions. His parents are dead; he rarely sees his brothers and sisters, and his wife's foster parents live at a safe distance. He receives minimum health-insurance protection, and should he lose his job he could draw 70 per cent of his pay for six months. Superficially he seems isolated and even, to a degree, free. However, he identifies himself with the "outcast" clique at the office, and for advice and counsel he invariably goes to three or four of his fellow workers who were his classmates at Tokyo University and who also are "outcasts." He knows that he is part of a still heavily paternalistic system whereby employees are rarely fired, even though they may be "outcasts," unless found guilty of crimes or unless there is a major disaster such as a depression. Modern and traditional forms of protection both are available to him to some extent.

He is intelligent but rather colorless and more than a little self-pitying. He says, "I am a product of the war," and throws up his hands without further comment. He does not expect to rise far beyond his present position; nevertheless, no matter how mediocre his work may be, his salary will slowly increase as he gains seniority.

His wife is a stronger character. She had a very unhappy childhood in an adopted family and now talks a good deal about her "liberation." Their frequent moves are largely a reflection of her restlessness, to which he can only comply. She would like for their life to become "stabilized," but she is not a good manager. Her children are poorly clothed and dirty; she hates to sew and likes to eat meat and Western-style cakes more than is good for their budget or her figure. Her great wish now is for some decent chinaware, as his is for a TV set. Behind her smile she is nervous; when I remarked how many electrical appliances they had, she snapped, "Yes, but don't make the mistake of supposing that this means the Japanese are really Western in spirit. They want the gadgets, but they will accept whoever is strongest. Now it is the United States, but it might be somebody else in the future. That is their nature." She feels freed from a despotic past, while he looks back with nostalgia on his childhood, when "things were better."

II & III: TWO FACTORY WORKERS

If Akira's postwar life has been turbulent, Toshio Segawa's has settled down. In fact, to Toshio the most wonderful thing is the way his existence has become "stabilized."

Toshio was born near Nagoya in 1920, five years before Akira, and in much poorer circumstances. Having had the misfortune to be the youngest of ten children of a farmer, he left home after finishing the compulsory six grades of school and migrated to Tokyo. For four years he lived here and there in the great, engulfing city; part of the time he worked in a small food shop run by one of his numerous brothers and managed to finish a commercial-school course when he was seventeen. However, he could not find a job and returned home for about a year to help on the farm. In 1938, with nothing else in prospect, he enlisted in the Army and was assigned to an engineering unit stationed near Shanghai. He served throughout the war in central China and in 1946 was repatriated to Japan, demobilized, and dumped in Tokyo with thousands of his soldier companions. He took refuge in a relative's home, did various odd jobs, and in 1948 finally landed a job as a boiler mechanic in a large textile-manufacturing plant on the outskirts of Osaka. The next year he married a girl from Kyushu who had been recruited to work in another section of the mill.

The Segawas have two children, a boy, six, and a girl, three. The family lives in a *shataku* (company house) on the premises of the mill. They have three rooms: six mats, four and a half mats, and four and a half mats, plus a smaller kitchen. Parents of both husband and wife are dead, and no other relatives live with them. The house is clean, next door to work, and costs them practically nothing. Although there is no private bath, the company maintains a bathing facility for its employees within the compound.

Toshio's basic wage is Y10,350 ($28.75) a month. With family allowance, efficiency allowance, other allowances, and overtime, his monthly wages average Y22,000 ($61.12). Average take-home pay is around Y14,750 ($40.97). Deductions are made from his pay for health insurance (Y480), retirement (Y270), unemployment insurance (Y160), union dues (Y420), special union fund for strikes (Y30), another special union fund, purpose unknown (Y20), life insurance (Y620), savings held in deposit by the employer (Y1,000), rice from the company store (Y2,915), taxes (Y200), rent (Y268), electricity (Y255), water (Y50), and gas (Y585). His wife earns Y3,000 a month at home by tying wires in radio sets for a large firm located nearby. Toshio has recently taken a 10 per cent wage cut because of the recession in cotton textiles, and his wife's work was arranged by his employer to help tide the family over. Thus at present their monthly income is about Y25,000 ($69.45). Toshio's annual bonus in 1958 was Y35,550 ($98.74), paid half in January and half in July.

The Segawas' total outgo (including payroll deductions) is about Y21,000 ($58.34) a month. They spend Y9,000 ($25.00) for food, or about 42 per cent of their total outgo. Of this, Y4,000 is spent for staples and only Y3,000 for "subsidiary foods." Y1,000 goes for seasonings. Their only concession to Western taste in food is for sweet cakes, which they all like excessively and on which they spend Y1,000 a month. Nearly all this food is bought at the company store at prices from 15 to 20 per cent lower than ordinary food markets.

Rent and essential furnishing expenses come to only Y600 ($1.67) a month. The Segawas spend an average of Y2,000 ($5.56) a month on clothes, most of them from the company store. The company maintains a nursery school which costs only Y200 per child per month, rather than the Y1,000 that Mrs. Kondō must pay. Expenses of the Segawa family for amusements, recreation, and social functions are small, though perhaps not as microscopic as they say they are. Until recently they made short trips twice a year to company-run resthouses at the beach or the mountains, where cheap facilities for sports and recreation were available for the entire family. The recent recession has curtailed these outings. They have no debts and manage to save from Y5,000 to Y6,000 a month.

Toshio works eight hours a day, six days a week, plus as much overtime as the company will allow. The factory has 750 employees, of whom 200 are men. Toshio never expects to go higher than his present position or to change jobs, but his wages, like Kondō's, will slowly rise until his retirement at fifty-five. According to him, his first wage at this company, while he was living in an unmarried men's dormitory, was Y5,000 a month. When he retires he expects to receive a lump-sum payment based on his basic wage—which is one reason why his employer seeks to keep the wage down and pad out the pay envelope with allowances.

In contrast to the Kondōs, Toshio Segawa's family has few electric gadgets or other labor-saving devices. Mrs. Segawa uses a foot-pedal type sewing machine, but in her words, electrical appliances are for *mukō no kata*, "the people over there," meaning in this instance employees who are university graduates, work in the company offices, and live in another section of company houses. The Segawas have few outside interests or hobbies. They read little; he gets the *Mainichi Shimbun* and a monthly trade magazine, and she takes a dressmaking and style journal and occasionally reads a women's magazine, usually *The Housewife's Friend* rather than the intellectual *Women's Review*. On the whole, they are more placid and content than the Kondōs, although they have less cash income and less "independence." They are saving more, and both husband and wife feel that their present condition is better than their childhood as they remember it. For him, things have settled down. He has security, and she, too, likes the protectiveness of big company life. They say they have no desire to own their own home. He approves of the labor union because, although it has accepted a wage cut, it has so far been able to resist layoffs successfully. The union is helping to make his job more secure, but he hopes it will not become involved in violent tactics. "Radical" tendencies of some of the top leaders distress him. With their neat, scrubbed children, and a bright vase of flowers in the alcove, the Segawas live in an environment very different from the appliance-cluttered bohemianism of the Kondōs.

Many thousands of other workers of Segawa's generation in the Osaka region and elsewhere would, if investigated, reflect similar characteristics: the highly mobile, often confused background; the struggle for education in a society that ranks people severely by their formal education; the more or less tractable acceptance of a meager level of living in exchange for security within a framework of paternalism.

Minoru Takahashi, for example, works in a small machine shop in Amagasaki, near Osaka. At forty he is one year older than Segawa and six years older than Kondō. The son of an accountant, he was born in Kobe, but his family moved to Tokyo when he was seven, and there he finished three years of commercial school. At that point he quit and went to work in a gas company, but he continued to attend night school and eventually finished a technical-school course in mechanical engineering. From 1939 to 1941 he was in the Japanese Army, and during the war he worked in a factory in Kawasaki making grinders and milling machines. Takahashi's wife, whom he married in 1943, is the daughter of a small merchant from Hikone, a town not far from Kyoto. They have three girls, fourteen, eleven, and five.

The Takahashis live in a rented house in a low-income section of Amagasaki, ten minutes from his workplace by bicycle. The house has three rooms, of five mats, four and a half, and four and a half, plus a tiny kitchen. The public bath is a five-minute stroll away (16 yen for adults, 8 yen for children). The family owns few appliances—a nonelectric sewing machine, an old electric washer that they bought on the installment plan (ten months to pay), an electric iron, and a bicycle. Other furnishings are those commonly found in Japanese homes—a chest of drawers, a low wooden table or two, a cheap dressing table without legs, a few pots and pans, a clock, radio, etc. Since Takahashi and his wife are Christians, a color picture of a praying child and an engraving of Jesus are prominently displayed. Over the chest of drawers is pasted a portrait of George Washington clipped from a magazine.

Takahashi's basic wage is Y14,500 ($40.28). With allowances and overtime his total wages are Y34,000 ($94.44), and his take-home pay is about Y30,000 ($83.33). Withholdings from his pay include the usual health insurance, unemployment insurance, taxes, and union dues (unlike most small firms, his has a labor union), plus savings held on deposit by the company and a small (Y345) item for "company birthday parties." His bonus in 1958 was Y32,000 ($88.89), or about one month's pay, but he says the union is still negotiating for another Y6,000 for each employee to be charged against the last year's bonus.

The monthly outgo of the Takahashi family totals about Y30,000 ($83.33). Of this, Y9,000 ($25.00) goes for food, including Y4,500 for staples, Y4,000 for "subsidiary foods," and Y500 for seasonings and condiments. The proportion of his rice expenditures to total food costs is about the same as Segawa's but much higher than Kondō's. For rent Takahashi pays Y4,200 ($11.66). When he rented his present house he paid a deposit of Y80,000 ($222.22), on which he will receive an 80 per cent refund if and when they vacate. This money was obtained from separation pay which Takahashi received when he was laid off from a previous company during the 1954 recession. All clothing for the family is paid for out of the bonus, and the company provides no store where purchases can be made at a discount. Heat and utility costs, as in most Japanese homes, are very small; although attitudes toward the necessity for warmth in cold weather appear to be gradually changing, heat is not economically important in most families. Electricity costs them Y620 ($1.72) a month, charcoal Y800 ($2.22), kerosene Y400 ($1.11), and water another Y400.

With the girls growing up, education expenses are beginning to be more considerable. The eldest daughter's junior-high-school tuition is about Y3,300 ($9.16), while the second girl costs another Y1,000. Both girls are taking organ lessons at a total cost of Y700 ($1.94) a month. Takahashi sends Y3,000 a month to his aged mother in Tokyo. Life insurance, taxes, gifts to the church and to relatives, and other social expenses eat up the rest. His total savings at present amount to only

Y5,000 ($13.89), and he is not adding to that amount. Like many Japanese men (including Kondō, but not Segawa), he feels that he was better off as a child, while his wife regards her present lot as much superior to her earlier one. Their primary goal in life is to own their own house, but they have no idea where the money will come from, even though they could build one for two to three thousand dollars, plus the land.

Both Segawa and Takahashi are relying on the bonus for most necessities beyond food, rent, and education fees. Neither has any interest in politics. Segawa says the politicians are all mediocre; Takahashi says that since the union organized his small shop (30 employees) a few years ago, some of the men have voted Socialist, but others have ties with local conservative bosses. Segawa and Takahashi both are living in a hive of "togetherness," Japanese-style, while Kondō has partly, but only partly, emerged from it.

IV: A MIDDLE-AGED "SALARY MAN"

Yutaka Aizawa is a section chief (kachō) in the production department of the Asahi Pharmaceutical Company, one of Japan's largest drug-manufacturing concerns. An eldest son, he was born 46 years ago in the town of Saga, in Kyushu. His father was a maker and seller of patent medicines, who moved with his family to Tokyo when Aizawa was in primary school. The family had means, and Aizawa attended good schools in Tokyo, eventually graduating from the Pharmacy Department of Toyko Imperial University before the war. In 1942 he entered Asahi as a drug expert. He married in 1943. His wife, who is forty, is a graduate of a prewar girls college in Tokyo. Her father is the former managing director of a small commercial firm. Now retired, he lives with his wife on an independent income.

Aizawa lives in his own home in the northern section of Tokyo. His father is dead, and his mother lives with the family. There are three children, thirteen, nine, and seven. Aizawa's work is near Shinagawa, 40 minutes from home by train. He normally leaves the house by 7:30 in the morning and returns around 10:00 at night. Recent high sales levels in his company have meant additional overtime for him and other employees.

Aizawa's basic salary is Y31,000 ($86.11), but when allowances are added for family, travel, seniority, efficiency, and overtime, his total salary is Y50,000 ($138.89). Take-home pay after withholdings totals around Y42,000 ($116.67) in a normal month but may run higher, depending on overtime. His monthly salary increases automatically by Y2,600 at the beginning of each calendar year. The usual deductions are made from his pay: income tax, retirement, health insurance, etc. His 1958 bonus totaled Y200,000 ($555.54), or about four months' pay, paid in the usual two installments in winter and summer.

In addition to the husband's salary, the Aizawas own an "apartment house" next door which they built three years ago for Y750,000 ($2,083.33) estimated total costs. This money was borrowed from their relatives and repaid by the month in 19 months. They also had Y250,000 ($694.44) worth of repairs done on their own home at the same time. All these debts are now paid, and the rental property is grossing Y26,500 ($73.62) a month. It consists of seven four-and-a-half-mat rooms with separate cooking space and is occupied by seven families. Finally, Mrs. Aizawa earns from Y2,000 to Y3,000 a month at home by repairing nylon stockings brought to her by the students of a nearby dressmaking school. Until recently she was making up to Y10,000 a month at this work but had to cut down to spend more time taking care of her family. The total income of the Aizawa family thus is around Y80,000 ($222.22) a month, plus the annual bonus.

Monthly outgo is Y63,000 ($175.00). With six mouths to feed, they spend slightly less for food than Kondō spends for his four. Total food expenditures for an average month are Y16,000 ($44.45). This includes Y4,000 for staples, Y10,000 for meat, vegetables, and other "subsidiary foods," and Y2,000 for seasonings. They usually eat meat and fish on alternate days. Since, like most Japanese, they have no refrigerator, Mrs. Aizawa buys vegetables daily from the markets, which check in the morning to find out what she wants and deliver later in the day. This system, known as *goyōkiki*, burns up a lot of boy-power on bicycles but is tremendously convenient for the housewife, who takes it for granted. Mrs. Aizawa uses 30 eggs a week to Mrs. Kondō's 35–40. She buys one pint of milk and half a pint of yogurt daily directly from a milk co-operative at about one yen a bottle cheaper than retail. She uses about one pound of butter a month in cooking, plus some vegetable oil and a little lard. Like many middle-class Japanese, the Aizawas are fond of ham and sausage, especially that sold by one of Tokyo's excellent German delicatessens. The children like cheese, but their parents have never become used to eating it—"just a matter of habit," as Mrs. Aizawa says.

Their house is paid for and costs them nothing now but upkeep and taxes. However, like many homeowners, they do not own the land on which it rests but must continue to pay Y2,000 a month for land. Heat and electricity cost them more than the other families I have described. Despite their relatively good income they still have no private bath and must go, apparently uncomplaining and by custom, to the public bath. Gas for cooking costs Y1,000 a month. Electricity is high at Y2,500 a month because of their numerous appliances: washing machine, electric room heater, electric *kotatsu*, iron, radio, TV set, etc. The latter was bought on the installment plan and is now paid for, but they must pay Y300 a month to the authorities to use it, as well as Y200 a month radio-listening fee. Like the majority of Japanese households they have no telephone.

Clothing is bought partly from the apartment income and partly from the bonus. Their clothing expenses are high, and in general the cost of clothes increases much faster than food or heat expenditures as incomes rise. There is still some truth, though less than before, in the generalization that the food of the Japanese is alike for all classes. But with a rise in income there seems to go a definite rise in clothing outlays, and clothing reserves build up at an increasing rate. At the beginning of each season Mrs. Aizawa buys something for each member of the family. Last fall she spent about Y20,000 ($55.56) for a *haori* for herself, a zipper cloth jacket for her husband, the same for one of the children, two child's sweaters, plus new underwear all around. Since she wears some of her kimonos for up to 20 years, Mrs. Aizawa has accumulated quite a number: by her own admission she has ten changes, plus five *haori*. In addition she owns one Western-style two-piece suit, five or six skirt-and-blouse sets, two one-piece dresses which she doesn't like, and four pairs of shoes. Japanese women rarely wear hats, and she has none. She owns three coats, a woolen one for winter cut in the typically Japanese wide-collar fashion, and two summer coats. Her husband has four business suits, three pairs of shoes, about ten white shirts, one overcoat and three light coats, including a poplin raincoat. The children are well clothed and shod. Much of this clothing was bought from a store run by the company at prices 15 per cent lower than retail.

On medicines and doctor's bills they spend about Y2,000 a month. (Her first figure was larger, but I discovered that she had entered milk under "health.") Admitted personal business expenses of her husband (gifts, parties, etc.) run to around Y5,000 a month, which Mrs. Aizawa insists she gives him as pocket money after he has turned over his entire salary to her. How much he spends on entertainment at company expense is not recorded. Y5,000 a month goes to his mother for incidentals. Insurance costs perhaps Y36,000 ($100.00) a year, and education about Y4,800 a month, including Y3,000 for junior-high-school tuition, Y1,500 for two children in primary grades, and Y300 a month spending money for the oldest child. Mrs. Aizawa budgets Y3,000 a month for home visitors and gifts and Y1,000 for books and magazines.

The Aizawas are saving about Y15,000 ($41.67) a month, in addition to insurance. Most savings are in bank deposits, and they have a nest egg of about Y150,000 ($416.66), which is likely to increase now that their property is paid for. They also own 500 shares of stock in the Hitachi Company, one of Japan's largest manufacturing firms. Some other stock was sold to help pay for the apartment building. They expect to receive a stock dividend this year and plan other stock investments in the future.

This family has two solid, middle-class objectives. They want to build a second story on their house to accommodate their growing family, and they want to provide security for their children in the future. Compared with Mrs. Kondō, Mrs. Aizawa is an excellent, if somewhat grasping, manager of her family's household affairs.

*   *   *

From the latter part of the nineteenth century to World War II Japan's leaders mobilized a frugal, industrious people who could be counted upon to make the major sacrifices necessary for rapid industrialization. Although the 1920's saw a brief interlude of weak "liberalism," no significant dissent was possible from policies that sanctioned and promoted great inequalities of wealth for the sake of achievement of Japan's "great leap forward."

Today the Japanese live in an era of "progressive conservatism," when conservative politicians and businessmen talk in terms of "welfare capitalism." A Socialist opposition which received 33 per cent of the votes in the last general election offers its own programs of social welfare. Money that once was spent for armies now goes for education and social security. All the families described above, and at least twelve million other workers, have some kind of health and unemployment insurance. A national old-age-pension bill is now before the Diet. The minimum wage is another matter, but it, too, looms in the future.

At the same time, although wages are steadily rising, those who are better off are gaining faster than those on lower wage levels. Equalizations of income that resulted from wartime destruction and postwar reforms are now being readjusted. In a recent government survey of several thousand urban workers' families, those in the lowest of five arbitrarily selected income brackets were found to have increased their disposable income by 25.4 per cent between 1953 and 1957, while those in the top bracket increased theirs by 41.6 per cent. Tax abatements favored those with higher pay. The wage differential between large and small manufacturing firms also has widened. When the wage level of firms with more than 1,000 employees is put at 100, the level of firms with from four to 49 employees fell from 81 in 1946 to 39.9 in 1955.

Japanese opinion differs on how far Japan can or should extend welfare programs. But all are agreed that social and economic progress in this overcrowded, resource-poor country depends on trade. Rising wages and changing consumption patterns challenge the government more urgently than ever to expand the sale of Japan's goods abroad. For a boom in domestic production and consumption without expansion of exports leads to larger deficits in the trade balance. In the words of the Economic White Paper for 1957–58, "It goes without saying that the trade balance sets the upper limits of the people's living standards."

The conviction that prosperity and welfare at home depend upon trade with the world prompts the government among other things to hang out slogans urging the people to save and thus indirectly to promote exports and provide more jobs. Most of my four families are doing their best to save, and Aizawa's savings program would please the Finance Ministry bureaucrats. Like Segawa and Takahashi, he lives within the more or less protected hive of Japanese industry, but he has passed beyond their level and now is able to invest his excess, to borrow and put up some visible evidence of progress—a $2,100 apartment house —which is seemingly so vital to the Japanese sense of well-being. Unless the scaffoldings are being raised and the streets being dug up some-where, spirits seem to flag.

Finally, the scale of living of these families may appear meager enough to Western readers, but by Asian standards it is far from meager. The people are drinking more milk, and they are also buying other less nourishing things. The white paper emphasizes that lower-income families especially crave TV sets, while "as regards washing machines, the lower the income level of household, the stronger its desire to buy one." The nature of these wants suggests the present level of consumer tastes and hints at future possibilities of the market. How far these possibilities will be realized is a question that cannot be decided by Japan's actions alone.

APPENDIX I

Tokyo Retail Prices of Selected Commodities
(as of September 1958, in US$ equivalents)

FOOD ITEMS

Rice (polished)	1 lb.	US$0.13
Wheat flour	1 lb.	.07
Bread	1 lb.	.08
Sardines	1 lb.	.12
Mackerel	1 lb.	.16
Cuttlefish	1 lb.	.11
Dried sardines	1 lb.	.34
Beef	1 lb.	.58
Pork	1 lb.	.58
Milk	1 qt.	.20
Butter	1 lb.	.94
Eggs	1 lb.	.31
Sweet potatoes	1 lb.	.04
Irish potatoes	1 lb.	.03
Leeks	1 lb.	.06
Radishes	1 lb.	.04
Onions	1 lb.	.03
Dried seaweed	10 sheets	.36
Bean curd	1 lb.	.06
Fried bean curd	1 lb.	.26
Pickled radishes	1 lb.	.06
Soy sauce	½ gal.	.47
Bean paste	1 lb.	.10
Sugar	1 lb.	.17
Edible oil	½ gal.	.96
Margarine	1 lb.	.44
Sake, 2nd grade	approx. ½ gal.	1.40
Common tea	1 lb.	.49

CLOTHING ITEMS

Men's trousers (summer)	1 pr.	$6.76
Men's trousers (winter)	1 pr.	9.14
Men's white shirts	each	1.63
Silk fabrics	1 yd. (36 in. wide)	1.02
Rayon fabrics	1 yd. (36 in. wide)	.53
Cotton fabrics	1 yd. (36 in. wide)	.24
Woolen fabrics	1 yd. (58 in. wide)	7.49
Sewing thread	spool (1200 yd.)	.32
Woolen yarn	1 lb.	4.00
Men's nylon socks	1 pr.	.42
Women's *tabi*	1 pr.	.64
Men's shoes	1 pr.	7.90
Tennis shoes	1 pr.	.88
Women's clogs	1 pr.	.30
Men's umbrellas	each	1.33
Tailoring charge, men's suits		23.37
Shoe-repair charge		1.22

HOUSEHOLD ITEMS

Charcoal	33 lb. bale	1.49
Firewood	1 bundle	.19
Coal	110 lb. bag	1.60
Window glass	1 small pane	.20
Board lumber	36 sq. ft. (approx.)	1.15
Electric bulbs (60 watt)	each	.17

MISCELLANEOUS

Haircuts		.43
Toilet soap	1 small bar	.08
Toilet paper	100 sheets	.04
Hair pomade	2 oz. bottle	.26
Notebooks	30 sheets each	.06
Pencils	each	.03
Movies	adults each	.31

Source: Bureau of Statistics, Office of Prime Minister, *Monthly Bulletin of Statistics,* November 1958.

APPENDIX II

Average Monthly Income and Living Expenditures of Four Urban Japanese Families

(annual bonuses are not included)

1. *Akira Kondō* (age thirty-four)

INCOME

Y40,000 ($111.11)

APPENDIX II (*continued*)

EXPENDITURE

Food	Y20,000	($ 55.56)
Heat, etc.	2,000	(5.56)
Rent	6,000	(16.67)
Education	1,400	(3.88)
Taxes	2,650	(7.35)
Insurance	1,000	(2.78)
Books, amusement	3,000	(8.33)
Total	Y36,050	($100.13)

2. *Toshio Segawa* (age thirty-nine)

INCOME
Y25,000 ($69.45)

EXPENDITURE

Food	Y9,000	($25.00)
Heat, etc.	1,500	(4.17)
Rent	600	(1.67)
Education	200	(.56)
Taxes	800	(2.22)
Insurance	1,500	(4.17)
Union fees	470	(1.30)
Social expenses	1,000	(2.78)
Amusement, etc.	1,500	(4.17)
Clothing	2,000	(5.56)
Doctor's fees	750	(2.08)
Total	Y19,320	($53.68)

3. *Minoru Takahashi* (age forty)

INCOME
Y34,000 ($94.44)

EXPENDITURE

Food	Y9,000	($25.00)
Heat, etc.	2,200	(6.11)
Rent	4,200	(11.66)
Education	5,000	(13.89)
Taxes	1,500	(4.17)
Insurance	1,500	(4.17)
Support of mother	3,000	(8.33)
Church tithe	3,400	(9.44)
Amusement, etc.	1,000	(2.78)
Total	Y30,800	($85.55)

4. *Yutaka Aizawa* (age forty-six)

INCOME
Y80,000 ($222.22)

EXPENDITURE

Food	Y16,000	($ 44.45)
Heat, etc.	5,500	(15.28)
Land payment	2,000	(5.56)
Education	4,800	(13.33)
Taxes	5,730	(15.91)
Insurance	3,000	(8.33)
Clothing	7,500	(20.83)
Doctor's fees	2,000	(5.56)
Personal exp., husband	5,000	(13.89)
Support of mother	5,000	(13.89)
Amusement, etc.	4,000	(11.11)
Total	Y60,530	($168.14)

APPENDIX III

Average Monthly Living Expenditures, All Urban Families
(as of July 1958, based on 4,000 families)

Food	Y12,052	(43.6%)
Housing	2,574	(9.3%)
Light and fuel	1,141	(4.1%)
Clothing	3,016	(10.9%)
Miscellaneous	8,859	(32.1%)
(including health, education, recreation, etc.)		
Total	Y27,642	(100.%)

Source: Bureau of Statistics, Office of Prime Minister, *Monthly Bulletin of Statistics,* November 1958.

CHAPTER *9*

BIRTH CONTROL IN JAPAN

March 30, 1956

The dramatic rise in the Japanese population from 72 million in 1945 to nearly 90 million in 1955, combined with vast losses of territory, has diverted attention from the steeply falling birth rate and obscured the fact that Japan is one of the few countries in the world now taking official steps to control population growth. Before World War II Japanese leaders used population pressure as one rationalization for expansion on the continent of Asia and encouraged pronatalist policies to feed their military machine; however, today's government has at least gone on record for a policy of birth control through contraception and is now spending a small sum of money for programs to achieve that end. This Report summarizes the major developments in the field of birth control since the war and examines recent governmental policies and actions in this field.

Bewilderment and misery in Japan at the war's end were deepened by the forced repatriation of about six million military and civilian personnel from all over Asia and by the birth of a flood of war-postponed children. The crude birth rate stood at 34.3 per 1,000 population in 1947, the "baby boom" year. But thereafter the pressure of economic conditions made family limitation more urgent than ever before. In the postwar inflation, prices left wages far behind, and housing and food problems became critical for millions of people. Education for children already born was expensive but essential for their success in the harsh competition for jobs. Farmers continued to want and to have larger families than city dwellers; but children who formerly had brought economic, social, and emotional benefits to parents now became more of a liability. In the ever-growing cities more women had to work to help support the families they already had, while unmarried working girls, including many who commuted from countryside to nearby city, were forced to postpone marriage and childbearing. By 1951 the birth rate had fallen to 25.2 and by 1954 to 19.9.

This picture may appear foreshortened, but it should be remembered that declining fertility is not merely a postwar phenomenon in Japan. Demographers have noted that the crude birth rate at the time of the Meiji Restoration in 1868 was over 40 per 1,000 population, a figure which is "still characteristic of the subsistence peasants living in the great rice deltas of Asia's mainland." [1] The birth rate remained high during the Meiji period, but it declined slowly to 36 in 1920, 32 in 1930, and 31 in 1937. Between 1925 and 1950 the postponement of marriage due to the loss of men to military service and other causes contributed to growing fertility limitation. On a broader scale it may be said that "the pressures and the stimuli of nonagricultural employment, urban life, education, increasing knowledge, and increasing wants" [2] all played a part in limiting fertility to some extent. In the interwar period industrialization did not alter the fecundity of the Japanese, but it did influence them to control it, despite the government's prizes for bigger families. [3]

Thus, although the total population has moved rapidly upward in the postwar years, a considerable decline in fertility has occurred throughout the society. Since the death rate has reached a point below which it may only imperceptibly fall, and then must rise, the Japanese population is expected to reach a peak of perhaps 110 million by about 1990, from which it will gradually decline and stabilize.

The reduction in the birth rate in recent years has been accomplished principally by the practice of abortion, which was made legal by the Eugenic Protection Law of 1948. This law originated in a committee of the Diet in which representatives of the Japan Medical Association

[1] Balfour, Marshall C.; Evans, Roger F.; Notestein, Frank W., and Taeuber, Irene B. *Public Health and Demography in the Far East.* (New York: Rockefeller Foundation, 1950), p. 19.
[2] *Ibid.*, p. 23.
[3] Taeuber, Irene B., and Balfour, Marshall C. "The Control of Fertility in Japan," reprinted from *Approaches to Problems of High Fertility in Agrarian Societies.* (New York: Milbank Fund, 1952), p. 2.

were influential. It legalized sterilization in certain instances and abortion when the local Eugenic Protection Councils—which the law established—considered it necessary to protect the health of the mother. Although the law used maternal health protection as its justification, it grew out of fears for public health during the rapid growth of postwar population and the economic disorders of the period. The real intent of the law was, therefore, economic, and it was meant to be interpreted liberally. In May 1952 an amendment removed the necessity for Council permission; thereafter the judgment of one of the 19,000 designated physicians was sufficient to authorize abortion. Physicians in the Institute of Public Health, Ministry of Welfare, in Tokyo estimate that about 70 per cent of the recent decline in the birth rate is attributable to abortion, about 30 per cent to contraception. Reported authorized abortions in Japan totaled 489,000 in 1950, 1,068,000 in 1953, and 1,143,000 in 1954. Unreported abortions are probably equal to the reported number, so that total abortions almost certainly exceed the annual number of live births.

Abortion is known to have been used in the Tokugawa period, although it has not received the same notoriety as the practice of infanticide. The extent of the early practice of abortion is not clear. A Tokugawa poem complains that "the baby doctors are building a cruel treasure house" (*chūjō wa mugotarashii kura wo tate*), i.e., getting rich by performing abortion. According to Dr. Taeuber, contraceptive procedures and practices designed to induce abortion are described elsewhere in the literature of the period.[4] Japanese religion and ethics seem to have played little part in controlling abortion; although Shintōism and Buddhism disapprove of the practice, there appears to be no strong proscription, and the basic distinction made in the West between abortion and contraception does not operate in Japan.

Most abortions are performed for economic reasons. In a Ministry of Welfare survey of 1,382 married women who had abortions between August 1, 1949, and July 31, 1950, 697 or 50.5 per cent gave economic reasons, 237 or 17.1 per cent gave health reasons, while 229 or 16.6 per cent said that they wanted a longer interval between children, which may be interpreted in economic terms. Sixty per cent of the cases were performed on an ambulatory basis—that is, the patient did not remain

[4] Taeuber, Irene B., and Balfour, Marshall C. "The Control of Fertility in Japan," reprinted from *Approaches to Problems of High Fertility in Agrarian Societies.* (New York: Milbank Fund, 1952), p. 2.

overnight at the place where the operation was performed. Average cost of the operation was about 2,200 yen (US$6.10). All operations were performed by doctors authorized under the Eugenic Protection Law. Of the 1,382 women, 679 became pregnant again at least once between their first abortion and February 1, 1952, or in a period of from 18 to 30 months after the operation. Of these, 312 had a second abortion.[5]

Legal abortion is very cheap to obtain in Japan. The women in the above survey were not paying an exceptionally small fee; they may even have paid more than the average, especially in cases where the patient comes under some social insurance scheme. The wife of a company employee with health insurance may have an abortion for as little as 300 yen (less than US$1.00). Cases costing 50 yen (14 cents) have been reported. One study of the problem asks, "Under such circumstances, which costs less, induced abortion or contraception?" [6]

Legalized abortion may be regarded as a premodern expedient for population control; and it need not be supposed that the more than two million Japanese women—about equally divided between city and country—who each year have abortions like to have them, regardless of the culture's ethical blankness on the subject. As a public health nurse with much experience wrote:

"Despite the seeming nonchalance with which mothers appear at the hospitals, clinics, and doctors' offices, it cannot be said that they come willingly to have an abortion. True, there are some very few women who come to the clinics, shopping bag in hand, en route to the market, who stop in to have an abortion and then proceed on their way. But their number is small. Many mothers are aware of the fact that there is such a thing as Family Planning, but, tragically, too often the price of an abortion is cheaper than a year's supply of contraceptives. Some doctors, oblivious of the precious charge of their profession, do not teach the patient who inquires how she may avoid repeating an abortion or direct her to where she may obtain such information."

Even when religious or ethical considerations are left out of account, abortion is inefficient, wasteful, and harsh. Figures show that the "high abortion rates of recent years have had no discernible effect on maternal

[5] Koya, Yoshio. "Preliminary Report of a Survey of Health and Demographic Aspects of Induced Abortion in Japan," *Archives of the Population Association of Japan*, II, (1953), p. 6.
[6] Muramatsu, Minoru. *Some Facts About Family Planning in Japan.* (Tokyo, 1955), p. 71.

mortality," [7] but the effect of repeated abortions on physical and mental health remains to be seen and studied. The possibility of large-scale damage to the female population has alarmed educated Japanese in and out of the government and led to publicity campaigns and programs for the spread of contraceptive information among the population.

Alongside legalized abortion, contraception has increased as a means of controlling the growth of population in postwar Japan. The Eugenic Protection Law of 1948 authorized the establishment of "consultation offices" in Health Centers for the "dissemination and guidance of proper methods concerning conception control"; however, it cannot be seriously maintained that the government thereby committed itself to a definite program. The Occupation maintained a "neutral"—i.e., hands-off—attitude toward the contraception issue, and the "consultation offices" were patronized by very few Japanese. Midwives who might have been easier for ordinary Japanese women to approach for guidance were barred by law (until August 1955) from dispensing contraceptives.

On the other hand, the press and popular magazines, particularly the numerous women's journals, often carried full and explicit information, and radio and television programs also gave wide publicity to the subject. Recent surveys by the *Mainichi Shimbun* reveal that magazines and newspapers have been by far the largest single source of contraceptive knowledge in Japan since the war and remain so today.[8] Contraceptives of all types have been manufactured and legally sold since new laws for the purpose were passed in 1948; however, as various experts have observed, the availability of contraceptives does not of itself insure that their use will become a way of life, especially where the practice of abortion rests on a long history and is cheap to obtain.

For the most part the general public has gone far ahead of the Japanese government in this matter. However, official government agencies have since 1948 taken slow steps in the direction of a population policy based on contraception. The center of effective work in this field is the Ministry of Welfare. The demographers of the Ministry's Institute of Population Problems (*Jinkō Mondai Kenkyūsho*)

[7] Taeuber and Balfour, *op. cit.*, p. 18.
[8] *Mainichi Shimbun* Population Problems Research Council, *Third Public Opinion Survey on Birth Control in Japan*, 1955, p. 22. See also Kokuritsu Yōron Chōsasho (National Institute of Public Opinion), *Jinkō Mondai ni kansuru Yōron Chōsa* (*An Investigation of Opinions on Population Problems*), May 1950.

have led in research on population since before the war; however, they have had little or no power to enforce their recommendations. On the medical side, the physicians and public-health personnel of the Ministry's Institute of Public Health, under the direction of Dr. Yoshio Koya, since the war have stood for a program of public education concerning contraception under government sponsorship. These segments of the career bureaucracy, reinforced by a few influential Diet members, businessmen, academic economists, demographers, and physicians, have pressed their superiors and the political leaders of the government for action.

The first government action after the Eugenic Protection Law of 1948 came on May 10, 1949, when the House of Representatives passed a resolution stressing the need for dissemination of contraceptive information as well as for emigration. This resolution produced no action, and a similar resolution on November 29, 1949, from the Population Problems Council of the Yoshida cabinet was equally without effect. This council was abolished in March 1950. Meanwhile the Welfare Ministry communicated frequently to the cabinet its alarm at the growing abortion rate, and the cabinet issued a new statement on October 26, 1951, as follows:

"The number of abortions is increasing each year. These are often necessary to protect the life and health of the mother. Occasional damage to the mother's health, however, makes the dissemination of the knowledge of contraception desirable . . .

"Recommendation: abortion has undesirable effects on maternal health. It is therefore necessary to disseminate contraceptive information to decrease these undesirable effects." [9]

This cabinet resolution was sufficient authorization for the Ministry of Welfare to prepare a specific plan for the promotion of contraceptive practice. This plan was announced on June 5, 1952, and distributed to all prefectural governors for appropriate action. It called for a program of individual guidance by doctors, midwives, pharmacists, and public-health nurses both in and out of the prefectural Health Centers and directed that facilities for such guidance within the centers be improved. The plan required that prefectural Health Centers furnish "educational guidance for industrial workers, women's associations, and other specific groups." In the sphere of training, the Institute of Public

---

[9] Muramatsu, *op. cit.*, pp. 35-36.

Health projected short courses for prefectural medical and health personnel, expected to return home to instruct local midwives, nurses, and doctors, in co-operation with the prefectural medical and nursing associations. A poster and leaflet campaign also was provided in the plan.

The Welfare Ministry's 1952 program provided an organized framework within which government physicians and others favoring conception control could begin to operate. However, it is obvious that the program's framers wanted to move faster than the cabinet officials who sanctioned the resolution of October 1951. Appropriations for the program in the 1952 national budget totaled 21,153,000 yen (US$58,750), an amount which, even when matched by the prefectural governments, provided an inadequate sum for nationwide implementation of the Ministry's ambitious program through nearly 800 Health Centers. Furthermore, these centers often were unenthusiastic about undertaking responsibility for another "program." Overworked staff doctors already must wage antituberculosis campaigns, inoculate for other contagious diseases, control rabies, and perform a hundred other miscellaneous tasks. As one sympathetic official remarked, "The Health Centers often are too worried about burying the dead to be concerned with birth control and contraception." The director of the Health Center in Nakano Ward, Tokyo, which must serve a population of nearly 300,-000, admitted to me that not over ten people a month come to the center for contraceptive advice.

The cabinet resolution of 1951 justified contraception on health grounds, but it did not venture into the muddy waters of national population policy. More recently, however, there have been further developments in this direction.

As stated above, the Welfare Ministry's Institute of Population Problems, though a center of demographic research, has suffered from lack of authority. In an effort to remedy this situation an incorporated private foundation was established in 1952, called the Foundation-Institute for Research of Population Problems (an unliteral translation of the Japanese title *Jinkō Mondai Kenkyū Kyōkai*). This body formed two committees, the Committee on Population Policy and the New Living Guidance Committee. The former committee drew up a set of recommendations for a national policy on population control. Later it was decided that these recommendations would have more force if they were given an official character; therefore, in 1954 the Minister of

Welfare was persuaded to establish an advisory council, called the Population Problems Council (*Jinkō Mondai Shingikai*), within the Welfare Ministry. The membership of the council closely resembles that of the Foundation-Institute.

On August 24, 1954, this new council issued an official resolution, consisting, in part, of the following:

"In order to solve the grave population problems which this country is facing, it is needless to say that measures should be taken to increase the capacity to support the population. In view of the present situation, however, where the heavy pressure of population is detrimental to the successful accumulation of capital as well as to the rationalization of industries, it is necessary for the government to adopt policies to curb the population increase.

"The movement for the popularization of the practice of conception control, which thus far has been put into operation, should be conducted not only from the standpoint of the protection of mothers' health, but also from the standpoint of family planning as a part of over-all population policies . . ." [10]

This resolution was followed by publicity and speeches by the Welfare Minister on the need for a population policy, and the 1955 national budget included the largest appropriation thus far for the program.

A word may be added here about private organizations for birth control and family planning in Japan. It is very difficult to evaluate the real effectiveness of private efforts, since in this, as in many other fields, "councils," "research bureaus," and "federations" fuse or divide continually into fragments of fugitive influence. Some well-known names dominate the "birth control movement," e.g., Mrs. Shizue Katō (the former Baroness Ishimoto) and Dr. Kan Majima. There are some other sincere exponents of birth control, but there are also some who are in it for the notoriety it brings them, and leadership is sometimes contested for reasons of social or political prestige or even for financial gain. It is possible, for example, that connections with contraceptive manufacturers could provide powerful enough motivation for supporting some particular method or other.

Also worth mentioning in the private sphere are the activities of the New Living Guidance Committee of the Foundation-Institute, mentioned above. The committee's program has a distinctly Confucian ring:

[10] Muramatsu, *op. cit.*, pp. 37-38.

"The fundamental requirements for our country to solve the distressing population problems we are now facing are that every individual live a modern, moral, rational, and well-planned daily life . . . To give proper guidance in the way of living to the general public along this line . . . is considered to be a matter of urgent necessity." [11]

The committee has concentrated on establishing family-planning guidance centers in industrial plants, and it has had substantial success at one plant, the Kawasaki Ironworks of the Nihon Steel Company near Tokyo. Several years ago the management of this large plant became interested in the possibility of saving money on family allowance benefit payments by reducing the number of children among the workers. This quickly aroused the suspicion of the labor union; this in turn caused the management to call on the New Living Guidance Committee for help. The committee first introduced cooking lessons for the wives of workers, who live in company houses on the factory premises; later knitting courses were offered, and then contraception was quietly introduced. In 1953, 750 married couples were selected as subjects of a "preliminary" test. Two midwives were assigned to make home visits to give guidance in contraception, and visual aids were used for group education of the housewives. After one year the birth rate dropped from 44.0 to 7.7. The rate of pregnancies dropped from 60.7 to 23.5. The number of abortions fell from 59 to 33, while the percentage of those practicing contraception rose from 39.7 per cent to 56 per cent. [12]

While experience at this factory is better documented than most, it is not unique. Several other large companies have experimented with the idea, and initial labor-union opposition has sometimes turned to co-operation. The Communist party and press have attacked this "capitalist-inspired" movement to "exploit the working class." However, some workers have gone beyond contraception. Last November the press reported that some 150 employees of the Yawata Ironworks, 120 of the Mitsubishi Chemical Company, and 150 of the Mitsubishi Dockyards (all in Kyushu) had volunteered for sterilization operations.

*   *   *

The productive-age population of this country (ages 15 to 59) is increasing at the rate of approximately a million annually. The number

[11] Muramatsu, *op. cit.*, p. 59.
[12] *Ibid.*, p. 99.

of completely unemployed today is reckoned at about 700,000, but the underemployed are perhaps ten times that number. Many marginal farmers would go to the city if they could find work there, but city offices are often overstaffed, as even a casual observer can see. It is estimated that around 750 job seekers a *day* arrive at Ueno Station, main Tokyo terminal for immigrants from the rural north. Few have offers of jobs, but all hope to live with relatives or friends until they can find work. Many are runaways.

Because of the people already born, the labor market will continue to receive over a million new job seekers annually for the next decade. It is this fact which is harassing the government's demographers and economic planners; this problem is more real to them even than control of the numbers of the yet unborn. Plans for massive industrialization, export expansion, and improved productivity occupy the energies of whole phalanxes of researchers, who work patiently among heaps of statistics in drafty offices. To Western observers they may seem often to retreat into theories, to fall back upon verbalization of problems. And these problems will multiply many times over if masses of new people continue to crowd indefinitely into a narrow job market.

In the face of these difficulties, it is evident that there has not so far been a concerted effort by the Japanese government to arrive at a national population policy based on modern methods of birth control. The cabinet and the Diet have been pushed into taking some steps by the force of press publicity, public demand for information, and needling from technical advisers on the staff level. The Welfare Ministry's 1952 action program is in sharp contrast with the cautious admission of the dangers of abortion revealed in the cabinet's 1951 resolution. It is not unreasonable to suppose that some government circles regard abortion as a method of birth control which can be turned off and on at will, thereby keeping control in the hands of the state, whereas contraception, once learned and practiced, would be hard to deny or abolish.

A Rockefeller Foundation team of experts who surveyed the situation in 1948 found an unwillingness "to face the magnitude of the population problem on other than a verbal basis." [13] A middle-level bureaucrat in the Labor Ministry, now assigned to the Economic Planning Board, assured me that Japan has no unemployment problem "like the United

[13] Balfour, Evans, Notestein, and Taeuber, *op. cit.*, p. 35.

States and the other Western countries." According to him, excess labor would always be absorbed in the myriad workshops of paternalistic small- and medium-sized industry. Somehow or other the slack would be taken up. As for birth control, he was willing to admit that something needed to be done now on health grounds; but he reserved comment on the future, when, he implied, changed national policies might call for a larger population.

Nevertheless, although progress in this field is slow, there is at present no discernible focus of political opposition to contraception. It is apparent that a process of gradual education is taking place; what the effect of this will be on Japan's population problems remains to be seen.

CHAPTER 10

ETHICS, YES, BUT WHICH ETHICS?

February 14, 1958

Most Japanese parents, observing the high rate of juvenile delinquency among others' children and the unseemly rudeness of their own, believe that the moral training now being offered by their school system is totally inadequate. Something has gone very wrong when schoolrooms can be turned into "blackboard jungles" and Japanese school children on outings can stage thieving raids on innocent food vendors and leave railway waiting rooms in a shambles. Tarō's bad behavior is what everybody is talking about; he seems to have lost all the old virtues without acquiring any new ones. Filial piety apparently means nothing to him; he hates authority and thinks "democracy" gives him license to do as he pleases without caring for the consequences. His teachers have filled him with contempt for the "absolutism" of his country's past leaders, but he has not learned how to control himself and to take his useful place in an industrious society. Many parents believe that something must clearly be done or they are done for.

Ever since 1950, when the American Occupation was drawing to a close, suggestions have been made for reforming "moral education" in Japanese schools. The Occupation replaced wartime ethics courses, which promoted the values of ultranationalism, with "social studies" and other expressions of the notion that the education system should fit the child, not the child the system. These reforms were accepted and pushed by a Ministry of Education purged of wartime officials and replaced by men who, in some cases, were genuinely devoted to liberal principles of education. Others wisely assumed the protective coloration of democracy, while the "new education" was welcomed by many teachers who, freed from the repression of the wartime government, moved in one step to the equally repressive regimentation of the leftist Japan Teachers Union (*Nikkyōso*). The new was embraced by different groups for different reasons, while the old, if not totally discredited, at least withdrew to regather its shattered forces.

With the end of the Occupation, Japanese nationalism swiftly reasserted itself, but conservative politicians, while predominant at the polls, found themselves operating in a greatly changed world. In 1952, when the Minister of Education announced that it would be a good thing for children to bow toward the Imperial Palace every morning and engage in other suitably "moral" exercises, he was laughed at and criticized in newspapers all over the country. His reactionary suggestions got nowhere. On the other hand, a booklet issued by the Ministry of Education at about the same time indicates the continuing influence of the new concepts of education.

Entitled "Notebook of Essentials for Moral Education," the booklet was prepared in the Ministry of Education (*Mombushō*) to help grade-school teachers to develop sound moral attitudes in children. Nothing is said of setting up a special course in morals or ethics; rather, teachers are urged to be patient, to co-operate with each other, and not to be swayed by the complaints of parents; plans must aim not merely at reaching formal goals but should stress flexibility, the need to show students the relationships which exist between things and to draw examples from everyday life. Constant evaluation of results is essential; school principals must encourage a democratic atmosphere. The booklet constantly stresses the empirical approach to problems, the importance of developing a child's inner potentialities, of giving him a sense of group responsibility and showing him how this relates to self-respect. It reflects on every page the educational philosophy of the American Occupation; and it is not without significance that this document is still pointed to by some elementary-school officials in the *Mombushō* as the best existing guide to professional thinking on the subject.

After 1952, as the Occupation receded farther into the background, enlightened professionals in education, like other rational elements in Japanese society, found themselves more and more dashed about in the gathering political storm. A polarization of forces clearly occurred.

Now the left, in this case represented by *Nikkyōso*, faces the right, represented by the Liberal-Democratic (conservative) party (*Jimintō*), or more exactly, by the more conservative elements of that party. Each provokes the other to new extremes, and the *tairitsu*, or opposition (one of the Japanese Marxist's two favorite words—the other is *mujun*, or contradiction), grows more and more intense. Every issue is entangled with politics, and "moral education" more than most, because it is a vital concern of everybody and, moreover, is full of emotional freightage left over from the war. The *Jimintō* slugs it out with *Nikkyōso* and hopes thereby to smash the Socialists, who count heavily on *Nikkyōso*'s half-million votes. Meanwhile, the supernationalists stir in their sleep and make growling noises in the direction of "Mr. Rockefeller's International House" and other symbols of "superficial Westernization." Tarō goes on being bad, while the really enlightened few feel abandoned and hopeless, and the majority of parents are disgusted with politicians, *Mombushō*, *Nikkyōso*, and Tarō all at once and overwhelmingly.

Without question political pressure is now being exerted on the Ministry of Education to "do something" about "moral education." Pressure originates at various points. It may come from organizations of veterans or former officers' groups. It may begin with shrine Shintō elements, who resent their disestablishment and would like to see Shintō supported again by the state and respected in schooltime rituals. The influence of such groups on this issue is apparently not yet strong. But pressure also comes from the highest echelons of the conservative party, where the small group of decision-makers, motivated by demands of political strategy as well as by pure nostalgia, see in juvenile delinquency and related phenomena a way to kill two birds with one stone: they can attack the "alien" reforms of the Occupation and so increase emphasis on patriotism and loyalty to the government and its policies; at the same time they can weaken the influence of *Nikkyōso*, and indirectly of the Socialist party, by tightening control over education from the *Mombushō* in Tokyo.

Pressure sometimes comes directly from individual Diet members or delegations who visit the *Mombushō* to present their demands. More often it is channeled through the Education Committee of the *Jimintō*'s Political Affairs Research Board (*Seimu Chōsakai*). The *Seichōkai* is composed of Diet members. It does not ordinarily draft legislation, but it communicates to the ministries of the government the policy wishes of party leaders; conversely, it sees that legislation and programs prepared by the ministries are agreeable to party rank and file. Thus the committees—especially the chairmen and senior committeemen—of the *Seichōkai* have great influence over the shape of legislation. The average age of the 16-man Education Committee is sixty-two, which obviously means that all the members were educated before the last war. The oldest member is eighty-three, the youngest forty-two, but only two are in their forties. The committee includes, among others, a former Home Ministry bureaucrat and governor of various prewar prefectures, several prewar cabinet officers, a former Rear Admiral in the Imperial Japanese Navy, a former Army officer who was an expert on Chinese affairs, the leader of the doctors' lobby in the Upper House of the Diet, and several former professional bureaucrats. Some of these men were purged by the Occupation. None of them has any professional educational background worth mentioning.

Importuned by these politicians and led by a Minister of Education who, unlike those of the Occupation period, is himself a politician, some technicians concerned with elementary education in the *Mombushō* feel considerable misgivings. As loyal bureaucrats they cannot rebel openly against the idea of more "moral education" for children. But their views are far from unanimous on the wisdom of such a course, and some of them fear that this may indeed be another step back down the long road toward the chauvinism of prewar times. They realize that, since elected school boards have been abolished, political control over education is easier to achieve than ever before; and they wonder how to check the attack on the values of democracy and respect for the open society which they see threatening. As one of them said rather wistfully, "We must lobby for our views; we must get materials and organize help from the right places."

One current expression of political pressure is the recent announcement of a separate hour once a week for "moral education" in public elementary and junior-high schools. (Ethics is already being taught as part of the social studies curriculum in the high schools.) This new policy is now in the process of being translated into "guidance" which will be passed out to the schools. First steps were taken in the top councils of the conservative party. Then the *Seichōkai* Education Committee called in the technicians from the *Mombushō* and talks began on what sort of guidance to provide teachers. These talks are still in progress, and final plans have not been decided upon. Present thinking in the *Mombushō* is represented by a provisional policy statement prepared there last November. Entitled "On Moral Education in Elementary and Junior-High Schools," it is a mild, reasonable-sounding document. Some such guidance may eventually go out to schools all over Japan.

1. *Aims*

(1) Moral education at present is conducted via social studies and all other courses and educational activities, but it cannot be said that results have come up to expectations. This method will not change henceforth, but a special new hour for moral education will be set up, in order to correct and strengthen the weaknesses of the present situation.

(2) Moral education in the new hour, in consonance with the development of children, will attempt to nourish an understanding of the basic forms of behavior in everyday life, moral emotions, and moral judgment. Along with the teaching of the other subjects, the new hour will foster practical moral strength.

(3) For teaching in this hour, various means such as reading materials and audio-visual materials will be broadly devised, following the development of the minds of children, and as closely as possible corresponding to concrete life . . . care must be given not to fall into mere memorization or cramming of moral precepts.

2. *Guidance targets*

(1) To produce an understanding of the basic forms of behavior of everyday life, and to induce these to be practiced.

(2) To assist the extension of individuality and induce the establishment of life attitudes.

(3) To heighten moral feeling and foster the ability to discriminate between what is good and bad, vulgar and fine.

(4) To heighten essential moral attitudes and practical will power as mature members of nation and society.

The rest of this document sketches the various teaching methods to be used in achieving the above goals. These include discussion of problems of everyday lives of students, reading, reports on books such as biographies, classics, historical tales, fiction, and other writings, talks by teachers on their experiences, use of radio and newspaper materials, audio-visual aids, school projects in health, safety, beautification of grounds and buildings, field trips, and so on.

Deliberations also are under way in the Subcommittee on Moral Education of the Council on Curriculum, a *Mombushō*-sponsored advisory group of university professors, school supervisory personnel, and others, not employees of the *Mombushō* but appointed by the Minister of Education. This subcommittee will consider whatever working papers are prepared by *Mombushō* officials and render technical opinions about what should be taught and how it should be taught. The membership of the subcommittee, by its very nature, is better informed on educational matters than the politicians of the *Seichōkai*. While presumably convinced of the need for new forms of "moral education," the subcommittee also is concerned with preventing the reintroduction of *shūshin*, the prewar variety of ethics. It has issued some moderately worded resolutions, of which the following is a sample:

Fundamental Policy on Moral Education

As a result of the great war, we sustained deep and grievous losses of enormous extent in every sphere. But in the midst of these losses, we unexpectedly gained one precious treasure—national awareness of the basic principles of respect for man's humanity. This has indeed become the leading principle in the education of the new Japan.

The Fundamental Law on Education laid down the framework of this essential spirit: its ideological background was respect for man and the ethics of the community based on this respect.

In order to put these value judgments into practice in education, first of all educators must study and understand their meaning and content. They must judge and evaluate our country's historical traditions from this new angle. They must retain what is excellent and expand it, and at the same time they must clearly recognize what is inferior and shore it up. They must work with awareness, in order to create a suitable social atmosphere for democratic Japan.

With the above value judgments as a basis, the selection of the objectives of moral education and the content of such education must be made without error. In order to enrich the educational content, materials arising from the individual and social experience of everyday life must be chosen; they must be drawn up out of the classical springs of East and West, of ancient times and the present.

At the prefectural level plans are also being made. Last week in Hiroshima officials of the prefectural department of education expressed their views freely on this subject. According to them, some reforms in the method of teaching moral values in the schools are necessary, but this does not mean that prewar ultranationalism will reemerge. The prefectural superintendent of schools insisted that there is absolutely no pressure on his education department from ultranationalist groups. One senses on the local scene a good deal of uncertainty about what is going on in the *Mombushō* in Tokyo. The degree of central control is not entirely clear; it is in fact in a transition stage, and local officials are rather apprehensive about *Mombushō* pressure; they talk of differences of opinion on "moral education" in the *Mombushō* in terms of personalities who favor this or that course of action, and some officials are apt to bluster a little: "No matter what the *Mombushō* says, we are not going to start teaching morals in April." Others accept the fact that what the *Mombushō* says goes, but they hope for a wide latitude of choice within the imposed framework.

The head of the guidance division of the education department in Hiroshima noted that no definite policy on moral education was yet forthcoming; but when it is announced, he expects that it will merely lay down some principles and leave the implementation to local officials. According to him, postwar approaches to moral and ethical training through general emphasis on "learning by doing" and development of individual potentialities have failed in his prefecture, and the failure has been due chiefly to the ignorance and ineptitude of teachers. Most teachers grew up before the war and were trained in the authoritarian environment of prewar schools, where all the emphasis was on rote learning, lecturing, discipline, and unquestioning obedience. Teachers brought up in such a system have taken hard to the new philosophy of group discussion, individual attention to students' needs, and so on— alien objectives under the most favorable conditions and even less likely to succeed in Japan's overcrowded, noisy postwar classrooms.

Especially distasteful to teachers have been calls on their time for such "extracurricular" activities as the "home room," which was supposed to become a sort of laboratory for the inculcation of democratic values but which (in this prefecture, at least) has turned into free play, baseball, and other amusements which leave the teacher free from unwanted responsibility. (Audio-visual techniques have taken very well, it seems, e.g., student radio programs are popular where funds are available for equipment.) Many teachers, in short, continue to yearn for more emphasis on textbooks and lectures. As the guidance chief explained it, "They don't, and won't, do something before children if they do it badly. Their honor and dignity are at stake, and they must feel that what they are doing they do well. In their teaching methods they have not yet emerged from their prewar attitudes; they are still unenlightened and conservative." These are the same teachers who will wrap the laborers' towel around their heads and follow the leftist rabble-rousing leadership of *Nikkyōso* into demonstrations against the government.

The Hiroshima guidance chief has plans to convert the ineffectual "home room" into a period for "moral education." His section is drawing up a handbook for junior-high-school teachers which divides each grade into months and sets up topics and targets for each month. This plan is still in the formative stages; topics are suggested rather sketchily, e.g., in May the seventh grade will study three topics, "Mother's Day," "How to Study," and "Meetings and What They Mean." May topics for the eighth grade are "Freedom and Rules" and "Positive Scholarship." The ninth grade will take up "Individualism and the Future" and "Life and the Social Environment." In June the seventh grade will study "An Ordered Life," "A Healthy Life," and "Correct Use of Words." The eighth grade will deal with "Communication Between the Sexes," "Life without Violence," and "Safeguarding Public Property." No one is likely to find fault with these topics; it is the spirit in which they are taught and the attitudes toward the children who are taught that matter.

From the papers I have quoted, prepared within the *Mombushō*, by the Committee on Moral Education, or by local prefectural officials, there are no positive grounds for predicting dire ultranationalistic consequences from the introduction of a special course on "moral education." But the memory of the prewar educational system is still so vivid to most Japanese, and suspicion of conservative intentions so deep, that any change tends to be viewed as a step in the wrong direction. One may reasonably doubt whether the elderly politicians in the *Seichōkai* committee have much desire to "evaluate historical traditions" from the "new angle" of respect for the individual and his humanity. Rather their purpose, which has been stated many times by leaders of the conservative party, is to remove from Japanese society the burden of "unsuitable" reforms, including a Constitution which was "imposed" on the country by "alien" forces and which is too "abstract" and "unsuited to Japanese conditions."

Jimintō politicians frequently use the word "abstract" when talking about the new postwar Constitution, and it is important to understand what they mean by this. They mean simply that the idea that all men are created equal and are due equal respect as men is an abstraction to most Japanese, because it does not fit their experience. In traditional Japanese society—and to a considerable extent even today—a man's relations with others depended upon who the others were, how they ranked in relation to one, how closely they were kin to one, and other specifics that were anything but abstract, that were in fact spelled out in great detail. Release from these customary rules has been a release into nothing for many, many Japanese, who naturally feel nostalgia for the certitudes of the past. I have had a university president and former Minister of Education explain it to me in just those terms: "The new Constitution puts too much emphasis on the individual and his abstract relationships to the world. It does not take into sufficient account the needs of the Japanese family, community, and national life. It must be revised and brought into better balance."

The meaning of "abstract" is brought home to many foreigners in Japan in a less "abstract" way without their realizing it. How often the outsider is struck by the rudeness of Japanese to strangers in trains and other public places. I have had my share of pushings and shovings and been knocked on the shins more than once by rushing old ladies with suitcases or parasols, without ever a *gomen nasai* for my pains; but if they know one, then nothing is "abstract," everything is at least covered over with a measured politeness which may not spring spontaneously but helps to repair the injured nerves and bones.

Very few people, Japanese or foreigners, are able to say with assurance how far the present government wishes to go or will go to bring back the past, in education or elsewhere. No one suggests, in calmer moments, that the social and political changes of the last 15 years will be entirely reversed. No doubt the freer postwar public opinion is a restraining influence. Yet the conservatives, among other things, have abolished elected school boards and want to revise the Constitution "to bring it closer to the realities of Japan's situation." The present Deputy Premier has stated privately that he favors abolishing women's suffrage and raising the voting age from 20 to 21. Fear has caused all sorts of people to feel a common antagonism toward "those politicians." In a country where freedom of expression has only lately been restored, reaction to the "reverse course" has become a fixed idea.

The wind blowing from the left may easily be tested in other reactions to government plans for "moral education" in the schools. In a long article in the February 1958 issue of *Sekai*, Arata Osada, president of the Japan Education Association, an organization of university professors, attacks the government from the familiar left-wing angle. Osada's article is full of innocent terms weighted with Marxist meanings. He begins innocuously by noting the futility of judging postwar students by prewar standards: "Graduates of today's schools no doubt are lacking in various ways; but it cannot be denied that, despite this, they contain within themselves the seeds of the virtues necessary to build the new Japan." However, the first question is not how to bring these seeds to growth by moral education; it is, rather, how to regain real independence from the U.S., which is keeping Japan "enslaved" by "all the unequal treaties."

From this it is a short step to "peace morality." "The morality of peace is perhaps the most important of all moralities today. Once the nature of hydrogen warfare is made clear, then the love of Christ, the compassion of Buddha, the humanity of Confucius, the greatest good of the greatest number of Spencer, Bentham and Mill all become impossible unless war is rejected and peace is safeguarded." After invoking peace and linking the danger of war to Japan's dependence on the U.S., Osada begins in a seemingly new direction to emphasize respect for "basic human rights." He soon turns, however, to Japan's "liberation" from the morality of feudalism. "We must move from a vertical morality which emphasizes respect between lord and retainer, parent and child, to a horizontal relationship which stresses the mutuality of individuals in society. . . . When we think back over the past 2,000 years of history, in our land there was the nation and the family, but there was no society in the modern sense. Society in this sense is the present first-stage capitalist society, the modern urban society, which was formed from the breakup of feudalism. But if we look a little further ahead, we can see that postwar Japan, indeed Japan from henceforth, will proceed to the stage where it will transcend modern urban society and will create a new human society." What Osada wants is a socialist society in which there will be no "cult of personality." When he refers to respect for "basic human rights" he does not at all mean these words in the sense in which they are used in Western democratic society. In his prose all the right words have all the wrong meanings. In case there should be any doubt, he is explicit: "Education in this human society will transcend the individualism of modern urban society, and will mean a practical attitude of offering self-sacrifice for society and mankind as a whole. That does not mean merely absolute respect for the character of the individual; it means sacrifice of the individual for the welfare of the whole body of society. . . ."

It should be clear from these excerpts that Osada no more speaks for truly liberal objectives in Japanese education than do those conservatives who regard the new Constitution as too "abstract" and who want to reimpose some part or all of the authoritarian paraphernalia of the past. The accuracy of Osada's estimate of the right wing's intentions should not, therefore, mislead the reader as to the true burden of his own intentions. He describes quite effectively how as a prewar student he once was expelled from the classroom: "I asked the teacher, 'Sir, why must we feel filial piety toward our parents?' To which the teacher replied, 'Why? The reason? Reason has nothing to do with ethics! Take reason out of the classroom! Osada, get out!' " From this he argues with some passion against the reimposition of a special course in ethics and "moral education." "Were not those who brought the morality of our country to ruin today the very ones who . . . received their moral education via the prewar variety of ethics? Did not the politicians of today, who are at the center of corruption, crime, and 'assignation politics,' themselves receive and perhaps even excel in ethics in lower and middle school?" One can scarcely quarrel with some other parts of his attack on the government point of view: "There is much emphasis on the fact that the ethics course was abolished by American Occupation policy, and that therefore, since Japan is independent, it should be restored. This argument is closely linked with the *Jimintō*'s doctrine of Constitutional revision. . . . But there is no reason to revise something just because it was done by the Occupation." While it is possible to agree with Osada's article on individual points, as a whole his arguments are marred by a heavy historicism; the new "reason" which he would install in education has as little to do as the old with individual freedom or individual growth. His own prescription for the future is clear: "The morality mankind will follow will be the new reason, which accompanies the advance of history from feudalism to capitalism and from capitalism to socialism."

I have paid some attention to Osada's article because he heads an influential national organization of university professors and his views are shared by many members of the university teaching community. They are not shared by all, of course; but although some rays of empirical light shine through the transcendental murk, many, if not most, influential professors seem to me to be still revolving around Marxism; the terms of their opposition to government's plans for a new hour in "moral education" are therefore predictable.

More dramatic outbursts of hostility may be expected from *Nik-kyōso* whenever the *Mombushō* finally announces its plans on this subject. The Teachers Union has just ended the first round of what promises to be a knockdown-dragout fight with the boards of education over efficiency ratings for teachers in elementary and secondary schools. The struggle over this issue has left local nerves frayed, but more trouble is bound to come when "moral education" is reinstalled in the curriculum.[1]

In this process of charge and countercharge, moderate opinion on any issue may be drowned out. However, interested bureaucrats or "technicians" are not the only ones who seek rational solutions to the problems of Japan's slowly opening society. Groups exist which wish to promote the growth in youth of decent moral attitudes, but to free them from too much pressure of authority; just as, in other fields, other organizations favor the spread of contraception, or the development of modern labor-management relations under a rule of law, or equality for women, and so on. These groups may be weak, but the educated community is not entirely divided between the partisans of extremes; it also contains some in whom a desire for disentanglement from myths of past or future is combined with a delicacy of nature which will not strain to be heard—too reserved, one may say, but nevertheless not without influence. There are some who realize that freedom involves responsibilities, that, for instance, the demands of individual liberty must be adjusted to the needs of the family as a social unit, and that freedom is not mere license.

A chapter on ethics in a recent social-studies text for high-school use includes the following comments on marriage: "To say that our present family life is unstable is no reason to dream of restoring the family system of the past, nor is it reason to make a thoughtless denial

---

[1] For a discussion of other aspects of the struggle over education, see Marius B. Jansen, "Education, Values and Politics in Japan," *Foreign Affairs*, July 1957, 666–78.

of family life. Marriage begins in respect for the instincts of both sexes. However, it is not merely an irresponsible satisfaction of instinct, but, as is written in the new Constitution, marriage begins in vows of human love by two sexes which are equal. These vows are taken in a religious ceremony attended by relatives and friends, which means that marriage and its vows form an eternal contract having the sanction of society. Marriage moreover includes important social duties, such as carrying on together the economic life of the family and bringing up children by mutual aid. On these points it differs completely from irresponsible free love. True love is not merely a temporary emotion; it leads to the establishment of a life in common. Husband and wife can contribute to the improvement of their common life only if they understand their mutual differences and shortcomings and 'make their long points longer.' For a husband and wife to live together lovingly and in equality as human beings does not at all mean discarding their differences or their individuality on either side. . . ."

The family's position in the whole society is conceived as follows: "Feudal society was based on the family and the master-servant relationship found pre-eminently within the family. The virtue of filial piety was made absolute in such a social environment, where there was no room for the development of a public morality. But conditions today have completely changed. The structure of today's society does not allow the family to be independent; it is called upon to fall in line with higher points of view, the public community, the nation, and mankind. A parent cannot compel a child to act against society or against humanity, nor can a child on account of his parent defend such actions or undertake them. There was a time when even the sale of the body could be prized as an act of filial piety. Nowadays such evil acts of parents demand re-examination; a truly loving child will endeavor to have his parents' evil deeds treated like crimes."

The author of these sentiments is neither a Marxist nor an ultranationalist. He is a professor of ethics in Kyoto University, a scholar brought up on the Chinese and Japanese classics and a specialist in the philosophy of Immanuel Kant. An "enlightened conservative" in all his instincts, he recently put the question this way in conversation: "Everybody agrees the Japanese need ethics, but which ethics shall they have? They are not Christians. The ethics of militarism are quite discredited, and they are not likely to accept the ethics of Marx. What they need above all is respect for the decency of man as man. Call it what you will, I call it humanism. I would have my students read Confucius and learn to be men of good character who treat all with due respect. I would also have them read Kant and Rousseau and learn the true meaning of reasonable thought and individualism."

Thus the dilemma that the partisan politicians and the union leaders seek to solve by new rules or new demonstrations against rules, when faced in the scholar's study, may be solved by including everything, from Confucius to Rousseau, in the belief, characteristically, that the resulting synthesis will somehow be better for having omitted nothing.

*   *   *

This Report has described some recent trends in the field of "moral education." In doing so it has used words like old, new, tradition, democracy, which are packed with different meanings, depending upon one's point of view. Any account of the process of change in Japanese society can therefore be misleading, and often is. To the American Occupation anything that was old in Japan tended to be associated with militarism and therefore regarded as bad. Occupation authorities often overlooked—or were ignorant of—prewar streams of rational, "liberal" thought. Yet these streams certainly existed, and many of the most successful reforms of the Occupation were built on beginnings made long before World War II. Even education, which was distorted to serve the chauvinism of prewar leaders, had in the 1870's and 1880's received the benefit of American advisers and looked toward opening opportunities to whole new classes of people, in line with the characteristic progressivism of that era.

To the Japanese, of course, "old" has different meanings, depending, among other things, on the age of the individual. Many among the postwar generation unquestionably have rejected authority; yet those who grew up before the war have nostalgia for the past, which they sentimentalize, as who does not? (The most touching re-creation of this nostalgia with which I am familiar is Tanizaki's beautiful novel, *Sasameyuki—The Thin Snow*—translated as *The Makioka Sisters* by Edward Seidensticker.) But all the polls show that nearly everybody rejects a return to the militaristic ethos of the 1930's. *Shūshin*, or the ethics of Japan's racial and spiritual superiority as taught before the war, appeals only to a lunatic fringe. On the other hand, democracy is regarded by many adults as placing too much emphasis on the rights of the individual and not nearly enough on his duties to family, community, and nation. Democracy is also thought to be too expensive for Japan. How can so poor a country, the argument runs, afford nine grades of compulsory education plus a bloated superstructure of second-rate colleges and universities that supposedly offer equal opportunity for all but actually give all a pitifully watered-down education, while the really ambitious boys still fight like tigers to get into a few good schools?

Sir George Sansom once remarked that it is easy to prove that the Japanese are a conservative people, or a revolutionary people, but that neither generalization is very useful in understanding the country at any point in time. Much depends on the imponderable demands of the moment, on the prevailing mood, on what he called the "inner life," the weight of the leading thought of the era. Not long ago, spending the evening with a friend in Shibuya, I found myself being tenderly warned off the stereotypes of "old" and "new" Japan. As my friend, a young assistant professor at Tokyo University, put it: "What matters is that the war period is over and we are in a new period of reconstruction. I feel in myself the synthesis of old and new, but I don't proceed by abstract principles but by practical situations, and I don't stand off and analyze the 'synthesis' very much. You are a kind of historical psychoanalyst"—he gave this last a disapproving tone.

A relativism which proceeds by practical situations and not by abstract principles may be profoundly unsatisfying to the Western mind. Yet it is characteristic. Reason may prevail, and gradual enlightenment spread, in "moral education" as elsewhere. But its spread is not, I think, inevitable. It will depend less on unchanging principles than on the demands of the Japanese moment, or world conditions, on the whole drift of the times and other movements which are complex and which cannot now be foreseen with any accuracy.

CHAPTER *11*

HOW THE JAPANESE DIVORCE

July 1961

Before World War II the known Japanese divorce rate fell consistently throughout the twentieth century. Many divorces were, of course, never recorded. Marriage remained essentially a social and religious ritual for the perpetuation of the family, a folk act requiring no license and no legal process beyond entry in the family register. Since this entry had no deadline and was frequently delayed, unregistered marriages often ended in divorce without leaving a legal trace. "Trial marriages" persisted, especially in rural areas: divorce in the countryside traditionally meant unilateral repudiation of wives who failed to produce sons or to please mothers-in-law. But as cities spread and the nation industrialized such practices grew rarer, and the time lag between the marriage ceremony and its legal registration narrowed. Repudiation of wives came to be frowned upon by those people with pretensions of "culture" and modernity; moreover, the parents of girls in the new cities and towns were often less willing than they had been in the more sedentary peasant society to receive their daughters again in their own households. For women the alternatives to wifehood were very limited. While their social position gradually improved, remarriage for divorced women remained difficult and their economic prospects dim. Here is one basic reason for the low divorce rate.

After the war the rate rose briefly, but from 1950 it again declined, and at present it has fallen to a point far below the American rate. Before 1945 women seldom were able to initiate divorce proceedings.

Today about two-thirds of all divorces are initiated by women, but their earning power outside marriage still is low and the risks of divorce great. Thus, although many observers have predicted that divorce must rise along with the increase in the more individualistic love-marriage, greater urbanization and industrial mobility, it has not yet done so, and today divorce as a problem of society does not receive nearly as much public attention as juvenile delinquency. The main reason for this is that divorce still is not seen by most Japanese as a "problem of society" but as an event, like marriage, which occurs within the family and ought not to be open to public scrutiny; juvenile misbehavior, on the other hand, has clearer and more immediate public consequences. Studies of divorce written in either English or Japanese are not numerous, but the handling of this problem in the family courts provides some useful insights into the social ideals the Japanese people now hold dear.[1]

Divorce is a legal act, but judicial divorce, granted by a judge in an ordinary court, is rare in Japan, comprising less than one per cent of all divorces. In most people's minds the conviction is deep-seated that marital problems cannot be solved by taking them into the cold realm of reason, law, and the courts. If possible, they should be worked out within the family itself, by talk between principals or mediation by parents or relatives, in an arena—at least in theory—of tenderness, warmth, and sincerity. The legal expression of these beliefs is divorce by consent (kyōgi rikon), a prewar method that has been carried over into the postwar period. More than 90 per cent of all Japanese divorces are reached in this way, the *only* requirements being that both husband and wife freely agree to end their marriage and affix their seals to a form at the local ward office. The marriage is then canceled in the family register and the divorce is complete. Before the last war such divorce by "consent" often was forced on wives by their husbands. Today this is less common, but recent studies show that some women still are pressured by their husbands or in-laws to agree to unwanted divorces. Personal seals are forged and other stratagems used to achieve that end.

In cases where one side cannot be persuaded or browbeaten to agree, or where there are unsolvable problems of the disposition of children

---

[1] For assistance in collecting material for this article I am indebted to Mr. Hiroshi Wagatsuma.

or property, a second-stage possibility is conciliation proceedings, which may or may not lead to the so-called "conciliation divorce" (*chōtei rikon*).[2] These proceedings are available at the domestic section of the Japanese family court located in each prefectural capital, with more than 200 branches scattered all over the country.

Family courts were first established in Japan in 1949 during the Allied Occupation. Earlier, various types of juvenile legislation existed, but marital problems reaching the stage of court action were dealt with in the ordinary courts. From 1949, under the pressure of American example, juvenile and domestic matters were consolidated in one family court system as a part of the newly independent judicial branch of the government, administered by the Supreme Court and its secretariat. Like some other Japanese administrative structures, this one had an impressive modernity when seen from the outside, but the content of the system and the people who operated it were somewhat less glitteringly new.

Conciliation divorce is an example of the virility with which informal Japanese social techniques can survive within imported forms. All divorce cases reaching the family court are subjected to conciliation proceedings for the purpose of finding a mutually acceptable solution. In each court district judges periodically select a list of conciliators (*chōtei iin*), who are ordinary citizens chosen for an annual term for family court service. Conciliators are required by the pertinent laws to be "people of deep human feeling" (*ninjō no fukai hito*), duly appreciative of virtue and social morality. Otherwise there are no formal requirements for the job. Higher education is not a prerequisite, and professional training in marriage counseling is neither required nor expected. In seeking candidates for conciliators, the judges solicit recommendations from local chambers of commerce, mayors' and governors' offices, lawyers' associations, and other local centers of power or influence. Wives of prominent local citizens frequently serve; a good many male conciliators are retired government officials or businessmen who have time to devote to the assignment. Some are lawyers. No money is paid for their services beyond a small honorarium and streetcar fares; but being a conciliator is a mark of prestige, and although appointment is for one year at a time, renewal is expected and

[2] *Chōtei* can also mean *mediation* or *arbitration;* I follow the usage of the family court officials.

as a rule granted indefinitely. When a leading family court judge recently suggested, in an access of reformist zeal, that a retirement age be set for conciliators, the idea met with widespread protests and had to be abandoned.

When a Japanese wife or husband appears at the family court, application for a hearing may be made either orally or in writing at a cost of only a few yen. Depending on the nature of the case, it may go directly to conciliation, or it may be referred to one of the family court investigators (*chōsakan*) [3] for special study. Whereas conciliators usually are amateurs and often are old with wisdom, investigators today are young professional caseworkers, university graduates from mixed backgrounds, sometimes from poor families. Many seek mobility upward through the system. One young investigator in Tokyo was quite clear about his motivation: born in rural Nagano prefecture, he had been offered a job on the *Yomiuri Shimbun*, one of Japan's largest newspapers, upon graduation from the university, on condition that he return to Nagano and represent the paper there; but since an investigator's job would keep him at the center of things in Tokyo, he decided on a career in the family court.

When the family-court system was born full-blown more than a decade ago, trained caseworkers obviously did not exist to give it life, and many ordinary court officials had to be recruited for the new work, just as many judges of ordinary courts had to take on new and unfamiliar responsibilities as judges of family courts. Since 1957, however, a national training institute for family-court investigative officials has been in operation in Tokyo, where university graduates in sociology, psychology, and education, who have passed civil service examinations and spent at least two years working in a family court, are brought in groups of around 50 for a year of special training in domestic and juvenile problems. The proportion of bureaucrats of orthodox background in the investigators' ranks has recently declined; in the current class of 42, only seven are graduates of university courses in "jurisprudence," the normal gateway to officialdom. The rest are social-science majors.

In a typical conciliation proceeding, an investigator is directed by

[3] The Japanese term means literally *investigating officer*. In juvenile cases these officials often have responsibilities similar to probation officers, but in divorce cases their duties are mainly investigative. The same officials do not handle both types of cases and there is little liaison between them.

his judge to interview the principals, collect background material, and prepare a report before the first hearing opens. At the hearing the judge and two conciliators (in divorce cases one is usually a woman) form a "conciliation committee" which meets around a table with the principals to hear their stories. Proceedings are secret and divulging them carries a fine and/or jail sentence. Husband and wife must both be present for a hearing to be held. Divorce conciliation always involves more than one hearing and may require many. Evidence is heard from both sides; the problems are discussed; the investigator's report is consulted, and the committee eventually reaches a judgment, which it offers to the couple. Their acceptance is voluntary. If both sides accept it, the conciliation is successful and has the force of law, whether it results in reconciliation of the couple or as is very often the case, in their agreement to divorce. If conciliation fails to secure any agreement, one party may go on to take judicial divorce action.

Investigators are not included in the conciliation committee and may or may not be required to be present at hearings. (In practice judges are often absent, since many cases are being heard simultaneously.) In any event they are not empowered to conciliate or arbitrate cases but merely to provide data and expert advice to the conciliators. Young investigators, with their newfangled notions of casework and the causes of marital difficulty, raise strong objections to this system of conciliation, which is more customary than scientific but which nevertheless has full legal legitimacy. They complain that their reports on cases are often ignored. Although many of them are married and have children, they are regarded by the older conciliators as too young to know how to deal with family problems, or anything else, for that matter. The investigators reflect the old lament of the "expert" against the "policy maker." They deplore the fact that the system's effectiveness depends to a large degree on the personal dispositions of the individual conciliators and judges rather than on their own supposedly more objective data.

They recognize that those conciliators who have a more modern, rational view, some training, and serious dedication to their task may be performing a valid service within a context that remains strongly Japanese. One of the most famous divorce conciliators, the wife of a university president, assured me that this was true: she said that her main task just after the war had been to advertise to women that they had new legal rights; today most women know this, and her efforts have shifted to getting more of them to protect their rights and use them in an intelligent manner. A number of conciliators, especially in the larger cities, are well read on the subject of marriage and divorce, and some short-term training (about equivalent to first aid for summer campers) is available to conciliators in various parts of the country. A few have traveled abroad and observed family courts in other countries. But investigators argue that too many conciliators are merely papering over the cracks of marital difficulty, enjoining couples to think right thoughts and sending them home either with divorces that could have been avoided or blithely confident that their problems have been solved, when the basic causes have not even been treated. One acquaintance of mine, a psychologist, tells of his own experience as a divorce conciliator in a family court outside Tokyo. He was rather young for the job, and his fellow conciliator was an elderly matron who, after dispensing paternalistic advice to distressed couples, had a habit of turning to him at the end of each session and asking in a loud, piercing voice, "Well, Professor, and what do *you* think?"

Here is a sample conciliation judgment in a divorce case taken from a manual for the use of investigators in training (translation mine):

1) Both parties vow that they will let bygones be bygones, and will regard marriage with a reverent spirit, co-operate and trust each other, and pursue a harmonious family life centered on the children.

2) In order to realize paragraph 1, both parties will perform the following in a respectful manner:

(a) To heighten self-awareness that they are husband and wife, they will exchange cups plighting their marriage vows in the presence of _____, the go-between. They will move to another house and take a trip.

(b) The defendant [husband] will completely liquidate all connections he formerly had with other women and will guarantee not to continue such immoral conduct in the future.

(c) The husband will hand over all his salary to his wife, and she will give back to him pocket money (not to exceed 20 per cent of his take-home pay).

(d) The wife will not neglect to keep her household accounts in a clear fashion.

(e) The wife will observe moderation in her contacts with her own family.

Up until 1956 such judgments were in no way enforceable by the family courts; since then it has been possible to levy fines for nonperformance, but a large number of conciliation judgments are poorly enforced, if enforced at all.

Conciliation is cheaper, more private, faster, and simpler than ordinary court litigation. Most cases are settled within three months of the first hearing, though a number drag on for years; on the other hand, a large number are dismissed in the course of the hearings. Public-opinion polls conducted by the government indicate that most people approve of the system, if divorce has to come to court at all. However, a large proportion of conciliation cases end in divorce, because by the time they reach court they are hopeless, and conciliation often really is concerned with the disposition of children and property and the payment of lump-sum "consolation money" to the wife. (Alimony in the American sense is not recognized in Japanese law.)

The conciliation system has been highly praised by some foreign legal experts as a unique Japanese contribution to international legal practice, with few counterparts in other countries. Conciliation as a device short of public judicial proceedings in ordinary court is not limited to divorce cases but also is very commonly used in Japanese commercial law, land tenancy and rent disputes, and other legal areas. It embodies a search for a harmony in which nobody is ever quite openly pronounced right or wrong; it pays homage to a "whole" with a life of its own, superior to and independent of its parts, to which everybody should be ready, at least in theory, to submit themselves. These concepts may have been weakened in various ways in the last 20 or 30 years, but in the social sphere, at least, they have by no means been destroyed. In the conciliators the values of the folk are carried on into a modern imported court system and given the force of law.

One segment of Japanese opinion objects to the conciliation system on political grounds. Professors of more or less leftist views are quick to point out that many of the basic laws authorizing the system were passed in the 1920's during the period of "Taishō Democracy," when the government felt strong protests from the people for more freedom and rights. According to this view, the government responded with conciliation as a stratagem to blunt and control these pressures from below. Conciliation in domestic disputes was legalized somewhat later, toward the end of the 1930's, and was not used widely as a method until after World War II. But these critics argue that divorce conciliators almost always are selected from among the most powerful conservative elements in the local community, and they see them as agents of a conservative "ruling group" that seizes every opportunity to oppress the people and enforce its own ideas of order. Though obviously most conciliators do represent conservative elements controlling Japanese society on local and national levels, representatives of labor unions and other Socialist-oriented groups are not totally excluded from the system, and judges, conciliators, and investigators alike deny that there is any deliberate political design in the choice of conciliators or any intention to "oppress the people." After talking for two hours with one university professor who was scathingly hostile to the system, I discovered that he himself served actively as a conciliator and had spent the whole previous day dispensing his own advice to couples at the family court.

Some Japanese psychologists and psychiatrists object to the whole concept of conciliation by laymen on the grounds that it is too unscientific and cannot by its nature get at the real causes of friction in the family. The psychologist regards the conciliator as a sort of shaman; but suspicion is mutual, and there is always the danger, in the solution of divorce problems as in party politics, that the people or the patients will be left with their needs unsatisfied. Little or no follow-up is made of couples who leave the family court, and the study of divorce by consent occurring outside the court is very difficult. Many people feel that the consent divorce should require some sort of court sanction. At any rate, the opposition is clear between the conciliators with their common-sense approach and often authoritarian behavior and the professional investigators with their more "objective" attitudes, which, unfortunately, may also be used in an authoritarian fashion.

A few farseeing people in the cities want to introduce more professional marriage-counseling services, but as of now such agencies are almost totally absent. So far marriage consultation has focused on bringing couples together for marriage, not on keeping them from drifting apart afterward. The most detailed studies of divorce in Japan therefore tend to be highly technical works by psychiatrists. However, as more family-court investigators are trained, they will add to the literature of Japanese marital problems from various points of view. The percentage of cases reaching the family courts is very gradually increasing year by year, and with the investigators' training institute serving, as it does, as a publishing center for books and monographs on family casework, the general interest of the public in the subject of divorce and its human solution may eventually be deepened. In the meantime, the clash between conciliators and investigators exemplifies the old wave motion of tradition versus change, "common sense" versus "science," the enfolding collective versus the intelligent self, that one sees constantly in the manifold processes and occasions of contemporary Japanese life.

APPENDIX

Four Japanese Divorce Cases

While making inquiries about the family court I acquired a book by Kazuo Hatashita, *Rikon no Shakaiseishinbyō Rigakuteki Kenkyū (A Social Psychopathological Study of Divorce)*, published in 1959 by the family-court training institute in Tokyo. This is a formidable, not to say forbidding, work of 935 pages, but it is an important work in its field. Hatashita is a psychiatrist formerly assigned to the medical section of the Tokyo family court and now chief psychiatrist at a large government hospital. His book is based on a close study of over 200 divorce cases, completed while he was serving with the court.

Hatashita classifies causes of Japanese marital friction leading to divorce under the following headings: Cultural (economic, religious, artistic, or political differences, or differences of general cultural attitude and value system); Human Relationships (relations between husband and wife or with relatives, and "triangle" relationships); and Personality Problems. Much of his work deals with personality disturbances and other problems of special interest to him; however, in the section dealing with "differences of cultural attitude and value system" he has included some case material of more general interest to anyone with a concern for Japan. From a large number of examples I have translated the four cases below.

These stories, with their tragi-comic themes of submission and rebellion, are of course meaningful in themselves and for what they tell of social change. The psychiatrist can use them for his analysis, the sociologist for his, the novelist for his. With others like them these couples speak of long-endured hurts, of the breakdown of stereotyped ideas of what a wife or husband should be, of new and misconstrued "freedom," of determination to have what has never been had, and so on. These "cases" share universal qualities, but they are also peculiarly Japanese and interesting in a Japanese context because they reached the court at all. They are like the tops of the subterranean mountains that form many islands in this part of the world. Here they are, in the bare, skeletonlike form which Hatashita gives to them (the headings and name initials by this writer):

1) *A young city couple of the postwar period, who lapsed into traditional attitudes after their infatuation wore off:*

"While K. was still a college student his mother died. The family had always lived in Tokyo, but K.'s father now took to traveling on business and rarely came home. K. was left to live with his younger brother in a household without rules or order. After finishing the university he went to work in a company office, where a casual friend introduced him to S., a girl clerk. S. had got her job through a family connection with the company president; her parents had conventional notions about bringing up their daughter, and she had met few boys and had little experience with them.

"S. and K. immediately fell in love, but the girl's family regarded K. as beneath her and strongly disapproved of the match. They put pressure on her to reject him and marry a man of their own choice, but she refused, and ten months after meeting K. she discovered that she was pregnant. K. then asked his section chief at the office to serve as go-between with S.'s parents, and the marriage ceremony took place two months later.

"Their married life began in a single rented room, and for a time things went smoothly. But before long S. began to complain about her situation. She wanted an electric washing machine, a refrigerator, a hi-fi set, and television. K. frowned on these expenses and told S. he expected her to conform to his idea of 'proper culture' and thus to demonstrate that their household was 'democratic.' S. rejected this odd definition of democracy and culture, began to pay more visits to her parents' home, and asked K.'s permission to leave the baby with the grandparents more often, so that the couple might go out together to movies and plays. K. resented this suggestion and opposed it.

"Their relations deteriorated and many quarrels arose from small causes. When S. forgot to buy a new jar of hair pomade K. upbraided her, but she refused to apologize. K. was suddenly transferred to a new job in another section of the company, where he was much busier than before, had to attend many sake parties, and was often late in returning home. He complained of fatigue and insomnia, but S. retorted that he was merely being silly: any man who did no more than K. did, and did it in a company he liked, as K. claimed to do, had no right, she said, to such complaints. She told him to stop annoying her with them and continued to press him to move to a room nearer her family, but he refused.

"When S. became pregnant a second time, K. wanted the child, but S. herself induced an abortion, saying that she wanted to enjoy life and having another baby so soon would damage her beauty. Soon after this she left home and moved to a room nearer her family. K. forbade her to depend upon her parents, but she would not move back to him. Finally S. went to K.'s father to try to get him to talk to her husband; but the father only delivered a moral sermon to K. and evaded the real issues between them. S. also was repelled to discover that K.'s father was living with a housemaid, and when K. tried to insist that she call this woman 'Mother' out of a sense of duty, she violently refused. S. and K. lived apart for two years before S. filed application for divorce conciliation proceedings at the family court."

2) *A young farm wife who demanded more equal treatment, and a husband who was unable to see his wife as a person:*

"The younger son of a farmer worked by day in a nearby town for the national railways but returned to his father's farm household by night. His wife also came from a farming family. They were married in 1954, and two years later the husband filed for divorce conciliation proceedings, with the following complaint:

" 'I am away from home from morning to night and hardly ever see my wife, but my parents say she is dull-witted and I think there must be something mentally wrong with her. If the rice is burning in the pot, she lets it burn; and even though she sees that my younger brother is busy, like as not she will tell him she herself is busy amusing the children, and he can damn well tend the fire in the kitchen stove himself. She never goes out to see me off in the morning or meet me when I return from work; she does nothing to look after her husband. When I speak, she is slow to answer, says little, and never tries to hold a conversation about anything. If I try, she leaves the house in silence. When she sews clothes the measurements are apt to be all wrong: if she makes a shirt one sleeve may be round and the other square. Her sewing is very odd, indeed. My father says that even after the diapers are dry she keeps turning the bamboo pole with the diapers on it around and around, over and over again. He says she goes out in the rain without an umbrella and stands like a fool under a tree by the brook behind the house. She collects bits and pieces of string and carries them around hanging out of her pockets. When my parents asked her to help them gather some greens, she pulled far more than was necessary. On my day off, when I asked her to help me in the fields, she refused.'

"Tests revealed that the wife was not mentally abnormal, and she had this to say about her husband's complaints:

" 'He says I am always acting as he describes, but actually my motives are quite understandable. He believes blindly whatever his parents tell him about me: for example, that business about the diapers. I was only performing a rational action to dry them more quickly; so who is crazy, my father-in-law or me? I do a lot of sewing and dressmaking to help out with the family budget, and even before we were married he griped about my work, and I have tried to improve. But I did graduate from a dressmaking school in the city, and if he is going to take my sewing mistakes as proof that I'm abnormal, then everybody who does such work must be abnormal. The mistakes I made were human mistakes; they were not made out of any special ignorance. As far as the greens were concerned, my mother-in-law scolded me for pulling too many, but where I was brought up we generally pulled a good deal more than I did on similar occasions.' "

3) *A middle-aged wife who decided that she had had enough and who took advantage of her new rights:*

"T.'s father, a fisherman, had no children by his legal wife but five by a concubine, of whom T. was the eldest. T. therefore was his father's heir and had to live in the family with his father's wife, who had been a prostitute before marriage and who treated T. harshly. Eager to get away from home, T. decided to become a teacher and went to live in a dormitory when he entered normal school before the Pacific war. In his fourth year of school T. was engaged by a Buddhist priest as a tutor for his son. T. moved into the temple and there fell in love with the priest's eldest daughter, several years his senior and a women's college graduate. Soon the girl became pregnant and had an abortion. Meanwhile T. graduated from normal school and, under the duty of paying back money borrowed for his education, went to teach in a school near Tokyo. His sweetheart followed by train, but during the trip she caught a contagious disease and died. Her mother, the priest's wife, had long been ashamed of local gossip to the effect that her daughter had seduced a younger man; now she insisted that T. marry the younger sister of his dead sweetheart. The sister was not asked for her opinion. Their marriage was duly performed, but the young wife did not live with her husband until he had paid his school debts.

"T.'s wife, Y., had five children in rapid succession; but since, as she said, 'he thought only of his sexual gratification,' she had herself sterilized after the fifth child was born. Except for one daughter who died in infancy, these children grew to maturity after the war. One girl worked in a Tokyo department store, another in a bank; the eldest son was in the university, while the younger son, hating life at home, enlisted in the Self-Defense Forces after graduation from high school. Y. complained that she had endured T.'s abuse, threats, and violent behavior for more than 20 years. As a young wife there had even been times when her father, the priest, had urged her to ask for a divorce, but she had borne her situation for the sake of her children. Now that they were grown, Y. saw no further reason for prolonging her predicament. She had become aware that certain legal rights were now available for women, including the right of initiating divorce proceedings, and she had finally decided to avail herself of these rights."

4) *A husband whose political universe collapsed with Japan's defeat, and a wife who felt debased by his postwar activities:*

"Before the war and up until Japan's surrender H. was a career official in a government ministry in Tokyo. His wife, E., was the daughter of a wealthy family with close connections in top *zaibatsu* circles. After the war H. was purged from government service; he spent much time brooding over

Japan's defeat, which he blamed on the selfishness and corruption of leaders in the wartime Tōjō cabinet. And he grieved continually that Japan had fallen to the status of a fourth-rate power.

"Before long H. became involved with a right-wing political group or 'movement' for the promotion of the 'national polity,' which sought to revive ultranationalist slogans and declared that today's decadent youth must somehow be made more patriotic. His wife had no sympathy for these activities. Her education had developed an interest in Western classical music, and otherwise she took a sophisticated interest in Western culture. She could live with her husband and endure whatever difficulties had existed between them as long as he remained in the bureaucracy, where his social position had been assured. But his new life seemed to her a disreputable and vulgar anachronism. She insisted that he leave the 'movement,' as he called it, and take a position in some private firm, which she, with her family connections, could help him get. But he disregarded her wishes, saying that he loved her and wanted to show her happiness but would not depend upon her for help.

"Later he degraded himself further in his wife's eyes by writing pamphlets, selling them in the streets, and even making street-corner speeches—actions which, according to E.'s account, made her want to vomit even to think of them. H. then took to drink and occasionally ran wild at upper-class business parties to which he still had social access through his own past connections and those of E. On one awful occasion, when E. tried to get him to stop drinking, he nearly choked her to death. E. finally gave up, and one day while H. was gone she returned to her own family. As she expected, he came to get her back, protesting that he cared deeply for her. But E. felt that his 'wild, banditlike love' was nothing but a form of misplaced kindness: she thought he really was more in love with his new political activity than with her; and she refused to return to their home."

*   *   *

CHAPTER *12*   ⊛

PAGES FROM A POLITICAL NOTEBOOK

March 9, 1958

Arriving at a new assignment for the first time or returning for another period of residence abroad means going rather rapidly through a series of phases before the routine settles down. First impressions are sharp, often incomplete, but still useful; and after the very earliest shock of arrival, when the swirl of baggage, taxis, and hotels ends, a period of intense activity begins, during which one seeks eagerly, sometimes too eagerly, to make or to renew "contacts," to come into relation (if not integration) with the new or remembered milieu. All the newspapers must be read, all the friends seen, "key" people spotted and reached, lines of approach laid down.

In such a period it may be very helpful to keep a written record of some sort into which early information and impressions can be regularly unloaded, deposited there against the future so that the mind can approach the next day on lighter, fresher terms. How long this period lasts depends on the place, time, and person: with me it usually takes a month to six weeks before the day begins to have a reasonably relaxed pattern, jobs can be sorted out and one thing neglected for the sake of another. Then, if the papers accumulate in the corner, let them, if what they contain is not germane to one's immediate thoughts or concerns. At first, however, most things are germane, and if they are recorded as experienced, when recording them does not yet seem less important than some other activity might be, the results may yield some fresh insights into the events which occurred during that particular period of reorientation.

With this thought in mind I have reproduced below some representative entries from a journal which I kept from late November of last year until early February of this year. Since the period of my return to Japan immediately preceded the opening of the 28th regular session of the Japanese Diet, much of the material concerns politics and is filled with the sort of detail that absorbs the student of Japanese politics. In December dissolution of the Diet and a general election seemed imminent. The Socialists, the press, and certain sections of the conservative party were calling for dissolution. The Kishi government had been in power for a year and had gone through one complete cabinet reshuffle without an election. In this context the day-to-day huddles of politicians took on immediate significance. The fact that dissolution did not come when many expected it does not diminish the interest of such negotiations, in a country where politics is so closely tied up with personalities. The election will come soon; meanwhile the sort of personal meetings that my notes record occur at all times; they are merely more intense when an election is in the wind. Some more permanent problems of politics also show themselves in these notes: the question of party versus bureaucracy, factionalism, formulation of party policies, and so on.

Some of the other contemporary concerns of the Japanese which also have political significance are briefly mentioned here: education, suicide, Russia's Sputnik, economic conditions, changing social customs. In one sense these entries may be regarded as the raw material from which judgments may later be formed; however, they possess an immediacy which is often lost in more formal studies.

A journal is bound to be a personal document, and I have felt obliged to delete some subjective comment and to select only those entries which have a general interest and relevance to current conditions. Material from which I have drawn extensively for earlier Reports has not been repeated. My sources have had to be anonymous; most of them are tried and trusted, and with one exception they are all Japanese. Some entries have been rearranged to give more unity, but I have not attempted to recompose in order to produce a consistent style or point of view.

*   *   *

November 29, 1957. On board S.S. "Cambodge," Kobe-Yokohama.

Landed today at Kobe, after nearly sixteen months' absence from Japan. On first glance the people look more prosperous than when I left, and the shops are crammed with merchandise in the arcades of Tor Road. Men's clothing seems less drab, but the same tightness and lack of smiles is evident on station platforms and in the trains. Kyoto has changed little—a few new buildings, but the old winter drabness, the trees being stripped of their leaves along Kawaramachi. I felt stared at, as always. Between Kyoto and Osaka, a new stop on the railroad is now at Takatsuki, where there are big factories, Meiji candy, National vacuum tube, and a new National television plant. Also a plant manufacturing stainless steel. In Kobe the new International Hotel is owned by the Asahi Beer Company, which also owns new hotels in Nagoya, Osaka, and Hiroshima.

Sitting in the Tōyōtei on Kawaramachi in Kyoto and eating an *ebi-macaroni*, I felt as though I had been away only for a weekend. I am glad we touched at Kobe before reaching Yokohama so that we could get a glimpse of the *Kansai*, which I specially like and specially sometimes hate. The first characteristic smell was the sweet perfume of hair pomade in the train. Only found in Japan, that particular smell.

December 2, 1957. Tokyo.

The house hoped for yesterday came today, a medium-sized Japanese house, not too far from the American School, and pleasant, with a small garden, expensive but livable, and we took it gratefully. The owner is a retired army officer, a lieutenant colonel of artillery, who lives with his wife and a grandson, who is in the fifth grade. They will be separate, but perhaps I can learn something from them. The house is prewar and so was not bombed out. Formerly a Japanese businessman's family lived here, and before them a Chinese. Now the elderly owners will live on the fat of American rent. From the upstairs one can look over acres of rooftops.

The drab gardens that should ideally be pruned and clean, and are so in the elegant picture books, still affect me by their quietness after coming from America, where gardens are colorful. These in Japan are in the interior, the filling-in of the "L" and protected completely from the street, so that one may see only a few treetops from the other side of the wall. They are owned by the onlooker inside, and even though they are muddy and misused and uncolorful, I like the glossy uniform of dark green they wear, and the gray of the stone vessel in which a depression has been cut for the rain to fall, and the gray *geta* with black velvet straps resting on the stone at the door. We must get a cat to keep down the rats and curl round the feet in the *kotatsu*. Tanizaki [a novelist] has a point in his praise of shadows. A year in Kyoto taught me that much, and I felt it again today when looking at this quiet house where we will live for a while.

December 7, 1957.

This is Pearl Harbor Day. I wonder how many Japanese are thinking of it. In the trams and in the streets the same immense preoccupation with the here and now seems to blot out past and future alike.

December 8, 1957.

[Premier] Kishi returned from his Southeast Asian trip today. He faces the twenty-eighth session of the Diet, with the budget the first major question. Kishi wants to place emphasis on road building and scientific education. He also wants to increase the ground self-defense force by 10,000 men. He has a four-year plan to establish a government university to balance scientific education with study of the humanities. Also subsidies to private schools and new research institutes.

Will Kishi dissolve the Diet before passing the budget? He is evidently moving in the direction of mobilizing support among groups now (heavily?) Socialist—youth and women. He hopes to turn anti-H-bomb sentiment, irredentist feeling toward Okinawa, Kuriles, etc., to the account of the *Jimintō* (conservative Liberal-Democratic party). He plans to strengthen links between central and local youth groups and to build an elaborate "youth hall" in Tokyo. The government's trade-union policies have hardened; the general confrontation of labor and management seems deeper; the Socialists may be moving more and more leftward. *Yomiuri Shimbun*, which tends to be conservative, sees the new Socialist policy draft as a clear indication of a leftward movement. Emphasis is placed on mass struggle, and parliamentary power seems less important to the left-wing Socialists than mass agitation based on Marxian dogmas. These tactics may well perpetuate conservatives in power and lengthen the period of their inefficient operations. With the conservatives working to organize more mass support and Socialist leadership confused, the prospects of a change in power diminish.

A forum of Japanese professors discussed Eisenhower's latest illness on the radio. Mainly they summed up the obvious and showed a fair knowledge of the weakness of the American Constitution on the question of determining incompetence of the President. They saw Ike's illness as a particularly hard blow for America now, with Sputnik and our own rocket failures and NATO coming up. "No peace, no war" seemed to be their verdict, with a widening of Russia's world influence and a narrowing of ours. One of them compared the present with the time immediately after the Pearl Harbor attack. Then America's resolution was aroused and she brought her already superior technology to bear. Now, even with determination, there is a technological gap to bridge and repair. The *Tokyo Shimbun* correspondent in New York has emphasized the whole fiasco of America's satellite-launching attempt, and one editorial tries to find some national characteristic in the story. Russia kept her efforts secret until she was able to announce her success; America became panicky over Russia's achievement and made too much publicity too hastily about her own launching. The eyes of the world were on America, and consequently her failure will hurt more than all of Russia's secret failures.

December 9, 1957.

The movement of people in the streets is sometimes inconspicuous, but it constantly goes on. One evidence of this is at station crossings. When a train is coming and the barriers go down, people begin to accumulate at them, like water forming pools behind an obstruction in a stream. At Yūtenji the streets may seem empty, but a sizable group will gather if the bars are down even for a moment. This constant wash and drift of people shows how packed this amazing city is.

Lunch with K. and H., who have moved in from Mitaka and are living in Higashi Nakano. K. had some interesting things to say, as usual, about the conservative party. He thinks that factionalism is less disruptive than at any time since the party mergers in 1955. He is now studying party organization. One key problem is organization on the local (*chōson*) level. Diet members have their machines, which often conflict with local party branches set up from Tokyo. The party must often endorse more candidates than is desirable, because all of them have some claim on party support and cannot be ignored. Each candidate may receive part of his support from party funds but supplement this by outside contributions in his local region. Thus in a three-seat constituency the *Jimintō* may find that it must support officially four or even five candidates, which may split its vote and allow the Socialists to threaten or even to win. K. thinks the conservatives thus are more concerned than ever with local organization problems.

December 15, 1957.

A Japanese Premier's timetable:

December 8: Kishi returned from Southeast Asia. Conferences with Shōjirō Kawashima, Secretary-General of the party, and Eisaku Satō, Kishi's younger brother. Kawashima later announces that there will be no dissolution of the Lower House in January.

December 9–10: Cabinet meetings on both days. Then formal courtesy calls by Kishi to Mōsaburō Suzuki, chairman of the Central Executive Committee of the Socialist Party; Shigeru Yoshida, Ichirō Hatoyama, and Tanzan Ishibashi, three former Premiers.

December 13: Conferences with Mitsujirō Ishii, Deputy Premier, and others.

December 14: Conferences with Shigemasa Sunada, chairman of the party's Executive Board, and Kiichi Aichi, chief cabinet secretary.

Thus within a week of his return Kishi has seen all of the top leaders of the party, some of them several times. His immediate circle includes Kawashima and Satō. The so-called "main-stream" group includes Ichirō Kōno, Director of the Economic Planning Board; Sunada; Bamboku Ōno, Deputy President of the party; Hisato Ichimada, Minister of Finance; Aiichirō Fujiyama, Foreign Minister. But these men have their own supporting factions, and Kōno especially is looking out for himself. The "anti-main-stream" of the *Jimintō* includes many of the old *Minshutō* crowd, Takeo Miki, Kenzō Matsumura, and Hayato Ikeda, an old follower of Yoshida. Also Hitoshi Ashida and the Admiral Nōmura splinter group.

After Kawashima announced no dissolution Ishii said that Kishi still is considering dissolution. Sunada then declared to the press that there would be no dissolution until the Diet passes the budget. Whereupon Kishi publicly announced that Sunada was presumptuous to make such a statement. Note the personal nature of all this. Each leader is thinking first of how Diet dissolution will benefit him personally, not the party as a whole.

December 16, 1957.

Love suicides are getting commoner. Now the niece of the last Emperor of the Ch'ing dynasty, Henry P'u-yi, and a Japanese college boy have killed themselves at a hot-spring resort in the mountains. It is the familiar story—their parents opposed their marriage and relented too late. I could not get this new case off my mind all day. Riding the #6 streetcar from Shibuya to Shimbashi, I felt the constraint of the people opposite—schoolgirls going home from school and wives with vain faces and woolen shawls about their shoulders; old men in black capes and black *tabi*. What a dangerous business to generalize about! A hotbed of subjectivism, in E. Sapir's phrase. It was I who felt constraint more than they. Getting off the train later at Yūtenji, however, I felt another sort of constraint. Schoolboys were making jokes at the barrier, and a young samurai type gave me a scowl as he swaggered by on his way to the bathhouse. The love-suicide theme had made me sentimental, but theories of sadness, humor, or "national character" evaporated in the bustle of the narrow street, where the main business was avoiding the bicycles and trucks of delivery boys.

Y. came to lunch and promised to take me back to see Yoshie Hotta [a novelist], who is just returning from a trip to Peking. His beautiful Zushi home, which we visited in the summer of 1956, has burned down, but he is living in another house on the same site. Y. is a winsome person and I like her very much. She says that she has become completely disillusioned with the Socialists. Their ignorance and gaucheness in connection with the "goodwill mission" to the U.S. last summer seems to have prompted this. The people they wanted to see in the States were all "has-beens" like Thomas E. Dewey, whereas they should have been seeing people (she said) like Lyndon Johnson and John Kennedy. The conservatives, she says, are pressing hard to get women's groups into their control. In Shiga prefecture they demanded that the head of the federation of women's organizations join the party or be replaced by a party member. She refused and has been replaced. In any case, the anti-prostitution bill has given women a sense of their power, and they won't be put back into the mold of prewar. This is Y.'s view; she is always the strong feminist.

M. [a psychologist] takes a different view. To him, the traditional division of female roles between wife and prostitute is reasserting itself, despite the coming legal ban on prostitution. The wife has always been regarded primarily as a child bearer, while the prostitute has filled the role of sexual partner. Immediately after the last war legal reforms disturbed this traditional dualism by introducing a civil code based on the idea of individual human freedom. Rapid gains were made for a few years for the new concept of woman as a wife combining both roles. But love marriage and related phenomena such as dating had no institutional basis in the society. The new system would require a basic shift of ethical values to succeed, a respect for the person as a person. M. says "decent" wives nowadays more and more accept a return to dual roles. They are thus committing a basic insult against human dignity by hiding behind their secure traditional status and condemning other women to sell themselves to their husbands. The "decent" wives are collaborating in the debasement of other women.

One woman, writing in *Fujin Kōron*, the "intellectual woman's magazine," says it is the "advanced" woman's duty to "act as a prostitute" toward her husband. While women in the West may express feminism by becoming more like men, taking men's roles, "advanced" women in Japan want to abolish a system whereby wives merely are supposed to procreate. Freedom for them lies in a fuller relationship with their husbands, not in a struggle to be individually independent from their husbands.

The cold is coming. I feel it in the wind that sweeps through Shibuya station. Whenever I see a young mother, fresh from the country, with her flat-faced baby wrapped in a lavender *nenneko*, the two of them leaning into the slope of Dōgenzaka, I always think of what I imagine Siberia must be like. Shibuya has a frontier atmosphere, full of mud and piles of sand and gravel. Will it never be finished? Ed Seidensticker is right: most of Tokyo looks as if it had been put up for the summer.

December 19, 1957.

S. came to supper last night. He was in good form, having just come from a meeting of the Central Committee of the Socialist party.

He says formal organization of the party is complex but means practically nothing. He estimates membership of the party at 40,000 nationwide. Decision making is all behind the scenes. He claims he "repeatedly warned" certain American scholars not to take formal organization seriously. Chief problem facing the party is how to transcend labor-union support and increase support among small industries and farmers. The basic split is on the top level, the class-mass split. But many other divisions exist. For example, there is friction between consumers' co-operatives run by unions in factories, which often sell to all and sundry at low prices (though this is against the law), and small retailers who are being hurt by the competition. Asanuma [Socialist Secretary-General] is tied in with the consumer co-op movement and so favors their activity, but in order to woo small business the co-ops must not be allowed to compete too strongly.

Socialist appeal to such conservative segments as small business is mainly negative. If Socialists can exploit the opposition's failures in this sector and convince small business it will get some specific favors, then it can win votes. The party is now trying to discover ways of countering the new Small Industries Law which the conservatives put through in the last session of the Diet to keep small operators momentarily pacified.

Peasant unions are extremely weak. They are led by and identified with individual Diet members. Apart from these leaders peasant unions have no real existence, according to S. The urban labor movement does have something of the character of an independent movement. Few union leaders are actually Diet members, but the movement as a whole is organized to give political support at election time to its own selected candidates. The Socialists would like to see peasant unions so organized, but here it faces an extremely conservative segment of Japanese society.

I thought S. was more relaxed than before and had more poise. His last world tour undoubtedly had a good effect on him in many ways. He is building a new house in Zushi.

S. says the *Sōkagakkai* [a religious sect claiming affiliation with Nichiren Buddhism] is especially strong in Districts One and Two in Osaka. Both districts return Communists to the Diet. The *Sōkagakkai* is fighting the labor unions, by teaching its followers that it is virtuous to submit stoically to whatever management requires. Unions in Osaka are deeply concerned.

According to S., anti-main-stream elements in the *Jimintō* are interested in delaying the general election because they think Kishi's popularity will decline the longer he is in power. Early last year his popularity was relatively high; his trips overseas were dramatic, though they accomplished little, and he was able to cash in on his anti-H-bomb appeals. Lately he has done less and less and is faced with diplomatic stalemates vis-à-vis both Russia and the U.S. Some in his own party are biding their time. Kōno, though nominally "main-stream" and supporting Kishi, is seeking a way to bring down the government to his own advantage, so that he can become party president and Premier.

December 20, 1957.

The need to catch up scientifically may be the thing that will end Japan's fragile "democratic" experiments with education. *Nikkeiren* [Japan Federation of Employers' Associations] as well as the *Seichōkai* [Political Affairs Research Board of the *Jimintō*] are calling in today's *Asahi* for a scrapping of the broad, unified curriculum in elementary and secondary grades and a return to the prewar selective European-type education, sorting out children by their presumed abilities and dividing the curriculum into college-preparatory subjects and industrial-vocational subjects.

Here is an issue of national importance on which the Japanese must take action soon. Business especially wants education tightened up to produce better-trained scientists and technicians for its laboratories and factories, close liaison between schools and workplaces, dispatch of lecturers from business to school, etc. Businessmen have long criticized the excessively theoretical content of education, the isolation of the schoolroom from the "real" world. The issue of scientific advancement for the state may bring the two "worlds" closer together at the expense of more egalitarian concepts of education installed by the Occupation. Japan intends to let nothing stop its efforts to keep up with other countries in the race for the "latest," whether it be a gadget for the home or for the nation. Here business and government will take the lead more or less together, and they will be attacked by intellectuals and Socialists out of power. But would not Socialists in power strive for the same ends?

December 21, 1957.

According to T., the left-right split in the Socialist party is simple when compared to the fragmentation within the conservative camp. He directly opposes K. on this. Not only do individual leaders have their bands of supporters and fight each other, but there are broad divisions between the so-called "party faction" [*Tōjin-ha*] and the "bureaucrat faction" [*Kanryō-ha*], depending on the background of the leaders.

Thus Miki, Ōno, Matsumura, Hatoyama are men who have had their careers primarily in party politics over a long period of time; whereas Kishi, Ikeda, Satō, Yoshida, and many others are primarily ex-bureaucrats.

Note T.'s typical professorial bias against the politicians, who are "dependent" upon the bureaucrats in order to run the country. As he explains it, having studied it in detail, the ties between the two are immensely close. In the Lower House nearly 30 per cent of the conservative party Dietmen are former government officials, as against nearly 10 per cent of the Socialist members. T. gave some interesting details on day-to-day working of politics. Party men go constantly to departments or ministries or summon bureaucrats to their offices for advice and materials from which to formulate platforms and plans. The bureaucrats they deal with often are their former subordinates, so that middle-level bureaucrats have great initiating power. From section chief (*kachō*) level up, departmental personnel and politicians are on intimate terms. It takes about twenty years to reach *kachō* level. According to T., then, bureaucrats are constantly manipulating Dietmen behind the scenes. He admits change since the war but insists that the trend is strongly away from Occupation ideals. The social system simply is not favorable to the growth of democratic attitudes and forms of action. T. reflects the intellectual's fear of the bureaucratization of politics— ghosts behind every door, and a reluctance to believe that real power has shifted to elected officials whose allegiance is to party. How often one gets this from professors: Japan is still "feudal."

December 22, 1957.

K. and H. came to supper. K. feels the basic hopefulness of his attitude toward Japanese political development is justified as long as the Constitution remains unchanged. The main essential change from prewar is that the Premier must now be elected by the Diet and must be a party man. This means the parties must be taken into account, since cabinet power is linked to party membership. K. feels that it is naïve to say, as T. does, that party men bow down to bureaucrats. They undoubtedly do in many instances, but a few party effectives do not, and they are able to tell the bureaucrats what they want and to get it. Here is a key to really effective party development: knowing what is available in the government, what to ask for, what to do with it after the government produces it. The *Seichōkai* drafts no legislation, but it is useful in feeling out what legislation will and will not be acceptable to the party. Standing committees of the Diet are another place where the politicians can learn the business of governing, how to run things and tell the technicians what to do. And if bureaucrats obstruct, politicians can make things difficult when the next budget comes around.

K. estimates that not more than twenty of the 291 conservatives in the Lower House have real political "weight." But as a type politicians are coming to represent larger groups of the population and have more real authority. The question is often raised, "Are 'extra-parliamentary' groups usurping the power of Diet and parties?" Many persons have disdain for parties. I recall the contempt with which one of the managers of the Yawata Steel Company spoke of "those illiterates" in the Diet. But the Constitution remains unchanged after twelve years; the parties are small and weak, but the various elites throng around (and into) them and use them to get what they want—business and bureaucracy, as well as labor unions.

Parties must develop a broader base. But they are more and more expressing the needs of larger groups of people—"pressure groups" such as farmers, teachers, doctors, etc. Even prostitutes get some protection in the Diet. And constituents come for help to the Dietman, who has some power over the bureaucracy. Diet candidates often are of poor quality, but the party leaders at least know this. Corruption still occurs, and organization is weak, but there is some knowledge that these things need tending to. How can one say, with T., that the parties are mere vassals of the bureaucracy? Yet evidence to the contrary is not always easy to get.

On Kōno, K. says he wants to use his Economic Planning Board to command implementation of economic policy, not just to formulate it. Kōno has Ichimada under his thumb: a common newspaper joke has it that the Finance Minister is a mere division chief in the Economic Planning Board. Kōno is not afraid to speak his mind or to accept responsibility, and this sets him off immediately. Sunada (who just died) was in his circle, but now there is no Kōno man readily available to take Sunada's place as chairman of the executive board of the party.

K. was struck by the fact that the party had given Sunada, who was a Christian, a fancy Shintō funeral. He spent two hours there listening to tributes.

Kawashima has no real power; Ōno is a man of dubious reputation. Where is there a conservative leader to take Kishi's place in the future?

December 26, 1957.

I saw [Deputy Premier] Ishii today for about thirty minutes. He is fatherly, smiling, and friendly but with a shrewd underlook that says he is a good negotiator. His office is off in a corner of the Premier's official residence, but it is nicely furnished and has a charming large color print of fisherwomen on one wall. The interview was cut and dried. He said everybody was coming to him asking when the Diet would be dissolved. But even Kishi doesn't know. Kishi would be glad to dissolve it in January; but the party is split half and half between the earlys and the lates (who want to pass the budget first). Ishii doesn't expect any great change in Diet strength to come from the next election. Compare this with Mizutani's [a Socialist Diet member] remark that the Socialists don't expect to win more than ten to twenty seats.

Ishii met Kei Hara [Premier, 1918–21] when Ishii was a young man in the Taiwan colonial administration and Hara was Home Minister and came to Taiwan on an inspection tour. That was before the First World War. One sometimes forgets how far back some of these people go.

More on bureaucracy versus parties: H. [a Foreign Ministry official] says the center of state power still really rests with the bureaucracy, but Diet members are "studying hard" and "improving." He says some Dietmen come to his office asking for "materials" but "we never give them anything important directly." Everything important has to go through the Parliamentary Vice-Ministers, who are the official link between ministries and Diet. "Theoretically, they are a link between government and people." This is another bureaucrat's view.

The bureaucrat's ideal is not conflict from which compromises are hammered out that will serve the best interests of the whole. Rather it is harmony and Confucian avoidance of conflict, mediation which will fuse the whole into as near a unity as possible, however specious it may be. When Ashida or other foreign-affairs experts get up in the Diet and ask questions on international problems, they already know the answers and are merely seeking to educate other Diet members and the people as a whole.

January 5, 1958.

In Kabe, a small town near Hiroshima, a young man of good family fell in love with a local girl. The boy's mother, investigating the girl's family discovered that she had eta [an outcast group] blood. The girl herself did not know this, but her parents did; they had moved from Hiroshima to Kabe long before to hide their identity and raise their children where they would escape discrimination.

When the girl learned the truth she drank poison but recovered in the hospital. When the girl's parents went to the boy's parents to seek to persuade them to relent, the boy's parents refused. The boy and girl attempted suicide together, but both failed. The boy showed every sign of intending to marry the girl, permission or not, until the boy's father, in protest against the match, drowned himself in the family's *well.* The boy's mother then vowed she would kill the boy if he insisted on marrying the girl. He probably will not. Thus the force of prejudice against the outcasts remains intense.

Japanese newspapers at the year-end are full of pieces about the new "space age," the age when men will set foot on new planets. The year 1958 will be year #2 of this new era. Mankind in general is threatened by the new scientific developments, and mankind hopes more fervently than ever for peaceful coexistence of the great powers with the small. I suspect the papers are more concerned over "weak Japan's" fate than over mankind "in general." The *Yomiuri's* editorial today stands apart from both the free world and the Communist one in analyzing the former's difficulties and the latter's accomplishments. At any rate, I doubt the genuineness of any real widespread feeling of shared experience—of peril or otherwise, with mankind "in general." If the "space age" contributes to an awareness of man's general plight and thus awakens interest in spiritual problems as well as scientific "challenges," it will have had some positive effect in Japan.

Perhaps a magnanimity and concern for the predicament of all is connected with the growth of a middle-class culture, a culture of the *chūkansō,* which some intellectuals profess to see developing along with the growth of mass communications. Maybe class lines are softening through increased mobility since the war and through the growing urbanization and spread of "middle strata," salaried men, professionals, and rise of the proletariat into middle class through wage increases. This sort of analysis is tempting but needs much care in its use. Unions are weak, and floods of people still pour from country to city. Half of Tokyo looks as if it slept last night in a *Tōhoku* village. The traditional ability of the people to restrain from consumption and accept "meagerness" as their lot works against the growth of a "leisured" middle class. The gulf between management and labor is still great, it seems to me. But perhaps "internationalism" can grow only in the "middle strata." And it is certainly true that the domestic market has expanded remarkably in the last four or five years.

January 6, 1958.

Eisaku Satō, Kishi's brother, has been chosen to succeed Sunada as head of the *Jimintō* Executive Board. His appointment was made over open complaint in the board; he was opposed by Ōno and Kōno, who fear they are being isolated. Satō has ties with the Yoshida faction of the party, and thus Kishi may have acted cleverly to unite opposing cliques before the general election.

The mechanics of Satō's choice are interesting. Party rules say that the board chief must be chosen by the board in an election. But Kishi got together with Kawashima, Ōno, and Kōno and indicated he wanted Satō. Miki's approval was sought and quickly obtained. But in the meeting Hideji Kawasaki got up and said he felt it was undemocratic for the chairman to be chosen behind the scenes. He asked if the party leaders meant to hold to the principle of election of the board chairman. Kawashima replied that they did—they had merely asked for Kishi's preferences first. Then somebody else insisted that the Premier's intentions be asked again. They adjourned the meeting and called Kishi on the telephone. He insisted that the board itself should carefully deliberate the matter and make its choice—seemingly he threw the ball back to the board. After further deliberation, however, they decided to throw it back to Kishi and phoned him again. After this conversation the board voted unanimously for Satō.

January 26, 1958.

G. says most students have made up their minds; they have accepted the Marxist interpretation of history. The most disturbing episode in his memory occurred during the visit to Japan of the Hungarian student "Freedom Fighters." Students in Tokyo and Kyoto refused to let them speak. G. said many students wanted to hear them, but there was no democratic students' organization to sponsor them, because none exists. Neo-fascist right faces Communist or pro-Communist left; or, as G. put it, "the Commies on one side, the *karate* devotees on the other."

With Y. today I went to Zushi to visit Hotta [see entry for December 16]. I had not seen him since the summer of 1956, and our meeting was not entirely satisfactory. He needs two or three hours to come to the subject he is thinking about, and there were too many other people present today, distracting his attention.

He visited India in the winter of 1956 and China last fall. His impressions of China were very favorable. He found China inspiring, especially to the lower classes, who now have "job, marriage, and old-age security." He said there are no prostitutes in Shanghai, no bums or beggars or gangsters. The city is amazingly clean compared to his last visit there at the end of the war. China seemed to him like America in the nineteenth century: all the young people want to go to the west and be pioneers. He is now reading a book on the Han dynasty and says he finds much in it that is similar to today's China.

He said nothing of purges, forced labor, loss of chance for human freedom. He thinks the U.S. should admit China's achievements and renew relations at the earliest possible moment. About India he felt things were "hopeless." The basic problem is lack of education and endless sectionalism. India is "not a country at all," has no unity, and is cursed with a multiplicity of tongues.

Jirō Yawata, chief of the political bureau of the Asahi *Shimbun*, writes that Kishi is caught between pressure from overseas and the wishes of the majority of the Japanese people. Japan is a small, weak nation allied with the Western camp. For its own safety it must rely on the United States and thus must accept weapons and be an accessory to America's defense of the western Pacific. The people, on the other hand, want disarmament, peace, prosperity, and the return of Okinawa, Bonins, and Kuriles. They also want the security treaty and the administrative agreement with the U.S. revised.

The Socialists thus have their usual range of targets: unpopular foreign policy, fear of war, irredentism (though these issues alone seem to me too weak to bring the Socialists into power). But ideological divergences and a shortage of top-notch people are operating to keep the Socialists weak. Many Japanese, perhaps most, have little faith in either party.

CHAPTER *13*   ✿   ✿   ✿

THE JAPANESE ELECTIONS
OF 1958: PREVIEW

April 30, 1958

On May 22, 1958, the Japanese people will choose a new Lower House of their National Diet in the first general election since February 1955. Nearly 52,000,000 voters are eligible to cast ballots, an increase of 2,800,000 since the last election. About three-fourths of those eligible are expected to vote for more than 900 candidates for 467 seats in 118 electoral districts.

Popular interest in this election is low, for several reasons. Dissolution of the twenty-eighth Diet was strung out all winter, until everybody, especially Diet members, grew tired of waiting for it. Now that dissolution has come the brief campaign period is a letdown. Political antagonisms also were obscured during a dull Diet session. Except for passing the budget the Diet accomplished little. In earlier sessions bills rewriting laws in education, labor, or the electoral district system caused disorder and fist-fighting on the Diet floor; nothing of the sort occurred this time. Again, in 1955 the conservative leadership's drive for Constitutional revision, implying full-scale rearmament, kept the Socialists tense and belligerent. Today the Constitutional issue lies in an advisory council; revision is blocked by Socialist Diet strength, and reports issuing from the council suggest that at least half of its members may oppose revision anyway. Free interpretation of the anti-war clause (Article 9) may be adequate to allow rearmament to proceed indefinitely, as, in fact, it does proceed. In this Diet Prime Minister Nobusuke Kishi avoided forcing through controversial measures. The Socialists, too, were quiet, bargaining for small favors. Dissolution came after public discussion of its timing by Kishi and Mōsaburō Suzuki, the Socialist leader. As the press rather scornfully noted, this was a "dissolution by talk."

Despite calm on the surface, however, two major political parties with substantially different platforms and policies now face each other for the first time in Japanese history. Before World War II voters could choose between conservative parties, and from 1946 until the autumn of 1955 an assortment of parties, conservative and "progressive," were available to the voter. Since 1955 conservatives and Socialists, though torn by harsh inner conflicts, have merged into two parties; and three weeks from now voters will be forced to register approval of one side or the other in a very real contest for political control of Japan. Here is the true interest of the coming election.

The conservative Liberal-Democratic Party (*Jimintō*) now holds 290 of 467 seats in the Lower House. The opposition Socialists (*Shakaitō*) hold 158 seats. Both parties are trying to estimate correctly the mood of the people and to represent themselves as the best hope of a revived Japanese nationalism. The conservatives maintain a heavy advantage, because a majority of the people consistently votes for them. But this majority has been declining in every election since 1952, along with a steadily increasing number of young voters and enfranchised women, many of whom favor the Socialists. In the search for votes now gathering speed, what are the main positions of the two major parties?

The Socialists continue to work the peace–anti-H-bomb theme for all it is worth. A *Shakaitō* planning-board official recently had this to say about his party's election strategy: "Postwar nationalism differs fundamentally from that of prewar, in that those groups which promoted Japanese imperialism have been basically discredited. At present pacifism is the masses' great *mystique*. And we link pacifism closely with nationalism: only through peace is national survival possible. Pacifism is the mainstream of the national soul. Of course, this is temporary. Ten years ago the mainstream was democracy, and we came close to convincing the people that the Socialists best represented the democratic way of life. Today interest in democracy has almost entirely disappeared among the inert masses. Peace has taken its place, especially since the Korean War. It is the current fad, everybody's desire, so each party strives to identify itself as the sponsor and protector of peace. This is why Kishi joined with Suzuki to back the Diet resolution calling for an end to H-bomb tests—although Kishi refused to declare that Japan should become part of a neutral, denuclearized zone. He must show that he is a peacemaker, but he is hampered by having to keep the U.S. satisfied that he is anti-Communist."

Following the peace theme, the Socialists pledge to oppose rearmament, gradually to reduce the existing military forces, and to use the savings to cut taxes. Japan's national sovereignty would be protected by a collective security pact signed by Russia, Communist China, Japan, and the United States. Such a pact would make unnecessary the present Japan-U.S. Security Treaty and the Treaty of Alliance between Communist China and the Soviet Union, and they would be canceled. (How this would be accomplished is not explained.) All of Japan's current troubles with Russia—territorial claims, fishing rights, peace treaty—would be solved by a "mission to Moscow." The Socialists repudiate the two-Chinas idea. They would restore trade and establish diplomatic relations with Communist China, and they would abandon Formosa. In this they have the silent or expressed support of a number of businessmen. They repudiate any connection with nuclear weapons, but they endorse the development of atomic power for peaceful purposes. In short, Socialist foreign policy, as presented to the voter, implies a fundamental realignment of Japan in the world to accord with the Socialist party's notions of coexistence and neutralism.

The goal of the conservative party, as the responsible agent of the Japanese government, is the regeneration of Japan's national power and influence, which were forfeited in a disastrous war. For a number of years after the war conservative leaders were overwhelmingly dependent upon the United States, and they were baffled by the prolonged inertia of the national will, which seemed to recoil into itself and to reject everything but a desire for peace and escape from responsibility. These conditions began to change after the Occupation ended, but only in the last two or three years have economic and psychological circumstances permitted conservative leaders to be more confident on the issue of rearmament. In working to bring the people around to the point where they identify rearmament, not peace, with nationalism, the Kishi government has shown that it understands the distinction between fear of nuclear weapons, which remains strong, and support for conventional rearmament, which is growing. One may of course ask how many Japanese really believe Japan should *never* have nuclear weapons. In any event, Kishi continues to insist publicly that he will not accept them. Conservative election pledges call for maintenance of national defense "to the degree appropriate to uphold national power," an expression allowing much freedom of action. Meanwhile, the Defense Agency has announced, without public uproar, that Japan plans to purchase 300 latest-type jet interceptors from the U.S. over the next three years.

Jimintō foreign policy has three main elements: international cooperation within the UN framework, friendly relations with the U.S., and a place for Japan in the new Asia. Party leaders regard close U.S. ties as essential to achieve their ends, and they are disposed to align Japan with the free world. In this their policy differs basically from the Socialists who, at least while out of power, espouse a neutralist position. However, to regard *Jimintō* foreign policy merely as "pro-American" is a sentimental oversimplification of the facts. The conservatives wish to reduce their heavy dependence on the U.S. in trade and other fields as rapidly as possible. The *Jimintō* wants as much freedom as possible to develop economic relations with Communist China, without breaking with the U.S. over diplomatic recognition; it seeks a greatly expanded sphere of influence in Southeast Asia and elsewhere, while remaining within a generally pro-Western orientation.

On domestic issues the platforms of the two parties are a good deal alike. Some political commentators have expressed fear that the people may have difficulty telling them apart. However, their differences are substantial. What has happened is that the *Jimintō* has moved over toward the Socialists on welfare measures. Both parties stress a welfare pitch. The Socialists have stopped talking about nationalization, at least for the time being; instead, they have adopted some vaguely worded references to state control of essential industries. On the whole they stand for control of production rather than expansion of free trade as the key to economic policy; but they say little about such complex matters and stress social welfare and the millennium that will result from their accession to power. Both parties promise tax cuts, old-age pensions, and other benefits. Kishi is against poverty, corruption, and violence (including labor-union violence) in the best Confucian manner. The Socialists, with their labor support, stress the minimum wage, which Japan does not have; they would soak the rich and the big corporations. Both parties are for the *taishū*, the masses of farmers, small businessmen, salary and wage earners who comprise the bulk of the voting population. Both parties support increased spending for scientific research and better facilities for scientific education.

These are the main issues; but how important are they in determining the outcome of the election? The extent to which Japanese voters are swayed by peace propaganda and antinuclear appeals when they decide on their candidates is uncertain. Many voters vote as they are told, or from ties of loyalty to some candidate, or hope of economic or other personal gain. The large "floating vote" of intellectuals, urban salaried workers, and professional men does not necessarily vote on the basis of issues; big names are likely to be more important. In general, businessmen and farmers vote conservative, while workers, especially union laborers in large plants, tend to favor the Socialists. But whatever the voting pattern, the merger of political groupings into two major parties since 1955 has at least helped to clarify the major issues on which antagonism exists. Voters have a somewhat clearer choice; and the *Jimintō*, especially, has been forced to think more about local organization to fight *Shakaitō* encroachment on areas traditionally conservative. This election is the first in which two party organizations have faced each other on a national scale.

Recently I traveled to two different prefectures to investigate conservative campaign issues and organization problems. Yamanashi is a mountain prefecture, containing Mt. Fuji and its chain of lakes, and noted for its scenery, silk raising, and grapes. The 1955 census gave it a population of only 807,044, after Tottori prefecture the smallest in Japan. There are 447,000 qualified voters. Population actually has declined slightly since 1950, due to the exodus of people to the big cities. Still, the population of Yamanashi is not exactly sparse: density in 1955 was 181.1 per square kilometer (Tokyo had 3,977 per square kilometer; the national average was 241.4).

The executive secretary of the Yamanashi prefectural *Jimintō* party federation, Minoru Matsuda, was ready and willing to talk about party problems and the coming elections. An experienced party official,

Matsuda expressed the views of some younger party leaders, who fear Socialist gains and wonder how to counter them. Yamanashi still votes conservative, but by a diminishing margin in recent years. In the April 1947 election the percentages showed 86.2 per cent conservative, 13.8 per cent for "progressive" parties, meaning mainly Socialists. In 1949 the conservative margin rose, but in 1952 the balance was 72.3 per cent to 27.7 per cent. In 1953 it was 63.9 per cent to 36.1 per cent; and in 1955, the last general election, 59.8 per cent to 40.2 per cent (nation-wide averages in 1955: Conservatives 63.2 per cent, Socialists 29.2 per cent, others 7.6 per cent). The trend clearly is toward the Socialists. The prefecture's one electoral district has five seats, filled at present by three conservatives, one Socialist, and one pro-Socialist independent (backed by the Japan Teachers Union).

Since the party mergers were completed, Matsuda and his head-quarters staff have been busy establishing local branches (*shibu*) of the *Jimintō* throughout the prefecture. Matsuda claims there are 38,000 registered party members in the prefecture but admits that only 20 per cent pay the nominal dues of 100 yen (27 cents) a year. About two-thirds of the geographical area is organized. Each of the 84 *shibu* at town or village level (*chōson shibu*) has its hierarchy of local executive officials, who tend to be identical with local power holders— village assemblymen and other notables. Each *shibu* also is equipped with advisers, a general assembly, and various functional branches, including a women's section and a youth section. Local branches in towns and villages are subordinate to the city-county (*shi-gun*) level, which in turn reports to the prefectural headquarters, where prefectural assemblymen predominate in party councils.

The paper organization of the party is symmetrical and impressive; however, it is largely artificial. Matsuda sees the essential power problem: "We are trying to get into relation to the life of the people. We want the farmers to come to us for favors from the local bureaucracy, instead of always going to individual assemblymen or Dietmen in their districts. If snails are eating up a farmer's crops, we want to be in a position to get the local office of the Agriculture Ministry to do something about it. Only by showing that we have real influence on the local level will the party develop power at the grass roots." However, Matsuda is only half-conscious of the role the party might play. He cannot be free of factional allegiances and prejudices; his position appears to depend upon the whim of the present governor. Questions about the local clique situation produce some heat. Yamanashi, I was told, is pro-Ishibashi (a former Prime Minister), not very keen for Kishi, and very hostile to Ichirō Kōno (a State Minister and contender for power within the party). And so on.

Loyalty to party has not yet supplanted personal influence in the crucial business of selecting candidates for the general election. The conservatives' three incumbents are all strong vote getters. In addition, two new candidates, both businessmen in their forties, look promising. One of the younger aspirants is strong in the home area of the pro-Socialist independent incumbent; the other is the son of a powerful local businessman, and his wife is head of the women's section at prefectural headquarters.

Matsuda believed that it would be foolish to run all five candidates and risk splitting the vote. In his opinion all five could not possibly win; he wished to jettison one of the incumbents. This man, he told me, "has not been a loyal party worker. He is not interested in party organization, and in the last mayor's election he supported the Socialist candidate." When the executive board met to decide on the list of candidates to be submitted to central party headquarters in Tokyo, Matsuda moved that they vote for four of the five candidates by secret ballot and thus abandon the principle of preferences to incumbents decreed by party rules. However, his motion failed to carry, and all five candidates were endorsed by voice vote. The moral of this incident is clear: once in the Diet, an incumbent's strength becomes solidified until it is nearly impossible to dislodge him from his party's nomination. By trying to do so Matsuda was himself disobeying party orders, although he declared that he was not really being disloyal but was trying to give the party a better chance to win. What other motives he may have had for throwing over one incumbent I cannot guess. In any case, the board feared that unless the incumbent was nominated he would bolt the party and take his supporters with him. His personal influence was what really counted.

According to Matsuda and others at party headquarters, the Socialists are gaining in Yamanashi because of weak *Jimintō* organization and because Socialist peace slogans are effective, especially among youth and women. The two main issues for local people are trade problems and nuclear tests. Raw-silk exporters still dream of restoring trade with China and Manchuria, and they blame the conservatives for not doing more to help them. Many more votes will be lost, Matsuda thinks, over the bomb-test issue. At first prefectural *Jimintō* leaders joined with the *Shakaitō* to form a "bomb-banning council." But as Communists came in to distort the movement the conservatives withdrew. On the domestic front the conservatives are being pushed toward a welfare state; but foreign policy differences are showing up more clearly and will have some effect in the coming election in Yamanashi.

In Chiba prefecture, *Jimintō* party organization is even less advanced than in Yamanashi. Bordering Tokyo Bay east and south of the city of Tokyo, Chiba has a population of 2,200,000, of whom 1,250,000 are eligible voters. The population mostly engages in agriculture, but there are also many industries, including steel mills. Chiba is known as a conservative stronghold. Of its 13 Diet seats in three districts, ten are held by the *Jimintō*, three by the *Shakaitō*.

Makoto Tsuchiya, the executive officer at Chiba *Jimintō* headquarters, is a typical local businessman-politician. He owns a starch-manufacturing business and sits in the prefectural assembly; formerly he was speaker of that body. As in Yamanashi, nearly everybody "who is anybody" connected with the conservative party is a member of the local elective assembly. Conversely, local elective officials are overwhelmingly pro-conservative. In Chiba all the city mayors, 68 out of 70 town mayors, and all village mayors are *Jimintō* party members or supporters. Fifty-one of the 59 members of the prefectural assembly are conservatives. Incidentally, there are no women among them. Nationally, out of 2,607 prefectural assemblymen, 1,767 are affiliated with the *Jimintō*, 477 with the *Shakaitō*, and 308 are independents, many of whom vote with the conservatives. The rest are from assorted minor groups or represent vacant seats.

Village party leaders in Chiba are either farmers who own their own land, or village businessmen, such as sake brewers, bedding makers, or other proprietors of local enterprises. At the city and prefectural level conservative leadership includes some large forestland proprietors, whose holdings were not taken from them by the Occupation land reforms, and businessmen like Tsuchiya. In Chiba conservative *shibu* organization has moved very slowly since 1955. While the local people are inveterate organizers of every kind of group or association, they have not been enthusiastic about new party branches. Tsuchiya, a local boss himself, and comfortably established in a hierarchy of personal influence, is not the sort of man to push a new, more impersonal loyalty to party very hard. Like many party functionaries, in Tokyo and elsewhere, he sees organization solely as a weapon against the spread of the Socialists, not in any more positive terms.

Tsuchiya has dutifully canvassed Chiba prefecture twice in the last year, held meetings with local leaders, and organized a few branches. However, real power in the prefecture remains in the hands of the national Dietmen, the Governor, and their financial supporters. Each Dietman has his *kōenkai*, or supporters' association, which works for him, especially at election time. Tsuchiya may try to incorporate *kōenkai* into local *shibu* and thus shift the focus of influence from the candidate to the party, but this effort is not very successful. For example, in Kisarazu, five *kōenkai* were merged to form one federation of locals (*shibu rengōkai*). On paper they are all one party organization, but loyalties to individuals remain strong, and conflicts between branch officials who support rival candidates are as fierce as ever.

Tsuchiya says that it takes from three to six months to get a branch going. Local opposition may claim that the party can do nothing for local people that cannot already be done better through the Diet member. In one town, Daieimachi, in the northern part of the prefecture, the people vote 80 per cent conservative, but in one section there is a small group of farmers who have opened up some new land and are living on it. Many of these people were bombed out of Tokyo during the war and returned permanently to the countryside. They have Socialist sympathies, and although they don't amount to much politically, if the conservatives organize a party local they will provoke these farmers into forming their own organization; confrontation and unpleasantness will result. The mayor of Daieimachi told Tsuchiya he wanted his town to be the last place in the prefecture to organize. Several other towns have expressed the same desire.

The Chiba conservatives are worried about *Shakaitō* gains among workers in small enterprises, where recent deflationary policies have cut production and raised unemployment. Socialist gains among youth, even in the countryside, are another problem. Local organizers worry about funds to carry on propaganda among groups susceptible to Socialist appeals. Conservative party members in the prefecture number only a few thousand, and most of these pay no dues. Party workers grumble that they have no steady source of working funds, whereas the Socialists are able to get contributions from *Sōhyō* (General Council of Trade Unions), which extracts money from union labor by the payroll check. As one woman party official told me, "People think we conservatives have plenty of money, but we don't see any of it around here."

The Chiba conservatives are sure of being returned to the Diet with a majority, but they are not too comfortable in their minds about the future. They feel, and say, that the U.S. is being beaten in the propaganda war with Russia, and they fear this will be reflected in the voting, although to what extent they do not know. They think the Socialists will pick up votes on the China-trade issue, as well as the nuclear-test issue. The conservatives in Chiba are quite openly for rearmament for national defense, and they seem to me basically friendly toward the U.S. But they are apprehensive about U.S. tariff policies and what the effect of these may be on their fishing and other export industries. They are afraid the Socialists will gain votes from this issue, too. They expect to lose one seat in the coming election; as they put it, "This is a conservative center. If Chiba loses one seat, what will happen in the rest of the country?"

No one doubts that the ruling conservatives will be returned to power. An upset is out of the question. But how great a majority will they get? This is the riddle of this election. The Socialists privately state that they do not expect to gain more than ten seats. Despite some local misgivings, *Jimintō* leaders seem confident of holding approximately to their present strength.

If the Diet balance remains about as it is, there is a chance that the two-party system which arose in 1955 will gain in strength and meaning. Slow growth of local organization could in time transfer loyalties from individuals to parties, with a corresponding decline of factionalism and greater concern for national issues. Japan would continue to be governed by a party representing, for the most part, the propertied classes; but tolerance toward the minority opposition might supplant a sometimes unreasoning, and unparliamentary, desire to smash it by whatever means. However, should the conservatives lose more than they expect to lose, say 20 to 30 seats, and the gap between the two parties narrow, anti-Socialist reaction might grow intense. More immediately, Prime Minister Kishi's leadership of the *Jimintō* would be threatened from within his own party. There the struggle for the succession already is visible; and given a shock at the polls, the shaky structure of conservative unity might collapse in a dust of cliques and factions.

CHAPTER *14*

THE JAPANESE ELECTIONS
OF 1958: OUTCOME

June 19, 1958

The general elections are over; the conservatives have won, and the Socialists are disappointed with their small gains. Fanatics on the extreme right and left got nowhere, while businessmen and all others who yearn for a stable government and a clear, pro-Western foreign policy feel encouraged, at least for the moment. The people, who never talk very much about politics anyway, have voted as they wished, or thought they should, or as they were told, but voted, and in record numbers.

Election Day, May 22, fell on a Thursday. The weather was good throughout the country; government offices and many private companies declared a holiday, and farmers were not yet busy harvesting winter crops or planting the new rice. The result was a record vote, though many people had predicted a poor turnout up until Election Day. Voting was an orderly, mainly silent business, unmarred by violence. Schools and other public halls were turned into polling places, filled first with long lines of men on their way to work in the early-morning hours and later by more and more housewives, many carrying market baskets and with their children dangling from straps on their backs. (More than 75 per cent of women voters voted. Out of 19 female candidates for the Lower House 11 were elected, three more than in 1955.)

178

In most respects the polling process looked like the one I watched last fall in the Philippines. There were, however, a few differences. In Japan identification of the voter is a good deal more cursory than in the Philippines. Here he merely hands the written notification he has received from the election administration agency to the poll clerk. He signs nothing; no fingerprinting or challenging of the voter is authorized, whereas in the Philippines, where "flying voters" have been known to move from precinct to precinct on Election Day, such safeguards are essential. Otherwise there were the same long lines of people, rich and poor alike, shunted in and out; the same overseeing officials striving to look dignified; the same narrow voting booths (appropriately steel in Japan, paper or wood in the Philippines). In Tokyo, no matter how dirty and drab the schoolroom, meeting hall, or basketball court, in the center of each a vase of flowers, dwarf pine, or azalea plant had been placed, "for culture," as one newspaper reporter said. The police were busy elsewhere. According to one poll clerk, "Before the war they sat around glowering at everybody and ran the election to suit themselves, but today they aren't even allowed inside the polling place."

Eligible voters totaled 53,275,123, nearly three million more than in the last general election in February 1955. Of these 39,751,650, or 76.98 per cent, voted, the highest percentage since the war, and 2,700,000 more than in 1955. The conservative Liberal-Democratic party received 408,660 fewer votes than combined conservatives got in 1955 and lost three seats for a total of 287. The Socialists gained 1,923,470 votes but picked up only eight seats, for a new total of 166. The Communists increased their votes by 271,914 by running many more candidates than in the last election, but they lost one seat and now hold a single seat in the Lower House. (See Tables 1 and 2.)

Voting figures and the balance of seats clearly reveal the continued dominance of conservative forces in Japanese politics. Socialist gains were smaller than most observers (and most Socialists) expected. With barely one-third of the Diet under Socialist control, their small gains ensure that they can block revision of the Constitution, but they are still as far from power as ever.

This election provided some evidence to support the generalization that the Japanese conservatives are stronger in rural areas while the Socialists are centered in cities where there is a large industrial labor force and a substantial floating vote. The Socialists received 74 per cent of the total increase in votes, and more than half of these votes (1,040,000) were registered in urban prefectures and big cities. Socialists increased by 320,000 in Tokyo, 230,000 in Aichi prefecture (in which the city of Nagoya is located), and 200,000 in Osaka. Socialists also gained votes in Hyōgo (Kobe) and Kanagawa (Yokohama). But with the exception of Tokyo and Kanagawa they lost seats in these places. (See Table 3.) Conversely, the Liberal-Democrats lost 68,000 votes in Tokyo and 130,000 in Aichi; they gained votes in Osaka, Kyoto, Kanagawa, and Fukuoka, but their total gain in all cities and urban prefectures is estimated at not more than 50,000 votes. A large percentage of the Communist vote came from sympathizers in Tokyo (170,805) and Osaka (182,428), Yokohama, and other big cities. However, the Communists were very nearly blanked in the Diet. Their one winner, Yoshio Shiga, who received 58,824 votes in Osaka's first district, was the lowest winning candidate on the ticket and only 2,000 votes ahead of the next candidate.

As the Socialists' gains were primarily in urban areas, the present outdated apportionment of seats worked against them. Apportionment of Lower House seats on the basis of population was carried out in 1946. Since then great population shifts have occurred; some cities have grown immensely, while rural prefectures have grown less fast or have in some cases shrunk. The most vivid example of these trends is, of course, Tokyo, where the population approximately doubled between 1946 and 1955. During the same period the population of Tottori prefecture, a rural area on the Japan Sea, increased from 580,000 to 610,000. As a result by 1955 in Tokyo there were 200,000 electors to each seat, but in Tottori only 90,000 to each seat. In the recent election, in the second district of Chiba prefecture (2 Chiba), 2 Gumma, 4 Saitama, 1 Niigata, 1 Nara, and 1 Nagasaki candidates were elected with from 30,000 to 40,000 votes. But in 5 Tokyo a candidate with 80,050 votes lost, as did one in 4 Tokyo with 72,260.

In other respects the election was a disappointment to the Socialists. Although their total votes increased, the party did not gain a majority of votes in a single prefecture. Moreover, the ranking of Socialist candidates among the winners reveals their relative weakness. Out of a total of 118 districts conservatives led the ticket in 91, Socialists led in only 24, while "independents" led in three. Conservatives ran second in 72, Socialists in 45; conservatives were third in 62, Socialists in 47. (All districts have from three to five seats.) Socialists gained seats in six districts out of ten where they had no seats at all before the election, but in a number of other places (notably 1 Osaka, 3 Osaka, 1 Fukushima, and 1 Saitama) they forfeited a good chance to gain more than they did by putting up too many candidates. (Conservatives also suffered from this difficulty.) In only 14 districts throughout the country do the Socialists now have a majority of Lower House seats.

Faulty apportionment alone cannot account for Socialist failures. No amount of rationalizing can explain away the defeat of 35 Socialist incumbents, including seven members of the party's 40-man Central Executive Committee. New candidates bring total Socialist strength to slightly above the party's former level, but the experience of some of these losers will be badly missed.

Socialist leaders themselves have acknowledged other reasons for failure in their own post-mortems. On May 24 Inejirō Asanuma, the party's Secretary-General, and Seiichi Katsumada, chairman of the policy board, in a talk with newspapermen claimed that the conservatives won many votes by promising old-age pensions, tax cuts, and other welfare measures. They complained that the conservatives had stolen their program and were "blurring the differences" between the two parties. Most decisive, according to these spokesmen, was the success with which conservatives exploited public distaste for strikes and labor "struggles." In recent months strife in the ranks of railroad workers and schoolteachers, two important affiliates of Sōhyō, the largest labor federation, has caused feelings ranging from inconvenience to moral anguish among millions of Japanese voters. In the campaign conservatives constantly pushed the idea that the Socialists are run by Sōhyō, and they had plenty of evidence to support their charge. However stubbornly the Socialists may claim that the public supports labor's cause, fear of labor violence, and especially fear of the effect of Teachers Union struggles on the education of Japanese children, was an important reason for conservative success in this election.

There were other reasons. The campaign period was shortened from 25 to 20 days, and some Socialists complained that their leaders did not have time to campaign very strenuously—a fact I find hard to believe after listening to some of their gravelly speeches in the final days. Beyond that the conservatives *are* the government, and they control most local elective bodies and officials of the bureaucracy. They had heavy financial support from the most important business firms and economic organizations. Times are better than ever for most Japanese; even though business is experiencing some recession and fears more, these trends have scarcely been felt yet by consumers, who flog themselves nearly to death on subways, sidewalks, and escalators to buy more merchandise.

From the election results one more thing stands out. Slogans of peace and anti-rearmament were not successful in pushing the Socialists along very much farther from where they were. This election was billed as the first test of a "two-party system" in Japanese politics, but the only real issues on which the two parties differed sharply were in the area of foreign policy. The Socialists tried to use the threat of suspended trade with Communist China to win votes, they espoused neutralism, and they failed to make substantial gains. (For the major election issues see Chapter 13, "The Japanese Elections of 1958: Preview.") Some Socialists recently have admitted that China's attempts to influence the election by shutting off trade and attacking the Kishi regime actually hurt Socialist chances, because Kishi quickly turned public resentment of these awkward interventions to his own account.

Reasoning along these lines, Masamichi Rōyama, author of numerous books on politics and a university president in Tokyo, on May 24 wrote in the *Yomiuri Shimbun* that the two-party system in Japan is an ideal which will be achieved only when the Socialists come nearer to balancing the conservatives in the Diet. No real sharing of political power can exist so long as one party controls nearly two-thirds of the seats in the Lower House. Rōyama believes that the people have supported the Socialists only out of dislike for rearmament. But now even this appears to have lost much of its meaning. "The people," he wrote, "have no wish to see the Socialists in power. Thus the Socialists have only a negative reason for being." Such a condition, Rōyama thinks, has serious implications for the future of Japanese politics. He fears that the left-wing Socialists may now turn to the Communists, who are waiting to receive them. Such a move would be mere defeatism; but in any case, Rōyama argues, the Socialists appear headed for nothing but frustration and difficulty in the near future.

* * *

Since World War II many books have been written about the revolution of Asian peoples. Asia is in ferment; it is "aflame," and the "voiceless Far East" has found its voice in an explosive roar that has blown out many of the Western settlements and made the position of others precarious. I recall how in Washington ten years ago the pins began to be moved farther and farther down the wall maps as the Communists took over China. India was torn apart, and in Indonesia a seemingly endless series of agreements and truces was made and broken and made again. Major wars broke out in Korea and Indo-China, while in Burma, Malaya, and the Philippines wars of attrition waged by ragtag guerrilla forces prevented governments from doing anything very constructive.

Today things are at a military standoff and some economic and political progress is being made; but as late as last fall, when I spent two months in the Philippines, I felt that the place was coming to pieces, there was no center to hold onto in past or present, no rewards for ability, only self-seeking and mediocrity instead of a vigorous spirit of service to common ideals.

The strongest feeling I have about Japan at present is that it is not at all coming to pieces, that as a nation it is in a firmer position than would have seemed possible ten years ago. This feeling has been reinforced by the conduct and outcome of the recent general elections.

During much of the most explosive postwar period, while the rest of Asia was heaving out the West, Japan was under the control of an American Occupation which for a time did some heaving of its own and put through many reforms from the top down, as most reforms in modern Japan have been put through. However, in postwar Japan there has been no prolonged discontinuity in the prestige and power of the businessman-bureaucrat elite, which for the most part assisted and co-operated with the military before the war. Although the military were put out and the old aristocracy declassed, no really new group or ideology took their place.

This elite can be seen with new clarity in the second Kishi cabinet, which has just been formed as a result of the general elections.

Ex-bureaucrats are combined with outstanding business talents and a few men of largely party background to compose a strong cabinet which, under a Prime Minister who himself is a former bureaucrat, will direct the course Japan takes at home and overseas in the immediate future.

These are competent, adaptable men, who have spent most of their adult lives in positions of increasing authority in an authoritarian society. Many of them have come into party politics only since the war, because that is where real power in the state now resides. They have "retired into politics" with an unerring instinct for the path to continued influence and authority.

Kishi himself, at sixty-three, is a former Minister of Commerce and Industry in the wartime Tōjō cabinet, an economic administrator with great experience in Manchuria and at home. After the war he was purged and spent three years in prison. Later he became active in party politics under the leadership of Shigeru Yoshida. Kishi has business connections with a paper-manufacturing company and is on the board of the Nittō Chemical Company. His ties with the steel industry are also close.

Kishi has filled the most important posts in this new cabinet with his own close associates. He has kept Aiichirō Fujiyama, sixty-one, as Foreign Minister, the only holdover from the previous cabinet. In the recent election Fujiyama made his debut in politics as an "imported" candidate in Kanagawa prefecture, near Tokyo. He is a nationally known businessman, has been president of the Dai Nippon Sugar Refining Company and the Nittō Chemical Company, president of the Japan Chamber of Commerce, and Chairman of the Board of Japan Air Lines. Fujiyama has had no political experience; he got a rough going-over by the Socialists in some of the committee sessions of the last Diet, and during the campaign he confessed that he didn't know very well how to present himself to the voters from the back of a sound truck. Nevertheless he made the effort, spent the money, and led the ticket. Fujiyama is an intimate associate of Kishi and a key figure in shaping overseas economic policy, which promises to become more aggressive.

Another key figure is the new Finance Minister, Kishi's brother, Eisaku Satō, fifty-seven, who got the job after some intricate maneuvering among the various factions of the Liberal-Democratic party. (Some newspapers call the new cabinet the Kishi Brothers Company, or the Kishi Relatives Association.) Satō is known as an able, vigorous man, whose prewar record is that of a "pure" bureaucrat. Like his older brother (and six other members of the new cabinet) he graduated from Tokyo Imperial University. After graduation in 1924 he went directly into the Ministry of Railways. Beginning as a stationmaster he moved through posts in the Shimonoseki freight office and other routine assignments before becoming a section chief. From 1934 to 1937 he studied in the U.S. as a Japanese government scholar. By 1941 he had reached the bureau chief level. In 1947 he became Vice-Minister of Transportation and in 1948 he entered politics as a protégé of Yoshida. Satō was Chief Cabinet Secretary in the second Yoshida Cabinet in 1948, elected to the Diet in 1949, Secretary-General of the Liberal party in 1950. His most recent job was Chairman of the Executive Board of the Liberal-Democratic party. Satō has little background in financial matters; but, as he told a newspaperman who asked about this, he intends to rely heavily on Takeo Fukuda, a financial bureaucrat of long standing who has just been named head of the party's Political Affairs Research Board. When the reporter noted that eight out of 17 of the new cabinet are ex-bureaucrats, Satō replied that he was astonished at the way people refuse to forget a person's past. It was a fascinating remark, that tells a good deal about the man and his colleagues.

A fourth key member of the second Kishi cabinet is Tatsunosuke Takasaki, seventy-three, the new Minister of International Trade and Industry. Takasaki is a businessman who served as head of the Economic Planning Board in the Hatoyama cabinet in 1955–56. Like Satō and Fujiyama, Takasaki has come into politics only recently. Not long ago he completed an extensive tour of Egypt and the Middle East on behalf of Prime Minister Kishi to look over the possibilities of extending Japanese trade and technical assistance in that area. His experience as an economic planner will undoubtedly contribute to Japan's overseas activities in the months ahead.

The background and quality of these men and their fresh hold on most of the vital centers of power must be understood if their policies are to be appreciated. Japan's "economic diplomacy" is taking the initiative on a world-wide scale. Every day brings news of more trade contracts, technical co-operation agreements, and tie-ins of one sort or another. Kishi's new cabinet, and especially the "inner cabinet," the men I have mentioned and a few others, can be counted on to push more and more dynamically to expand Japan's economic influence, and open up more sources of raw materials and markets for this country's manufactured goods. With their own vigorous, *ad hoc* way of operating, these men will provide more aggressive direction than before for Japan's trade drives and Japan's assistance in the development of less industrialized areas from South America to India, Africa, and Southeast Asia. (For a sample of recent overseas activity in one country, see *Japanese Interest in India* (LO-4-'58), an AUFS publication.) They will couple protestations of friendship for the U.S. with suggestions and perhaps threats that they must seek elsewhere unless the U.S. buys more from Japan to balance the dollar deficit. As one high official blandly remarked just after the election, "Dollars are overconcentrated in the United States. They must be redistributed."

At home the conservatives face many problems, but the basic one is this: can they realize and meet the needs of a society in which production is rapidly expanding and social divisions becoming more complicated and diversified? The Kishi government's education and labor policies, for example, ought to reveal a good deal about its image of what the state should be. A series of moves within the last three or four years has virtually stripped education of any local autonomy and put control back in the hands of the Ministry of Education in Tokyo, where it was before the war. In its determination to smash the Teachers Union the government has stubbornly insisted on returning teachers to the control of bureaucrats and making them cogs in an educational machine that will vend a standard ethic out of standard textbooks. This process is not yet complete and is not likely to match the prewar situation; but it cannot be overlooked that the new Education Minister was an official in the notorious Home Ministry and rose to become its Vice-Minister before the war. Nor will men like Satō, Fujiyama, and Kuraishi, the new businessman-Labor Minister, give much encouragement to a labor movement that engages in incessant political demonstrations and "struggles." The new Constitution guarantees broad freedoms, but respect for these freedoms has not yet become a unifying habit.

For a long time the Japanese have called out for someone to give them a new lead. In the recent elections they showed that they do not at present trust the Socialists to provide one. The new conservative regime, with its fresh mandate, may shape a national policy clear enough for all to see and follow. Parliamentary government is the order of the day and, barring some catastrophe, seems likely to remain so. However, Kishi's "progressive conservatism" still is largely in the realm of promises; he still has to deal with opposition in his own party; and his record and the records of some of his associates are more reassuring in terms of energy than of purpose.

TABLE 1

Voting Returns by Party, May 1958 Elections

		May 1958	February 1955
Liberal-Democratic party	22,976,786	57.8%	63.2%
(Combined conservatives, 1955	23,385,490)		
Socialist party	13,093,986	32.9%	30.2%
(Combined Socialists, 1955	11,170,514)		
Communist party	1,012,035	2.6%	2.0%
(Communists, 1955	740,122)		
Miscellaneous parties	287,990	0.7%	1.3%
(Miscellaneous parties, 1955	496,624)		
"Independents"	2,380,792	6.0%	3.3%
(Independents, 1955	1,229,892)		

Source: Japan Autonomy Agency, May 24, 1958.
Note: "Independents" are put in quotes because in most cases they were conservatives running without party endorsement. Of twelve such "independents" elected, ten joined the conservative party after the election. The remaining two are pro-Socialist.

TABLE 2

Postelection Balance, House of Representatives

		New members	Incumbents	Former members	Before dissolution	In February 1955
LDP	287	26	215	46	290	297
SP	166	34	121	11	158	160
JCP	1	0	1	0	2	2
Misc.	1	1	0	0	0	2
"Indep."	12	5	0	7	2	6
	467	66	337	64	452 (15 vacancies)	467

TABLE 3

Voting Returns by Prefectures, May 1958 Elections

	LDP	SDP	JCP	Misc.	"Indep."	Total
Hokkaido	908,930	860,797	44,639	6,560	15,099	1,836,025
Aomori	337,242	132,027	8,314		72,673	550,256
Iwate	326,338	208,848	6,651		57,782	599,619
Miyagi	456,321	234,429	7,933	45,021		743,704
Akita	355,041	161,370	10,785		68,118	595,314
Yamagata	423,864	144,245	8,031	4,985	90,487	671,612
Fukushima	501,285	357,234	9,023	41,760	42,903	952,205
Ibaraki	589,857	259,833	12,648		14,175	876,513
Tochigi	472,716	215,913	8,197		1,855	698,681
Gumma	503,443	233,156	11,075		47,853	795,527
Saitama	569,701	326,362	17,566	13,263	77,100	1,003,992
Chiba	653,317	230,809	19,035	8,341	9,772	921,274
Tokyo	1,581,840	1,419,110	170,805	57,173	205,837	3,434,765
Kanagawa	629,561	499,649	49,908		112,333	1,291,451
Niigata	571,939	417,736	18,756		137,889	1,146,320
Toyama	361,360	117,063	7,514			485,937
Ishikawa	318,189	102,506	9,998		34,943	465,636
Fukui	267,912	101,754	2,965			372,631
Yamanashi	232,932	86,092	5,742	1,670	62,680	389,116
Nagano	577,420	362,808	46,366	744	50,603	1,037,941
Gifu	485,413	247,837	11,297			744,547
Shizuoka	882,767	309,742	33,053		31,337	1,256,899
Aichi	887,222	648,681	38,492	1,098	188,103	1,763,596
Mie	397,950	195,982	5,763	3,439	133,272	736,406
Shiga	233,597	157,584	7,387		4,144	402,712
Kyoto	408,691	294,365	45,834		47,328	796,218
Osaka	892,907	710,709	182,428	12,750	6,907	1,805,701
Hyogo	863,777	578,266	35,735	31,047	89,717	1,598,542
Nara	180,104	101,164	4,103		90,217	375,588
Wakayama	273,296	118,638	10,161	41,256	20,931	464,282
Tottori	167,113	87,215	4,634		37,013	295,975
Shimane	300,390	139,531	14,083			454,004
Okayama	507,768	263,859	17,640	838	3,027	793,132
Hiroshima	621,120	313,215	11,599		76,135	1,022,069
Yamaguchi	500,448	231,357	16,381			748,186
Tokushima	244,801	102,289	4,379			351,469
Kagawa	298,145	119,207	1,940		40,489	459,781
Ehime	529,387	204,045	4,852	143	7,043	745,470
Kochi	222,965	133,534	4,486		66,924	427,909
Fukuoka	911,265	698,194	39,076		40,315	1,688,850
Saga	320,889	118,382	7,157			446,428
Nagasaki	396,808	177,199	7,727	3,500	116,105	701,339
Kumamoto	567,889	176,418	7,616		92,908	844,831
Oita	364,253	176,105	5,966		49,183	595,507
Miyazaki	285,776	128,309	3,124	14,402	64,018	495,629
Kagoshima	592,837	190,418	11,171		73,574	868,000
Total	22,976,786	13,093,986	1,012,035	287,990	2,380,792	39,751,589

Source: Japan Autonomy Agency.

CHAPTER *15*

THE POLICE BILL CONTROVERSY

November 28, 1958

The police bill crisis is over and the Japanese Diet, nearly paralyzed for six weeks, has been restored to its normal course. Solution was reached through talk: both sides, ruling conservatives and opposition Socialists, responded to public opinion and compromised their demands. What was the excitement about, and what can be learned from it about the current state of Japanese politics?

Everything began on October 8, when the government suddenly sent to the Lower House a bill to revise the Police Duties Performance Law. As its formal reason for submitting the bill, the government cited the need to enlarge powers of interrogation, search, and arrest and otherwise to enable policemen "to perform their duties so as to meet the needs of today's social conditions." This was a reference to greatly increased gangsterism, juvenile delinquency, drug addiction, suicide, and other disorders which the police at present feel unable to handle within their severely restricted powers. The government also admitted unofficially that the bill sought to control labor unrest and violence, including zigzag parades and demonstrations in and around public buildings.

One of the two basic statutes governing the police (the other is the Police Law itself), the Duties Performance Law was passed in 1948 under the American Occupation. In eight brief articles the law defines the limits within which a policeman must carry out his duties. It limits preventive arrests and restricts powers of personal search and detention; e.g., drunkards and would-be suicides may not be questioned without their consent. It bans police intervention in criminal cases unless it is "certain that a crime is about to be committed." Like the postwar Constitution, the law clearly reflects the concern of the Occupation, especially in its early years, with protection of the individual from the abuses of police power that afflicted Japan before 1945. It recalls an era when protection of civil liberties was believed to require restraints, now said by many to be excessive, on all forms of control.

Since 1948, and especially since 1952, when the Occupation ended, pressure has been exerted by the police to revise the law. This pressure has been formally channeled through the National Public Safety Commission, a small appointive body attached to the Prime Minister's office, which originally was set up to take over-all responsibility for the "democratic" police system. Supervision by the NPSC has tended to become nominal. In 1954, near the end of the long regime of Prime Minister Yoshida, the basic Police Law was revised to abolish local police autonomy and recentralize control in the prefectural capitals. Thereafter the authority of the central Police Agency in Tokyo grew steadily stronger, and the police bureaucracy worked harder to widen the sphere of the police's operational powers. However, the politicians did not respond at once to these promptings. The 1954 Police Law revisions had produced a parliamentary crisis, complete with fist-fighting and other violence in the Diet. The revisions had been rammed through, but the affair had left an ugly memory, and none of the conservative leaders felt ready to attempt new moves in the area of police powers.

By this autumn conditions had changed. The government of Prime Minister Kishi, in power since early 1957, was returned to power with a nearly two-thirds majority in the general elections of May 1958. Although the conservative party's total vote declined, Kishi's personal position was fortified by cabinet shifts after the elections, which left his own clique and those of his close associates stronger than the cliques of his rivals within the party. Meanwhile, the public was profoundly repelled by the tactics of the Japan Teachers Union, a Communist-infiltrated body which resorted to teacher strikes, school boycotts, and violent demonstrations against the government's new efficiency ratings for teachers and the introduction of ethics courses in the public schools.

lrresponsible interference with the education of their children touched millions of parents on their most sensitive nerve. Other strikes, including a particularly bitter one at a large paper mill in Hokkaido, led to calls for countermeasures by the government.

Against this background, the government was emboldened to respond suddenly to the urging of the police and send in a bill to make substantial changes in the Duties Performance Law. The new proposals would allow immediate body search of those suspected of carrying weapons; they would permit detention of those "who it is feared will cause annoyance to the public," including drunks, mental cases, and children under eighteen, without their consent. More significantly, in criminal cases the revised law would allow preventive arrests not, as at present, when it is "certain that a crime is about to be committed," but when it is "clear that a crime is going to be committed." The definition of "clear" initially would be left up to the individual policeman, who also would have power to take preventive steps in situations "when it is clear that there is danger of a considerable disturbance of public peace and order." [1]

These proposals may seem mild and unexceptionable to foreign readers. However, they represented a broad extension of police powers. Within Japan public opposition was loud and immediate, indicating that while police treatment of the public has vastly improved since the war, large numbers of people are frightened at the thought of granting them wider discretion, at least not without more discussion than the government seemed to regard as necessary.

Protests came, predictably, from the labor unions and the Socialist party. By October 11 all three main labor federations had announced joint opposition to the bill. From the leftist *Sōhyō* leadership came anguished cries of "neo-fascism." The Socialists, furious and frustrated, began strong-arm tactics in the Diet. Their "action corps" of Dietmen occupied committee rooms and used force to block committee meetings and plenary sessions of the Lower House. On the night of October 14 there was a fight in the Local Administration Committee chamber, in which the private secretaries of Dietmen of both parties were pushed forward to give and take most of the punishment. The morn-

[1] *Dai Sanjikkai Kokkai, Sangiin, Chihō Gyōsei Iinkai Kaigiroku (Proceedings, Local Administration Committee, Upper House, 30th Diet)*, October 21, 1958, pp. 3–4.

ing papers gravely reported that cleanup squads had removed fourteen baskets of shredded documents and other debris from the scene. The dispute seemed to be taking a familiar and rather sordid course.

It soon became apparent, however, that the government's sudden move had touched off wider fears than had been supposed. By October 21 the bill had been attacked by many large and small organizations of professors, scientists, and other intellectuals. The Federation of Press Workers Unions, the Broadcasting Workers Union, the Japan Council of Science, the Japan Publishers, Essayists, and Novelists (PEN) Club, and the Japan Historical Research Association all opposed the bill. The Young Women's Christian Association came out against it, reportedly taking part in a political movement for the first time in its history in Japan. The YWCA's protest was given more force by the fact that its director, Mrs. Uemura, had been a member of the National Public Safety Commission from 1948 to 1954. In her statement she declared: "I know from my contacts with top police leaders that they are good people. But I cannot believe that lower ranking police who do the actual job with the public have the good sense and restraint necessary to keep from abusing any new powers. Nothing is more mistaken than the government's argument that police have much more power in such democracies as the United States and Great Britain. In those countries respect for human rights is deeply ingrained in all social institutions and in men's minds. Moreover, they have developed a legal system and other social means to redress any possible damages to human rights. We cannot discuss in the same dimension the police law of Japan, which is still an infant in the development of democracy."

Although the government may have had misgivings over the breadth of public opposition, throughout the rest of October it showed no signs of modifying its intention to railroad the changes through the Diet. On October 15 the Speaker of the Lower House attempted to calm the Socialists and others by setting up interpellations on the bill. Prime Minister Kishi denied that there was any intention of infringing on individual freedom; he insisted that the "basic human rights of the many should not be sacrificed for the few," and he declared that the bill had been introduced to "get rid of social unrest." He publicly staked the prestige of his administration on the bill and promised to use all his power to see it passed. On the night of October 17 the Lower

House voted 244 to 147 against withdrawal of the bill and sent it to the Local Administration Committee for routine consideration. Once reported out of this committee, it was sure to pass the Lower House.

As the end of October approached, public uproar grew more intense. The press overwhelmingly opposed the bill, and those papers that supported it urged that it be changed to prevent feared abuses. The Socialists and many who had no use for them by this time had conjured up another police state. At the same time, signs of opposition appeared within the conservative party itself. On October 21 State Minister Takeo Miki told me during an interview that the government had handled the bill very unskillfully indeed. (He used the word *mazui;* other pro-government critics have called the action *"oroka-na"* [stupid], or *"kodomo-mitai"* [childish].) Miki said the bill probably would pass, but with revisions to satisfy public opinion, and he left no doubt that he and others would use the affair to embarrass Kishi in the internal struggle for power in the party.

Indications of conservative party disunity increased during the early days of November. The temporary Diet session was supposed to recess on November 7, and nothing had been accomplished. As a gesture to public opinion, open committee hearings were being held, but they were time-consuming and perfunctory. The Socialists, stalling for time, planned non-confidence motions against the cabinet. The government had sacrificed everything to the police bill, and it now was clear that the bill could not pass in time. From the left came rumblings of first-class violence if the Diet were extended. The conservatives had insisted on a brief session and had promised no extensions; for them to reverse their position could provoke real disorder. The Diet would again be presented to the world as an unruly, immature farce.

Sources differ on details at this point, but it seems clear that Prime Minister Kishi refused to back down and decided on a subterfuge to extend the Diet session. The Socialists on November 4 had surrounded the Speaker's rostrum and were ready to prevent him by force, if necessary, from occupying his chair to call the House to order and announce an extension. However, instead of the Speaker, the Vice-Speaker, surrounded by a strong-arm squad of conservative Dietmen, slipped into the chamber, rang a bell from the floor calling the House to order, and ran through a motion to declare a thirty-day extension. Conservative *banzais* drowned out Socialist protests. The whereabouts of the Speaker during this melee has never been made clear; he appears to have followed his instructions from the party leaders to the letter, and according to some reports, he was not even in the Diet building when the extension was declared.

After November 4 the situation deteriorated for the conservatives. Kishi had had a good case for revision of the police bill, but the methods he had used were not adequately justifiable. The Diet extension, though not strictly illegal, was brought about through pure intrigue. Ultraconservatives in the party had been urging strong action; now they were not unhappy to see Kishi in trouble. The multiple cliques of the conservatives, that since last year had been frozen in a tableau of seeming unity, suddenly sprang to life and began moving in different directions. Conservative Kenzō Matsumura began a round of conferences with ex-Prime Ministers in an attempt to solidify the anti-Kishi forces around himself. Takeo Miki openly attacked Kishi's handling of the crisis. At a meeting of party leaders on November 5 there were demands that the Speaker and Vice-Speaker resign and the *status quo ante* be restored.

The Socialists responded to the Diet extension with a complete boycott of all sessions. On the morning of November 5 some four million organized workers held '"workshop rallies" and temporary work stoppages occurred all over the country. Trains of the national railways were delayed for more than an hour during the early-morning rush. The Socialists announced an emergency national convention for November 12 and formulated three demands: the police bill revisions must be withdrawn; the Diet extension must be declared void; and the Speaker and Vice-Speaker must resign.

With the Diet paralyzed by the Socialist boycott, the pace of events slowed. Kishi, recognizing that little could be done until the Socialist convention was over, began a series of conferences with the elder statesmen of the party, including the ex-Prime Ministers. His object was to hold the party together and shore up his threatened prestige, but he got little comfort from these conversations. The public supported the November 5 labor protest, or at least condoned it. The kind of sharp distaste that people had felt for the Teachers Union earlier this year had dissipated; to a considerable extent popular sentiment now turned against the government. Among thoughtful people fears were expressed for the life of parliamentary government in

Japan. The *Asahi Shimbun* ran a sober four-part symposium on November 8, 9, 11, and 12, entitled "Parliamentary Government and the Two Political Parties." The gist of the commentators' opinions was that although some changes were needed in the police laws, the government's behavior had been inexcusable. The people would not countenance passage of such important legislation affecting their personal lives without long and careful consideration and debate by qualified commissions and study groups. The police bill should be shelved until public opinion had been investigated; but the Speaker and Vice-Speaker of the House should bear immediate responsibility for the dubious extension of the Diet. Above all, parliamentary rules should be better observed, and mutual trust between the parties should grow.[2]

For their part the Socialists, recognizing that public opinion was warmer toward them than it had been for years, managed to keep their balance and not throw away an opportunity by violent tactics. Labor was united against the bill from the start, but the Socialist party had rejected a bid from the Communists for a united front. The Socialist convention was far quieter than had been expected. The party issued an inflammatory manifesto in which the workers were exhorted to resist the oppression of monopoly capitalism, but a good many commentators regarded this as window dressing. What mattered was that the convention gave its two leaders, Chairman of the Central Executive Committee Suzuki and Secretary-General Asanuma, a free hand to settle the dispute over the police bill, thus opening the way to negotiations with the conservatives. Although there were rumors of dissatisfaction among certain Socialist factions (e.g., the Wada group was unhappy, and some of the right-wing Socialists grumbled over the convention resolutions), the party maintained an outward appearance of unity and seemed determined not to exhaust its momentary credit with the people.

Once the Socialists turned toward talk and away from action outside the Diet, the bargaining began. Among the conservatives, one segment, led by Ichirō Kōno and Bamboku Ōno, insisted that the bill be passed as it was, even without the participation of the Socialists in the Diet. But they were bucking the trend toward negotiation. Kishi's

---

[2] Participants included Masamichi Rōyama, President, Ochanomizu Women's University; Tadashi Hasebe, a political analyst; Jōtarō Kawakami, a moderate Socialist Dietman; Tanzan Ishibashi, former conservative Prime Minister.

brother, Finance Minister Satō, argued for negotiation and concessions to the Socialists, if necessary, for the sake of party unity. By this time the conservatives also had taken up the cry for "normalization of parliamentary government," which they as well as the Socialists earlier had ignored.

For over a week both sides dickered, standing off with their demands. Finally, on November 23, Kishi and Suzuki met and after three and one-half hours of talk reached a solution, at least for this stage of the affair. The Socialists finally accepted the extended Diet session as a *fait accompli*, but both sides agreed the Diet would recess after passing the supplementary budget. The government promised to suspend Diet discussions on the police bill, thus killing it for the remainder of the temporary session. It further agreed, as a concession to public opinion, to submit any future revisions of the bill to consideration by a group of suitably eminent citizens and otherwise to publicize its intentions in advance. Bipartisan talks were scheduled to decide concrete measures to strengthen the position of the presiding officers of the Lower House, in order to prevent their being used as pawns in the future. Some suggested that they be removed from party affiliation, while others proposed that the Vice-Speakership be given to the Socialists. New elections are to be held for these posts when the regular Diet session convenes on December 10; thus, in effect, the incumbents have resigned. After the negotiations had ended, conservative die-hards vowed to pass the bill unchanged in the regular session. Socialists pronounced the results of the talks a great victory.

*   *   *

The police bill revisions were conceived by government officials working with one group of conservative politicians, among whom were some with long careers in the bureaucracy. Who moved whom would be difficult to say; the needs of one served the other's purposes. Their goal was closer control of certain spreading types of crime, as well as the activities of labor unions. Many of those who proposed the revisions are conscientious, able people without ulterior motives. The same cannot be said of some others.

All thoughtful Japanese believe that they must find some way to deal with the dreadful symptoms of maladjustment in their expanding industrial society. But the Japanese have *had* their police state. Less than twenty years ago many intellectuals, labor leaders, and Socialist politicians were in jail, while millions of ordinary citizens felt the pressure of the police in their daily lives. The personal history of that era, and particularly its tragic intellectual history, remains to be written, at least in English. These memories retain a vividness that most foreigners cannot appreciate. Japanese police today probably are no better and no worse than police in many countries; however, they are looked down upon; jokes are made about them, and behind the jokes lie fear and a feeling of "never again." To most people the police bill revisions sounded like a voice from the past. Today's police operate under restrictions, imposed during the Occupation, which in some respects leave them too weak to cope with present-day disorders. But the record of violations of civil rights by police in recent years leaves plenty of room for misgivings about allowing them wider individual initiative. Although such misgivings may be inevitable in any society, the government in this case did nothing to relieve the public's fears; on the contrary, by its dubious actions it inspired fears.

The police bill episode reveals the archaic disposition of some of the top leaders of the conservative party. In their passionate desire to be rid of a disorderly opposition they have bungled and isolated themselves from public opinion. They have acted like reactionaries, not conservatives. Last May, summing up the results of the general elections, I wrote: "At home, the conservatives face many problems, but the basic one is this: can they realize and meet the needs of a society in which production is rapidly expanding and social divisions becoming more complicated and diversified?" By their handling of the police bill they have not realized these needs. As a result, Kishi's position as leader of the government and the conservative party has been weakened. Before this affair many regarded him as a vacillating politician; their distrust now has been confirmed.

Kishi's failure has threatened to break up the conservative camp. It is difficult to judge now how deep the hurt really has gone; but the cliques are revolving, and some Japanese observers believe that if an election were held today, the Socialists would make spectacular gains and might poll half the votes. This position will, of course, change as time dulls voters' memories. But the conservative failure has placed in peril Kishi's chances of succeeding himself as party president in the elections next March, and it may affect the Upper House elections next May.

The Socialists committed their share of violence. In the early stages of the affair they were as ready as ever to jeopardize parliamentary process. However, they managed to handle themselves carefully enough to block the bill. Their gains were due to the intensity of public fear of revival of a police state, not to any sudden or prolonged passion for the Socialists themselves. As a party they remain deeply divided, but they were astute enough to cash in on public sentiment in this issue.

For once public opinion seems fairly clearly to have deflected both sides away from the extremes and toward the middle. At lunch recently with a magazine editor in Tokyo, I remarked that this year had seen military take-overs in Pakistan, Thailand, and elsewhere, but that in Japan a political clash of considerable proportions had been settled by a compromise that left both parties promising to respect the framework of parliamentary government more carefully in the future. I ventured to suggest that the contrast was encouraging. My companion agreed. "But surely," he added, with a gesture of condescension, "you don't compare us with such places. Compare us with Europe, if you like, but not with those other countries."

The conservatives went too far and were caught out where blustering statements could do no good. The Socialists saw that here was the support of the mass base they (or at least most of them) had been seeking for so long. For them it must have been a tantalizing glimpse of the following they need to reach power. The final question then becomes: how significant is this momentary centering for the future of Japanese politics? To this there can be no sure answer. No doubt the picaresque atmosphere of politics, with its "struggles" and "countermeasures," will go on as before. But for a brief, fascinating moment the storms and alarms abated, and the two parties were found arrayed toward the center of the stage.

CHAPTER *16*

THE PRINCE AND THE POLITICIANS

March 30, 1959

In this quiet spring of 1959 the attention of the Japanese people is fixed on the April 10 marriage of their Crown Prince to Miss Michiko Shoda, daughter of the wealthy president of a flour-milling company. This exotic event completely overshadows the tedious Machiavellianism of the politicians who run the country.

Nearly 14 years after the surrender, Japanese politics still is short of unifying, propelling symbols. The present Emperor is finished as a rallying point for the whole nation. Those who were grown before the last war may still regard him with reverence, but the war generation has ambiguous feelings toward him, and young people are for the most part indifferent or irreverent. After the war nationalism turned inward and became negative, focused on the idea of "peace." The concept of an unique polity, with the Emperor as its spiritual head, destined to expand Japan's "Imperial Way" over other peoples, was obliterated and is nowhere visible today. Rightist organizations do exist and occasionally wave their flags or scatter their handbills, but it cannot be maintained that they have much significance. Their membership, estimated by government sources at 65,000 persons, shades off into the miasma of the big city underworld, and they are not believed to receive any important support from the business sector of the economy.

At the same time, popular distaste for the elected power holders of both principal political parties has increased in recent months. The conservative party, frustrated last November in its clumsy attempt to force new police powers through the Diet, has relapsed since then into confused clique fighting. Recent newspaper polls show that Prime Minister Kishi's popularity is at a lower point than at any time since his assumption of power early in 1957. On important issues, such as trade with Communist China and revision of the Security Treaty with the United States, his ruling party remains divided along factional lines. On the Socialist side, factional and ideological quarrels reinforce each other to produce disunity. With both parties jockeying for advantage in the Upper House elections in June, the Diet moves so slowly as to appear dead.

The young Prince, now about to be married, has not been soiled by these struggles and disillusionments. He was a child during the war and bore no responsibility for it. The stigma of a lost cause could not attach itself to him as it did to his father, and he grew up in an atmosphere far more open and humanizing than anything that had been permitted before. He traveled abroad, engaged publicly in many sports, and was photographed falling on his skis. He had liberal-minded tutors, including a gracious American lady who wrote a book about him.[1] More thoroughly than his father could ever be, the Prince was disassociated from all the supposed attributes of divinity. Though he remained remote from the masses of the people, he was considered to be a human being.

Last November, when the royal engagement was announced, Dr. Shinzō Koizumi, the Episcopalian ex-President of Keiō University, former tutor of the Prince and key figure behind the choice of Miss Shoda, declared to the press that "the most important guide I have to offer [to the Imperial family's future] is *The Theory of the Imperial Household*, by Dr. Yūkichi Fukuzawa, founder of Keiō University. It was written in 1892 but is still appropriate. In a word, the Imperial Family should be something like a source of warmth. It should be absolutely neutral. It must transcend politics and be the fountain of kindliness. The business of punishing the wicked should be taken care of by the administration, and the Imperial Family should be concerned only with the business of rewarding the good. This is indeed a broad vision."

Fukuzawa was a convinced exponent of Westernization in his own day, and his "broad vision" seems to have combined some of the at-

[1] Vining, Elizabeth Gray. *Windows for the Crown Prince.* (Philadelphia: Lippincott, 1952.)

tributes of the Confucian good prince with constitutional monarchy. However, his day came before television and an unrestricted press, and he could not have foreseen what their effect would be on public opinion. Today, in the heyday of what Japanese intellectuals like to call their new "mass culture," the Crown Prince and Miss Shoda are being given the form of adulation most characteristic of their times: they are being treated like movie stars. No longer is it necessary to write guardedly in a special vocabulary about members of the Imperial family. Instead, their every move is being transmitted everywhere throughout the country, as if they were matinee idols. For the flood of tabloid weeklies, whose combined circulation runs into many millions, this material is made to order. As everyone knows by now, Michiko is the first "commoner" ever to marry a future Emperor; her plebeian origins and the supposed love interest in the royal match are being relentlessly exploited by the press. Nationwide contests are being held to locate girls who look like Michiko or who were born on the same day. Details of her trousseau are the common knowledge of girls in the Nagoya textile mills. The wedding is being heavily commercialized, with souvenir makers rushing to cash in on the occasion and purveyors of other commodities competing for the label of her favor.

In all of this there is a good deal of compulsive curiosity but not much affection. The warm role that Fukuzawa proposed for the Imperial Family, and that the managers of the present marriage seem to approve, has not yet materialized. The Japanese have moved from an attitude of awe toward the prewar Emperor, in a military uniform on a white horse, to the Hollywood star worship of the Prince, in white flannels on the tennis courts of Azabu.

However, if the Japanese cannot feel for their Prince and his bride the kind of warm affection that binds the British to their Queen and makes them want to protect her from the vulgar glare of publicity, at least publicity has performed an important function. It has helped to rehabilitate the Imperial institution. Some of the British in Tokyo were shocked at the choice of the bourgeois Miss Shoda; they feared that she means the end of the monarchy, and they may be right insofar as the prewar type of divine Emperor, utterly remote from the people, is concerned. But most Japanese prefer the present publicity treatment of the Crown Prince to the primitive seclusion of prewar times. Stars may be cold, but they are human like ourselves, not gods. The Imperial institution has never been so completely divested of its supernatural aura. On the other hand, mass acclaim and publicity add to its glamor, and it is more firmly planted than at any time since the war. Not since the early postwar years has public attention been focused on the Imperial family to such a degree and in such a positive way. But the focus now is in predominantly human terms; as the ladies of Kagoshima recently remarked to a Japanese reporter, they could scarcely be expected to bow low before the photograph of such a girl as Michiko Shoda.

The choice of Miss Shoda is a good example of the Japanese talent for adapting to new circumstances. Fourteen years ago the symbol of power was an American general in an embroidered cap. He was not resisted. Today power lies with the flour millers, not with the declassed aristocracy. A few rightist irreconcilables may gnash their teeth over Miss Shoda and write scurrilous pamphlets, which they are free to print, concerning the number of young men who, they say, have rejected her, or the supposedly baleful influence upon her of Christianity. But most people are simply pleased with the choice and happy in their new stars. On April 10 there will be parades, and people by the millions will line the streets in an atmosphere quite different from the stricken silences of royal passages in earlier times. (Other millions will stay at home to watch the proceedings on television.) After the tired politicians, the Prince and Miss Shoda make a refreshing pair.

The politicians themselves may be grateful for the publicity surrounding the throne at this time, when their own confusion is so evident. In fact, there is usually this leeway in Japan. The attention of the public slides about on the surface of things, while the turgid stream of day-to-day problems flows along underneath, freighted with the ambitions of venal politicians who often seem willing to drift and default on their responsibilities for governing. Nevertheless, real power lies with them and their businessmen associates. As the Crown Prince matures and establishes his own family, he may in time become the warm figure of Fukuzawa's imagination. But the unexampled glare of publicity that has surrounded him makes it unlikely that he could ever be used, as his father was used, by extraparliamentary forces behind the scenes. He will play a ceremonial, symbolic role; but barring some catastrophe, he is not apt to be available as a shield behind which the designs of others could be legitimized and imposed upon the people.

CHAPTER *17*

A JAPANESE MARXIST

March 15, 1961

On the northern outskirts of Tokyo, where suburban developments give way finally to cabbage fields and scattered farmsteads, stands an unpretentious country house of prewar vintage, entirely surrounded by a tall hedge. To reach the house one must pass by lumberyards, a dog and cat hospital, and a police box, and skirt around patches of road repair and construction that are a part of every local scene. But the neighborhood is quiet and the house isolated at the end of its lane, with nothing to mark it except an old pine tree, which has been drawn on the map one carries, and which overarches the low-lying tile roof of the house and gives to the whole property a very Japanese look. At the entrance, too, everything is conventional. A dull-faced serving girl pushes aside the frosted glass doors; a middle-aged wife watches while shoes are removed; and her older husband, in brown kimono with winter underwear showing at neck and wrists, hovers behind, waiting to lead the guest into the interior.

Here a gas stove has been turned up for the foreign visitor's benefit on a bitterly cold day. It is the room of a scholar, with a litter of paper and ink on the matted floor; and seated on a cushion at a low table under a hanging lamp, the guest feels dropped into a sort of silo of books; Japanese books, English books, books in French, Russian, and especially German, that rise on three sides of the room and overflow across the floor and the *tokonoma*, while on the fourth side through the glass panes of the paper doors can be seen the old-fashioned garden, where straw squares have been placed on the ground to make walking possible over the midwinter mud.

Across the table the host smiles and rubs his hands against the edge of a green ceramic *hibachi*. His wife reappears with cups of black tea and a plate of soft pastries and then retires. And once more the attempt begins to join minds a little and if possible to understand how this man, who lives on a government pension and looks as if he meant no harm to anybody, has been so influenced, dominated, even obsessed by the books on his walls that for most of his adult life he has preached the destruction of the political and social order which produced him; how this quiet, bespectacled, retired professor, Itsurō Sakisaka by name, as Japanese-looking as the pine tree in his garden, has responded to the impact of Western ideas by becoming one of the most dedicated and celebrated Marxist theoreticians in Japan.

* * *

Sakisaka, an eldest son, was born February 6, 1897, in Ōmuta, a little coastal town not far from Nagasaki, on the island of Kyushu. His family had lived in the area for at least five generations. His paternal grandfather was a samurai and scholar of the Chinese classics in the service of the lord of the local feudal domain of Miike. At the Meiji Restoration of 1868 this grandfather, who was then about thirty, went off to fight against the collapsing Tokugawa regime. He got as far as the area north of Tokyo, where he was wounded and returned home; but after the Restoration he did not serve in the new government but instead opened a small school in Ōmuta, where he taught until the new public education system went into effect in 1872. Afterward he turned to farming and disappears from the record; he died the year Sakisaka was born, but as a boy Sakisaka admired and romanticized him, and he still treasures a faded photograph of this grandfather, who, he says, was a "much better-looking specimen" than his father. He remembers that during his childhood the house was full of Chinese books, and he recalls poring over old wood-block editions which he could not read then and cannot, he confesses, read very well even today.

Sakisaka's parents come out blurred as individuals but familiar as types of that period. His father began as a minor functionary in the Mitsui Trading Company, and thus a thread that would reappear later

in the boy's life had its origin very early. For Mitsui is nearly synony-
mous with Ōmuta and Miike, and to a modern Japanese the three
names together mean only one thing: coal.

Coal was discovered in Kyushu in the fourteenth century and used
for heating by local farmers in Tokugawa times. After the Restoration
the central government ran the mines for two decades and then sold
them to private interests, principally the Mitsui family. In Sakisaka's
childhood around the turn of the century the Mitsui mines were being
rapidly developed as a power source for the north Kyushu steel and
chemicals complex and the system of rail transport that was to articulate heavy industry on a national scale and support Japan's rise as a
world power. This was a period, also, of primitive working conditions,
when women stripped to the waist in the sweltering underground heat
worked alongside men cutting at the coal face, and when horses used
to haul coal from the mines were stabled underground, sometimes removed permanently from the sunlight.

Sakisaka's mother came from a family of small coal merchants, but
neither of his parents went beyond primary school. They were the
heirs of provincial samurai who failed to adjust to the demise of the
old regime. Looking stiff and uncomfortable in their ill-cut Western
suits and dresses, they were part of the new white-collar horde, the
first generation to experience the full meaning of industrialization in
Japan.

Sakisaka has written down his own memories of those days of long
ago: "I think it was a happy circumstance that both my parents were
very ordinary people, because I was born a commonplace child and
brought up in commonplace surroundings. Ōmuta then was a coal
town of about 15,000 people. My friends in grammar school were
mainly the children of miners and farmers; a very few came from
mining company families. I studied little and spent an ordinary childhood. The Russo-Japanese War came while I was in the first grade,
and I remember having a great deal of fun reading war books and
looking at war pictures, playing soldier in the hills and fields around
Ōmuta. I remember reading a history of the war, *Robinson Crusoe*, and
a collection of fairy tales. So you can see that I was the usual sort of
mischievous boy, and my idols were the usual ones, Admiral Tōgō
and General Nogi. Even after I got into middle school I was thrilled

by General Nogi's bravery and thought that I, too, would be a soldier. It's a good thing I didn't, because I would not have been up to committing hara-kiri!" [1]

At about this time, in 1911 or 1912, the family met financial trouble. Sakisaka's father lost money for the Mitsui Company in the soybean market and was forced to take responsibility and resign. Shortly before this one of the boy's uncles also had left the company and failed in a venture of his own, and now his father was to experience a similar failure. Fortunately another uncle came forward to help tide the family over, and the young Sakisaka soon entered the Fifth Higher School in Kumamoto. Now he began to prepare seriously for the university, and his character took on a clearer shape: "I saw that for such a person as I, who had no special brains or qualities, there was nothing to do but study. This resolution was to run through my whole life. When I entered higher school I was put in a class specializing in German. I went at German with good health and stolid confidence. The only way for me to learn it was to repeat it over and over endlessly, because I had no natural gift for languages. But looking back now I can see that entering that class had great meaning for my whole life. Because Karl Marx wrote in German."

Entering higher school in 1914, Sakisaka passed through some of his most impressionable years during the First World War. As a nation Japan was prospering as never before. Though nominally on the Allied side, her active participation was limited to naval patrolling and some local actions around German concessions in north China. But Japan profited greatly by exporting to the markets of South and Southeast Asia, from which Great Britain and the continental nations were temporarily absent. Japanese industrialization now was approaching maturity; but the process was accompanied by widespread social unrest and maladjustment. The government failed to control inflation, prices of food and other commodities rose sharply, and rice riots broke out all over the country in 1918. Then, almost as Sakisaka was graduating from higher school and making the long journey to the capital to enroll in Tokyo Imperial University, Japan fell into a severe depression, from which it never really recovered during the next decade. While the nation wallowed in the familiar cycle that eventually was to become

[1] Sakisaka, Itsurō. *Watakushi no Shakaishugi* (*My Socialism*). (Tokyo: Shiseidō, 1959), pp. 14–15.

world-wide in its effect, a revolution in Russia succeeded in establishing a new and apparently different kind of regime, one which could not fail to absorb the attention of many young Japanese.

The general atmosphere of those times has been sketched by a well-known non-Marxist economist, who was some years younger than Sakisaka: "My youth was a time of *sturm und drang* in a quite different sense from the present. Japan was going through the great depression and the social tumult following the First World War, and conditions were incomparably more difficult than they are today. The country was in the grip of a nationalism which was soon to turn to imperialism on the continent of Asia. Inequalities of livelihood between various levels of people, discrepancies in income and wages were immeasurably greater than they are now. Agriculture was in the hands of landlords and the farm tenancy system. . . .

"The social movement was under heavy government suppression. Armed with the Peace Preservation Law and the Police Law, the authorities were clamping down not only on Communists but on non-Communist Socialists as well. Marx's *Capital*, Lenin's *Imperialism*, and other works were legally permitted to be sold, but when university students got hold of them and tried to use them in reading clubs, the police would always find some pretext for impounding them. Communists, labor-union organizers, and members of youth leagues associated with them had to resign themselves to years in jail for no worse things than reading such books. Capital punishment for the leaders was clearly provided for in the laws. All those who could be identified with Socialist parties were placed under strict police surveillance. The police intervened to warn or silence speakers during election campaign meetings and elsewhere. In short, it was a dark period, when freedom of speech was crushed and there could be almost no freedom of assembly. Within the controlling bureaucracy the military was growing stronger than civilian elements; social security measures were almost entirely lacking; labor unions were weak, and even defensive struggles for purely economic motives were subject to police repression. Under such conditions the conviction gradually became implanted in the minds of intellectuals that the large numbers of poor people could not be rescued from their poverty, freedom of speech and assembly could not be restored, and political and economic control by a few people could not be done away with by peaceful, parliamentary, democratic means.

What especially spurred them in this direction was the Russian Revolution of 1917 and the birth of the Comintern." [2]

Sakisaka describes his own social awakening: "From the fifth year of middle school [*i.e.*, the eleventh grade] I liked the life of a student, but the thought of becoming a serious scholar had not entered my head. Then, in 1916, in the second year of higher school, I read Hajime Kawakami's *Story of the Poor*, which was running in installments in the Osaka *Asahi*. It was so absorbing that I could hardly wait for the newspaper to arrive. At that time Kawakami was not even a Socialist but a mere humanist. But his story dealt with the problem of poverty in society, and from it I learned a strange thing: that the workers, who produce all the wealth of society, either are poor or do not know when they will become poor. I suddenly lost my desire to study jurisprudence at the university and decided to go into economics. . . .

"In the *Story of the Poor* I first heard the name of Marx. In 1918 I entered the economics department at Tokyo University and there first read the works of Marx and Engels. At the same time I read the writings of Toshihiko Sakai, Hitoshi Yamakawa, and Kanson Arahata [all early Socialists and founders of the Japan Communist party] one after the other. When I read the *Communist Manifesto* and Engels' *Socialism from Utopia to Science*, I knew that I could not again be separated from the fascination of those ideas. I realized that this was the way my life must take. For more than forty years I have continued in the same direction, and I am not likely to change before I die." [3]

In his college days Sakisaka also read many of the books that his classmates were reading: the naturalistic novels of Ōgai and Soseki; Dostoevski, Tolstoi, Heine, and Goethe. *Faust* was a favorite. His interest in painting was also great and seems to have begun before his conversion to Marxism. Today he is fond of Daumier and Goya, though how much because they fit the party line and how much because they are compassionate artists would be difficult to say. He is quite visibly proud of his collection of facsimile reproductions of Western paintings, mainly of the eighteenth and nineteenth centuries. When I tried to get him to discuss more recent art, he claimed that

[2] Inaba, Hidezō. "Nihon no Shakaishugi" ("Japanese Socialism") in *Shakai Kaikaku e no Teigen (Proposals for Social Reform)*. (Tokyo: Keisō Shobō, 1960), pp. 54–56.
[3] Sakisaka, Itsurō. *Watakushi no Shakaishugi (My Socialism)*. (Tokyo: Shiseidō, 1959), p. 18.

he felt no great excitement for much of it, and especially not for Picasso. But at one point he remarked: "There is no painting that I really dislike"—to use his own characteristic Japanese construction. He says that he once wanted to be a painter and that he influenced a younger brother to become a painter in the Western style.

However, from his college days most of his time was spent on the new scriptures he had discovered. He took no interest in sports, confining himself to occasional walks in the suburbs; and he appears to have done little serious work with the professor of agricultural problems to whom he was formally assigned. At that time Japanese translations of Marxist writings were proscribed, and he was forced to wade through many of them in German originals. His comment echoes the perplexity of many others in Japan and elsewhere: "When I read the original of *Das Kapital* I found it completely incomprehensible. I could read the German all right, as far as the grammar went; but the meaning was most formidably difficult."

Upon graduation from Tokyo University in 1921, Sakisaka was given a typical choice, one that many student Marxists have been given since: to enter the Sumitomo Bank or remain at the university for further study leading to a professor's post. He eagerly accepted the latter and was shipped off the next year to Germany, where he enrolled in the University of Berlin but spent most of his time at home reading Hegel, Marx, and German poetry, visiting museums and buying books and manuscripts on Marxism. In late 1924 he returned home armed and crippled with the typical qualifications of a Japanese university professor of his generation. Like his colleagues, he had marked off a theoretical domain; within it he built his castle and prepared to spend the rest of his life fortifying it and defending it from attackers. As he himself put it, "An ordinary boy such as I had to despair of creating anything new. At most, all I could do was to try to understand Marx's theory and apply it to what had happened subsequently and to the situation in Japan." The young man who only a few years earlier had whipped the school bully and played soldier on the slag heaps of Ōmuta now was ready for a career as a professor of economic theory. Soon after his return he was married and named Assistant Professor of Economics at Kyushu Imperial University in Fukuoka.

From this point on Sakisaka's life loses much of its particularity and becomes part of the larger history of Japanese Marxism and the "social movement." And just as the timing of his earlier education had a bearing on his original attraction to the literature of Marxism, so the timing of his return to Japan affected his role in the Marxist controversy that had already begun and that would continue to the present day.

The Japan Communist party was founded in July 1922 by a handful of radical Socialist intellectuals with close Comintern guidance and direction. At this time Sakisaka was in Germany. From its inception the party was under heavy police pressure, and in 1924 a serious split occurred, leading to its temporary dissolution. When Sakisaka reached Japan to take up his new academic duties, this split had been formalized and a new attempt was being made by the "orthodox" Communist group to re-establish the party.

The controversy was desolatingly arid to non-Marxists but vitally meaningful to the faithful. It revolved around the interpretation of the stage that Japanese capitalism had reached and the definition of the enemy that must be destroyed if the Socialist revolution was to be successful. The "orthodox" group accepted the Comintern thesis that Japanese society was still essentially "feudal," dominated by an archaic Emperor system and feudal landlord-tenant relations. Admittedly, capitalism in Japan was further developed than in other Asian societies; but the essentially feudal big businessmen and their bureaucratic, militaristic cohorts who ran the country were closely linked with international capitalist imperialism. Socialism, therefore, could only be achieved in two stages. First would come a bourgeois revolution, in which the disciplined Communist party would lead in the liberation of the oppressed peasants and petty bourgeoisie. This would then be quickly followed by a revolution of the proletariat to establish socialism.

Critical of this line was the group, led in 1924 by Hitoshi Yamakawa and others, who maintained that Japan was already a well-developed capitalist society, in which the two fundamentally opposed classes were the bourgeoisie and the proletariat. According to this view the bourgeois revolution, which the Communists insisted must come first, had already come at the Restoration of Meiji. What was required now was a strengthening of the working class, especially in large key industries, until a workers' revolution could achieve Socialist utopia in one stroke. Japanese "monopoly capitalists" rather than international capitalist imperialism were seen as the prime enemy. Some members of this group were skeptical of the strong domination of the Comintern over the party; some objected to violent tactics and a frontal assault on the Emperor system. And Yamakawa, a founding member of the Communist party in 1922, argued in 1924 that the times were not right for such a party; the proletariat was still too weak, lacking almost utterly in class consciousness; until the labor movement could be built up, indoctrinated, propagandized, and made into a revolutionary instrument, the small, illegal Communist party could achieve little to further Communist goals.

Though there was not then, nor has there since been, any substantial difference between these two groups on the ultimate goal of Socialist revolution in Japan, the difference on means has had a stubborn history, running through all the shifts of doctrinal line and personal factionalism that have characterized Japanese left-wing politics for the last 40 years. The slavish adherence of the orthodox Communists to the Soviet-dictated line led to their increasing theoretical impoverishment; while the relatively more moderate views of the Yamakawa group appealed to the common sense of many intellectuals, who saw around them the rapid growth of Japanese industrialism and felt the monopoly capitalists to be their natural foe.

Yamakawa never returned to the Communist party after 1924.[4] At the end of 1927 the Yamakawa group started its own magazine, Rōnō (Labor-Farmer), in which it attacked the Communists and answered the charge of "right-wing deviation." By 1928 Sakisaka, now a full professor at Kyushu University, had associated himself with this group; from now on he was a full-fledged member of the Rōnōha (Labor-Farmer faction) and devoted his own theoretical training to the promotion of its goals, engaging in polemics against the Communists and calling for his own version of proletarian revolution that would at some point sweep out the bourgeoisie and achieve socialism.

The Japanese government tended to be uninterested in these nice distinctions between factions of left-wing intellectuals, and in the spring of 1928 Sakisaka was caught in a roundup of Communists and Communist sympathizers. It was his first arrest, and apprehended along with him were some distinguished colleagues, including Professor

---

[4] Swearingen, Rodger, and Langer, Paul. Red Flag in Japan. (Cambridge: Harvard University Press, 1952), p. 20.

Kawakami of Kyoto University, the same whose *Story of the Poor* had turned Sakisaka toward Marxism. Because of lack of evidence Sakisaka was not subjected to criminal prosecution, but he and several others were discharged from their teaching posts, and his brief academic career came to an end.

From 1928 to 1937 he made his living as a contributor to *Rōnō*, *Kaizō* (*Reconstruction*) and other intellectual journals of the period. For a time he also took an active part in politics. After universal manhood suffrage was granted in 1925, a variety of proletarian parties began to form, coalesce, and divide, and Sakisaka made speeches on behalf of candidates of some of these and engaged happily in polemical writings. Available evidence indicates that he has never been a Communist party member. During this period he was especially close to one left-wing leader, Mōsaburō Suzuki, who was to be prominent in the Socialist party after World War II; and thus some of the groundwork was being laid for his later activities.

At the same time, as Japan moved steadily toward aggression on the Asian mainland, Sakisaka read the signs of approaching trouble for himself and his friends. Although he and his wife had no children, it was becoming increasingly difficult for them to live on the income of a radical journalist. Even translating was precarious if one's name was familiar to the police. So he began to think of some other shelter: "From the fall of 1931, at about the time of the Manchurian Incident, I saw that I would not be able to support myself by writing, and there was nothing left but to become a farmer. We moved to a small house in a deserted area in the Tokyo suburbs, where we turned the whole garden to cultivation, occupied an adjoining vacant piece of paddy, and opened up some land that had not been cultivated before. In all we had about a third of an acre. And there we worked at subsistence farming, growing various kinds of potatoes. . . . The young people began to be mobilized and sent off to die, and we had very little contact even with other intellectuals. One of my uncles broke with us completely; an aunt wrote my wife a letter heaping blame on her for what we were doing. There is a saying that blood is thicker than water, but blood seemed to us then very thin compared to our connections with those who believed as we did. I received help especially from Junzō Inamura, who was to become a Socialist party leader after the war."

Sakisaka's public activities dwindled after 1931; and in 1937 he was again arrested along with several hundred others, indicted, and detained for two years in Tokyo's Sugamo Prison, the same that later was to house Japan's war criminals. As he bitterly remarked, "Kishi was a year ahead of me at Tokyo University, but I was senior to him at Sugamo." In 1940 he was released and allowed to return home, but he was prohibited from writing or other activity and spent the war years raising potatoes.

*   *   *

If Sakisaka had not survived the war, he would have remained almost totally unknown, a name on a list of names in somebody's footnote. But with Japan's surrender and the arrival of the Occupation forces, he and his contemporaries who had survived were exonerated and given a new freedom and respectability. After a lapse of 18 years he was reinstated as Professor of Economics at Kyushu University and, according to his own account, was asked by the Occupation authorities to serve as a representative of the academic world on a committee to study the breakup of the *zaibatsu*. He says he declined this honor, preferring to return to his academic duties. It soon became obvious, however, that these duties included a range of activities which merely re-expressed his lifelong political beliefs, now legal and less hampered by fear of persecution or reprisal.

He returned to Kyushu in 1946 and, living at first in Fukuoka, began to lecture on *Shihon Ron* (*Das Kapital*) and the development of modern Japanese capitalism. He was now nearly fifty, a veteran theorist of the "social movement," who had been writing and preaching class war for almost 25 years. Unlike some others of similar persuasion, he had not collaborated with the military either before or during the war. Although he and his fellows had never been subject to the sort of treatment that the Nazis reserved for their enemies, he had nevertheless revolted against the central notions of the political system and had suffered isolation, imprisonment, and ostracism for his beliefs. Perhaps most important from a Japanese standpoint, he had proved his "sincerity" in a position, albeit a position totally antagonistic to the powers that be. He had remained an undeviating follower of the proletarian doctrines and the national communism of his master, Hitoshi Yamakawa.

This was a period of nearly total economic and spiritual breakdown, peculiarly favorable to the spread of Marxist materialism in Japan. With his double authority as a *sensei,* or teacher, and a Marxist theoretician of proven experience, Sakisaka quickly re-established himself and gathered around him a group of faculty assistants and student helpers, whom he indoctrinated in his ideas. Before long, new postwar graduates of his lecture courses were ready and willing to spread that gospel.

Before long, too, Sakisaka had begun to create a laboratory for the application of his ideas. For this he chose Ōmuta—or rather, Ōmuta chose him. An hour and a half from Fukuoka to the south, Ōmuta had grown from 15,000 to 70,000 since Sakisaka's youth, but it was still a coal town. Here he had been born and brought up, and here before World War II the Mitsui Mining Company had developed the great Miike complex of mines until they produced a substantial share of all Japan's coal and employed many thousands of people. Mitsui was the company that had forced his father to resign years before; Mitsui was the backbone of the coal industry; and Mitsui was the epitome of Japanese capitalism, where the ties between entrepreneur, bureaucrat, and politician were so diffuse, yet so intimate, that one could never say with precision where private interest ended and government or semi-governmental decision-making began. All the traditions of modern Japanese capitalism were focused in this company, just as all the intensity of emotional and intellectual alienation from it was concentrated in Sakisaka.

In early 1947 he was invited by the new labor union at Miike to give lectures and indoctrination to its members, and a close association soon grew up between Sakisaka, his younger university assistants, and a group of young unionists, some of whom had served in the Japanese Army in north China and Manchuria. At war's end these young soldiers drifted back to Japan and took jobs in the mines for lack of other employment. Few of them were university graduates, but a number had graduated from engineering schools and military courses of one sort or another, and compared with the rank-and-file local miners, they considered themselves to be intellectuals.

Unions had been illegal much of the time before the war and had no experience in working for purely economic goals. To the union, relations between the company, the cabinet, and the ruling conservative party were so close that Mitsui *was* the government. The union, therefore, had to engage in political activity to protect itself and improve the lot of its members. To do this it needed theory, and Sakisaka and his assistants were on hand to provide the "theoretical armament" considered necessary. In the summer of 1947 the Miike Political Culture Association was established, with a small library of Marxist literature and reading clubs for young unionists. A leader in this activity was one Shigeo Haibara, a returned army engineer who was receptive to Sakisaka's indoctrination from the first and who later became a union executive. The Culture Association put out its organ, *Miike*, and formed "social science study groups" to "raise the cultural level of the workers." Sakisaka began a lecture series on Engels' *Socialism from Utopia to Science* at the Ōmuta branch temple of the Higashi Honganji, headquarters of the largest Buddhist sect in Japan. The flavor of these lectures may be suggested by the title of one of them: "Are We Being Extinguished?"

By this time Sakisaka had moved his home to Ōmuta and was commuting to teach classes in Fukuoka. The "Kyūdai scholars group" had joined forces fully with the union leaders at Miike, and the company called the union's complex of local organizations the "Yamakawa Communist party," thus recognizing the original source of Sakisaka's ideological message. Warnings were issued by the company, but the union's "educational" activities were legal, and in this period the union as a whole was still relatively docile and weak.

Sakisaka's personal relations with union leaders grew close. He fraternized with the workers, drank sake with them in their dormitories, and held meetings with their wives in the company housing compounds. Here high walls enclosed the living areas of most miners and their families; the paternalistic environment which long before had been arranged by management also was a convenient arena for an intellectual like Sakisaka, now an elder statesman of the old Rōnōha theoreticians, casting about him the prestigeful light of the *sensei*, and perfectly in his element indoctrinating the workers in the aims of proletarian revolution. Over and over he pounded into the rank and file that they were being exploited—that Mitsui was skimming off the profits and giving back only a small fraction of the take in wages; that office workers were guarding management's interests and making three times as much as miners in the pits, and so on. Most of his listeners were young men from poor farms who had little class consciousness. Mitsui's wages and working conditions were better than other mines, yet his arguments had increasing effect, and by 1949 over 200 people were attending his weekly lectures.

Sakisaka himself realized that the situation at Miike was an extreme example of intellectual influence and ascendancy over a labor union, which was perhaps not matched elsewhere in Japan. In his preface to the union's official history, published in 1956, he wrote: "Has there ever been another union in which workers and scholars, each knowing his role and intimately linked with the other, fought to fulfill the historical mission of unionism and science as they did at Miike?" And he continues with a sample of his message to the workers, written in a clear, simple style: "The labor movement is not like the movements of Confucius, Christ, or Buddha. It is a movement of ordinary human beings. For this reason there are bound to be cracks in it. No matter how small these cracks are, they must be sealed. When we have won a great victory and feel confident of our strength, what must we think about first? We must see whether there are any wounds in our body, which is the union. Are there fissures somewhere in our organization, which we thought was hard as a stone? If there are, then capital will take advantage of our carelessness to creep in." [5]

In this way Sakisaka exerted increasing local influence, and as the 1940's ended, he began to emerge on the national scene. Here there were two key developments: Sanbetsu, one of the principal labor federations, came under heavy Communist influence, and in 1950 a split occurred and a new federation, the General Council of Trade Unions (Sōhyō), was created. Soon after, the Japan Socialist party split over the San Francisco Peace Treaty, and the left-wing Socialist party formed a close relationship with Sōhyō. In the process some of Sakisaka's friends and former associates emerged as leaders of the Socialist left, and the left-wing overshadowed the more moderate, non-Marxist right-wing Socialist party. Left Socialists also were far more powerful and influential than the Communists. Though Communist leaders who re-entered the national spotlight after the war liked to pose as martyrs who had fought the "fascists" in the 1930's, actually nearly all of them either had been in jail or out of the country, and so out of circulation, for long periods. Their obvious loyalty to Soviet goals and directives made them abhorrent to most Japanese, while their

[5] *Miike Jūnen* (*Ten Years of Miike*), Ōmuta, 1956, introduction, p. viii. (Published by the Miike union. Not for sale.)

violent tactics and insistence on the abolition of the Emperor system were poorly timed and had a disastrous effect on their popularity.

Sakisaka had long been close to Mōsaburō Suzuki, now to become a leading Socialist politician of the early and middle 1950's; and he had formed close ties with Kaoru Ōta, a former section chief in a chemical company, who entered the labor movement after the war and became head of the federation of synthetic chemical workers unions (Gōkarōren) and later chairman of Sōhyō. The well-known Socialist Association (Shakaishugi Kyōkai) was closely connected with chemical union headquarters; its organ, *Socialism*, edited by Yamakawa himself until his death in 1958, continued to expound Rōnōha Marxist theory.

By 1952 or 1953, then, Sakisaka was operating on two fronts, Miike and Tokyo. He continued to teach at Kyūdai, but he spent much time in Tokyo and assumed the role of leading theoretician of the left Socialists.

Sakisaka's doctrinal influence may have been greatest during the period 1952–55, before the formal reunification of the Socialist party. His personal fame, however, reached its peak during the great strike at Miike that extended through most of 1960 and that, though now settled, may explode again in the future. Here a whole career of dedication to Marxist theory came to its disturbing climax.

As the 1950's passed, the Miike union grew steadily stronger and more radical in tone. It struck for 63 days in 1952, and in 1953, after a 113-day strike, it succeeded in forcing the company to reinstate some 300 workers who had been discharged. After this it became more belligerent under the direction of the National Federation of Coal Miners Unions (Tanrō), a key component of Sōhyō and one of the largest federations of unions in the private sector of the economy.

Meanwhile the coal industry, like its counterparts in other countries, was facing high production costs and pressure of competition from imported fuel oil. Many small mines went bankrupt, while big operators like Mitsui looked to the government for help. In Tokyo officials put higher duties on oil imports and to a degree protected the coal operators, but the government did little to solve the basic problems of the industry. Unemployment spread, and the demand for coal declined. At Miike the Mitsui Company, which since the war had tolerated the union and acquiesced in many of its demands, now began to gird itself for battle and lay plans for rationalization of its portion of the coal industry. On its side stood the other coal owners, the Japan Federation of Employers' Associations (Nikkeiren) and the government, which was increasingly determined to bring industrial costs down and make Japanese heavy goods more competitive in world markets. All these forces decided that the time had come to fight, and they chose to fight at Miike.

On the other side, Sōhyō and Tanrō ignored the energy revolution that was obviously taking place and blamed the coal depression on pressure of United States capital in league with the Kishi cabinet. Labor could not bring itself to accept rationalization, which would mean layoffs and a whole change of attitude toward management and the conservative government. Miike was seen as a deliberate battleground where "all labor" would oppose "all capital."

By 1958 Sakisaka and his professors' group were holding almost daily meetings at Miike. He told the union leaders that they held in their hands the power to paralyze the industrial economy of Japan; but the workers would never be conscious of the need for revolution until it was made clear to them that capitalism of necessity oppresses them; until capitalism was destroyed, their oppression could not be ended. These workers must be organized into a class army, which would also be joined by farmers' organizations. Once the class army was fully aware of its role, the whole productive apparatus of the country could be brought to a stop. Then the working class would establish power, form a revolutionary government, revise the present Constitution, and communize the means of production. The role of the Socialist party in this process was to be the vanguard of working-class revolution. Socialism could never come through parliamentary means alone; the party must also guide, rally, and lead the working class; it must avoid bourgeois ideology, social reformism, and leftist adventurism. Most important, the working class must not become an expendable tool in the hands of party bureaucrats.

On a more immediate level Sakisaka told the union that new technology in the mines would merely mean loss of jobs. Miners with little more than a literacy education were reported to be reading highbrow magazines like *Shisō* (*Thought*), full of difficult articles on socialism and other intellectual subjects. Miners and their wives were quoted in the press as saying that "Sakisaka-*sensei* has opened our eyes."

After his retirement from Kyushu University in March 1960, he devoted his full time to Miike. The workers were being heated to a fine pitch by intellectuals who told them that "the government, the capitalists, bureaucrats, judges, press, radio, all of them alike are our enemies." Rōnōha doctrine emphasized "peaceful" revolution, but the miners were being incited to stop work and to sabotage mining operations. Man-day output fell far below the average of Japanese mines. In the view of one conservative newspaper, it seemed "obvious that Professor Sakisaka's ultraleftist ideas do not help the workers. . . . A professor of economics should be sufficiently prepared to recommend to management and labor a joint action to protect their common interests, instead of setting them to quarreling among themselves."

By early 1960 both the Mitsui Company and the union at Miike had lost the capacity to see that they had common interests. As part of its rationalization program the company sent out dismissal notices to more than 1,200 miners, including some 300 specifically named persons who were described as activists who had "overstepped the limits of conventional union activity." The union saw in this a threat to its very existence. When it ignored the notices, the company called a lockout, and the union responded with an unlimited strike.

The Miike strike was one of the bitterest in Japan's bitter labor history and involved repeated violence, one death, and many injuries. The union was split in two; families were divided against each other and against themselves. Housewives armed with clubs invaded the homes of rival union members; pitched "sea battles" were fought in the waters of Ōmuta port; management was intransigent, the union was incorrigible. Both sides were badly bled, and the police and the Kyushu courts were caught in the middle and driven to distraction trying to enforce law and order. During the strike the Communist party sent in its cadres, Zengakuren student nihilists hurled themselves at the police and got in the way of the strikers, and the strike was linked for a time with the even greater turbulence of the anti-treaty demonstrations in Tokyo.

Through it all Sakisaka stuck to his extremist position, exhorting the strikers to fight to the bitter end. When the union finally found itself exhausted, heavily in debt, and isolated from public opinion, he had nothing to suggest but martyrdom. If the union had to go down in flames, abandoned by the rest of the Mitsui unions, then it was worth doing for the cause. As the theoretical godfather of the union, he never yielded, and at one time in late July 1960, it appeared very likely that a full-scale battle between pickets and police might cause hundreds of casualties on the company's property. Finally, however, the local union executives, Tanrō and Sōhyō leaders, and the Mitsui management, all had had enough. A third conciliation offer from the government's Central Labor Relations Council was accepted by both sides. Management got substantially what it had demanded earlier, and new dismissal notices were mailed. But many of the dismissals will be contested in the courts for years to come; and Sakisaka, in his latest writings on the strike, boasted that the company had lost, the union had scored a great victory and must now shore up its ranks and prepare for the next encounter.

*   *   *

Sakisaka's career represents one Japanese response to the problems of industrialism and the import of foreign ideas. To the question why he became a Marxist there can be no complete answer in a short space. He is worth a book, and the movement of which he has been a part is worth a bookshelf.

As a young man he saw that the society he lived in was full of evils and abuses accompanying forced-draft industrialization, in an era when Japan was desperately trying to catch up with the West. Technical society demeaned his parents in his own eyes. And when someone came along who said that the source of such evils and abuses lay in the private ownership of property and that if this ownership system were changed, they would disappear, there apparently was nothing in his background or earlier life to cause him to doubt or deny this argument and to seek elsewhere for the cause of the difficulty. Family relationships, contact with teachers in school, friendships—none of these existed as determinants of individuality working to prevent him from accepting the narrow notion of class struggle and class war. On the contrary, they probably contributed in a negative sense to his acceptance of such ideas.

From his middle school days he was a dogged and methodical schoolboy, proud of his ordinariness (today he would be glad to have it shortened to "orneriness"); and when he came to Marxist writings he was moved by them, took them up, and doggedly made them his special intellectual province. In this he was very like many of his Japanese "social scientist" colleagues, whose chief claim to fame often still lies in their scriptural knowledge of foreign theory and their memorization of foreign texts which, once mastered, harden into a kind of imperious orthodoxy. Thus Japanese university professors, who have been rightly called "transformers" passing foreign ideas into more general public circulation, today still tend to make a fortress of their special subject and to sit within it, enhancing the magic powers of their role but isolating themselves from outside change and reality. The Japanese phrase for this mode of behavior is *ikkoku ichijōshugi*, the principle of one castle to one territory. However, as another professor remarked, "Sakisaka chose a very large territory, and he has had to deal with many pretenders. This may help to explain his extreme inflexibility."

In such a situation the timing of the encounter between imported ideas and the Japanese receiver assumes great importance. Japan has been a remarkably isolated society, and foreign ideas have come in successively in waves and are still arriving in this manner today. Their effect on a given intellectual is likely to be determined not only by his personality and the circumstances of his upbringing but by his age and impressionability at the moment of collision, as well as by the prevailing temper of that moment, or what the Japanese currently call the "mood." Many observers of Japan have remarked on the desire, which goes back to ancient times, to be on the side of the new.

Sakisaka was at his most impressionable during the First World War and the Russian Revolution, and he went rapidly into Marxism. By no means all Japanese of his age and period made the move as definitely as he did; but the majority of them were stirred by the mood of social change and felt varying degrees of alienation and ambivalence toward the conservative society of which they were a part. The diversity of their reactions is well described by one writer: "Japanese intellectuals are by nature petit bourgeois individualists, not necessarily fit for a life of action among the masses. In those days [post-1918] some of them abandoned their study or work and gave themselves to communism or related movements. But many felt that, even if their ideas went that far, there was a distinction between thought and action. They maintained that while their lives were bourgeois, their thought could be Marxist. Others were unable to make such distinctions between revolutionary Marxism and the still-feudal family system in which they lived, and they ran away and tried to escape from one or the other. Others were Democratic Socialists, who wanted to reach socialism by a different route from the Communists; still others found their own destiny in the midst of bourgeois society and the bureaucracy, in the classic pattern. Thus intellectuals made various gestures; and this was not true of intellectuals alone; it was a general condition. But in intellectuals the range of vibration was especially great. And though their ideas and their mode of action were very diverse, the thinking of all of them was influenced by the notion that socialism and the liberation of humanity could not be achieved only through parliamentarianism or other 'quiet' means."

The same writer describes his own initial encounter with communism: "The awakening of my social consciousness came late and, as it were, by accident. I might have spent my life as a spiritual idealist, or a Christian, lecturing on classical literature and philosophy. But a friend of mine happened to say to me once that social poverty and degeneration do not arise from individual character, but from the social structure which is the genesis of character. If that social structure is not destroyed, the ideal society will never come. And here is the way to destroy it. Thus my friend explained to me and prevailed upon me, and my heart was extremely agitated by what he said. My feelings were so strong that I can remember them even today. Through my friend I experienced a sort of spiritual revolution. But unlike some others, I could not bring myself to go off immediately to the front lines of the movement for social revolution. This was mainly because of my rather spiritual, literary environment, which prevented me from giving myself to 'isms.' I could not agree at all with what materialism maintained. To my way of thinking, the Socialist movement was an idealistic movement for human liberation, which included within it even communism. To a certain degree I was receptive to communism, but even in those days there was a great ideological rigidity among Japanese Marxists. My friend prevailed upon me to make my thought conform to militant materialism, in clear opposition to Christianity. But it was hard for a person interested in any religion to be a materialist. . . . I thought once of killing myself, but I lacked the courage to commit suicide. For a year after this spiritual upheaval, I watched my close friends abandon their studies and go off to front-line activity.

But I could do no more than offer them a certain amount of co-operation. And in a very vague fashion I devoted myself to social reform and social activities." [6]

Finally, there is the question of Sakisaka's political significance. Although rather an extreme case, his career demonstrates that intellectuals can and do stand behind labor unions, provide them with theory and incite them to action. Sōhyō and the Miike union have used him and his theory in their fight against management. They also have used other intellectuals; Sōhyō has its stable of them, and Zenrō, the other large labor federation, has its own. These are merely signs of the fact that labor is primarily a political movement in Japan. And since left-wing Socialist leaders have been imperatively close to Sōhyō and dependent upon labor for funds, the "Sakisaka theory" of socialism, with its strong syndicalist overtones, has been reflected in party "action programs" and policies.

Since the last war Marxist-influenced intellectuals, a large and articulate portion of the intellectual community, have not ceased profoundly to distrust the conservative government, while within that government are many who still harbor scorn and bitterness against opposition and yearn for the days when labor unions and opposition parties had fewer legal defenses behind which to oppose a tightening of national controls. Sakisaka has not been abroad since his student days, and he has remained blind to the changes in capitalism. Nevertheless, since the war his inflexible, disruptive theories have continued to have considerable appeal. By European standards Japanese socialism remains in a kind of archaic dawn, dominated by an ideology that is already a bankrupt possibility in the West, and that has led to tyranny everywhere it has prevailed. Recent European Socialist visitors to Tokyo have expressed amazement at this state of affairs.

Such is the prison within which the Socialist party has been enclosed; but to escape requires a willed act, and it is most unlikely that the old leftist politicians and labor veterans of Sakisaka's generation are capable of such an act. They remember too much; they have been out of power too long, and their attitude toward parliamentary govern-

[6] Inaba, Hidezō. "Nihon no Shakaishugi" ("Japanese Socialism") in *Shakai Kaikaku e no Teigen* (*Proposals for Social Reform*). (Tokyo: Keisō Shobō, 1960), pp. 56–58.

ment is too vague. If the Socialist party is to widen its support and reach power as a parliamentary party, leadership will have to come from younger men.

At the moment of writing this, a new controversy has arisen within the party over a plan for "structural reform," calling for a step-by-step progress toward socialism through new policies designed to attract more support for the party "within the framework of capitalism." Party membership is to be expanded and broadened and the party, rather than the labor federation, made the real headquarters of Socialist "action programs." The precise origin and full dimensions of the plan are not yet clear; one well-known scholar and former associate of Sakisaka has termed it a tactical means of broadening support and "escaping from the chains" of classical Marxist theory before coming to power as a parliamentary party. But some right-wing Socialists are attacking the plan as merely another attempt to gain popularity while concealing the true revolutionary goals of leftist leadership; and younger leftist leaders, though they may seem to be more "pragmatic" than their elders, still cannot resist playing around with popular movements, with all the risk of Communist penetration that that involves. The tradition of militant opposition to government is too emotionally rooted, too fundamentally romantic, to die easily; and one sometimes wonders whether it is not as much related to the samurai vendetta of past ages as to Marxist revolutionary ideology. But whatever the origin of this type of behavior, the calculated participation by Socialist politicians in the riots and violence during the last year has not reassured those who hope for a stable parliamentary system in Japan.

Sakisaka, at any rate, knows where he stands on "structural reform." He scorns it as nothing but "social reformism," and though some young critics deride his fanaticism and tell him to grow up politically, other young followers are glad to come and sit at his feet. There, in his quiet suburb, comfortably ensconced in his impressive library of books on socialism, he can look back on a life of work in that cause and forward to an old age full of polemics, stumping tours, and "struggles," interspersed with trips to the remote hot spring in his beloved Shinshū mountains, where he is painstakingly putting together his magnum opus —a life of Karl Marx.

SIX MONTHS AFTER THE STORM: THE JAPANESE ELECTIONS OF 1960

January 24, 1961

The uproar over the adoption of a new Security Treaty with the United States has ended, and the Japanese political scene has returned to normal. The conservative politicians continue in their vigorous, *ad hoc* way to push the country forward, while the humorless Socialists, unable to capitalize on the exhilarations of last summer, when they felt they momentarily had a mass movement behind them, have subsided into doctrinal and factional quarrels and wait hopefully for new conservative mistakes. The political conditions that produced the disorders of May and June 1960 have changed; but the emotionalism of the people that helped to produce violence has not disappeared. New up-heavals wait for new issues; nothing is resolved, but everything is stored up.

In the broad center of the political stage, the confrontation of con-servatives and Socialists that has been the governing theme of politics here since the war was reconfirmed in the general elections of Novem-ber 20, 1960, the eighth since 1946 and the twenty-ninth since the first elections in 1890. The elections were held to provide a fresh mandate for the government of Prime Minister Hayato Ikeda, who had taken over from the beleaguered Kishi regime last July but had postponed the date of the election in order to turn the attention of the people from street fighting to such tranquilizing matters as tax cuts, social wel-fare programs, and plans to double the national income.

The pre-election atmosphere was superficially no different from any other similar period in recent years. Candidates mounted their sound trucks and blared out their appeals and promises in lonely hill villages and crowded city neighborhoods. Money was handed out for votes, and politicians raided each other's territories for support in the same old way. A common saying was *nitō ichiraku*, meaning that a candidate who spent 20 million yen could win, but one who spent only 10 million could not. (Both sums were far beyond the officially approved limit.) Pretend-candidates with no hope of success were glad to forfeit their election deposit money in exchange for the penny postcards and other materials given them by election committees, which they could then sell to more serious candidates at a profit. Despite these and other amusements, however, the campaigning seemed to an American observer a rather unexciting process, and the corruption that existed was relatively tame, hardly to be compared in scope or daring with that which corrodes the vital energy of some other Asian countries, and not worth the weight of shame brought down so unremittingly on the heads of Japanese readers by the self-righteous newspapers.

Ikeda's diversion of the people's attention from foreign devils to domestic economic matters was proceeding with great success, which even the Socialists privately acknowledged, when the surface was again shattered by the assassination on October 12 of Inejirō Asanuma, Chairman of the Socialist party, by a seventeen-year-old student rightist. This mad act occurred during an official speech meeting of the heads of the main political parties on the stage of Hibiya Public Hall in downtown Tokyo and was caught by live television and shown, knife and blood and all, to millions of Japanese. With three political stabbings in six months, the past seemed to be repeating itself with horrible immediacy. The nation's leaders spoke out soberly against terrorism, while the newspapers less soberly predicted that Japanese democracy was doomed. But when the conservatives tried to use the incident to sponsor a resolution condemning violence of either left or right, the Socialists predictably retorted that they had committed no violence; *their* demonstrations of last summer had been "protection of democracy." They accused the conservatives of close links with ultranationalist fringe groups and immediately put up Asanuma's widow to run for the seat of her husband. Police investigations have failed, at least publicly, to link the assassin with any politician or group in the conservative party, but in the exchange of recriminations Asanuma himself was lost. A few weeks later the assassin committed suicide in his jail cell and the affair apparently had ended. The newspapers stopped writing about terrorism and turned again to the corruption of politicians. In the elections which followed, Asanuma's murder gave the Socialists some votes but was not a decisive factor in the outcome.

The conservative Liberal-Democratic party (Jimintō), which has been in power almost continuously since 1945, was kept in power with the largest parliamentary majority won in any postwar election. The Socialist party (Shakaitō), long confirmed in opposition, also made substantial gains; but the Democratic Socialists (Minshatō), a right-wing Socialist faction that broke away from the parent party in 1959 and formed a new party in early 1960, were smashed and reduced to an insignificant minority. Conservatives and Socialists both claimed great victories, while those who had hoped for the emergence of a more liberal "center" party were disappointed, and the Minshatō survivors retired to engage in self-critism and "renovation of the party structure." Except for the Minshatō collapse, however, the results surprised no one. Many people who were inflamed against Kishi last summer as a symbol of everything nightmarish in the Japanese past, and who later were stunned by the assassination of Asanuma, still voted for a new conservative Prime Minister when given the chance. Most Japanese are still conservatives; but this does not mean that they necessarily approve of what conservative candidates do after they have been elected. On the contrary, the election also indicated that, in the midst of unprecedented economic progress and prosperity, a wide and growing sector of the people prefers to cast its votes for the opposition. Thus both sides could point publicly to success and privately consider failure. And in the debacle of the third party the fundamental opposition of conservatives and Socialists was further institutionalized.

Eligible voters totaled 56,554,475, over 3 million more than in the last general election in May 1958. Of these 39,509,104, or 73.5 per cent, voted. This was the third lowest percentage since the war, primarily because Election Day was a fine fall Sunday, when excursions to mountain and sea resorts or suburban golf courses were more urgent than a trip to the polls for thousands of city residents. The disenchantment of many city voters with both political parties also contributed to the low city percentages. Osaka had the smallest turnout, with 63 per cent, followed by Tokyo with 63.4 per cent, Kanagawa (Yokohama) with 64.1 per cent, and Kyoto with 64.2 per cent. On the other hand, in Shimane Prefecture, on the Japan Sea, 86.5 per cent of those eligible voted; in Yamanashi 84.6 per cent. Other rural districts recorded similarly high percentages.

The conservative party received 22,740,258 votes, or 57.6 per cent of the total. This was a decline from 1958 of approximately 236,000 votes, or 0.2 per cent. Thus in spite of an increase in the electorate, and even though the highest voting percentages were in rural prefectures where conservatives are strongest, conservative votes did not increase, but declined slightly. If more people had voted in cities, where a majority of new voters favor Socialist candidates, the Socialist percentage of the vote might have been even higher.

Conservatives won 296 seats in the Lower House, a gain of nine seats over their 1958 position. Their ability to gain seats while losing votes may have been in part the effect of a slight reduction in the number of conservative candidates (from 413 in 1958 to 399 in 1960). The votes they secured counted for more. With the adherence of three so-called "independents" to the conservative party since the elections, and the succession of a conservative to the seat of a deceased Democratic Socialist, the conservative party now has 300 seats out of 467, an overwhelming majority, but not quite the two-thirds majority it needs for its long-planned revision of the Japanese Constitution.

Description of the Socialist vote is complicated by the fact that the party nominally was united in the May 1958 elections but had split in two before November 1960. In 1958 the united Socialists received 13,093,986 votes, or 32.9 per cent of the total. In 1960 the orthodox Socialist party got 10,887,134, while the right-wing heretics in the Minshatō got 3,464,144. Total votes of the two Socialist parties combined was 14,351,278, or 36.3 per cent for the "Socialist camp." (If the 1,158,722 votes received by the Japan Communist party are added to these, the total for the "renovationist camp" amounted to 39.2 per cent as compared with 35.5 per cent in 1958.)

Although the vote gap between conservatives and Socialists has gradually narrowed in the last four elections, the two parties still are separated by over 8 million votes. The Socialists won 145 seats in the Lower House, 21 fewer than they had in 1958, but 23 more than they had left after the Minshatō bolt of early last year. Their gain of 23 seats precisely matched the losses of the Minshatō, which dropped from 40 seats to 17. Socialists and Democratic Socialists together hold one-third of the seats. The Communists rose from one seat to three.

Comparison of new candidates is one interesting way to get at the basic differences between the two major parties. The conservatives put up 399 candidates, but only 58 of these were "new men" (278 were incumbents, 63 former incumbents). Twenty-nine of the 58 were elected. With the three new "independents" freshman conservatives now total 32.

Their average age is 49.7 years. Before entering politics ten of the 32 had careers principally in the government, including prominent posts in the Ministries of Welfare, Labor, Construction, Finance, Justice, Education, Agriculture, and Transportation, and in the Prime Minister's office. One common pattern is for a vice-minister (*jikan*) to retire from the bureaucracy and enter politics, since he has no chance of becoming a minister without election to the Diet under the present system of "responsible government." (Constitutionally, only a majority of the cabinet must be Diet members; in fact, all cabinet ministers customarily hold Diet seats.) Officials of lower rank may also move into politics: several of the ten men above were former bureau chiefs (*kyokuchō*) in their respective ministries. If an individual has been employed in such ministries as Construction, Transportation, or Agriculture, where large sums of money are dispensed for local projects, he may have been able to develop a local base of support while remaining in the government; if so, he can move directly to the Diet. On the other hand, a senior official in such ministries as Education or Finance often must move through an intermediary position in some other organization. For example, a former bureau chief in the Education Ministry became the director of the Social Communication Education Association and later was elected to the Diet. A onetime Labor Ministry official served as adviser to the All-Japan Industrial Safety Association before his election. Such organizations are clustered about each of the government ministries; ex-officials who retire into them can use the expertise and personal connections which they accumulated in government jobs; and these groups form the nucleus of their support at election time.

Eleven of the 32 new conservatives were primarily businessmen. They included one sake brewer and the presidents or executives of a

TV service company, two textile concerns, a bakery, a marine transportation company, a sulphuric-acid manufacturing plant, and an auto company. Three others were officials of farmers' and fishermen's cooperatives or credit institutions and had rural connections. (Some of the others, of course, also had rural connections.) Three of the 32 were former prefectural governors; three were former mayors of cities, towns, or villages; seven had been speakers or vice-speakers of prefectural assemblies, and nine had been or were members of such bodies. However, only seven had any official experience as functionaries in the local apparatus of the conservative party—a reflection of the fact that party organs are weak; the essence of conservative strength is still the personal tie between a boss and his followers.

Twenty-three of the 32 conservatives were university graduates. Of these, 14 were graduates of Tokyo University. Three others graduated from Waseda University and four others from universities in Tokyo. Only two of the 23 were alumni of universities outside Tokyo. This underscores the continuing importance of a university education, as well as the great prestige of a Tokyo University diploma as a passport to high position, especially for those Japanese who were educated before the war and are now in their prime of life and career.

The Socialist party put up a total of 186 candidates, 49 of them new. (Of the rest, 119 were incumbents, 18 former incumbents.) Of these, 26 were successful. Their average age is 45.9 years. Only two were primarily former bureaucrats and without experience in party organs. Sixteen came from labor-union backgrounds, and 24 of the 26 had either been officials in labor unions or officials in local or regional party organs or had combined both functions. In other words, Socialist candidates usually come up through the party apparatus. However, this apparatus is weak, and the really effective focus of local support and organization is the regional labor federation and the local union. Nearly all of the 16 successful union candidates came out of unions affiliated with Sōhyō, the leftist-led federation that supports, and to a large degree controls, the Socialist Party. Five were schoolteachers from Nikkyōso, the Teachers Union; two were from communications unions (Zentei), two from railroads (Kokutetsu and Shitetsu), one from coal mines (Tanrō), one from steel (Yawata), and so on.

None of the successful Socialists was identified as having significant business background. Three were lawyers and one a physician. Finally, there is a noticeable difference in educational level between the two groups. Whereas 23 of 32 new conservatives are university graduates, only nine of 26 Socialists finished their university studies. Of these, four are from Tokyo University, two from Waseda, and one from Chūō University in Tokyo. Only two went to universities outside Tokyo. Most of the rest attended trade or labor schools, or normal schools in the case of the teachers.

Summing up, two-thirds of the new conservative Diet members are either pillars of the local business community, with wide ties in the life of the local people, or they are former officials who in many instances worked up through regional outposts of government ministries, are allied by education to the business class, and command the respect still due the government bureaucrat. No data on their relationships by marriage is available; but it is fair to assume that a considerable number of the ex-bureaucrats are linked to business interests, and conversely, that businessmen have ties to government officials through their sisters, mothers, and wives. The same pattern holds true for other conservative members of the Diet and for members of the government up to and including the Prime Minister and his cabinet.

On the other hand, more than half of the successful new Socialists are from unions of government employees or large industries such as coal or steel. They are bureaucrats of the labor movement, who have spent much of their energies in "struggles" against the more senior bureaucrats and businessmen who go into the conservative party. Although they are often incited by leftist intellectuals to engage in "people's movements," the intellectuals themselves tend to stay in their libraries and seldom run for election.

Some political observers who were jaundiced with both conservatives and Socialists saw in the Democratic Socialist party a possible mediating force or "center" party that would somehow stand for truly democratic social reform without preaching class struggle or taking periodically to the streets. But the November elections demonstrated that this was mere wishful thinking. The Minshatō is not a party at all but a faction under the personal influence of one man, Suehiro Nishio, an elderly politician who has been in the Diet since 1928 and was Deputy Prime Minister in the Ashida coalition cabinet of 1948. Nishio and his associates (who are not beyond fighting among themselves) represent the far right-wing of Japanese socialism. They ex-emplify the difference between the older generation of non-Marxist reformers who were involved in the "social movement" in industrial areas around Osaka and Tokyo from long before the war, but who remained relatively conservative, and the Marxists and advocates of various versions of syndicalism and quasi-communism who came to prominence in the Socialist party after 1945.

The Minshatō break of 1959–60 was motivated by both personal and ideological differences, but from the beginning the new party was in a poor position to win votes in an election. In the most prac-tical sense, its members by their defection automatically lost the support of Sōhyō, the core of labor's voting strength, and were forced to rely upon the much smaller Zenrō federation, whose affiliated unions include many thousands of weakly organized women textile workers. In district after district, candidates who had been elected as Socialists in 1958 were beaten as Democratic Socialists in 1960. In some cases new candidates deliberately put up by the Socialist party against their defected rivals were successful. In others, conservatives were able to take advantage of Socialist confusion to gain seats. In a few places a candidate was popular enough to survive switching to the Minshatō, though usually with a heavy decline in voting strength. Thus in the third district of Tokyo, a lady candidate who led the ticket as a Socialist in 1958 with 78,000 votes squeaked by in third place this time as a Minshatō member with 54,000. But in Tokyo 4, another lady, who was first as a Socialist in 1958, lost as a Democratic Socialist in 1960. Similar results occurred in Tochigi 1 and 2, Kanagawa 2, Chiba 1, Gifu 1 and 2, and elsewhere. Most of those Minshatō candidates who won made a poor showng. Only one, the party leader, led the ticket in his district. One ran second, three third, five fourth, and seven fifth. Twenty-eight ended as runners-up; in other words, a large pro-portion of the party's total vote was thrown away.

Minshatō candidates were mostly old men who projected a faded image. The average age of the 17 survivors in the Lower House is 59.17 years. Their background and education are very mixed; eight are university graduates, several held posts in the government, a few others are businessmen with experience in the organization of producers' co-operatives.[1] One or two came up through the right-wing factions

---

[1] For a description of a typical right-wing Socialist and his activities among the producers' co-operatives of Kyoto, see Chapter 7, " 'Mizuchō' in His District."

of large labor unions in government or industry. Most are relatively unknown.

In trying to straddle the conservative-Socialist gap, Minshatō policies ended by being merely vague. They attacked both sides for "attempting to bring into Japan the cold war existing between the United States and the Soviet Union." They advocated diplomacy on the principle of "co-operation with the Free World" but also stood for restoration of ties with Communist China and abolition of the Japan-United States Security Treaty "in stages." Their economic platform promised a "middle class" income of 50,000 yen ($141.66) a month for the "standard family"; but details were scarce. They wanted the best of both worlds without having to accept the consequences of joining either. In this they were little different from the two major parties; but the images and programs that they conjured up lacked freshness and clarity. They had at their disposal neither the negative nationalist motifs of the "peace movement" and the antitreaty demonstrations, nor the conservative government's record of economic achievement and prospects of higher material goals, with their more conventional nationalistic implications.

A number of moderately liberal intellectuals, who were frightened by the violence of last summer, hoped that the Minshatō would increase its Diet strength, although they refused to run on its ticket or do much more than hold "encouragement meetings" and write articles deploring the state of Japanese democracy. Some of these people were dashed by the Minshatō failure. Other intellectuals gloated over their discomfiture and expressed the orthodox Marxist view that the Minshatō and the Zenrō labor federation were tools of the monopoly capitalists, who were using them deliberately to check the growth of "renovationist" forces, meaning Socialists and Communists, in Japan's politics. There was an element of truth in this: Prime Minister Ikeda took a soft line toward the Minshatō in the campaign and praised some of its candidates, in a tactical attempt to cut into the Socialist vote. As usual, such "fifth column" methods were derided by intellectuals full of grim Marxist piety.

* * *

In the United States a revolutionary politics no longer has meaning, and it is difficult for Americans to understand why it can have meaning elsewhere. Japan, they may say, ought to have a healthier parliamentary system than it now has. The Japanese economy has gone much farther than any other Asian economy toward modernization. The rate of economic growth in recent years has been among the highest in the world. Production and consumption have rapidly multiplied and changed in structure; wages have risen much faster than prices, and social security benefits have widened. Inequalities of income and wealth, though obvious, are less marked than before the war. Savings and investment are both high; and greater productivity in industry is providing new jobs, in some fields more jobs than there are people to fill them. A massive and rather frightening movement of people into cities has been combined with a falling birth rate. The 1960 census reveals that in 26 mainly rural prefectures there has been an absolute fall in population in the last five years, while in the other 20 prefectures population has, of course, increased. This is a phenomenal change. For the first time in modern history new rural births are failing to replace migrants as fast as they move to cities or faster.

A technological revolution is already affecting agriculture and small industry as well as large industry and will eventually bring about deep changes in the lives of all the people. Yet last summer, at a peak of prosperity for the nation as a whole, there occurred a series of riots and violent demonstrations that were entirely political in character and had not the slightest overtone of economic protest or discontent.

The most obvious reason for political turmoil is the widespread fear of involvement in a war not of Japan's making. This feeling, which amounts to an obsession, can easily be exploited when suitable issues appear by hard-core Marxists and all others who hope to gain from turbulence and disorder. The wild storms of last summer against Kishi and the Security Treaty blew up from this sick center of fear—fear of war and fear of the ugly past's returning—in which highly excitable groups of students, unionists, professors, and plain townspeople of all sorts, who had no implacable ideological hatred of one another, were incited by a few activists who played on fear for their own purposes.

However, the cold war is only the proximate cause of the rigidities and hysterias of Japanese political life. The economic transformation of this country has been very uneven and has far outrun social and psychological changes. The peculiar oppressiveness of prewar political history corrupted or embittered intellectuals and bred endless rancor. After the war the discrediting of the whole precious *mystique* of Japanese uniqueness led to the search for something—anything—in which to enfold the naked self. The weakness of Japan in the post-war period has been galling to submerged feelings of nationalism, which are just as much the property of intellectuals and Socialist politicians as they are of conservative businessmen and bureaucrats.

As long as power rests in the elected parties in the broad center of politics, conservatives and Socialists will to some extent force change upon each other. The conservative party may be a haven for retired bureaucrats, but most of its money comes from businessmen, who have more political power and influence than they had before the war; and with a free press and a system of free elections such as Japan is fortunate enough to have, conservatives must react to Socialist proposals; rather than sending out repressive ordinances, they must present an image of themselves that is more and more modern. Failure to do so can mean loss of power, no matter how much is said about the docile, perpetually conservative majority. Today "progressive conservatism" has more meaning than ever before in such fields as social security, public welfare, and labor relations; advances in these and other areas may be slow and grudging, but they are not imaginary.

The Socialist party is a grab bag of theoretical incongruities and rival cliques. Dominant leadership is influenced by Marxism of a peculiarly Japanese variety, and its slogans closely resemble the Communists'. However, personal or factional differences are at least as important as doctrinal squabbles among party leaders; and some Socialist politicians, who have more emotional interest in parliamentarianism than leftist professors and labor leaders do, are advocating a stronger party organization and more positive domestic programs as well as the usual struggles against American bases and treaties. These tendencies are not new and they need not be exaggerated, but neither should they be ignored.

Intellectuals are seriously disaffected. But support for the Socialist party is far from solid among even the members of Sōhyō-affiliated unions. Young members of the bureaucracy often vote Socialist, but there is no suggestion that such a vote indicates a fundamental distaste for parliamentary government; rather they regard the Socialists as a valid alternative to the conservatives; and as they grow older their vote tends to shift to the conservative party. Likewise, though there are some morale problems within the small Self-Defense Forces, there is no hard evidence of disloyalty or disaffection from civilian control within a parliamentary system.

In the last year there have been some very disturbing signs. Leftist violence, in which the Socialists took a leading part, has produced a rightist reaction, and rightist extremist groups are more noticeable than at any time since I first came to Japan six years ago. Ties between conservative politicians and ultranationalist groups are obscure but are known to exist, at least on the level of individual contact. A conservative member of the Diet told me recently that, although he did not believe in violence in the abstract, Asanuma's assassination served him right for having agitated the mobs of last May and June. This person, a very old-fashioned sort, denied that the conservatives had any official connection with right-wing organizations; he blamed the whole sorry mess of the summer on the cold war; and he implied that if only America would go away and leave Japan alone, while continuing to buy Japanese goods and to protect the country from its enemies, all would be well.

Rightists have held public meetings to memorialize the boy assassin, whom they have made into a martyr. Not long ago a rightist group unfurled a swastika flag on the crowded Ginza. On the other hand, leftist college students are organizing high-school auxiliaries and waiting for the next move. The radical student organization, Zengakuren, represents the way of pure darkness. Most of its followers may be sentimental boys who are led by their emotions; but its young ringleaders have the same fanatical, elitist mentality as the young army officers of the 1930's. They are just as sure as the officers were then that the farmers and other "little people" who vote for the conservatives do no know what they are doing and need "guidance." (Fortunately, the farmers are thriving at the moment and regard the radical students as rather foolish.) Though one extreme masks itself in communism, "Trotskyism," or plain anarchism, and the other mumbles in an archaic accent about the Emperor and the noble race, both point back to the closed Japanese past, and both mean only one thing: militant nationalism.

In this rather nervous atmosphere, everybody here is waiting with a good deal of anticipation to see what the change of administration in the United States will mean. The Japanese are amazed at Kennedy's youthfulness. If only, some of them say, Japan could be governed by a forty-three-year-old! Although the Ikeda government officially deprecates the influence of the change on Japanese-American relations, there is a general hope that less will be said from now on about "massive retaliation" and that a fresh and more flexible attitude toward Communist China and the Soviet Union will help to relax tensions and reduce the chances of some new explosion that would again rip up the political ground. Naturally there is a lot of wishful thinking in this. The Japanese are still buying time for their Western-modeled institutions to develop an inner meaning and become a binding faith. For this, economic prosperity alone is not enough, but without it there is no hope, in my opinion. Except for the Communists and the fanatical right, there is little irreconcilable ideological hostility within the Japanese in their attitudes toward one another. But neither do they want to serve as the bloody arena for anyone else's hostilities.

APPENDIX I

Voting Returns by Party, November 1960 Elections

		November 1960	May 1958	February 1955
Liberal-Democratic party	22,740,258	57.6%	57.8%	63.2%
Socialist party	10,887,134	27.5%	32.9%	30.2%
Democratic Socialist party	3,464,144	8.8%	—	—
Japan Communist party	1,156,722	2.9%	2.6%	2.0%
Miscellaneous parties	141,940	0.4%	0.7%	1.3%
Independents	1,118,906	2.8%	6.0%	3.3%

Source: Asahi Shimbun, November 22, 1960.
Note: Most independents were conservatives running without party endorsement. Of five independents elected, three joined the conservative party after the election.

APPENDIX II

Post-election Balance, House of Representatives

	New members	Incumbents	Former members	Before dissolution	May 1958	February 1955
LDP	296	29	226	41	283	287	297
SP	145	26	103	16	122	166	160
DSP	17	1	13	3	40	—	—
JCP	3	0	1	2	1	1	2
Misc.	1	1	0	0	0	1	2
Ind.	5	3	1	1	2	12	6
Total	467	60	344	63	448	467	467
					(19 vacancies)		

APPENDIX III

Voting by Prefectures, November 1960 Elections

	LDP	SP	DSP	JCP	Misc.	Ind.	Total
Hokkaido	885,232	805,749	108,191	36,920	3,567	75,214	1,914,873
Aomori	400,308	135,549	10,579	6,544			552,980
Iwate	383,028	174,719	41,050	10,840			609,637
Akita	338,299	185,920	45,132	14,152			583,503
Yamagata	466,484	174,497	4,526	8,092		2,485	656,084
Miyagi	396,770	215,867	46,946	9,305	23,630	41,389	733,907
Fukushima	569,349	213,709	127,466	16,082		22,748	949,354
Ibaraki	566,033	245,212	37,674	16,169		35,844	900,932
Tochigi	406,125	174,456	45,874	5,523		59,097	691,075
Gumma	465,761	214,604	43,578	13,886		35,529	773,358
Kanagawa	685,921	325,769	202,744	62,479		5,502	1,282,415
Chiba	661,453	184,006	72,961	12,909	827	25,682	957,838
Saitama	577,128	270,827	55,497	17,042		26,975	947,469
Tokyo	1,539,594	1,248,561	327,627	160,809	12,170	33,835	3,322,596
Niigata	638,511	431,572	62,393	25,269		1,279	1,159,024
Nagano	548,810	368,241	36,926	53,349		7,317	1,014,643
Yamanashi	243,098	136,207		5,525		1,495	386,325
Shizuoka	845,886	270,696	108,849	21,162		39,462	1,283,053
Aichi	1,040,680	481,949	170,645	42,651	894	5,122	1,741,851
Gifu	443,820	179,853	72,121	12,683		57,606	766,083
Toyama	337,256	100,225	25,941	6,947		28,956	499,325
Ishikawa	259,028	87,589	54,757	23,497		45,522	470,393
Fukui	244,327	110,442	11,588	3,808			370,165
Osaka	873,210	486,090	355,357	213,326	2,226	13,381	1,943,590
Hyogo	846,976	427,460	212,639	35,772	1,400	66,120	1,590,367
Kyoto	368,769	230,928	112,142	70,349		5,627	787,815
Shiga	142,940	109,595	40,645	6,127		100,560	399,867
Mie	436,163	170,742	40,301	8,863	1,868	53,538	711,475
Nara	251,373	84,263	23,124	3,974		11,289	374,023
Wakayama	288,374	107,983		17,165		11,211	424,733
Kagawa	280,038	93,499	28,606	5,745	213	54,754	462,855
Tokushima	280,077	52,740	33,599	5,248	2,462	4,265	378,391
Ehime	447,711	164,572	85,047	9,749		12,182	719,261
Kochi	259,710	93,257	49,620	9,572			412,159
Okayama	459,682	232,339	54,380	16,847	4,668	15,986	783,902
Hiroshima	614,794	188,080	113,431	19,083		95,294	1,030,682
Tottori	184,239	75,927	23,564	6,928			290,658
Shimane	320,828	77,888	54,483	9,862	408		463,469
Yamaguchi	460,701	141,382	100,384	9,828		2,647	714,942
Fukuoka	820,905	520,469	185,842	74,324		14,796	1,616,336
Saga	251,956	103,919	4,307	7,792	75,978		443,952
Nagasaki	463,178	168,254	56,986	9,614			698,032
Kumamoto	560,116	177,228	19,842	7,863		600	765,649
Oita	314,009	119,564	87,828	7,445	10,134	42,330	581,310
Miyazaki	287,579	146,899	29,727	6,230		22,463	492,898
Kagoshima	584,029	177,837	42,227	9,463		42,299	855,855
TOTAL	22,740,258	10,887,134	3,464,144	1,156,722	141,940	1,118,906	39,509,104

Source: *Asahi Shimbun*, November 23, 1960.

CHAPTER *19*

ATOMIC CROSSCURRENTS IN JAPAN

April 29, 1959

In the country of Hiroshima and Nagasaki after World War II no subject was more sensitive than atomic energy. Deaths attributed to radiation disease were ticked off one by one in the local press; lurid museum exhibits engraved at a glance the horror of the two atomic moments on the minds of millions who saw them; and annual demonstrations led by political propagandists in the "peace cities" and elsewhere kept the attention of the people focused on the hideous destructiveness of the past. In such circumstances the government was unable or unwilling to publicize very effectively the peaceful applications of nuclear energy or lead informed opinion to a wider realization of the positive possibilities of nuclear science.

This situation is now changing. The official decision to push atomic energy for peaceful purposes was taken as long ago as 1956. Since then agreements have been signed with the United States and Great Britain for exchange of atomic materials and information, and the Japanese government has begun a moderately paced program of reactor construction and research. Much more might be done in the realm of public information; but more and more people are coming to accept and take pride in Japan's atoms-for-peace program. As the scientist-president of Tokyo University put it recently, "When I was a boy I remember how frightened the people in my village were when the first electric lights were introduced. They thought that if they touched the light bulbs they would die. But pretty soon one farmer said to his neighbor, 'Your house is brighter than mine. I'm going to get bright lights, too.' The same thing is happening with atomic energy today. Our experience with it has been profoundly negative, but popular attitudes are slowly changing. After all, we cannot afford to lag behind the West. The problem is not whether nuclear energy should be developed, but how and when and at what speed."

Government interest in the industrial uses of the atom, and especially in nuclear power, has been influenced by some hard economic facts. As industrialization advances in Japan more emphasis will be placed on the heavy industries—iron and steel, chemicals, and other large consumers of electricity. But energy supplies are limited. Most of the advantageous sites for hydroelectric power are already being exploited. Low-grade soft coal reserves are substantial but not inexhaustible, and coal mining is expensive and inefficient. Nearly all of Japan's petroleum must be imported. In 1956, 23 per cent of all energy consumed was derived from imports; but by 1975, 48 per cent will have to be imported, if predicted growth rates are maintained. Government planners believe this will be true even if domestic production of fuel is increased to the limit and consumption of energy made more efficient. These imports cost money, but Japan's foreign-exchange position is chronically precarious. Thus, while it has not yet been proved to everyone's satisfaction that nuclear power can be produced safely and at rates competitive with oil-fired thermal power stations, the government has judged that any prospect, or any possibility, of cheaper power sources must be exploited.

At Tōkai-mura, two hours north of Tokyo, a nuclear research center has been laid out on 800 flat acres fronting the Pacific Ocean. Tiny by United States standards, the Tōkai installation is by far the largest in Asia. Administrative and housing facilities, radiation and other laboratories, a waste-disposal plant, engineering workshops, and reactors are scattered on landscaped grounds along wide, paved streets in one of the most modern industrial settings in Japan. Admission to visitors is free, and more than 2,000 people tour the grounds daily. (An estimated 20,000 a day go up to see the view from Tokyo's new TV tower.) One small (50 kw.) research reactor of American design and construction has been in operation there since mid-1957. A second research reactor of American design but primarily Japanese manufacture is nearing completion, and foundations are now being laid for a third research reactor for which all, or nearly all, of the equipment will be Japanese-made. In addition, a letter of intent was signed earlier this month for the purchase of an improved Calder Hall-type British power reactor of 150,000 kw. capacity, and negotiations are underway for import of an enriched uranium-type power reactor from the United States. Total installed nuclear power capacity is expected to reach 600,000 kw. by 1965, although the program is now running somewhat behind schedule. A nuclear fuel refining and fabricating plant, US-designed and constructed by Japanese engineers under American supervision, was dedicated three weeks ago on land adjoining the research center at Tōkai. This plant is intended to make the Japanese independent of foreign fuel processing, although most raw fuel will have to be imported.

To direct the nuclear program an elaborate hierarchy of organizations has been set up. The Atomic Energy Commission is responsible for policy formulation; the Atomic Energy Bureau of the Science and Technology Agency for administration; the Atomic Energy Research Institute, at Tōkai, for government-supported research; the Atomic Power Company (an 80 per cent privately financed organization) for power reactor import and construction; the Atomic Fuel Corporation (wholly government-owned) for uranium prospecting and refining, and so on. This administrative structure is answerable to the cabinet and the Diet. In addition, numerous government laboratories and research institutes are engaged in research on radiation, isotopes, and other branches of nuclear science, while basic and applied research are being carried on at government and private universities in a number of cities, notably Tokyo and Kyoto. Finally, five "atomic power groups" have been formed by combinations of large private business enterprises anxious to share in the supply of equipment in this new field. These groups for the most part parallel the new zaibatsu-type interests that have re-emerged in the last few years.

The pattern of technological borrowing and adaptation established in the preatomic age is being carried over into the era of nuclear reactors and nuclear power. Advanced, already workable models, based on long and expensive development abroad, are being brought in, with a view to further research and development in Japan. Since World War II the American share in the total of imported know-how has been very large, and American influence in the nuclear field obviously is strong today. But in borrowing nuclear technology, as in other, earlier fields, the Japanese want to choose what they think works best and is most adaptable to their own conditions.

The thinking behind these methods was explained to me recently by Daigorō Yasukawa, president of the Atomic Power Company. Yasukawa is a typical older-generation businessman, who has spent a lifetime in the electrical industry both in and out of the government and whose interests tend to fuse with those of his government to a degree Western businessmen often find difficult to understand. Long ago he studied electrical engineering at Westinghouse in the United States. For many years he was president of his own electrical manufacturing company, and during the war he served as the government's electric-power tsar. Purged by the Occupation, he later headed the government's Atomic Energy Research Institute at Tōkai but left it to take over the Atomic Power Company. "We import the finished product," said Yasukawa, "not the principle. Our job is to get engineers to construct the product, to find the best Japanese subcontractors to bring foreign ideas to concrete form, as far as possible on Japanese soil, and adapt them to Japanese needs. Our decision to import the Calder Hall reactor was based on purely technical grounds. The British reactor is producing power and its fuel is cheaper than American enriched uranium. We are convinced that it will work safely and economically for us. At this early stage in the import of reactors we are not much concerned with Japanese scientists who do basic research. Their research is necessary for sound future development, but if they oppose our methods of importing reactors, that's just too bad. Our job can be done best through private companies with as little government interference as possible. Of course the government is behind the whole program, but bureaucrats have a tendency to get in the way. At Tōkai I could get little done because of the Finance Ministry bureaucrats. That is why it was decided to set up the power company mainly with private funds."

Yasukawa is scornful of skeptics who point to the many unproven aspects of the program. With the cost of conventional fuels rising and more and more fuel having to be imported, he sees atom-generated power as the only course for Japan. A businessman with wide ties in the utility industry, he is convinced that nuclear power plants, though much costlier to build than thermal or hydro plants, will become steadily cheaper to operate because of the fuel component; and he predicts enthusiastically that Japan will have one nuclear plant in each of its nine utility-company districts in the not-too-distant future.

However, in moving into the nuclear field the Japanese have commenced a technological adventure full of hazards and ambiguities. Under the surface of progress strong differences of opinion persist. Many scientists and others distrust the whole program. Professional skepticism, emotional fear, and political propaganda are found in different minds to different degrees. Few would deny the cliché that Japan must not "lag behind" the West. But all do not agree on what should be done to prevent this from happening.

Doubt especially surrounds the power program because the cost of producing electricity from nuclear fuel is still obscure. Some Japanese engineers and other specialists in the energy resources field seriously doubt that nuclear power in Japan can become competitive with oil-fired thermal plants as soon as its exponents say it will. They emphasize that Western scientists are much less hopeful than they were a few years ago about nuclear power costs; especially since last year's Geneva conference on the peaceful uses of nuclear energy they have begun to have grave doubts about the program. One highly respected specialist in water-power development, Dr. Kōichi Aki, Professor of Engineering at Tokyo University and Counselor in the Science and Technology Agency, thinks that Japan should reorganize its decrepit coal industry and build more reservoirs to increase the output of the hydro system already in existence. He is dubious about the present nuclear development program. Japan has no uranium deposits of any value, and it should not tie itself to a program that, he thinks, will mean indefinitely large imports of foreign raw materials and technology for an unpredictable length of time. Import of technical know-how is fine for things like cameras, transistors, and other machinery, especially small machinery, that requires much manual dexterity but relatively little electricity to develop. Finished metal products such as electronic and optical equipment are, to Dr. Aki, ideal expressions of Japanese industrial talent and, furthermore, can be produced within the capabilities of present resources. The money that is being sunk in the import of a British power reactor (nearly $100 million) should, he thinks, go into more basic research and exploitation of conventional power sources, construction of large oil tankers and sea-front industrial areas, improvement of the inadequate road transport system, expansion of domestic aviation, more rational land utilization, and improvements in other branches of the domestic economy.

Instead of assuming that the present industrial structure is inevitably set and must naturally lead to greater emphasis on heavy industry, Aki argues that the present trend to bigness will cause strains in the economy which it will not be able to withstand even with nuclear power. In his view, instead of importing foreign technology across the board as their Meiji grandfathers did, Japanese leaders should be planning for an international division of production functions in Asia. If the production of aluminum, for example, requires such high doses of electricity that the Japanese aluminum industry operates at only about 30 per cent of capacity, the proper remedy might be for some other country to make aluminum, rather than for Japan to try to provide enough electricity via the dubious atomic route to make its full capacity. Aki denies that he is at odds with men like Yasukawa over the main goal of a strong Japanese economy. He merely thinks that Yasukawa is too conservative about "changing the industrial structure."

A formal expression of these opinions may be found in a first-draft of a "long-range plan for promotion of science and technology" prepared and printed in Japanese by the Science and Technology Agency in February 1959. This draft of a policy represents the views of the "nonatomic" bureaus of the government's scientific apparatus. Included are some interesting statements concerning the role of innovation and foreign technological borrowing:

"In Japan many of the elements of technical innovation have been imported in finished form. We are deficient in experience of the development process by our own efforts. . . . Ever since the Meiji era we have been importing foreign scientific know-how, with the object of reducing the gap between ourselves and the advanced countries. In the process we have expanded our production by a relatively painless method. But this is precisely the cause of our present weakness in science and technology. From about 1935, with the experience gained up until then from foreign technology as a base, we seemed about to break out of our imitativeness and become original and creative. . . . But this process was interrupted by war and the military demand for quick results. After the war we began once more to import technology; but the experience of the last ten years has finally brought about the necessary conditions for technological independence, and the creativeness foreshadowed in prewar times may be about to be realized."

Other noted scientists and members of the Japan Science Council favor a slowdown in the nuclear reactor program. Dr. Seiji Kaya, president of Tokyo University, feels strongly that basic research is being sacrificed for the sake of too rapid import of foreign nuclear know-how. He agrees that Japan must have the know-how, but he thinks too much haste is being shown, and he is distressed at the neglect of research as evidenced by the structure of government budgets. In his view, politicians ignorant of the needs of basic research are easily persuaded by profit-minded businessmen to appropriate large funds for power reactor import, while the Tokyo University nuclear physics budget is a mere pittance. Kaya's pride in the achievements of Japanese physicists is combined with distrust of the motives of politicians. Kaya defines himself as "neither a Communist nor a capitalist but a Japanese." He talks a good deal about Japan's duty to work for a better world order through the UN "before the world we live in now is destroyed in a fight over Quemoy or some such place." And he describes in half-joking, half-serious fashion his plan to join Nobel Prize-winning physicist Hideki Yukawa in a public demonstration at the Diet to lobby for more research funds.

Other lesser-known scientists present similar arguments which can be summarized as follows. Japan could well wait for a decade to import a power reactor. Developments in the nuclear fusion field may produce a safer power source than the present fission reactors. In any case, much more study is needed. But because the businessmen are in a hurry for profits, Japan will be used as a "testing ground" for Britain's Calder Hall reactor. "Why," asked one young chemist, "are we always tied to the United States or England? We should give more and not take all the time."

Such misgivings sometimes shade off into the language of the Communist press, whose readers are told that the "monopoly capitalists'" decision to import reactors is pushing Japan into an unsafe program whose ultimate goal is nuclear rearmament and war.

Doubts also are articulated by influential non-Communist journalists whose distrust of conservative politicians is profound. They see three current motives for development of nuclear energy in Japan: profit, position in the field of nuclear industry, and acquisition of technology. The second motive is strongest now, i.e., the large private industrial concerns are jockeying for position as suppliers of nuclear equipment, and they are willing to sacrifice profits in the early stages. Scientists and most government officials have only the third motive, acquisition of technology. But the government is under such pressure from business to go ahead and make tie-ins with foreign suppliers of technology that nuclear reactors are being imported too rapidly and without thought of a basic policy. As a consequence of importing from different foreign sources, it is alleged that Japanese know-how will be dispersed and fragmented rather than concentrated on one type of reactor, whether it be the British natural uranium or the American enriched uranium type. It would be better to start with a research reactor program and wait to see which foreign power reactor proves to be best. But Japanese business, say these journalists, is a disgustingly easy mark for American and British "salesmanship."

Businessmen reply to these accusations by ignoring them. Yasukawa and other Atomic Power Company officials insist that the decision to import the Calder Hall reactor was made on the best of all grounds: it was producing power. They admit that cost figures still are uncertain, but they insist that Japan cannot afford to wait passively until all the unknowns of nuclear power are settled. Neither, they say, can the country afford to indulge in idealistic dreams of international production-sharing in Asia. One look at the political realities of contemporary Asia should be enough to prove the fantasy of such an idea. Similar views are expressed by conservative party members of the Atomic Energy Committee in the Lower House of the Diet. Scholars may oppose the program as much as they wish, but the government will go ahead with it. Men like Yasukawa regard intellectual opposition with some scorn: "First they were against Calder Hall on account of supposed earthquake danger. This was eliminated by design changes in the reactor. Then they attacked it on grounds of general safety, disposal of waste gases, etc. This also was argued down. Now they have fastened on the cost factor. But the country must go ahead anyway. Atomic power will be competitive with the best thermal plants in Japan in ten to fifteen years. That is, it will be if we can keep the bureaucrats from putting too many brakes on progress."

Working alongside the distrustful scientists and the aggressive businessmen, government officials concerned on a day-to-day basis with administration and planning of the nuclear power program are trying to implement an economically feasible policy. They must neither wait passively for further nuclear progress abroad nor indulge in a ruinously expensive "crash program." Atom-conscious bureaucrats in the Atomic

Energy Bureau laugh at the idea of Japan's being ready to stand on its own feet technologically. "This has been said for years," one of them remarked to me, "but we are no nearer than ever to such a state of affairs. Technology abroad moves ever faster than we are able to move." However, they are not happy over this situation. The same officials are dissatisfied with businessmen who are eager to import foreign reactors but reluctant to take more risks to develop a local nuclear technology.

The question of providing business with "incentives" enters in at this point. If the whole program could be linked with some more powerful incentive, say some officials, so that the government would purchase equipment on a larger scale, then investment in local know-how could be better advanced. As one official put it recently, in a sudden access of frankness: "In your country the peaceful uses of atomic energy grew out of the war and military developments, and your budgets are overwhelmingly military. In Japan we are having to go at things the other way round. The Constitution and the basic laws of atomic energy prevent any military application of the nuclear program. Our agreements with the United States and other countries for supply of nuclear fuel also contain clauses governing the use of by-products. But conservative politicians would like to link the program with national defense to give the businessman a better reason to take risks with large research programs for heavy water and other nuclear equipment. This may not be an ideal solution, but it would be a practical one. We push the businessmen to develop more original products; they push us to import more reactors, and meanwhile projects like the atomic ship are languishing. To some of us that is even more important than power plants."

From this it should be clear that the thinking of some "nuclear" officials is running far ahead of the present program. Public opinion still opposes military application of the program, but recent statements of the Kishi government that Japan might legitimately possess "small" nuclear weapons for "self-defense" did not provoke nearly the uproar that they would have four or five years ago. Ten years from now, perhaps sooner, Japan will be producing ingredients required for atomic bombs. Use of the by-products of the atoms-for-peace program is now controlled by international agreements and domestic laws; both could, of course, be altered in the future.

However, "non-nuclear" officials faced with solving present-day economic problems do not believe that atomic power is the only need, or perhaps even the principal need, of the Japanese economy. The government is committed to a nuclear power program, but some influential persons take a conservative view of its possibilities. This brief guide through the maze of pros and cons on the subject may suitably close with a recent statement by Saburō Ōkita, chief of the bureau of long-range planning of the Economic Planning Agency and one of the ablest of the government's economic planners. Somewhat more hopeful about nuclear power than Dr. Aki, Dr. Kaya, and other scientists, he is somewhat less enthusiastic than Yasukawa and other champions of the program in the government: "Economic progress is a gradual, slow process. We had the *jinrikisha* alongside early industrial machines. Of course nuclear power will eventually save on fuel imports, but we must think in terms of over-all technological improvements, the effects of automation and the like. We also need to train more technicians, not only in the nuclear field but in other fields as well. We must increase the technical specialization of our export products, with the focus on articles that require less energy, more brain power and special skills, such as cameras and small machinery. I now have a section of my research staff working on a 20-year projection of the economic effects of the nuclear power program and other technical developments. This will be ready by the end of the year, but our thinking is still very ambiguous on the end effects of nuclear power, because of the vagueness of the cost factor. We just don't know when it will become competitive with thermal plants."

CHAPTER *20*

THE UTOPIA OF THE
CONSERVATIVES

April 10, 1961

By the end of the 1950's the Japanese economy had recovered in nearly
every way from the ruin of the war. Japan's share of world trade was
smaller than in prewar days, and many glaring problems remained in
transportation, domestic housing, and public facilities. But despite the
predictions of Marxists and other skeptics, Japanese capitalism was not
in decline; on the contrary, economic plans that had been considered
too bold a few years earlier were being fulfilled ahead of schedule. The
annual average rate of growth was officially put at 11.5 per cent from
1947 to 1952, and 8.3 per cent from 1953 to 1959. In 1959 the rate shot
up to more than 17 per cent, by far the highest in the world. These
figures astonished and delighted the central authorities. Growth economics became a favorite theme of the mass media of communications.
Economists studied the latest Western theories of the subject and
argued knowingly about their application to Japanese conditions. "Rate
of growth" was a cliché of everyday speech, like "instant" foods.

In the spring of 1959 the government ordered a review of current
programs and preparation of a new ten-year plan by the Economic
Deliberation Council, a top-level advisory organ on economic policy
which includes on its committees leading figures in business and industry, high government officials, and academic experts. At the same
time, another group was set up in the Council, including some of the

249

same experts, for the purpose of projecting Japanese economic growth another decade beyond the ten-year plan. This longer projection was not expected to be internally consistent at every point; it would not form an official plan but would, it was hoped, provide an expansive, unguarded vision of what the Japanese future could and should be like.

The Kishi government, which was then in power, did not last to see these studies result in documents which could be used for political purposes. However, Kishi's successor, Hayato Ikeda, who came to power in July 1960, inherited the fruits of these labors; and he has had the wit to identify his regime, at least temporarily, with the modern mass desire for a better life rather than with outworn Confucian slogans concerning the abolition of corruption and poverty. Not noted for the richness or variety of his ideas, Ikeda has made economic growth his whole policy, because he is a former Finance Ministry official and that is what interests him most. No doubt the danger in this is that it is easier to produce economic blueprints than political blueprints, and Japan badly needs a chart through the shoals of political change. But however abrupt or prolonged his decline may be, and however harsh the disagreements over his policies, Ikeda has at least turned the people's attention deliberately from the rancid past toward a future filled with revolutionary implications for life in Japan. And he has sanctioned the publication of a model for the modern welfare state in an Asian setting.[1]

ASSUMPTIONS AND EXPECTATIONS OF
CURRENT ECONOMIC PLANS

The planners' image of the Japanese future is bound by several assumptions. The first of these concerns people, the richest raw material this country owns and the most vital ingredient in its industrial progress.

The dramatic fall in the Japanese birth rate in the last ten years has not been fully understood in the West, because the impact of that fall on Japan's economic position still lies largely in the future. The stereotype of an exploding population in a tiny land area lingers on, both

[1] *New Long-Range Economic Plan of Japan (1961–1970)*, Economic Planning Agency, Tokyo, February 1961. Approved by the cabinet December 27, 1960. Authorized translation by the *Japan Times*. The longer, 20-year projection is available as *Nihon Keizai no Chōki Tembō*, Japanese Government, Tokyo, December 1960.

here and abroad. And paradoxically, this stereotype will seem more than ever justified during the next few years.

This is because the birth rate just after World War II was very high, and children born then, between 1947 and 1951, are now on the verge of entering the labor force. For the next several years a flood of new people, more than one million annually, will need jobs. Here is one key to the government's encouragement of such labor-intensive industries as transistor radios and other electronic equipment.

However, this influx of new, young labor will be temporary, because in 1948 the government legalized abortion, and since then the birth rate has fallen spectacularly, until it is now only 17.1 per thousand, lower than in most Western countries. It is still falling, and although the death rate is also very low, the rate of increase in population has shrunk to less than one per cent per year.

This means that as this decade passes into the next, the planners believe Japan is likely to face serious shortages of labor, unless the available human resources are better educated and used in a more "rational and modern" manner. No significant political pressure is now apparent to change the law permitting abortion for economic as well as medical reasons; and even if abortion were outlawed at some time in the future, little could be done to reverse the trend of labor supply for a number of years. Contraception is becoming a significant social practice. The proportion of older people in the population is rising, and this will force measures for more adequate social security, vocational training, and retraining for mature workers who lose their jobs in the new wave of higher technology.

The planners' second assumption is that technological innovation will become more rapid and will eventually affect every branch of agriculture, manufacturing, and the service trades. The race to catch up with the West will never stop: "This is an age of technological reforms and rapid scientific progress supported by economic growth continuing at a high level." Such statements are scattered through current plans. There is never a thought of going back; the good lies in a higher sphere of technical society.

The Japanese people have shown that they can quickly adapt techniques imported from elsewhere. But the planners now urge that domestic research, invention, and export of local know-how be more heavily stressed. To encourage creativeness, they believe much closer relationships are required between business and the universities. There should be more interchange of talented people between these two worlds, and the university professor should somehow be brought into the "more fruitful service of the national community." This assumes great changes in the intellectuals' role in many fields. Graduate schools should be greatly strengthened and research funds increased, especially in science and engineering. Engineers and skilled technicians in private firms should assist in teaching new technical knowledge in the universities until enough new teachers can be properly trained.

The third assumption is that world production and trade will continue to expand. No major war will destroy the world's economic foundations; depressions will be controlled and co-operation on economic matters between nations improved. In the ten-year plan the annual rate of growth for world trade is guessed at 4.5 per cent for the next decade. The advanced industrial nations will trade briskly with one another. "It is expected that East-West trade, as well as Japan's trade with the Communist bloc, will gradually reach more normal conditions." However, trade with the underdeveloped countries will be sluggish because of their chronic exchange difficulties.

The expansion of the labor force, progress in technological innovation and training, and the rise in world trade will combine to push rapid economic growth in the next few years. The planners' fourth assumption is that government's role is to provide a suitable environment for this growth. Japanese economic plans are not of the Socialist type, with targets for each industry minutely spelled out and operating control in the hands of government officials. Rather they are perspectives of what everybody, it is profoundly hoped, will agree is in the best interests of Japan's capitalist economy.

Nevertheless, they do contain targets and propose ways of reaching them; and there is more than a suggestion in current plans that the government intends to provide a large degree of "guidance" to insure that general goals are successfully attained. The government, in the words of the plan, "is at all times responsible for positively cultivating factors for economic growth and eliminating adverse elements. It is also responsible for keeping the value of currency stabilized, maintaining economic growth, and minimizing business fluctuations through proper application of fiscal and monetary policies." The major task of carrying out the objectives of planning is left to private business; the private entrepreneur is expected to be "community-centered" enough to respond to government plans by making his own long-range plans and by taking actions on his own which will lead to generally desirable ends. This is an old relationship, which before the war served one set of ends and today serves another. What is wanted are public-spirited profit seekers, full of vitality and "national sense."

Given these main assumptions, the Economic Deliberation Council foresees dramatic changes that will open up a whole new era of national possibilities for this country. Earlier plans stressed the need for equipment investments and modernization of private industrial plants. These ends continue to have high priority, but current plans strike a new theme: "What should be emphasized is the revision of various systems and institutions currently in force. Heretofore little importance has been attached to the roles played by such systems and institutions in economic growth."

The planners expect, first, a vast increase in public investment, which is essential if Japan is to take the leap into the new millennium of science and technology. Transportation and communications systems, now choking economic growth, will be rebuilt and expanded. Roads, which today prevent travel almost as much as they permit it, will be enormously improved. By 1980 an expressway will extend from Sendai north of Tokyo to Fukuoka in Kyushu—surely one of the more bracing dreams in the planners' book. New road systems also will be created between and around the great industrial centers on the Pacific shore. Rail transport will be greatly extended, with much new double-tracking. Harbor installations will be expanded and mechanized to accommodate the larger tankers and ore boats bringing in energy fuels in ever greater quantities for the new age. "Nowadays," declares the ten-year plan, "a modern city is defined as a city 'having an airport.'" Consequently, domestic and international air facilities will be incomparably more complex and large-scale than at present. Today only about five persons in 100 have a telephone; by 1970 nearly 20 will be so blessed.

Over the next decade or so the traditional construction industry, which, like poor roads, strangles progress, will be transformed by modern machinery, permitting more rapid construction of new housing, sewage and water-supply systems, roads, hospitals, welfare centers, and parks. New laws will provide "a unified standard for compensation, an appraisal system, and measures to permit the start of work even before the conclusion of the purchase contract." In this sentence, as in many others, a whole process of sociological change is concentrated.

Tokyo has become a monster out of control, and nobody, not even the planners, seems to think much can be done about it. However, by 1980, and probably much earlier, public facilities in Japanese cities will be startlingly transformed. There is even mention in the plan of building a kind of Japanese Canberra at the foot of Mt. Fuji, with universities, government offices, and other institutions in a cooler, more pleasant environment than the bayside now affords.

Industry will continue to be concentrated in four major centers on the Pacific, from Tokyo-Yokohama through Nagoya and Osaka-Kobe to northern Kyushu. Here are the best harbors and the only plains to support large urban populations. The planners agree that these areas will always be central, but a new industrial zone will be built along the coast between Osaka and Tokyo, as well as smaller industrial centers in Hokkaido, nothern Honshu, and elsewhere, all linked by the new and better roads and rail lines. Laws and regulations will discourage new industries from building in the old centers; but land, water, and labor resources will be made more easily available in new areas. The ten-year plan stresses that the location of new industries and the redistribution of old ones are problems requiring rational foresight, if the murky air, filth-filled rivers, sunken land areas, and general dilapidation of the industrial sections of Tokyo, Osaka, and other big cities are not to be repeated elsewhere.

While this new physical framework for industrialism is being created, the structure of production will also change. The percentage of people in farming and fishing will fall steadily, and agriculture will decline to European proportions in the national product. Private owner-farmers will continue to be the backbone of agricultural operations, but farming will be extensively mechanized and "marginal" producers encouraged to leave the land or to join in co-operative farm management corporations of from 50 to 100 acres for paddy crops and 100 to 150 acres for dry farming. The working population in agriculture will fall by 25 per cent in the next ten years. Meanwhile, the structure of farm production will change, with rice and other cereals diminishing in relative importance and livestock, dairy products, fruits, and vegetables becoming more significant. These trends in agricultural production have been evident for several years.

With more people freed from agriculture, and with the new labor force rapidly increasing, the heaviest growth for the next few years will come in the machinery and heavy chemical industries, particularly machine tools, electrical and electronic equipment. Japan produced slightly over 22 million tons of crude steel in 1960; the ten-year plan estimates 1970 production at 48 million tons. For the time being industrial wages will remain relatively low, and the pressure for increased productivity will not be felt with particular force by thousands of small- and medium-sized industries. However, as the 1960's pass and the supply of fresh labor dwindles more rapidly, labor unions will be in a stronger bargaining position, wages will rise, and employers will be forced to take other measures to increase productivity. These trends, too, are already visible, though still in their early stages.

With industry as a whole moving toward higher forms of production and more complex techniques, the demand for skilled labor will come to resemble Europe; the gap between small and large industry will narrow, and the Japanese will no longer be able to avoid modernizing their management-labor relations. Here the ten-year plan is explicit and quite revolutionary in terms of traditional practices and attitudes: "Interindustrial migration of labor must be carried out on a fairly large scale within the program period. The traditional practice of employment for life in one company and wage scales determined by seniority alone are to be revised to keep pace with technical progress in order to create a new system, which will determine wages according to the vocational proficiency of each individual." And the plan continues: "Full employment and a high living standard are the two ultimate ends for a modern state to accomplish. Because of perennial surplus manpower and subsequent underemployment, Japan has long needed to improve its backward labor employment methods. This plan is definitely directed toward drastic modernization of the conditions and structure of employment in this country. The structural change in the employment situation, coupled with the modernization of the industrial structure, is likely to exert a potent influence on the structure of national income distribution. . . .

"The seniority system in industry tends to dissatisfy young and competent employees and gives undue favor to mediocre employees with long service and little creative ability. Economic development in the age of technical innovation requires a basic labor force with talent and judgment." Reforms should accordingly lead to the principle of equal pay for equal work, smooth labor turnover, and the shift of the labor movement away from the enterprise-centered union to the industrial-type union, more characteristic of the West. "Thus, though some aspects of economic development will remain in embryo, the working environment in general is expected to be modernized to an extent comparable to that in advanced Western countries by the end of the plan period."

By 1970, too, the people as a whole will have an immensely higher standard of living than they now have. Per capita income in 1970 will be $579. This is somewhat lower than West Germany and France (in 1957) and of course far lower than the United States. But the Japanese compare themselves with Europe more than with the United States; $579 is higher than present income levels in Italy and Spain. Consumption of durable goods and electricity will rise enormously. The "life environment" will be improved: "in comparison with the miserable social situation during and immediately after the war, these foreglimpses of our future life will, if realized, prove the high ability of the Japanese people, and Japan will be able to stand proudly before the world."

Social security and social welfare services already are an accepted part of urban life in Japan. They will be greatly strengthened and extended to cover farmers and workers in very small shops, because "it is the responsibility of the government of a modern country to build it into a welfare state." Vocational training and unemployment insurance will help to soften the blow of technological unemployment, a phenomenon largely avoided up to now by paternalistic devices hampering "modern" productivity and efficiency. A meaningful minimum-wage system will be established "so as to eliminate the fear of poverty and unemployment, thus taking a step closer to the long-awaited goal of full employment and rich living." Such a goal was unheard of in prewar Japan.

To achieve this new age exports are expected to triple in the next decade. Export targets have been set up for each major commodity. Textiles, until now the mainstay of Japanese sales abroad, will decline to about half their present value, as Japan's traditional textile customers develop their own industries. But machinery exports will rise from 25 per cent to over 40 per cent of total exports by value. The United

States and Canada will continue to be Japan's best markets, while Western Europe will rise in importance. Asia will take a large share of Japanese goods, but the percentage of total exports sold to Asia will fall. Exports to the Communist bloc will resume but will be small in scale, not over 6 per cent of total exports, because, in the language of the ten-year plan, "trade with them still is believed to involve considerable difficulties."

Imports will be liberalized, partly because foreign pressure for freer trade is strong and will increase, partly because the planners realize that the economy as a whole will benefit from less protection, even though some sick industries must be allowed finally to die or to reincarnate themselves in a new form. Obviously there is much caution and strong pressure against relaxing imports; removal of licensing restrictions will be offset to some degree by higher tariffs. But the planners assume that the general trend is toward more freedom of trade. Many of the reforms now being urged in the ten-year plan are a direct reaction to the expected stiffer competition from foreign imports.

Among imports, finished products, energy fuels, and raw materials for iron, steel, and other metals industries will expand sharply. Food imports will fall. North America will remain Japan's largest supplier, though not, perhaps, quite to the same extent as today. Europe and the Middle East will continue to be important sources of raw materials and finished goods, while South and Southeast Asia will decline as sources of supply. More Japanese merchant ships will be built to increase freight earnings. The tourist industry, which in 1959 earned only about $40 million, will earn $260 million by 1970.

Although the planners take a dim view of trade with Asia in the next decade, they urge the government to commit itself to a policy of greater economic co-operation to develop new, convenient sources of raw materials, such as Indian iron ore, and to insure an eventual market for Japanese consumer goods as well as capital equipment. Therefore, the ten-year plan calls upon government and business to invest in overseas resource development; it asks government to grant more credits, loans, and tax benefits to stimulate exports, and to expand technical assistance now being offered by Japan, both by training more foreign students in this country and by dispatching more Japanese specialists abroad upon invitation of foreign governments: "Considering that stagnation of exports of primary goods is one of the basic causes of current payments difficulties in underdeveloped nations, Japan should in some cases increase its purchase of primary products with the eventual aim of expanding Japan's exports."

SOME IMPLICATIONS OF CURRENT PLANS

It is easy to be cynical about these plans. The gulf between economic utopia and the stumbling crudities of Japanese political life has never seemed greater than in the past year. In the words of the London *Times*, "So far Japanese politicians have shown no inclination to strengthen their political institutions, preferring to concentrate—in Mr. Ikeda's case admittedly with striking success—on buttressing the economy. The same pointlessly single-minded determination was apparent in prewar Japan before the militarists took over."

Obviously, the political hack from X district who sits in the national Diet is limited in vision and sees such plans in terms of votes—good roads and more social security are a part of his campaign platform every election time, anyway. Obviously, too, many Japanese are attracted only by that portion of the ten-year plan which promises to double their income, without appreciating what its other implications may be. Not long ago, during a visit to a provincial city, I felt the raw heat of local politics in a conversation with a young American businessman in town to arrange for local distribution of his company's product. He was frankly disgusted with the political jungle he had found there. "Take K., for example. His group has been fading for years, he desperately wants the product, but so does N., who owns half the real estate downtown. Both K. and N. live in Tokyo and put up a big front, but their roots are here. And the former mayor also came around, picking his teeth behind his hand, and implied that he had powerful backers. The trouble is that most of them happen to be in the *pachinko* [pinball] racket—gangsters on the gambling fringe, probably including some Koreans. He was mayor for one term, and he set himself up in it.

"All you've got here are bosses and their paid-off followers. Nobody represents anything but himself and his crowd. The essence of local politics is the struggle for money and power. While the bureaucrats in Tokyo try to keep the bars up against foreign investment and talk about the danger of Japan's being 'colonized,' these local people are crawling on their hands and knees for preferment. It's sickening to watch. Then you meet a really capable bureaucrat, like T., educated, sure of himself, and relatively disinterested, and the contrast is tremendous. But T. doesn't represent anybody either, except the government. He is also in a hierarchy of his own, that can get things done sometimes a little faster than the politicians, but that has little relation to representative institutions. His bosses have to respond to pressures from the politician, but these pressures are mainly selfish, and if they help the 'people' it is usually as much an accident as anything planned."

Last year's massive upheavals left an uneasiness at the top of the conservative party, and the new economic plan is in one sense a diversionary gambit to reduce political tension; Prime Minister Ikeda has said as much publicly. Other conservative leaders have communicated their own nervousness, but a number of them also hold to a long-range view which, though it may not quite match the dream world of the Council's planners, is nonetheless hopeful. One such politician, a former member of several conservative cabinets and a close associate of the present Prime Minister, remarked that the conservatives may seem to be tangled in political trivia from day to day, but they have their sights set on objectives a decade from now, when the new economic plan and the United States-Japan Security Treaty both will reach full term. By then economic levels will be far higher than the present, though perhaps not twice as high, as the plan boasts, and the people's mood will have settled down. The conservative government will have corrected the more offensive "excesses" of the Allied Occupation, but it will also have created a new and more progressive image of itself in the public mind. Greater social security, welfare, the relocation of industry, the reduction of income discrepancies between small and large industry and between country and city, all will be in progress. Basic laws in education will have been amended to strengthen the ethical and patriotic content of the school curriculum and to reduce the influence of professional leftists in the Japan Teachers Union. The labor movement cannot be abolished, nor should it be; but with the progress of the economy into a new stage of labor scarcity, the political struggles of labor federations will subside, and there will be a cooling off of the violent differences on foreign policy that now divide conservatives and Socialists. Through their welfare state policies the conservatives will have robbed the Socialists of their appeal. Japan, like France, will be an independent, nationalistic power, with some ability to keep itself to itself and to mediate between East and West, while remaining tied in basic self-interest to the West. "If there is no revolu-tion," these goals will be within reach a decade from now.

How far economic ideals are revealed wedded to political ideals de-pends on whom one talks to. Most bureaucrats, politicians, and business-men still think in terms of abundant rural labor, low wages, imported technology, company consciousness, cheap exports, high dividends, heavy bank loans, and high interest rates. Nor is economic aid to under-developed countries viewed with uniform enthusiasm. When I sug-gested to former Prime Minister Yoshida that it might be a good idea to give more to Southeast Asia against the future, he replied that he had visited the area recently and had come to the conclusion that "you can't do business with beggars." An Osaka trading company president elaborated on this theme: "The attitude of Indians, Indonesians, and others coming here for money has been arrogant. They seem to think that just because we have money again we have to give it to them. Rather, they should show some appreciation for getting our hard-won cash. Of course, we should respond to American requests that we aid Southeast Asia by giving as far as we are able. We should go farther than the Germans in helping other countries. But I would hate to see the Japanese government spending our good, hard-earned money in countries where the recipients can't and won't use it properly. Private business deals are one thing, but government aid is open to corruption and waste or misapplication. Your American record is none too clean on this score, either."

Trying to predict the success or failure of the government's long-range plans is futile. Granted the assumptions of the planners about world conditions and domestic trends, the chances are good that some portion of them or some degree of all of them will be accomplished, though perhaps not in a form recognizable to government planners. Japan has changed beyond imagination in the last ten or fifteen years.

Before the ten-year plan was approved by the cabinet last December it was submitted to the various factional leaders of the conservative party for their suggestions and sanction. If it fails, rivals of the Prime Minister will naturally consider that failure fair ground for attack. But within the party there appears to be no real opposition on anything like conceptual grounds to the welfare statism of the plan. The current fiscal budget already has on it marks of the planners' concepts in agri-culture, economic co-operation, and elsewhere.

More to the point than predictions is the frame of mind behind the plan. Many Japanese think it is far too optimistic. But, as one official rather gaily remarked, "The optimists are in power." Today there is considerable acceptance of the idea that Japan is entering a period of change at least as great as that experienced in the Meiji era. This notion is fed to the literate population through the mass media. Early industrialism is passing into a new stage that finds the leaders more or less consciously grasping for new technical accomplishments. Technological innovation is regarded as inevitable and as a good. Secular progress is a great good.

Finally, the planners believe that the people will be equal to whatever challenges are presented to them. A new self-confidence is being expressed. Economic tasks, at least, will be successfully performed. Recently the director of the Japan Development Bank, who is regarded as the moving spirit behind the ten-year plan, was asked to explain his views on postwar economic growth. He replied: "I think the basic cause is the release of individual capabilities. The Japanese, in my opinion, are in no way inferior in creativeness, both mental and material, to anyone else in the world. What affects economic growth is the manner in which this latent creativity is permitted to come into play. . . . With the over-all situation promising productivity at European standards for Japanese in all fields, we can safely assume that growth in future will continue to be rapid." [2]

Inflation may knock down their plans, foreign tariff walls curtail their exports, or pressure of imports bring recession; but these are the presently dominant concepts of Japan's governing group. By comparison, the conservatism of the Japanese left is more than ever noticeable. For the Socialists not only are against war or rearmament; they also oppose freer imports of commodities and technology, and they are shouting out against the rationalization of industry. More and more it is they who are seen to be defending the *status quo*, while planners endorsed by conservative political leaders move into a new range of possibilities that could forever alter many of the old sureties and make Socialist utopia seem irrelevant and unnecessary. Such, at least, is the planners' dream.

[2] *Oriental Economist*, February 1961, p. 86.

CHAPTER *21*

JAPAN'S SEARCH FOR AN
OIL POLICY

February 25, 1962

Industrial Japan is one of the world's greatest and most competitive oil markets. In the present fiscal year oil accounts for about 15 per cent of total imports and costs nearly half a billion dollars, the largest single import expense of the Japanese nation. But this is only the beginning. Today coal supplies more energy than oil or water power, but in the next decade oil will become the most important energy source; the coal industry is in decline and most suitable hydroelectric sites are already being used. Some natural gas has been found, but domestic oil reserves are small and the prospect of future discoveries unpromising. Recent world discoveries of oil have reduced interest in atomic power in this country as in some others. The government estimates that imported energy will rise from less than half the total now to nearly three-fourths in 1980. In this, as in so much else, Japan is becoming more rather than less dependent on the outside world.

Until 1920 domestic oil production sufficed for most local needs. For example, Sazō Idemitsu (seventy-seven), founder and president of Idemitsu Kōsan, the most important independent oil company, got his start by selling fuel to the new fleet of oil-powered fishing craft based in the Moji-Shimonoseki area and operating off Korea. This was in 1914, when Japan was an ally of the West and nearly all petroleum demand was met by domestic crude oil. But during the First World

War industry expanded, the demand for oil rose, and domestic refineries could not keep up with it. In the 1920's new refineries were built along the Pacific shore of the island chain, but more and more petroleum products were imported in already refined form. In 1920 only one-fourth of heavy fuel oil demand was imported; by 1930 the figure was 96 per cent.

As relations with the West deteriorated in the 1930's Western companies controlling oil supplies were in conflict with Japanese governments concerned with protecting local interests and securing new crude oil sources. Oil was a vital objective of military bureaucrats seeking wider empire in Asia; the need for oil and other materials, like the need for living room, became a justification for winning empire. In 1934 the Petroleum Industry Law established a permit system for refineries, regulated crude imports, "thruput" rates (oil has a language of its own), and other matters. The government forced greater centralization of the industry after the invasion of central China in 1937. By the late 1930's and early 1940's the search for new sources of oil and other materials turned the Japanese toward Southeast Asia. Nationalism shifted into wholly military channels and the oil industry was put under direct operation of military men. In the summer of 1941, as Japan and America moved toward the war which had been implied for so long, the United States declared an embargo on oil shipments to this country.

Lack of oil was a decisive cause of Japan's defeat. Refineries, especially those on the Pacific coast, were heavily damaged by bombing, but even if they had not been bombed they would have suffered from shortage of crude oil. The story of the intervention of American submarines across oil supply routes from Java, Sumatra, and Borneo still needs to be told in detail. Convoy after convoy of Japanese tankers was found and sunk in the South China Sea or in waters much nearer Japan. By the middle of 1944 the Japanese economy was dying of thirst for oil.

After surrender refinery equipment that was still usable was designated as reparations for the countries Japan had overrun. However, this policy was reversed when the decision was made to rebuild the Japanese economy. Until 1949 refineries were left in ruins and oil needs filled by Occupation forces, but from early 1950 refinery operations were recommenced on a large scale.

The rebuilding of the Japanese oil industry was made possible by capital and technical know-how from American and British companies. In return these companies concluded contracts for purchase of their crude oil and participated in the management of Japanese firms. Whereas in prewar times most oil had come from America in the form of refined products—gasoline, heavy fuel oil, lubricating oil, and so on —after 1950 most came in crude form by tanker from Middle East concessions and was refined in Japan. Only those products for which demand exceeded refinery supply, like heavy oil, were imported. This was in line with world-wide trends; since crude oil was abundant and cheaper to import than refined products, this policy saved foreign exchange and promoted technical progress in Japan, not only in oil refining but in other related industries. In 1960 less than 10 per cent of all oil products consumed in this country was imported, but 98 per cent of crude oil was imported.

STRUCTURE OF THE JAPANESE OIL INDUSTRY

First, then, come the international companies and their affiliates. These are formed into groups: the Caltex group, the Shell group, the Standard group, the Tidewater group, each with its foreign supplier of crude and its affiliated Japanese companies engaged in refining or selling or both. Foreign companies as a rule have a half interest in their affiliates. However, together these international groups account for more than half the total sales of major oil companies. The Nippon Oil Company (Nippon Sekiyu), a member of the Caltex group, in 1960 led the field of some 14 Japanese companies with 20.1 per cent of the market.

Apart from the international groups are a number of Japanese refining and marketing companies, which are called "independents" because no foreign capital is invested in them. However, none of these companies is really independent of foreign supplies of crude oil. All need capital for development, and in order to get it they accept "tied loans" from foreign suppliers of crude. This is the key equation: domestic refiners needing capital and crude, foreign suppliers eager to sell crude which they have in overabundance and ready to underwrite foreign bank loans. Idemitsu, largest of the independents, last year received a $6 million loan from the Esso International Oil Company in return for a six-year crude purchase contract for 24 million barrels of crude. But Idemitsu may buy and borrow elsewhere; he is not limited in his purchases to Esso. In this sense Idemitsu is independent; producing no oil, he buys crude where he can, refines it in his new, modern refinery, the largest in Japan, and sells it through his own marketing organization.

At present Idemitsu is demonstrating his independence in still another way: more than 20 per cent of his imports of crude now come from the Soviet Union, and he has contracted to buy six million tons of Soviet crude over the next six years. These purchases are being made within the framework of the current Japan-Soviet trade agreement. Several smaller companies also have recently bought Soviet oil.

Besides the foreign-affiliated companies and "independent" refiners, some Japanese themselves produce crude oil. Most of the meager domestic production comes from wells in northwestern Honshu controlled by the privately owned Teikoku Oil Company. In 1955 the government established the Japan Petroleum Exploration Company (Nihon Sekiyu Shigen Kaihatsu K. K.) to explore oil reserves on land and offshore. A little oil has been found but nothing very significant.

Much more important is the new Arabian Oil Company, the first Japanese enterprise ever to produce Middle Eastern oil. Arabian's president, Tarō Yamashita (seventy-three), is a former trader in rice and wool who, like Idemitsu, followed the flag into the Asian mainland long before the war. There he became President of the Nissan Steamship Company, the Chōsen Chemical Industries Corporation, and many other colonial ventures. Again like Idemitsu, Yamashita could say that the government told him what to do, but he profited from doing it, became one of the top industrialists in the empire, and was nicknamed "Manchuria Tarō." After the surrender he was purged by the Occupation; by 1949 he had been "depurged" and returned to prominence in the industrial boom during the Korean War.

In the summer of 1958, in the face of strong opposition from American and British companies, Yamashita won a 44½-year concession from Saudi Arabia and Kuwait in the Persian Gulf offshore "neutral zone" and formed a company to exploit the oil wealth it contained. After some severe discouragements, including fires, underwater explosions, and the skepticism of many Japanese government officials and conservative businessmen, Yamashita struck oil of good quality and quantity in 1960. More than a million tons of this "Khafji" crude have already been shipped to Japan. Arabian estimates that production will reach ten million tons annually by 1963, or nearly one-fourth of Japan's total expected crude oil demand. Since Yamashita's success (he now has 25 producing wells) the government has had a rather fresher appreciation of the immense advantages that his venture represents.

Finally, the Japanese government, as part of its policy of "economic co-operation" in Southeast Asia, in the summer of 1960 signed an agreement with Indonesia to assist that country's oil organization, Permina, to restore and expand production of oil wells in the Atjeh region of north Sumatra. Japan is supplying equipment and technicians for geological surveys and drillings; in return this country will receive around 40 per cent of any increase over the base level of production. The Japanese side has set up the North Sumatra Oil Development Company, with majority control in government hands but nearly a third of the shares subscribed by private Japanese companies. The chairman of the new company, Ataru Kobayashi (sixty-three), was for many years before the war an influential figure in banking and life insurance. Although the project has been delayed by bandit attacks and other difficulties on the scene, a small amount of Sumatran crude now is beginning to arrive in Japan.

Thus in addition to large purchases under supply contracts from Western oil companies, a growing quantity of crude oil has begun to reach this country from diverse sources, some of them new. The term "special crudes" has been invented to describe oil coming from (1) Soviet Russia, (2) domestic Japanese fields, (3) north Sumatra, and (4) the Arabian Oil Company's Middle East concession. Since Arabian has not yet built its own refineries and the Japanese government owns no refineries, the government so far has required other refiners—including, of course, those who have contracts with Western suppliers— to accept Arabian's crude, as well as north Sumatran crude, on a pro-rated basis.

This has caused some unrest in the local oil industry. More important, the handling of these "special crudes" has obvious international political implications. The Russians are selling oil to Japan at prices substantially lower than Middle East crudes, even after Japanese buyers receive their customary discounts from the Middle East "posted price." Idemitsu's purchases have been strongly opposed by the Western oil companies, who view the Russian oil offensive with alarm. Last December the United States Department of Defense banned purchase of jet fuel for its Air Force units from Idemitsu, on the grounds that even though, as he claimed, Russian crude might be "segregated" at his refinery, his cheaper source of supply gave him an unfair price advantage over his competitors. This action precipitated no public demonstration; but as imports of Soviet crude increase so do the chances of trouble in Japan's foreign relations. (During a recent interview Idemitsu told me that the government "ordered" him to buy Soviet oil to help fulfill the terms of the trade agreement with Russia. He failed to mention another strong incentive: since allocations of foreign exchange for import are based in part on previous import volume, cheaper oil means a bigger share of the next exchange budget.)

Interest in these problems is growing today, when the government has promised to end import controls on crude oil in the next few months. If it holds to this pledge, some new method of regulating the industry must evidently be found. But the government is not searching only for new oil policies; oil is closely related to the freeing of Japanese imports as a whole.

IMPORT LIBERALIZATION AND STEPS TOWARD A
NEW OIL POLICY

Postwar Japanese industry had an astonishing rebirth, but it grew up in a thicket of import restrictions. Foreign currency was never free: in its exchange budget, prepared twice a year, the government assigned quotas of currency to importers who could qualify for them according to various formulas, such as previous import volume, sales, capacity of plant, etc. Import allocations had an over-all simplicity that greatly appealed to the official mind. By using them officials could continually intervene to turn industry into paths thought to be desirable by the persons in power.

Until the late 1950's these controls accorded, or could be interpreted to accord, fairly well with the facts of Japan's economic life. To foreigners who expressed delight at growing prosperity officials responded with glum warnings. All this was shallow; Japan had no resources to speak of, too many people. Industry was structurally weak, with most workers in tiny shops that were low in productivity and capital. Japan had to trade to live, as the saying went, but many countries discriminated against Japanese goods, and trade balances, especially with the United States, were consistently unfavorable. Of course,

Japan was not to be compared with India, China, or the rest of Asia; but this country had far to go to "catch up with the West." If the foreigner ventured to suggest that Japan's own protectionism might be contributing to low productivity and discrimination against its goods, officials would respond with a whole battery of arguments, which boiled down to fear that if imports were wholly freed hundreds of local businesses would be blown down by the typhoon of foreign competition. In the Japanese phrase the wolf would be at the front door and the tiger at the back.

However, as the decade of the 1950's ended, these arguments began to meet heavy foreign counterdemands for lowering of trade walls. By 1960 Japan's exchange reserves reached $2 billion; productive capacity as a whole had enormously increased, the domestic market had expanded, and a whole new order of consumption was growing up, especially in the cities. The general trend in the West was toward lower trade barriers; and more and more informed Japanese began to argue that they would have to raise the level of their free imports, at least to some extent, if they were to have a strong case against exclusion of their own products from Europe and America. The government's decision to "liberalize" imports was not spontaneous but resulted from foreign pressure, specifically pressure from GATT and the International Monetary Fund, and was based on tit-for-tat calculations of reciprocal treatment.

In early 1960 came the first announcements that some commodities would be freed of foreign currency restrictions governing their import. These were mainly goods that Japan did not import in any quantity anyway, like ceramics or canned foods. But the list gradually widened to include such things as soybeans, scrap iron, and other products from the dollar area. Because the Japanese raised tariffs "temporarily" on some items and otherwise sought to cushion the shock of freer trade, they were accused by foreigners of hypocrisy or worse. But once the basic decision had been made to liberalize imports it seemed clear that, barring a major exchange crisis, the government would continue in that general direction. In the late summer of 1961 the pace was speeded up when, as part of a deal with the International Monetary Fund to postpone the abolition of exchange controls, Japan pledged to free a large portion of total imports by October 1, 1962. Many of the products that Western businessmen wanted to see freed were not freed: passenger cars, electrical generators, electronic appliances, color TV, machine tools, and many others. However, crude oil was included in the list.

The announcement that crude oil imports would be freed of foreign currency restrictions was made on September 26, 1961. Since then all the principal players in the game of Japanese oil, plus a good many others, have been busy exchanging opinions and taking positions on a new oil policy in their own characteristic way.

Favoring liberalization of crude imports with as few controls as possible are the international oil companies, which wish to expand their share of the market. However, since oil policy is a matter for the Japanese themselves to decide, the foreign companies are not able to intervene directly but must express themselves through diplomatic channels or through their affiliated members in the Petroleum Association of Japan. Relations between foreign companies and their affiliates are not without problems. Japanese businessmen naturally are adept at using government policies or regulations as a shield behind which to gain points from their foreign associates. If the government decides to change its policies, there is little or nothing foreign businessmen can do about it. By accepting Arabian Oil's crude or Sumatran crude at government request Japanese refining companies may be violating the principle of "exclusive" crude supply from their foreign connections; but all contracts for the import of oil, like everything else, are made contingent upon government permission in the first place. Foreign companies can and do protest, but in such matters the government cannot be bound.

Idemitsu, a freewheeler and the largest and most powerful of the independent refiners, wants free imports and few controls. Similar views are being expressed by the electric power companies, which are interested in an abundant supply of cheap energy and are less concerned with how it is supplied. In its latest memorandum on the subject, dated December 19, 1961, the Electricity Industry Association emphasized that world oil is expected to be in surplus supply for some time. Energy will have to be imported in increasing quantities; atomic energy may eventually take the place of oil, but for the next 15 or 20 years the most important thing is to have a "many-sided" oil supply, which would include the Western companies, Japanese independents, Arabian Oil, and any other sources that can be developed. The tanker fleet should be expanded in order to save on foreign freight payments. While everyone is sorry about the plight of the coal industry, the only solution is to rationalize and bring down coal production costs. The memorandum states that people who lose jobs in coal should be shifted to other industries (easier said than done, as the government has discovered in the last five years). Coal might be helped out by building more factories and power plants near the producing areas (a scheme that is regarded as impractical by many economists), but in any case the problem of regulating the oil market will best be settled by agreements between producers and consumers without government interference. Nothing will be gained by raising oil taxes: this merely raises the cost of energy and weakens Japan's over-all competitive strength in world markets. Since the electric power producers might wish to do some of their own refining in the future and are now experimenting with burning crude oil in power plant boilers, the electric industry opposes passage of any new Oil Industry Law to replace import controls.

Very different views are held by the domestic producers of oil, by Arabian Oil, the North Sumatra Oil people, and the smaller independent refiners. Throughout the fall and winter this group's association, the Oil Mining Industry League (Sekiyu Kōgyō Remmei), circulated a series of memoranda to the Diet, government agencies, and private business, advocating an elaborate new system of laws and regulations to replace the present quota system. These papers stressed that Japan's oil policy should not be based merely on a desire to diversify the sources of energy supply; rather Japan, like the European countries, should actively fight against international oil capital and try to limit its control over the national oil market. Oil duties, consumers' taxes, and other means should be used to strengthen "national capital" in the industry, in order to develop larger domestic resources and expand Japanese overseas facilities. According to these views, a new Oil Industry Law setting out government controls is absolutely essential but is not enough: some means must be found to guarantee "national capital" a definite share of the market—30 per cent is the figure most often mentioned nowadays, leaving 70 per cent for "international capital." (One oil economist employed by a foreign-affiliated company suggested that this figure was pulled out of the air because it fit the French model.) Up to now, state the reports of the League, the Japanese oil industry has had to depend on foreign capital and has thereby lost its freedom of action. To redress this situation the government should get into the oil business. The League proposes that an "oil stabilization fund" be established to subsidize crude production and development and make loans for tanker construction and new storage facilities. Since "special crudes" are uneven in price and quality, with Soviet crude lower than Middle East prices and domestic crudes higher, and since Arabian Oil's crudes are facing price and refining difficulties, the League urges that a "national policy company" (*kokusakugaisha*) be established to purchase "special crudes" and sell them to refineries, which would have to accept them at a pooled price. Opponents of this plan criticize it as excessively clever; they believe that if the government ran such a company it would collapse through inefficiency or open Japan to a flood of Soviet oil, which might be cheap at first but suddenly become expensive later.

The League's other proposals concern government assistance to help stabilize the price of domestic crude, preferential treatment for products made from such crude, and reduction of the multitude of taxes that now surround the local oil prospector. In general the intention of this group is to use the abolition of import controls as the occasion for building a new industry structure which would express the "will of the nation" and put the nation (*kokka*) behind the domestic oil interests.

Somewhere in between the advocates of liberalization with few controls and lobbyists for stringent controls are others, like the Mitsubishi Oil Company, whose president came out against government controls in principle but hinted that some new framework of regulation would be required to prevent disorder in the industry. On the whole the Japanese oil companies are less enthusiastic than foreign companies about removal of all import restrictions. They fear that excessive competition (a talismanic phrase) would result in the total exhaustion of the local industry. The in-betweens have hit upon the face-saving idea of temporary controls; thus the president of the Petroleum Association, to which nearly all refiners belong, put out what he labeled his "private plan." According to this, the goal of energy policy should be cheap energy, available to all users by their free choice and refined in the place of consumption. Private enterprise should work for these ends without government controls—the less controls the better—because controls only tend to drive up prices and lead to further inefficiency and confusion. Furthermore, controls go against the "spirit of liberalization" to which Japan is now committed. Yet, suggests the plan, some "small steps," such as a permit system for new oil refineries, government approval for new facilities, and "necessary regulation of demand and supply," may be inevitable as "temporary measures," say for five years. "Special crudes" in principle should be handled on a purely commercial basis, but if the government decides to establish some new system the industry should co-operate, especially if the new system were temporary.

While the various groups in the oil industry were expressing themselves in diverse ways, rumblings were heard from Miyakezaka, the hill in the center of Tokyo where the Diet was getting ready to open its regular session in December. The chairman of the Lower House Committee on Commerce and Industry, a conservative party member who himself earlier headed an "energy mission" to Europe, issued a pear-shaped statement to the effect that energy policies must be formulated from an over-all point of view, but "national security" (he used the English words) must also be considered. It was dangerous, he felt, to depend entirely on imported sources of energy: "Even though it is uneconomical for the time being, domestic energy should be the focus of our national energy policy, from the point of view of national security." The government should not be confused by the "mood" of trade liberalization but should set up an energy agency or ministry to supervise policy for oil, gas, coal, hydraulic and atomic energy. Under the ministry should come a public corporation to direct energy development, stabilize prices, and pool resources.

Another conservative party group, the "Over-All Energy Countermeasures Diet Members' Council" (chairman: Yasuhiro Nakasone), came out for an Energy Ministry. With the true politicians' instinct this group stressed local area needs and the effect of energy development on local employment, while suggesting what would in effect mean a greater centralization of power than now exists. The council's report, circulated to the same people who were reading (or being given copies of) all the others I have cited, recommended that priority in energy policy be given to coal (which still has the most votes), followed in order by domestic oil, natural gas, water power, overseas oil development through "national capital," and, finally, purely foreign oil. Atomic energy was regarded as full of problems requiring further study.

In sum, the oil producers want protection, other industries want cheap and abundant energy, and the politicians are for everything, especially the local people and national security.

Meanwhile government authorities responsible for any new oil policy were not sitting idly by, reading other people's memoranda. On October 3, 1961, one week after the announcement that oil imports would be freed, an oil study mission sponsored by the Ministry of International Trade and Industry (MITI) left Haneda airport for a two-month tour of Europe, including a stopover at the Arabian Oil Company's operating base in Kuwait. This was the latest of several energy missions: a coal study group visited Europe last August; an electricity group is scheduled to depart in the near future. These missions are in a tradition of European visitations that have been going on since the early Meiji period. They are part of the continuous process of finding out how Europe solves its problems and then rejecting, adopting, or adapting those solutions to fit Japanese needs.

The oil mission included representatives of the Japanese producers, refiners (both foreign-affiliated and independent), the electric industry, officials of the Economic Planning Agency and MITI. It also included several examples of what are sometimes called *gakushiki keikensha* (learned men of experience)—professors or other intellectuals who are expert in some subject or other and are used in an advisory capacity by government bureaus. They are to be distinguished from "progressive" (i.e., leftist) intellectuals, whose services are neither desired nor requested. Three famous men of the former type accompanied the oil mission: Yoshitarō Wakimura, Tokyo University professor and authority on international oil problems; Hidezō Inaba, professional economist and respected writer on domestic economic subjects; and Hiromi Arisawa, the mission chief, a former professor of economics and specialist on energy policy.[1]

After the mission's return it issued a report dated December 22,

[1] All three of these men were involved to some extent in the "social movement" before the war and either lost their jobs or went to jail in brushes with the military. Since 1945 all have served in government positions or as advisers to government bureaus. One of them, by his own account, now serves on 40 government committees and is chairman of 18.

1961, surveying the European oil picture and noting the peculiarities of each country's approach to energy problems. A good deal of attention was given to the role of government in the oil industries of Italy, France, England, and West Germany. The report is weighty reading; from a mass of data about prices, pipelines, and tariffs it concludes that (1) liberalization of trade is all very well, but some "new order" must be set up to replace import controls if the Japanese coal industry and the small oil operators are to be saved from ruin; but (2) whatever "new order" is established should be based on a "co-operative attitude" toward international oil capital. Since the mission included representatives of all interested groups, its conclusions were written to please everybody.

On the same day this report appeared another more important document was circulated in mimeographed form: the "Interim Report on Oil Policy" of the Energy Council (Enerugi Kondankai), an eight-man group set up last August to advise MITI on energy policy. Representatives of industry were excluded from the council, but four of its members also had been members of the oil mission.

The Energy Council report is a statement of principles on which Japan's new oil policies should be based. All the members agreed on two points: a "cheap and stable supply" of oil must be assured; and oil policies must be framed "in accordance with the principle that a fixed proportion of the domestic oil market can be placed under the influence of the country."

After agreeing on these principles the council issued a majority and a minority report (the minority consisted of two). The majority report notes the main oil industry problems: disposition of "special crude" imports, fear of excessive competition, anxiety that after October 1 foreign oil interests may be in a position to break small Japanese operators and monopolize the local market. The majority recommends that refined oil products, as distinguished from crude oil, should continue for some time to require government allocations of foreign exchange. This would protect local refiners from an uncontrolled influx of cheaper foreign products. In addition, though crude itself should be freed for import, the government should devise schemes to support domestic producers, just as the governments of Europe and America have done. As a basic first step the majority approves the draft of a new Oil Industry Law, already drawn up by MITI officials, and urges its speedy passage in this Diet session. Beyond the general regulatory provisions of the law the report recommends that the government establish some kind of public or semipublic corporation to provide long-term arrangements for refining of "special crudes." Two plans for such a company are put forward; the plan most favored corresponds closely with that being lobbied for by the Oil Mining Industry League. Finally, after recommending that the government virtually go into the oil business, the Energy Council majority cautions that bureaucrats must not be allowed to have a monopoly of power over the industry; there are some ringing expressions to the effect that "freedom of action by enterprises should be respected."

The minority report, representing the views of Professor Wakimura and one other member, declares that there is no need for an Oil Industry Law. To put the government into the business would only result in waste, inefficiency, higher prices, and losses for the economy as a whole. What is necessary is not a lot of strict regulations concerning refinery operation but a greater emphasis on Japanese production of crude oil and more Japanese tankers to haul it. Domestic producers may need some government help, but Arabian should have no difficulty, the minority believes, since it has already announced plans to build its own refineries and can find a sufficient market for its oil if an effort to do so is made among Japan's steel and power companies.

The draft outline of the new Oil Industry Law made its appearance in December at about the same time as the Energy Council's report. The earliest version I have seen was dated December 16, but discussions had gone on within MITI for more than a year. The process by which the law was prepared was characteristic of most legislation, which originates in government bureaus, not in the Diet. The original draft was written by a young man in the Mining Bureau of MITI, a quite junior official but a career officer, not a specialist in oil, who acted on orders of his superiors, meaning, ultimately, Eisaku Satō, the Minister of International Trade, and other cabinet-level officials. As is the usual custom, the drafter took his draft around to the various councils, committees, and business associations I have mentioned, or representatives of those bodies went to MITI to see him. He also visited the Commerce and Industry section of conservative party headquarters, where there are some headquarters staff who have worked in MITI or who have some interest in oil, perhaps through connections with oil companies. However, his meetings with party officials were not a specially vital step in the process; to him they were rather perfunctory. (When I asked him whether he had showed the draft to any Socialists he replied: "We don't bring them in until the final stages are reached.") The initiative was MITI's, not the party's. As one senior MITI official put it, "We had the *gimu*, the obligation for policy-making." In MITI, after a year of discussions, a consensus had been reached that for the sake of the entire economy the import of crude oil must be "liberalized" as part of the general and progressive abolition of import controls; but some kind of alternative controls clearly was essential to prevent foreign monopoly leading to price rises. Everybody had his usual chance to say something to the point (or off the point) of this matter; for sheer volume the mimeographed memoranda in the Japanese language that well up out of Tokyo offices and government bureaus can hardly be exceeded anywhere on earth. Basically, however, MITI had decided on some form of control before the talking began and felt responsible for enforcing it. By sending the oil mission to Europe the government could be sure that Japan had the latest information on the subject. But the role of the mission and the Energy Council was mainly to confirm, rather than radically to revise, MITI's policy line.

The Oil Industry Law has not yet been submitted to the Diet, but it is supposed to reach the floor during this session. It is being criticized as too restrictive in some quarters, mainly those that use energy rather than produce it, and some changes may have to be made in the law's provisions. This is all to the good; times have changed since 1934, when the first Oil Industry Law was passed. The new law might, of course, be diverted by more sensational legislation; however, though it may be watered down, there are no present plans to withdraw it.

Essentially, the law would require that oil refiners have permits from MITI before they can operate (in the first draft importers also were to be put on a permit system). In order to get permits the scale of oil refining, storage, and other facilities would have to conform to standards set by MITI. Changes in refinery capacity would require MITI approval; refiners and importers would have to submit annual plans, which would be subject to some control; MITI would also be empowered to set "standard" prices. In exercising all of these powers MITI would "listen to the opinions" of a new high-level Oil Deliberation Council, also to be created by the law. As presently written, the law would be permanent, but it might be reconsidered after ten years, "like the U.S. Security Treaty," one MITI official explained to me with a smile. No mention is made in the law of any "national policy company," but some such scheme seems likely to be brought up sooner or later.

CONCLUSION

All these announcements and proposals, full of complicated and technical-sounding language, were hardly noticed by the Japanese public. Coal excites them; it stands for something human—cave-ins or explosions where men die, peasant faces rising out of mine shafts, "struggles" with management. As late as 1960 a great mine strike nearly paralyzed politics. Oil is different. Only two per cent of consumption is produced within the country, all of that in a remote area on the Japan Sea where nobody wants to go. The rest comes in by ship from far places and is pumped into pipes of refineries at the water's edge, invisibly. From there tank cars or trucks take it to where it is consumed. Coal employs more than 200,000 people, who are a charge on the conscience of the politicians, or some of them. Far fewer work in oil. The coal pits are alive; oil refineries are a mass of pipes and gauges, passionless, tended by humans but dehumanized. Their "thruput" is "automated"; they are up to date and dead.

True, the public knows that most crude oil is controlled by a few foreign companies; it has a vague idea of international oil imperialism. Foreign capital is more prominent in oil than in any other industry in Japan; foreign money and technology have equipped the refineries and are deeply involved in the new petrochemical industry, with its host of weird but useful new products. Foreigners sit on the boards of several of the biggest Japanese oil companies. The Japanese left seeks to interpret these facts to its own advantage; but there is no public memory of oil strikes, no image of unemployed workers on relief grumbling away their time in oil shantytowns. Wages in the oil industry are near the top of the industrial sector. The sweated oil worker, slave of foreign oppression, does not exist as an issue to inflame Japanese politics.

Nevertheless oil, an international commodity, pumps through the national body and vitally affects the national interest. Without energy, without oil, nothing moves, and nobody is more committed to movement than the Japanese. The people may not be concerned with oil as long as it is abundant, but government officials and planners are. Nearly all Japanese would agree that their country, poor as it is in oil resources, cannot allow free access of foreigners to the Japanese oil market. Whether they are "right" or not, a large majority fears this would lead to disaster.

In the last year or two Japanese crudes produced in the Middle East and Southeast Asia have begun to arrive in this country for the first time. Because refining facilities are tied closely to British and American interests and rely on exclusive crude supply contracts, some difficulties have already arisen over the refining of this oil. These problems may increase; they may be solved by putting the government into the oil business in some way. One thing, however, seems certain: Japan cannot be prevented from trying to develop its own sources of oil supply. This is not at present a matter of noisy "oil nationalism." Most informed Japanese believe that for the larger part of their supply of crude oil they will have to depend indefinitely on foreign sources; however, they can be counted on to try to expand their own reserves, at home and abroad. This means they will give some kind of protection to Japanese producers as well as refiners. In any case, "liberalization" of crude oil imports will not mean a free oil market. Import controls will be followed by some new framework of regulations, arrived at by the customary diffuse, round-robin method of reaching consensus that I have described, and rationalized by reference to European example. All independent countries have an oil policy, and Japan is no exception.

Finally, the Japanese government is not only sensitive about a Western oil monopoly; it also takes a cautious attitude toward Soviet oil. In 1960 Soviet crude was 3.5 per cent of total imports; in 1961 it was 6.4 per cent, and 10 per cent is being called the "danger point." Young MITI bureaucrats may banter with their oil industry friends and ask why they don't buy more Soviet crude; but when forced to reply whether such action would be supported by their superiors, the young bureaucrats are likely to fall silent. Russia clearly seeks to invade the Japanese oil market for its own reasons. But the oil industry here is closely tied to Western interests; Western technology and capital, I repeat, are vital to the growing petrochemical industry as well as to refinery expansion. These close relationships flow from basic political decisions aligning Japan with the West. These decisions are certainly not immutable, but they are a matter of the deepest national interest and would not be changed lightly. Oil crises, like textile crises, could put a strain on Japan's relations with America and Europe; but to change these relations in any fundamental way more than oil or textiles would have to be considered.

PART THREE ❀ ❀ ❀

JAPAN IN ASIA AND
THE WORLD

CHAPTER 22

ON THE "ORPHAN JAPAN"

February 28, 1959

In an article last year about Japan's efforts to expand its market in India, I concluded with the observation that India meant different things to different Japanese, but that knowledge of the country was limited because very few Japanese had been there or were likely to go.

With travel to South and Southeast Asia now rapidly increasing, the theme of Japanese ignorance of other Asian countries has been taken up by more and more writers in recent months, and nowhere more eloquently than in an article entitled "Recognition that Japan Is an Orphan," that appeared in the October 1958 number of the magazine *Chūō Kōron*. The author, Miss Chie Nakane, is a lecturer in the Institute of Oriental Culture at Tokyo University. Brought up in Peking, she graduated from Tsuda Women's College in Tokyo and received her master's degree in history from Tokyo University Graduate School. Later she became interested in anthropology and spent three years doing field research in north and south India and one year at universities in Europe under a grant from a Swedish foundation. Upon her return to Japan last year she was requested by the editor of *Chūō Kōron* to report on her observations of foreign countries, and her article was given the place of honor in the magazine.

Miss Nakane's essay is addressed to scholars and other intellectuals. With her own impressions of the outside world still fresh, she argues that Japanese intellectuals should spend less time constructing elaborate theories about the "Asian" or "European" character of Japan's cultural development and give more attention to learning the facts about societies other than their own. One object of her essay was to reply to a long article by Professor Tadao Umesao of Osaka City University, which appeared in the July 1958 number of the same magazine. In his article Professor Umesao, an ecologist, presented a geographical theory purporting to account for the many close resemblances between Japan and Western Europe. Dividing the Old World into the First Region (Japan and Western Europe) and the Second Region (everything in between), Umesao maintained that racially, linguistically, and from the point of view of religion, the countries of the former represent far more homogeneous cultures than those of the latter, e.g., Southeast Asia or the Balkans. This is primarily because Japan and Western Europe both are remote from the great "Dry Zone'" which cuts across the Old World from northeast to southwest and which has played a great part in racial migrations and cultural diffusion. Western Europe and Japan both are industrialized areas which originally lay outside the boundaries of civilization; both borrowed the cultures of the civilized centers; both, it is alleged, have passed through various stages— feudalism, absolutism, and bourgeois revolution—to reach their present level of capitalist development. Other writers besides Professor Umesao have stressed the "European" nature of Japanese culture; these arguments are not new, but, as Sir George Sansom pointed out long ago with respect to Japanese-English similarities, they rest on a series of ingenious parallels that should not be pushed too far.

Miss Nakane is skeptical of all such formulations. Obviously moved by her foreign experiences, she concludes that Japan belongs essentially to no one but itself and that what it needs today is not theories of cultural affinity but more facts about other countries to serve as a guide for autonomous thinking and acting. She would like to buttress the desire for "independence" with more information. Since this attitude is uncommon in Japan, where emphasis in the social sciences still is laid on theory rather than empirical research, I have, with the author's permission, translated the major portion of her article, omitting those parts concerned mainly with her academic views on the role of personality and social structure in national development, and focusing on sections which bear in a more general way on Japan's ignorance of contemporary Asia and on what should be the nation's proper course in the future. For one of the pleasant things about this country is that even young anthropologists can sometimes have a chance to explain their foreign policy views in a national magazine.

*   *   *

Japan is very proud of being the most Westernized country in Asia, but do the Japanese know Europe in the same way that the Indians know England? In no country in the world are scholars so expert in the new theories of foreign countries as those of Japan; in no country are foreign theories so loved. We are familiar with European literature, art, learning and technology; but all these things have been imported in abstract form as fragmentary elements of culture, and what we think of as "Europe" is very abstract and to some extent Japanicized. For example, the influence of Europe in literature since the Meiji Restoration is obvious, but European life and the Christian tradition, which form the basis of European literature, are not necessarily grasped. Formal academic theories, particularly in the humanities and social sciences, are well understood, but little concern is shown for where the materials came from out of which such theories were constructed. The theories of Western scholars are the fountainhead of our scholarship and are respected like the law itself; day and night we study them one after the other, Marx or Max Weber or Toynbee and so on, but we do not construct our theories from our own materials. In the natural sciences this may not matter, since experiments will quickly reveal errors, but in the humanities and social sciences, where there is not the same degree of scientific procedure, fakers may pass as fine scholars.

In all the former colonial countries there was much personal intercourse with the mother country, and through colonial policies and administration, colonies were brought into contact with the thought, action, and manner of living of the mother country. Education was carried on by foreign teachers in foreign languages, and students could learn directly from the teachers of the mother country through long study abroad. For these reasons the depth of the experience of these countries through human contact with Western Europe far surpasses the imagination of the Japanese. The Indian people may not know the works of Goethe or Balzac, but through Englishmen they have realistically experienced the European world; in India there was direct contact and confrontation, opposition was pressed in every direction, there was a process of resistance and conquest. This contact with Europe was an excellent thing from the viewpoint of knowing one's adversary, and it is a great strength in the circumstances of India's emergence on the international stage at the present time. The same thing has been true, more or less, in all the other countries of colonial Asia. In this sense Japan is at the greatest disadvantage; here is one weakness of Japan's present diplomatic position.

Just because Japan is situated in Asia and has some comprehension of things European does not mean that it is fit to become a bridge between the two. While we rejoice that the feelings of Egypt, Iraq, and the other Asian-Arab countries are good toward Japan, they may at any time change and become hostile like China. It is essential first of all to know each country well. How many Japanese who sympathize with the utterances of Nehru and Nasser really understand India or Egypt? The important thing is why Nehru speaks as he does, not the contents of his speech. And why he speaks as he does is conditioned by India's place in the international arena, by various internal conditions, and by tradition.

While listening to Nasser's words last summer, how many Japanese were able to call to mind the burning desert heat; the flowing of the mother Nile, which brings fertility and gives to man the happiness of endless life; the functioning society made up of the many various types of people who dwell in that river's fertile plain; the prayers of fanatical Islam, and the people playing in the night clubs, like apparitions of the Farouk era; the poor who live on a level with animals; the wandering nomads; the cunning merchants of uncertain nationality who fatten by filling their stomachs with colonial corruption; the whirlpool of thought and emotion, like Shanghai in the old days; the premodern personal relations; the terrible confusion in the social and economic spheres after the departure of European and American influence, and so on? Japanese intellectuals like to blame colonialism for all the confusion and evil in the underdeveloped countries. If that is true, were India and Egypt ideal places before the arrival of British power? Japanese intellectuals are accustomed to think of nationalist movements in terms simply of "organized labor" or the "aroused masses." How far do they understand the effort involved, and the actual record of India's or Egypt's emergence out of the quagmire of today, which is an accumulation of the long history of the past that it has been their fate to bear? What is necessary today is for Japan to have sufficient materials, and interpretations of those materials, to understand and judge the various phenomena which are arising all over Asia. . . .

When I went there I discovered that the Europe I had been told about in school was very different from the real Europe, just as I was shocked when India far exceeded my imagination of it. To mention only a few examples: among the English, who are always depicted as solemn and cold, were some who were good-humored and kind; indeed, they helped me whenever I was in trouble, without fail. In Italy the waiters in restaurants were handsome and considerate and served the food in a pleasant manner. Even though I knew Michelangelo and Giotto I had no knowledge of such things. In a certain town in Sweden, the richest country in Europe, which boasts of its most modern way of living, I found a dirty privy such as one would see in a Japanese farmhouse. When I came close to people living in the cities of the small countries of Europe, which seem so very modern, I, who had been brought up in Tokyo, felt that they were very countrified. Except for London, there is no city in Europe with such massive concentrations of people as Tokyo or Osaka. Of course, Paris and Rome are magnificent old cities, but Stockholm and Amsterdam are small, about on a par with middle-sized cities in Japan. When I returned to London I was as happy as if I had returned to Tokyo from a trip to the country. On the other hand, the life of farmers in Denmark and Holland is amazingly modern and gave me a feeling that I had come very thoroughly to Europe. The social influence of the aristocracy is very strong everywhere in Europe; capitalists and workers are sharply divided, and the opposition between them in the social and economic spheres is everywhere extreme. By comparison Japan seems a democratic country; in Japanese society the aristocracy (which, after all, no longer exists), capitalists, and workers are all much nearer one. Only after living in England, where vegetables, meat, dairy products, cotton cloth, and other necessities of life are for the most part not produced but must be imported, and where from fall to spring the sun shines hardly at all, can one understand why the English wanted India so much. And the English who were cruel to the Indians are just as cruel to those of their own who break the rules.

I have mentioned only a few examples, but the point is that only by living in Europe, seeing it at firsthand and accumulating and consolidating one's experiences, can one come to know the place. And unless we truly understand the countries of Europe we cannot understand either their history or the movements of the international situation.

With the exception of China we know no more about Asia than we do about Europe. Today we are having our first contacts with the countries west of India. The inclination of the Japanese to look toward Europe, resulting from many years of contact with European culture, is a great obstacle to our understanding of Asia today. India and Egypt can never be understood so long as modernization and living standards are the only criteria used. But the Japanese, accustomed to a modern way of living, and with a tendency to place all value on European things, are unable to appreciate the countries of Asia. There are superb things in every country. Why is it that the Japanese, who value Christian culture highly, cannot do the same for Hindu culture?

Aside from a few people who have a mania for Asia, Japanese living in the area say they hate it and want to go to Europe or return home to Japan. This is because they know very little about Asia. People say that I like India; but it took three years of living in India before I could understand the country calmly and before I reached the stage where I was happy there. It was not merely a question of staying in India; fortunately, by pursuing research in cultural anthropology, I was blessed with the most favorable conditions by which to know India. Even so, I still like Peking and Rome better than Calcutta.

The Japanese newspapermen who had to transmit interpretations of the

Baghdad uprising last summer were perplexed over how to do their job, because they knew nothing whatever of Western Asia. To know a country it is necessary to know the language and have considerable experience in the area, to know its history, social structure, and culture. When I traveled in the Arab world last year there was only one member of our embassy in Egypt and one in the Baghdad legation who knew Arabic. Although these two studied extremely hard and did their work with enthusiasm, they were on a very low level in their missions. Japanese diplomacy would be strengthened if there were such people at the ambassador or counselor level. Those Foreign Service officers who could speak Arabic said, "We will spend our careers in the Arab world," and they showed by their forlorn manner that they felt they had been diverted to the back streets of the diplomatic corps. Our Foreign Service officials all over Asia are dreaming only of being transferred quickly to Europe or America.

I had a pleasant talk with a man from our embassy who could speak Arabic. We sat and drank beer beside the Nile. After a year in Europe I was overcome by the scene: the flowing of the vast Nile; the long-skirted, loose-falling garments of the Egyptians, and their slow, deliberate gait; the pyramids in the desert with the fierce sun on them; the inexpressible serenity of that old country, and the chaos and energy of the newly rising country now standing at the focus of the world's attention. My companion spoke quietly of the ancient struggle between desert and Nile, and then he remarked, "The other day a Japanese who had been a student in Paris came here and denounced everything about Egypt, saying only, 'Paris is good, Paris is good.'" My friend's voice was sad, and I suddenly felt the lack of education of many Japanese intellectuals, and cold chills ran up and down my spine. When I was in India it was the same: Japanese who came there said merely what a dreadful place it was, how hot, how dirty. Many Japanese seem able to see things only by such shallow standards. Then there is the opposite type, who goes to Asian conferences and praises Asia merely because it is Asia. Neither type does Japan any good.

How can Japan, in its peculiar position and weak as it is in knowledge of conditions in foreign lands, make a contribution to mankind? In an international sense Japan has until now been a country cousin of the world. Japanese receptiveness to the completely disparate cultures of China and Europe has seldom been paralleled in history; but this power of understanding has never been used correctly, because there has not been much direct contact with other peoples. We must get rid of our vice of knowing other countries merely through ideas and not by their actual conditions. The world is growing narrower, and the number of Japanese going abroad, as well as the number of foreigners coming to Japan, is increasing. If the energy of the Japanese, the living, creative strength of more than 90 million people, is properly and wisely brought to bear, who knows what contribution Japan may be able to make to mankind in the future?

Truly to understand the countries of Asia, the Japanese should avoid too much inclination toward Europe or too fanatical an attachment to the Asian-African bloc. I believe that to overvalue Asia and low-rate Europe, or the reverse, means that the Japanese cannot really understand either and is proof that their understanding of Japan itself is not clear. We must escape from such shallow, biased, and emotional concepts. Individual likes and dislikes are all very well, but the failure to understand the value of different cultures causes trouble.

Only when the Japanese have a true understanding of other countries will they have a good understanding of their own peculiarities. In its weak, disadvantageous position, Japan must play its part skillfully in the international arena. Because it is weak, it must not wantonly join any large group or take its color from that group. If it does it will inevitably get into an impossible position and have to pay dearly for the loss. Japan must make more of itself. What matters is somehow to maintain a free position and take flexible actions. That seems to be the special privilege of an orphan. And Japan's international position will only be clear when it is consciously realized that Japan is an orphan. Thus the question is not whether Japan is culturally between Europe and Asia or politically between liberalism and communism. It is not a question of preserving neutrality. In certain situations it might be best to join the Arab-Asian group, but at the same time it is necessary to consider relations with the powers of Europe and America. It is a question of autonomously looking at practical realities and acting. If we are wise, I believe we can do this.

CHAPTER 23

THE JAPANESE IN INDIA TODAY

New Delhi
November 14, 1961

On the grounds of the Japanese Embassy in New Delhi, set well away from the white-painted chancery and the other buildings, stands a small teahouse made entirely of materials imported from Japan. Its unpainted wooden walls would in the humid Japanese air gradually take on a darker, richer texture, but here they have merely been dried out by the hot Indian sun, and the ornamental scrollwork on the balcony is beginning to warp and crack. In the garden pool, where one might expect to find stones placed artlessly in a row across dark water covered with lilies or lotus flowers, a mustachioed Indian gardener with his clothing hiked up about his thighs sloshes around in two or three inches of muddy slime on some obscure errand. The teahouse is wan-looking; it does not make its point; and a rolled-up tennis net that somebody has dropped in the entrance-way evidently is used more often than the tea utensils lying on the dusty *tatami* floor.

The Japanese in India today in a sense resemble their teahouse: deposited in incongruous surroundings, they have great difficulty communicating with others and others with them, and they keep very much to themselves. For the most part they are an unloved and unloving group. It did not require the five weeks I have spent in this country to learn that most Japanese here would rather not be here; that they regard the Indians as a shiftless, sanctimonious lot who talk of saintliness and idealism but are woefully lacking in honest performance; or that the Japanese in their turn are believed by the Indians to be opaque, uncommunicative, and untrustworthy, clever imitators who have worked hard and got themselves an industrially advanced society but who lack any real tradition of humaneness.

How often I have thought in the past weeks how much they are missing of each other! Could it possibly be, for example, that no Indian had ever caught and fully appreciated as I had the grace with which a Japanese businessman, in a Calcutta restaurant, stopped in the middle of a sentence to mimic the way Indian women at his factory walk with baskets of earth on their heads—a stroke of inimitable theater by (as it turned out) a talented amateur *kabuki* performer? Or that no Japanese had sat as I sat in a Bombay hotel room and been quite entirely caught up and absorbed while a South Indian newspaperman who talked with his wrists, elbows, and shoulders as well as his mouth gave me a five-hour lecture on what was right and what was wrong with his country?

However that might be, there is clearly a kind of gross failure to register on both sides, which has to be acknowledged before one can go on to write about the more objective relationships that exist between Indians and Japanese. Indians use all sorts of clichés to describe this failure: they say the Japanese are not "with it," they don't "click," or "we don't use the same wave length." Partly, of course, the problem is language. Japanese are notoriously poor at English, while educated Indians speak English with a relish unknown to any but a tiny, untypical handful of Japanese. But beyond language there are all the great differences of politics, history, social manners, cultural background, and temperament. Many Indians and foreigners in India dislike the Japanese because of World War II or because of their unsavory commercial reputation in the past. Little factual information about Japan is available in India. The Japanese Embassy's public relations efforts leave much to be desired, and the few "friendship" associations that exist are mainly used for commercial purposes. When the Bombay Indo-Japanese Association opened a Japanese-language class, 50 people came to the first session; but most of them were company presidents who preferred golf to the rigors of Japanese verbs, and by the third meeting only one loyal student remained. A few Indians are being trained in Japanese subjects under the auspices of the Indian School of International Studies in Delhi; it is hoped that they will eventually spread their knowledge by teaching in Indian universities. Beyond this an occasional Indian shows some interest in the "simplicity" or "tranquillity" of Japanese life—something of the quality of grace in narrow circumstances gets across to a few with an appeal partly esthetic, partly religious—but the Japanese are regarded by most as clannish, shy, ambiguous, not given to clarifying their purposes even when they know them, imitators with a cruel streak, "chrysanthemum and sword" people. Japanese and Indians often use the same stereotyped expressions in describing each other: the other side is too cautious, untrustworthy, negotiates too slowly, and so on.

Thus the teahouse sits on the Indian plain without getting much of its message across. Nevertheless, between 1,200 and 1,500 Japanese are living in India today, and the vast majority of them have no more time to think of teahouses than the Indians do. As a matter of fact, the building was donated by a mission of leading Japanese iron and steel manufacturers who visited India early in 1960 to negotiate an iron ore development scheme with the central government. Along with their commercial interest they brought a little culture and deposited it—after proper ceremonies presided over by a tea "master" also imported intact for the occasion—on the unfamiliar grass among the strange plants, in an atmosphere and light that make this traditional structure look like a banal cottage.

This very well sets the tone of Japanese activity in India at the present time. Like the steelmakers, most other Japanese are here for commercial or technological reasons. In Japan steel production is steadily rising, with a target of 48 million tons set for 1970; to reach this goal the Japanese must have iron ore and manganese, among other things. Both are available in India, the former in very large quantities and of excellent quality. At the same time, Japanese plant and machinery manufacturers are eager to increase their exports, and the Indian market obviously is expanding.

India seeks technical assistance from the world in order to transform a stagnant society into a modern one at high speed. This process is already under way, and it is one of the great dramas of this age. There is no need to make too much of Japan's part in Indian development. Japan and India both look to the West far more than to each other. Japanese participation in Indian economic growth is still primarily in the stage of export promotion and cannot begin to compare with that of America, Great Britain, Soviet Russia, or even Western Germany. Long criticized for their imitativeness, the Japanese are now being reproached for their excessive stinginess, their lack of "moral commitment" to Indian needs, their "bankers' attitudes." To these charges the Japanese reply that they have joined the "aid India club" and are doing what they can "within their means." Clearly the definition of means varies, depending upon whether one is Indian, American, or Japanese. However, though the two countries are separated politically and are planets apart culturally and temperamentally, Japan today is associated in a small but growing way with international efforts to assist India. Japanese nationals are active in a number of fields where they are competitive and have something to offer. What follows in this Report sums up Japanese participation so far in the great Indian effort to reach economic "take-off."

JAPANESE GOVERNMENT LOANS AND CREDITS

Japan's debut as a creditor in Indian economic development took place with the signing of the first yen credit agreement in February 1958. By that time the acute foreign-exchange shortage that has afflicted India since the early years of the Second Five-Year Plan (1956–61) already was being felt; the 18 billion yen ($50 million) credit was the chief fruit of a state visit to Japan by Prime Minister Nehru.

This was Japan's first postwar loan to any government, and the decision to grant it was taken at the highest levels in Prime Minister Kishi's government. Conservative Finance Ministry officials argued that Japan itself was very short of foreign exchange and that a credit to India would invite unfulfillable demands from other countries in the same area. These arguments were overcome by others in the Ministry of International Trade and Industry and by powerful organizations of businessmen who maintained that Japan must engage in economic co-operation with the underdeveloped nations to maintain its competitive position in those expanding markets for the new products of Japanese factories: the chemicals, electrical equipment, construction machinery, and other capital goods that were growing rapidly in importance in Japan's total output. It was also argued that Japanese sources of raw materials must be diversified and extended, and that since mainland China was cut off as a source of iron ore for the foreseeable future, Indian iron might be developed into a major source of supply for Japan's booming steel mills.

These views began to be reflected in the reports of many Japanese economic survey missions that visited South and Southeast Asia. As one summed it up:

It is obvious to everyone that the economic development of Southeast Asia is essential to improve the welfare of the people of those areas and raise their living standards. On our trip we received the strong impression that the development of the region is also an essential condition for the maturing of Japan's own economy. Industrialization in these countries is inevitable if economic levels are to rise. Much must be done in agriculture, but industry is the only way to give jobs to these rapidly growing populations. The advanced countries must not be frightened at the thought of creating competitors to try to prevent the industrial advance of these backward lands. If one industrial country fails to help, the process will go ahead anyway with the help of others, and the country that hesitates will have lost its position entirely. Japan must still import capital, but we must also become an exporter of capital to less developed areas. There may be limits to what we can do, because our national income is low compared with the other industrial societies; but we must not shirk doing what we can.

Less than a month after the first yen credit agreement was signed, another agreement was concluded in New Delhi between the Indian government and a Japanese government-sponsored steel mission for a long-term loan of $8 million to be used (along with a larger amount from the United States Development Loan Fund) to develop iron deposits at Kiriburu in the Rourkela district of Orissa State, some 200 miles from Vizakhapatnam on the Indian east coast.

Both these agreements were concluded without any profound Japanese awareness of Indian conditions, and both have been slow in fulfillment. When the yen credit became available, the Export-Import Bank of Japan, which was to supervise its expenditure, did not even have a representative in New Delhi. Each contract with Japanese suppliers of machinery involved long and sometimes heated negotiations between the Indian Embassy in Tokyo, the Japan Plant Export Association and other agencies concerned. Although the credit was supposed to be obligated within three years, nearly 10 per cent of the funds remained unused in August 1961. Of the used portion roughly two-thirds went into the Indian public (government) sector. Electrical machinery was most important; some of it went into power generating stations, e.g., at Bhakra Dam, where the Hitachi Company supplied five turbines and two transformers, along with two technicians to help install them. Other public sector purchases included two coal washeries, vehicles and equipment for road-building projects, and one seagoing vessel. Japanese machinery was also acquired for two plants to manufacture communications equipment (principally porcelain insulators) and for six other assorted small-scale industrial establishments. One-third of the first yen credit was set aside for the private sector, where a total of 44 contracts have so far been concluded, involving supply of equipment for rayon and paper plants, two small ships, and a small number of assorted industrial machines. In most cases Japanese technical personnel have come to India to supervise the installation of equipment and a number of Indians have been sent to Japan for short-term training.

The Kiriburu iron-ore project has moved very slowly, but production is expected to begin within the next year, and by 1964 Japan hopes to receive two million tons annually from this area. Payment for this ore will be an important source of foreign exchange for India. However, since most of the Kiriburu ore is scheduled for eventual consumption by India's own steel mills at Rourkela, the Japanese are now more interested in the large deposits at Bailadila, south of Rourkela in the same general area. To develop these deposits a steel mission (the same one that donated the teahouse) signed an agreement with the Indian government in March 1960 for a long-term loan of $21 million for machinery and equipment. In return Japan expects by 1966 to receive four million additional tons of ore annually, also to be paid for (rather than being credited against the loan). If present imports are maintained, in another five years Japan may be buying between eight and ten million tons a year and will be the largest market for Indian iron.

Conversations with Indian government officials responsible for negotiating the Kiriburu and Bailadila agreements reveal something of the Indian attitude toward collaboration with Japan in this and other fields. A Joint Secretary in the Ministry of Commerce and Industry spoke with a sense of suppressed excitement about Indian plans and the philosophy of the "mixed economy." He named off the government enterprises for which he had some administrative responsibility, calling them "my iron mines," "my foundries": "Take my wrist-watch factory in Bangalore, for example. [He pointed to a huge map of India on the wall behind him.] First we imported the watch movements complete from Japan. Now we have brought in the machines to make the movements and cases from local raw materials. We brought in 12 'Japs,' too, with their wives. The factory isn't built yet, but we have put them in one of the unused bays at H.M.T. [Hindustan Machine Tool] and they have already made a few prototypes. We've given one to the Prime Minister and a few others. The first watches will sell for about 95 rupees [about $20], not cheap enough for the masses, but once production gets under way the price will go down. We like these yen credits, you know. We get the know-how, machinery, and technicians with no political strings attached. Of course, if the interest rates were lower, they would be even better."

He went on: "In some cases the Indian government just has to set the pace. Clinical thermometers are another example. You would think that anybody would know how to make thermometers, but you would be wrong. Indians didn't know how, and foreign companies would rather export to India than invest in India. We wanted self-sufficiency, so we set up a public sector company in Calcutta, the National Instruments Co. It has a technical assistance contract with the Mitsui Trading Company, which acts as agent for a Japanese thermometer maker. We pay Mitsui a technical fee and a small royalty and we get the know-how and can stop importing thermometers. That is our preferred technique all along the line.

"I would like to see the Japanese buy 15 to 20 million tons of iron ore from India. We will also sell them pig iron. And yet in the back of my mind I still wonder a little about all this iron. I told some of the 'Japs' when we were negotiating, 'You can't help but have relations with China again in a few years, and China is your natural market. How can you make such long-range commitments for iron from India?' They replied, 'Yes, relations with China may eventually come, but in the meantime we have to make 48 million tons of steel by 1970 and need iron to do it.' They are buying ore everywhere, not just in Asia but in South America as well.

"I liked Japan very much when I went there to visit, but I really can't communicate with those chaps, you know. They spread out to conquer or to trade, but they seem to me a supremely home-centered, home-conscious people. On the other hand, I must say the Indian negotiators put a strain on our relations by being too commercial-minded and asking too high a price for iron ore."

Besides the first yen credit and the two iron-ore agreements, Japan has granted three other government-backed loans to India in recent years. The first of these, a "suppliers' credit" for $10 million, was agreed upon at the meeting of the World Bank consortium in August 1958 and was spent mainly for electrical and textile machinery. A second credit for $10 million, guaranteed at the March 1959 meeting of the consortium, is being used for the same types of machinery in both public and private sectors. The latest credit, known to New Delhi as the "second yen credit," for the yen equivalent of $80 million, became effective in October 1961. The most important single project under this credit will be a urea fertilizer plant to be located at Gorakpur, in Uttar Pradesh. The second yen credit also involves other projects and is meant to cover only the first two years of the Third Five-Year Plan. Further credits are expected to follow in due course.

Even after all these loans and credits, totaling $150 million so far, Japan's share of world plant exports to South and Southeast Asia is only around 5 per cent, compared with Britain's 30 per cent, America's 25 per cent, and West Germany's 15 per cent. However, through these measures, as well as through constant efforts to expand commodity trade, Japan hopes to establish firm technological relationships with Indian industry. In addition to these multipurpose loans the Japanese are currently responding to Indian needs in several special fields.

ASSISTANCE TO SMALL-SCALE INDUSTRIES

To help India develop small-scale machine industries the Japanese government is collaborating in the establishment of an Indo-Japanese Prototype Production and Training Center on the outskirts of Howrah, a suburb of Calcutta, in West Bengal. Here is a field in which the Japanese have had particularly rich experience at home, where a pattern of small industries long ago was developed to fit the conditions of Japanese economic life: an abundance of literate skilled and semi-skilled labor, adequate power and transport, and a relative scarcity of capital. Small industries acted as a sponge to take up some of the excess population moving from farm to city, and large manufacturers grew accustomed to subcontracting with small shops for a variety of parts and processes. In the web of Japanese industry tight personal relationships grew between large and small enterprises. Since World War II the productivity of small industry as a whole has greatly risen; machinery and techniques of production are being steadily modernized.

In India, on the other hand, what manufacturing industry existed before the war was in the hands of a few large interests like the Tata family, while small-scale plants supplied with power-driven machinery, as distinct from cottage industries of the type encouraged by Gandhi, hardly existed at all. Today, with the Indian population largely illiterate, per-capita income at about $60 a year, and at least half the national income still derived from agriculture, most Indians do not have money to eat adequately, much less to go into business, and what capital is available is controlled by merchants and moneylenders whose horizons tend to be commercial rather than entrepreneurial. Too many of them want a quick profit and the quality of the product may be damned. Until very recently there were no credit facilities to speak of for would-be entrepreneurs, and today they are only beginning to function.

Indian government specialists in small-scale industries know these things and much else besides. They feel strongly that in order to absorb many of the 17 million new people who will be added to the labor force during the next Plan period, and to spread the economic power of this developing country more widely and if possible more evenly, people must be encouraged to engage in small productive enterprises; workers must be trained in new skills and provided with machines according to some scheme they can afford. Government is committed to promoting "ancillary industries" in many fields, some of them fields in which the demand for products is as yet uncertain. The great emphasis of Indian planning is on heavy, basic industries like steel, power, and transport. But a strong and explicit Socialist flavor permeates the plans, and small industry is very appealing to government officials whose ideal, at least, is to raise up the poor and keep the rich from getting richer at the poor's expense. In India's "Socialist pattern of society" small industries have an important economic and moral place.

Indian interest in Japanese co-operation in this field dates from the visit of President Rajendra Prasad to Tokyo in 1958. He came back full of enthusiasm for small factory development, and in August 1959 a mission of Japanese specialists toured India for two months and submitted a report to the central government. In January 1960 an agreement was signed, setting up the Howrah training center. Japan is contributing machinery worth around $1 million, plus a staff of 20 instructors. In Tokyo the government has selected a technical director for the project, while the machinery and teaching staff are being taken from various Japanese firms. The Indian government has appointed a director with administrative responsibility for the project and is bearing the cost of the land, building, and power facilities, as well as local accommodations and transport for the Japanese staff.

The Howrah center is the third such project undertaken by the Indian government. (One, at Rajkot, near Bombay, has American assistance; another, at Okla, near Delhi, is with German collaboration.) The center has three stated objectives: (1) to train engineers, foremen, and shop workers for small-scale manufacturing industries (according to the government's rule of thumb, any business with less than 50 lakhs of rupees, or about $1 million, in fixed assets is a small business); (2) to develop and produce prototype machines, tools, and accessories for reproduction on a commercial basis; and (3) to develop special types of machinery suited to Indian conditions. Each Japanese vocational instructor will have an Indian counterpart, and as many as possible of them will be sent to Japan for several months. Six people already have been selected from Indian government bureaus and are busy studying Japanese in preparation for assignment to the center. It is hoped that some of the Japanese who come to teach will know English, but interpreters are certain to be needed, at least in the initial stages.

At first the center will concentrate on making a few types of machines for which there is wide demand: wire-drawing machines, thermo-plastic extruders, die-casting machines, and the like. Trainees, 250 of them at a time, will be brought to Howrah for several months and housed in the same area with their instructors. Candidates for training also will be chosen from the technical staffs of the Departments of Industries of the states and the various small industries organizations of the central government. Machines produced will eventually be turned over to private entrepreneurs, by a method not yet decided, for commercial reproduction. The center will then shift to other types of machines.

When I visited the 120-acre site, most of it still marshy and planted in rice, Japanese machinery was being installed at one end of the main building by young Japanese running around in coveralls, baseball caps, and sneakers, while at the other end long files of Indian laborers were pouring cement or moving gravel and sand by the basket-on-the-head method. The young Indian director indicated with a sweep of his arm where shops, houses, and other buildings were to stand. He was eager for the arrival of Prime Minister Ikeda from Tokyo later this month to inaugurate the project. "We are just imitating what you in the United States have already done," he said, "to help small people to learn and get on their feet." And he confided rather proudly to me: "Our whole mind is on ourselves, and we will take from everybody as long as there are no strings attached. I was in a private company before I joined the government, but in this country the public sector is far more exciting and important. We are going to spread the economic power more evenly"—he sounded like a quote from the Five-Year Plan as he gestured again toward the distant palm grove, while disregarding the cluster of dismal brick and straw hovels of the local construction gang that filled up the foreground of the scene.

Back in Calcutta I talked with the Japanese technical director of the Howrah project. At sixty, he is nearly 20 years older than his Indian boss; a Kyoto University graduate in electrical engineering, who went into the colonial administration in Korea before the war. Afterward, like many other professionals, he lost out when the empire collapsed and found things difficult at home; finally he wound up in New Delhi, where he spent six years as a member of a private Japanese business consulting service. I had known his type before in many an economic research institute or other such establishment in Japan, and I met others like him during my stay in India, engineers from the old South Manchurian Railway Research Bureau now writing papers on ramie cultivation in Assam or on the subcontracting system in automobile manufacture for Indian research bureaus.

The Japanese director at Howrah told me that private business in Japan had opposed the project but had been overruled by the politicians. But mostly he was preoccupied by the problems of working alongside Indians. His points were simple ones, and he put them simply. Indians, he said, "always will say they know how to do a thing, whether they do or not. Try to tell them how, and they say they know. This leads to mistakes and maybe will ruin a machine. Tell an Indian sweeper to sweep up and he will sweep up, perhaps; but he doesn't know what his sweeping has to do with anything else. Because he is a sweeper only, he performs an isolated act, he does not feel integrated in a productive process. Just so India is importing machinery from all over the world, but Indians are not changing their mentality to absorb and integrate the machinery in a new industrial society. They are merely copying machines without changing their own thought processes. And caste gets in the way at every stage: the man on the lathe must have another to bring him his materials and a third to clean up the mess he makes around his machine."

ASSISTANCE TO AGRICULTURE

In agriculture, too, the Japanese are beginning to make a substantial contribution to Indian growth. India is not primarily a wet rice culture, as is Japan; but the Ministry of Food and Agriculture in New Delhi estimates that a third of the cultivated area of the country is in paddy. Where rice is grown Indian yields are among the world's lowest. The Indian plow has been in use since Vedic times, and cultivation practices are extremely primitive. Most of the rainfall in India comes during the monsoon, and irrigation and drainage works need a great deal of improvement. Farmers are likely to use either too much water or too little, or to use it at the wrong times. Chemical fertilizers are too expensive for most, and credit is controlled by moneylenders or landlords. Animal manure is burned for fuel rather than being used on the fields, and the harvest is threshed by primitive methods that often damage the crop.

Indian interest in Japanese rice culture began a decade ago, when the government of Bombay sent a small agricultural mission to Japan. There the Indians observed a combination of practices which add up simply to very intensive cultivation of rice on very small plots of land. They saw how Japanese farmers carefully selected and disinfected seed, how they planted them at a relatively low seed rate in beds raised above the level of the surrounding fields. They watched, and participated in, the transplanting of seedlings, from bed to field in neat rows, far enough apart to allow interculture by specially designed but simple tools. They learned of the necessity for very heavy applications of fertilizer according to a set schedule, and some of them stayed long enough in Japan to observe Japanese methods of harvesting, drying, and threshing the rice. Above all, they were impressed by the enormous amount of personal care each farmer gave to his crop at every stage from seed selection to harvest; how he fertilized and weeded and sprayed during the growing period, and how he stopped work altogether at a point well before the maturation of the crop.

On their return, members of the Bombay mission began experiments of their own which soon drew the attention of top leaders, including the President and the Prime Minister. Soon after a campaign began under the direction of the Minister for Agriculture, a man of peasant origins, who saw that the spread of more intensive methods of rice cultivation could help solve the shortage of food grains that afflicts this country and holds back its development in every sphere.

Since then improved rice-growing practices, more or less inspired by the Japanese example, have gradually spread and productivity of this crop has slowly risen. In a 1959 report on "India's Food Crisis and Steps to Meet It," a top-flight team of American agriculturists sponsored by the Ford Foundation recommended that "in attempts to increase acre yields, the Japanese method of intensive cultivation of rice should be extended to practically all irrigated areas. . . . The essential elements of the 'Japanese method' are related and the lack of any one of these elements is likely to reduce the efficiency of the others." The report also recommended that consideration be given to the widespread use of Japanese-type weeders, hoes, and small garden tractors.

The economic position of the average Indian farmer, the social organization of farm life, and the force of traditional farming practices all operate to prevent the rapid spread of an alien approach to rice culture, no matter how "rational" or "scientific" it may be. It is all very well to talk about the need for heavy applications of fertilizer, but where does the money come from to buy it? Transplanting seedlings in rows sounds easy and practical, but it takes far more labor than the traditional method. Who wants to go to the trouble of preparing a raised seedbed and keeping the water level adjusted in it according to fixed principles, especially when the water supply itself is uncertain? New doctrines sound fine in the laboratory or the experimental station, but these and other complaints have arisen, and there have been many criticisms of the "Japanese method." The name itself has offended a good many people. One Planning Commission official laughed when I mentioned it: "They call it the Japanese method," he said, "but I have the impression they took it from the Chinese originally." The Ministry of Food and Agriculture has been forced to emphasize that certain portions of the "Japanese method" would naturally have to be modified to suit Indian conditions. "Our drive," says one of its reports, "is not to be based on blind imitation of the Japanese."

During most of the 1950's the Japanese government itself did little or nothing to promote wider knowledge of Japan's agricultural practices in India. However, by 1959 this situation had begun to change. The new Japanese ambassador in New Delhi, Dr. Shiroshi Nasu, was a well-known agricultural economist, former professor of Tokyo University, and author of several volumes on Japanese agriculture. Indian officials found that Dr. Nasu had a keen interest in raising rice production, and shortly after his arrival in India he found an opportunity to turn his interest to practical use. He learned of four young Japanese, all younger sons of farm families, who had traveled to India some time before as Buddhist missionaries of the Nichiren sect; at an *ashram* in Bihar they had fallen out with their leader, an older Japanese priest who had been a member of the secret police during the war and now had turned into a religious fanatic who treated his young charges rather more harshly than they believed they deserved. They had therefore resolved to cease being missionaries; but because they had learned to speak Hindi, and because nothing awaited them at home, they were searching for some way to remain in India. As a result it was decided that they should settle on a small plot of land in the district of Saharanpur, in Uttar Pradesh, on the Grand Trunk Road about 110 miles north of New Delhi. There they were to set up a model Japanese rice farm under the joint sponsorship of the Japanese Embassy and the government of India.

This is not the place to go into all the details of the Saharanpur experiment. Three acres in all of India, and that in an area where rice is not the principal crop, was a small beginning indeed. Funds for the project were meager; the embassy had to pay farmers out of its "public relations" budget (which, to judge from results, must have already been very small). Farm implements donated by Japanese manufacturers failed to arrive on schedule; the plot was too small to be typical of Indian farming conditions; irrigation facilities and seed stocks were substandard, and there were many other difficulties. Still, in two years' time the four Japanese on their plot had quadrupled the average rice yield for the area. Their fame spread through the district and the state, and visitors even began to come from other parts of India to look at what they were doing. Their annual reports, translated into readable English, were handed over by the Japanese Embassy to the Indian Ministry of Food and Agriculture, which printed and distributed them all over the country. Many requests came for the Japanese farmers to lecture and give demonstrations, and their value was not entirely confined to agricultural techniques: "On one occasion," their report reads, "we talked for about two hours on village life in Japan, the marriage problem in the villages, compulsory education, and land reform." During my own Indian visit the young farmers had returned to Japan to marry Japanese girls, but all four couples were expected to return to India to continue their work.

The Saharanpur experiment cannot compare with the agricultural pilot program suggested and sponsored by the Ford Foundation in India, which involves a concerted effort to bring to bear all the factors necessary to raise agricultural productivity in 16 selected districts, one in each state. Nor have the Japanese been notably co-operative with this and other projects in agriculture. Here one hears the same old complaints: the Japanese are too shy and retiring; they can't or won't communicate; the specialists they send to India have not always been their best in a given field but have been either unseasoned youngsters or second-rate older men. However, there are some signs that Japanese assistance is about to increase. Early in 1962 a mission of Agriculture Ministry experts is expected from Tokyo to complete arrangements for three new demonstration farms, one in the Sambarpur district of Orissa, one at Shahabad near Patna in Bihar, and the third at a place undecided. Each of these farms is to be from ten to fifteen acres, and five farmers will be stationed in each to demonstrate multiple-crop intensive farming on the Japanese pattern. The Japanese government will pay their living expenses and give them a small stipend, while the Indian government will pay the "running expenses" of the farms. Japanese machinery will be brought in and demonstrated, and there are reports that a factory licensed by one of the Japanese farm machinery makers will be set up very soon in India.

If these experiments succeed, they might be expanded after two or three years. In addition, it is surely not without interest that two headquarters officials of Japan's ruling conservative party—one the chief of the party's youth bureau—recently visited India to sound out the government concerning the possible dispatch of a "Japanese Peace Corps" to India. They are reported to have represented themselves as personal emissaries of Prime Minister Ikeda, who himself arrives next week on a state visit. At the Delhi headquarters of the American Peace Corps they asked many questions about how it was to operate and particularly how it was being financed. The Indian reaction to their visit is unknown to me, but it seems clear that the dispatch of Japanese to India in various fields is still in its early stages, and while it may be controlled so as never to reach very large numbers, it is likely to increase in the future. Some other projects are now being negotiated. For example, a center for training people in fish canning and processing at Mangalore, on the southwestern coast, is under discussion by the two countries.

ASSISTANCE FROM PRIVATE JAPANESE SOURCES

I have already indicated that a portion of the yen credits granted by the Japanese government was made available to the private sector in India for collaboration of one sort or another between Japanese and private Indian firms or between Japanese firms and firms partly owned by central or state entities in India.

The most common type of arrangement has been for straight licensing of technical processes or designs, with payment of a cash technical assistance fee, a royalty, or both. A good example is the licensing agreement between the Tokyo Shibaura Electric Company (Toshiba), a large manufacturer of electrical equipment, and the Radio and Electricals Manufacturing Co. (Remco) in Bangalore, Mysore State. Remco is 60 per cent state-owned, 40 per cent private. Its managing director is a Mysore government official who was trained at General Electric in the United States. The firm employs 2,500 people and makes cables, radios, and other electrical equipment. In 1950 Remco wanted to start making watt-hour meters for home installation and needed foreign know-how. Toshiba, which itself has been licensed by GE for years, agreed to supply and install machinery, import parts unobtainable in India, and give training and guidance in production of these meters, for which the demand was rapidly expanding. Indians were trained by Toshiba in Japan and Japanese technicians were sent to Bangalore. Production started with 5,000 meters a month in 1952; at first all parts were imported and meters merely assembled in India. Management and sales were left entirely up to Remco, and Toshiba received a royalty with a guaranteed minimum and fees for technical drawings. Today there are no Japanese at Remco; production stands at 15,000 a month; machines to make meters are themselves being manufactured, and all but one or two parts are locally produced. The Remco meter won a gold medal at a Mysore State exhibition, and Remco is now supplying approximately half of total Indian production. Most of the other half is made by another Indian firm, Jaipur Metals and Electricals, which is licensed by another large Japanese manufacturer, the Fuji Electric Company.[1]

The Toshiba-Remco arrangement involves a fairly rapid shift away from dependence on imported parts and toward self-sufficiency. This is the Indian goal. Foreign exchange simply does not exist for imports, and it is much cheaper to pay for the know-how and end up with something to show for it. Large Japanese firms like Toshiba, with a variety of products which are well established in the home market and can be exported elsewhere, are apparently content to license their know-how with Indian companies. Toshiba has licensed several other firms besides Remco.

According to figures supplied by the Japanese Embassy in New Delhi, Japanese capital investment in India, apart from technical licensing agreements involving no capital participation, amounts to only about one per cent of the total foreign investment in this country. Indian government policy prohibits capital control in foreign hands except in rare cases where the need for the technology is overriding or there are other special considerations. Japanese capital is busy at home, where most companies are heavily overborrowed at the commercial banks. The climate of investment in India is regarded as risky and unpredictable. Japanese fear that more and more of their products will be shut out of the market as soon as they can be made in India; but if they come in and set up a "joint venture," it may be difficult or impossible for them to import parts or raw materials necessary to operate. As one businessman put it, "They are trying to force us to invest, but suppose I put up a factory on a promise of import licenses

[1] These details are contained in a study entitled *Teikaihatsukoku Kōgyōka no Gijutsuteki Jōken* [*Technical Conditions for Industrialization of Underdeveloped Countries*], published by the Asia Economic Research Institute, Tokyo, November 1960.

and then government policies change. I might wind up with a factory with chimneys but no smoke coming from them. My own government won't back me up and the Indian government certainly will not. Taxes are too high, and repatriation of dividends is uncertain, no matter what the regulations say." All the arguments against investment are brought to bear, and too often the Japanese businessman looks at India and turns away with a shudder.

Up to now only a few companies have been interested enough or confident enough in the Indian future to take the risks and enter into joint ventures with Indian partners.[2] Most of them are small-scale enterprises. The best known is probably the Pilot Pen Company, which controls a major portion of the Japanese home market for fountain pens and ink. In 1954 Pilot set up a factory in Madras with an Indian partner. The Indian side has 70 per cent, the Japanese 30 per cent. The pens being sold in India are inferior to Pilot's home product, but they are also cheaper in price.

Another enterprise which illustrates the way in which technology taken from the West is being passed on by Japan to India is the Hindustan-Kōkoku Wire Manufacturing Company near New Delhi. In this case blocked yen assets of the Gosho Trading Company seized by the Indian government during the last war were released a couple of years ago. Gosho then went into partnership with a wire manufacturer in Japan, and together they formed a joint company with Indian interests. The factory, now about to go into production, will make high-tensile steel wire for use in aluminum conductors, at first using steel rods imported from Japan and later locally made rods. Until 15 or 20 years ago Japan had to import such rods from Germany or elsewhere. Machinery for this plant is being partly financed under the government-backed yen credits, but the raw materials imported from Japan must be paid for. The Indian side estimates that the rods will be made in India within two or three years; in the meantime, if all goes well, the company will have established itself in a growing market.

Finally, in addition to licensing agreements and joint ventures, one totally owned Japanese company now operates in India: the Indo-Asahi Glass Company at Bhurkunda, in Bihar State, about 300 miles from Calcutta. In this unique case the Japanese won the bidding to

[2] As of August 1961, Indo-Japanese technical licensing agreements totaled approximately 40 cases and capital investment nine cases.

take over a defunct glass plant from the Indian Industrial Finance Corporation but were unable to find any Indian willing to put capital into the business with them. Because the Indian government wanted to promote the technology of glassmaking, and the Japanese were venturesome enough to see the possibilities of the market and go ahead despite risks and difficulties, the Bhurkunda plant today is one of the two principal sheet-glass suppliers in the country; Indo-Asahi plans to build an additional factory near Bombay and sooner or later to manufacture automobile glass and other special glass products.

CONCLUSION

In writing about Japan and India one begins with differences and goes on to record "activities" and "projects," some of them quite hopeful and logical. Surely the Japanese have something to offer India in such fields as small industry and agriculture. However, one comes back finally to a deep sense of unlikeness. For an American who has lived long in Japan the scene here is full of ironies. I am quite sure that I shall never forget being served Coca-Cola by the proper bureaucrats at the Japanese Embassy, with the wry apology that it was the only cool thing available. Nor shall I forget my friend K., the correspondent of a large Tokyo daily, who had made his existence in Delhi bearable by developing an interest in Indian sculpture and graphic design. "If I hadn't had these hobbies I would have gone crazy before now," he told me one night, while his Indian cook was serving us the approximation of *tempura*, made with local ingredients, that he had been painstakingly taught to prepare. "When I first came I tried to get to know Indians, but they only invite you to them when they want to get something from you, and I soon became disillusioned." And he spoke despairingly of how he was awakened every morning by an Indian woman pounding spices in a bowl on the cement floor in the apartment overhead. Nor am I likely to forget the garden of the Grand Hotel in Calcutta, where at one end a three-quarters-naked Japanese dance team billed as the "Golden Sisters" ran through their routines for the assembled American tourists, while at the other end the hotel's squadron of cats patrolled back and forth under the tea tables after the huge rats that came up from somewhere looking for spilled delicacies. On a more serious plane there are profound differences to consider, as I suggested at the start of this article. Especially I was struck by the difference in what concerns Indians and Japanese most. Indians seem preoccupied with themselves in quite a different way from the parochial but nervous Japanese. The most vivid issues here are national integration, making one nation from many languages, religions, regional and ethnic loyalties; economic growth and "take-off" at some date hopefully close but still in the future; anticolonialism, hatred of the Portuguese in Goa and the dying colonial regimes in Africa. Habits of caste and social thinking of which the Japanese director at Howrah complained will take at least a generation, and probably much longer, to change in any fundamental way. The press quotes Nehru as saying that a Chinese attack on India would mean world war but that such a war would not be fought on the borders of India. Japanese similarly say that a Chinese attack on Japan would mean world war, but their exposed position in their small, densely packed, vulnerable country forces them to the realization that they would again be destroyed, as India has not been destroyed by war in modern times.

In India many of the founding fathers, so to speak, the original leaders of the nationalist movement, are still alive and in power, and Nehru at least possesses remarkable charisma. In Japan, by contrast, the national leaders of the early phases of industrialism long ago passed from the scene. Today's leaders operate under a burden of lost confidence in politicians and are confronted by an alienated intelligentsia. Japan thus is preoccupied by a different set of problems: ideological hostilities in politics and the maturing of meaningful political institutions; assurance of economic stability at a relatively high level of industrialization; and a social synthesis or sense of purpose that will somehow define Japaneseness satisfactorily for a people already long united in race, religion, and language, but anxious in mind and spirit. Nehru likes to say that India got its free political institutions before its economic growth. Japan has had a century of economic growth, but its political institutions are still weak and pointed uncertainly into the future.

In fact, Japan is in a peculiar halfway stage, an in-between position; it is industrially advanced relative to India, but still far behind the United States and Western Europe in most respects. It is expected by the United States to make a contribution to Indian growth, and in addition to acting in its own commercial interests there is evidence that Japan is trying to help India out of general Free World motives. But India looks to America (as well as to Russia and Europe) for really important aid, and Indians still regard Japanese goods and people with suspicion. Conversely, a good third of Japan's total trade is with the United States. Both countries, I repeat, look more to America than to each other.

However, given these limitations and differences, Japan's role in India definitely is growing more important. Last year Japan's exports to America rose very little, while exports to India went up more than 40 per cent over 1959. South and Southeast Asia take more than a third of Japan's exports, and the region as a whole is a vital source of many raw materials. These are still the fundamental imperatives of Japanese policy in the area. However, in this, as in so much else in Japan, the method is to act case by case, in a pragmatic manner, without any clear-cut declarations of policy. "Good will" visits of politicians on both sides lead to economic assistance by fits and starts. Various ministries in Tokyo still contend among themselves, as they have for years, for a dominant role in overseas economic activities. As one official commented before I left Tokyo in September, "We are still groping toward some kind of centralized organ to co-ordinate economic collaboration." After listening to that sort of language for an hour or so one is likely to feel that it may be just as well they have not found such an "organ."

For their part Indians seem quite willing to take what they believe Japan can most profitably give them, but there must be "no strings attached"—the phrase is repeated to the point of tedium. As one key official in the Planning Commission put it, "Japan's idea of what Asia is has differed from India's idea." Their plans, he said, may achieve more than India's plans; their "uninhibited capitalism" may even go further in its own way with welfare schemes than India does. But India's values and India's planning policies are its own: "We can communicate meaningfully with Americans but not with Japanese. And for you, too," he gratuitously assured me, "India with all its mysteries is easier to understand than Japan."

Finally, a highly placed member of Prime Minister Nehru's personal staff described his own feelings in a similar way: "When I visited Japan a few years ago I liked the place, especially the grace of the women, their politeness, and the industry everyone showed. But I couldn't reach them verbally, and because of memories of the war I felt a sense of distrust. India will get what it can in the way of technical know-how and machinery, and it will pay for it. But there is no question of closer political ties with Japan. We are nonaligned and Japan is aligned. When the Japanese Prime Minister comes, there will be talks and a communiqué saying the usual things. But treaty ties or anything of that sort are out of the question."

I asked him whether Indians resented American aid to Japan, as some other countries in Asia did. "No," he replied, "we feel no resentment. India, too, has received massive aid from the United States and we are grateful for it." He smiled and closed off the subject: "After all, there is nothing in the Indian ethic to produce resentment over someone else's being given help."

CHAPTER 24

JAPANESE ACTIVITIES IN BURMA

Rangoon
November 30, 1961

The Union of Burma is a loose Buddhist society made up of many diverse peoples who in 1948 were released from more than 60 years of British law-and-order rule to become a Socialist state with much political nationalism but little capital and few technical skills or developed industrial resources. Today the country has by no means recovered from the destruction of World War II. Primary production is below 1939 levels. Transport and communications are still very poor; Shan and Karen insurgents roam the countryside, blowing up trains and murdering the passengers; the government must spend more money to maintain peace and order than for agriculture or industry. Buddhist monks and novices, armed with the knowledge that theirs is now the official state religion, invade mosques and clash with the Muslim minority. Student leftists stone the American Embassy and, looking outside themselves for the cause of their difficulties, accuse the United States of plotting with Kuomintang guerrillas to bring down the Rangoon government.

A ramified bureaucracy suffocates nearly all economic activity with controls and delays. One small example: the Japanese Embassy in Rangoon estimates that it takes six months for a notice of Colombo Plan scholarships to circulate around the various states. "Burmanization" has ended foreign control of trade and business, but private capital formation is extremely small. The Ministry of National Planning reports that 70 per cent of all "industrial loans" are made by private sources, while only 10 per cent come from commercial banks and 15 per cent from the state. "With gold and jewelry as security the rate of interest is about 24 per cent." There is no industrial bank (though one is being discussed) and no securities market. Most people distrust banks: "Were it not for the preference of the general public to hold currency rather than bank deposits, the expansion of bank credit would have been much greater."

Burmese life expectancy is below 30 years, and the death rate of 30 per thousand per annum is one of the highest in the world, nearly four times Japan's. But the population is relatively small and most people have at least something to eat, though most are ill-nourished and many, especially the hill peoples, abjectly poor. Rice exports provide three-fourths of Burma's foreign exchange; the government buys the surplus from farmers at a depressed price and sells it abroad. This means that the country is heavily dependent upon world rice prices but also that there is little internal compulsion to change. In India the gulf between aspiration and fact is frightening, but the aspiration to advance is real. Something must be done: the commitment to modernization has been made by the leaders. In Burma such a commitment is not so clear. Except for a scattering of intellectuals, a handful of Army officers, a few officials, perhaps a few others, progress is an ambivalent value, industrialism a goal of dubious worth. Most people are more eager to earn religious merit by contributing to the erection of pagodas, or prestige by adorning their wives with precious stones and gold bangles, than they are to save and invest in productive enterprise. Much money goes into gambling and movie houses, little into factories. The Prime Minister is a devout man who withdraws occasionally for interludes of meditation. No doubt there is something admirable in this; it also helps to win votes but does little to increase the gross national product. Indeed, the good as it is conceived in Burmese life seems largely unrelated to modernism.

In short, Burma is a weak agrarian state going nowhere very fast, wedged between two enormous, more dynamic neighbors. Sharing borders with India and China (as well as with Pakistan, Laos, and Thailand), it adopts a policy of neutralism and prides itself on being a "neutral among the neutrals." One official told me, "If the world would leave Burma alone, there would be no need for industrialization."

However, the world has not left Burma alone in recent history and is not likely to, because it is strategically located and possesses valuable resources. Like other former colonies on the fringes of the Asian continent, it has become a demonstration area in which more advanced states and international organizations carry on their "programs," not always co-operating very much with one another, but all eager for political advantage. One of the most important of these states is Japan. During the last war Japan spurred the nationalism that led to Burma's departure from British rule. In 1945 the Japanese took their own ignominious leave. In 1961 they have returned, not as an army to overrun and occupy, but in small numbers to contribute goods and constructive skills. Japan's assistance through war-damage reparations and in other ways is vital to Burma's national plans for the future; at the same time Japanese activities in Burma provide an ironic contrast to past dreams of an Asia marshaled to their desires.

JAPANESE REPARATIONS PAYMENTS TO BURMA

On November 5, 1954, Japan signed a peace treaty with Burma and agreed to pay $200 million in goods and services as reparations over a ten-year period. This was the first of four such agreements—the others were with the Philippines, Viet-Nam, and Indonesia—and the Burmese government was careful to reserve the right to additional claims should other countries get more than it did.

Since then reparations have been Burma's largest and steadiest source of foreign assistance. When payments began in 1955 the Burmese government decided to use a large portion of them for basic power and transport projects essential to the creation of an industrial base. The most impressive of these projects, and the most important single industrial achievement in postwar Burma, is the Balu Chaung hydroelectric power plant. Here is a clear example of the way in which Japanese skills are being brought to bear on basic resource development in Southeast Asia.

Balu Chaung grew out of a 1953 visit to Burma by the president of the Nippon Kōei Company, a firm of Japanese consulting engineers. Nippon Kōei is a postwar reincarnation of the old Yalu River Hydroelectric Company, which in the days of the Japanese Empire supervised the construction of world-famous power plants on the boundary between Korea and Manchuria. After the war senior engineers of this company found their way into Nippon Kōei, and the company sought business in the newly independent, developing countries, where it was familiar with local conditions and had long experience.

The Burmese government had surveyed many locations for its first water power development, but Japanese experts recommended a site in the Kayah State in east-central Burma on a tributary of the Salween River. There the Balu Chaung River drops more than 2,000 feet in a few miles through a series of waterfalls. The area is rugged and remote; the falls themselves had never been precisely surveyed. Access roads had to be cut through the hill forests and jungles so that heavy equipment could be moved in. Machinery and supplies arriving in Rangoon from abroad had to be transshipped by rail and road over an indirect route through wild territory controlled by Karen dissidents and bandits.

After more than two years of surveys and preparations of the work area construction got under way in 1956. The Burmese Electricity Supply Board had over-all charge of the project; it employed Nippon Kōei, which in turn contracted with the Kajima Construction Company, one of Japan's largest building firms. Many leading Japanese manufacturers as well as Western firms furnished equipment; a major part of the cost was charged against reparations.

The first stage of Balu Chaung was completed in March 1960. At the peak of construction activity more than 250 Japanese were at work there, from engineers and designers to foremen, carpenters, riggers, and pipe fitters. The first power plant has an installed capacity of 84,000 kw.; two other plants are to be built to bring the total installed capacity to 240,000 kw. Transmission lines and substations have been built to the Rangoon area; towers are in place and lines are now being taken north to Mandalay. Contracts are being let for the second stage of the project, which calls for construction of a large reservoir, also under supervision of Nippon Kōei. The same company has been engaged in similar projects in Southern Viet-Nam and Indonesia.

The first stage of Balu Chaung cost about $25 million, nearly one-fourth of all reparations dispensed to Burma in the first six years of the ten-year program. Another large sum went for Japanese rolling stock, locomotives, rails, and other equipment for the crippled Burmese railways, and for trucks and passenger cars to help rebuild the battered road transport system. Most taxicabs in Rangoon today are small

Japanese three-wheelers, painted bright orange and mounted with a small chassis.

The reparations program thus began with the acquisition of considerable quantities of capital goods and equipment. But even as payments were getting under way the Burmese economy ran into serious difficulties. The export price of rice fell precisely when the government was depleting its foreign-exchange reserves by heavy imports of machinery for poorly planned enterprises which few Burmese knew how to set up or operate. A steel mill was built without adequate knowledge of available raw materials or markets for steel products. A government silk-reeling factory, begun with reparations equipment, failed to thrive because of the inefficiency of bureaucrats in charge; a government milk-products plant received its machinery before a decision had been made on one important raw material: suitable cows.

Industrial projects which had been planned but not started were quietly shelved during 1955 and 1956, and Burma began to request more consumer goods as reparations from Japan to help check inflation. Textiles, canned sardines, and many other goods arrived in quantity. Galvanized iron sheets for roofing soon were a large item in the reparations budget. Other miscellaneous goods for direct consumption left little or no permanent trace on the economy: earthenware, glassware, electric bulbs, radios, fans, sewing machines, watches, cameras. Some imports, like pool tables and hi-fi sets, were of doubtful urgency. At the same time, however, a certain amount of small-scale machinery was brought in and turned over to private enterprise on a long-term basis. Japanese sources estimate that 90 per cent of the loans extended by the Burmese Government's Loans Board in recent years really have been in the form of reparations goods. During my recent visit to Burma I talked with several Burmese who had gone to Japan for brief periods of training in the use of machines for extraction of oil from rice bran and similar machinery suited to Burmese needs.

While consumer goods increased in reparations payments, normal Japanese exports to Burma also increased; since 1958 Japan has led the world in exports to Burma. However, sales of Burmese rice fell sharply as Japan approached self-sufficiency in that staple food. At one time last year the Burmese cut off trade entirely in an effort to force Japan to buy more rice. A mission from Tokyo recommended that Burma follow Thailand's example and grow more maize in order to reduce its dependence on rice exports. The mission noted plaintively that if the issuance of entry visas for Japanese were "expedited" and the activities of businessmen "facilitated" trade might be enlarged between the two countries. Such expressions suggest some of the annoyance the Japanese and others feel in dealing with the obscurantist Burmese bureaucracy.

Also related to reparations is one small but meaningful project, the Japan Agricultural Machinery Service Center at Okkin, in the suburbs of Rangoon. If Nippon Kōei and its Balu Chaung power plant symbolize Japanese technical competence in large engineering works in the foreign field, the Okkin center reveals the ability of Japanese to adapt to grass-roots conditions in tropical Asia and spread their skills without fear of personal consequences.

Late in 1958, while the army was in power in Burma, the government signed a contract with the Japan Agricultural Machinery Overseas Service Association for equipment and experts to set up a center to service farm machinery coming into the country as reparations and to introduce Burmese farmers to various kinds of modern tools and educate them in their use. The association is a nonprofit body supported by farm-machine makers. To support the center the Japanese government offered a small annual subsidy, while the member companies contributed the machinery and tools.

On a budget of less than $40,000 a year, a director and five Japanese assistants were selected from various agricultural extension bureaus all over Japan and dispatched to Rangoon. There, in modest buildings on a three-acre plot, they have assembled a large assortment of farm tools: dusters, sprayers, pumps, small tractor-cultivators, threshers, dryers, reapers, plows, small rice mills. The program, though tiny by Western standards, is beautifully suited to local needs. Groups of Burmese, many of them young staff members of agricultural bureaus in Lower Burma or the states, are brought to the center for short periods of training. Communication is not a problem, as it is between Indians and Japanese. Many Burmese learned Japanese during the war, while some of the Japanese speak adequate Burmese. In a well-equipped machine shop students learn how to repair and maintain farm machinery. Most important, the Japanese have two trucks on which they load tractors and other tools and take them all over the country to give demonstrations.

When I visited Okkin one staff member had just returned from a safari to Upper Burma, where he had lived in villages for several weeks, shown off his machinery, and given advice to farmers.

The Japanese director, an enthusiastic man with 30 years of experience in such educational work, told me proudly that his center was succeeding because his staff accepted the risks of traveling in the countryside and living off the country. He saw his work as something more than mere export promotion: "What we are really doing here is fighting communism," he told me. "The Chinese have granted Burma an $84 million loan; the Russians have given a hospital, a hotel, a technical school. The UN is here with its many agencies, the Ford Foundation, the Asia Foundation, and the American aid people have their own programs. But Japanese experience is perfectly suited to the scale and conditions of Burmese farming. By introducing them to our machines, even in this small way, we are trying to change their ideas about all farming: to get them to plant more maize, to learn horticulture and animal husbandry, to grow more vegetables, to irrigate properly, to raise new crops that will reduce their dependence on rice." When I told him about what a few Japanese farmers were doing in India and expressed my admiration for all such projects, he complained sadly that his budget was too small and urged me to ask American officials to co-operate with his center to help Burmese agriculture.

PRIVATE JAPANESE ACTIVITIES

In addition to $200 million in goods and services the original reparations agreement called for private loans to Burma totaling $50 million over ten years. Although both governments agreed to encourage such loans, not a penny of this money has been used so far.

Many joint ventures have been proposed by Japanese or Burmese, but all have foundered during negotiations. A fish-processing plant failed to materialize because of uncertainty over the market for ocean fish. A Burmese proposal for a ceramics plant failed because Japanese makers feared loss of their normal export markets. Burmese government planners wanted a shipyard to build large vessels for export, but the Japanese vetoed this as unrealistic at Burma's stage of development. Similarly the Burmese suggested an automobile assembly plant which would, it was hoped, be able to turn out complete automobiles within five years; the Japanese pointed out that the capital requirements of such a scheme were beyond Burma's resources. Japanese fertilizer manufacturers have long wished to build a plant in Burma, but raw-materials supplies are uncertain and the market has not been carefully explored. Negotiations for a cement plant, coal and iron mining, and a number of other proposals failed to mature and had to be postponed or abandoned.

Japanese in Burma speak despairingly of the difficulties of negotiating such joint venture arrangements with a Socialist regime. The Burmese government up to now has required that at least 60 per cent of all equity capital remain in the hands of Burmese nationals. Investment laws until very recently guaranteed no nationalization of joint enterprises for ten years; but with the government changing hands from civilians to military and back to civilian groups, and with internal order still a serious problem, very few Japanese have been interested in taking the risks and enduring the frustrations of operating in Burma, even if they could find Burmese with capital to invest. Americans in Rangoon refer to the one airline representative stationed there as the "American business community." The Japanese community is not much larger.

About 200 Japanese now live in Burma. Most of them are embassy staff and dependents or technicians assigned to the Balu Chaung project. The Bank of Tokyo hopefully keeps a "liaison officer" in Rangoon. The Asia Economic Research Institute, a government agency with headquarters in Tokyo, supports one young graduate student who is specializing on the Burmese economy. (When I suggested that there might be something of interest in Burmese culture besides economic statistics, he did not respond.) Three private firms, all small, operate with Burmese partners. All three were in Burma before the war and have long-established contacts in the country. One, the Pilot Pen Company, owns a 40 per cent interest in a small factory and supplies nearly half of the Burmese market for cheap fountain pens and ink. Pen parts are imported from Japan and merely put together in Rangoon. (In India the same company now makes nearly all parts from local materials.) Pilot makes a profit by paying very low wages, selling directly to agents, and avoiding middlemen. Its difficulties are many: import licenses are issued when the spirit moves Burmese officials and often must be bought at a premium. The company tries to keep at least six months running stock in hand to meet emergencies.

The other two companies are a pearl-culture farm and a small deep-sea-fishing enterprise. Not long ago the pearl farm was attacked by bandits and lost most of its assets; the fishing company also suffered when one of its trawlers, which had been supplied as reparations, was seized by the Burmese Army.

RECENT NEGOTIATIONS

By March 1961 more than half of the $200 million in reparations had been paid to Burma. Beginning with overblown plans for economic development largely based on recommendations of American advisers, the Burmese government in the mid-1950's had to retrench and shift to imports of consumer goods. By late 1958 Prime Minister U Nu was forced to turn over his government to the Army. His retirement was temporary, however: in the elections of February 1960 he and his party returned to power with an absolute majority. Since then Burma has been marking time, growing slowly in total output, but as dependent as ever on rice exports and with falling foreign-exchange reserves.

Today the politicians in power are still suffering to some extent from the shock of failures in the 1952–55 period; but they are again calling on their planners to produce blueprints for progress. The Second Four-Year Plan, commencing in the present fiscal year, emphasizes the diversification of agriculture and the continued rebuilding of transport and communications. Officials responsible for the plan stress that there is no thought of trying to achieve self-sufficiency in everything. Rather the new plan proposes, at least on paper, to give more encouragement to the private sector and to build up textiles and other light industries while relying on imports for heavier and more complex goods. Nearly half the money for the plan is expected to come from foreign loans and grants, including a portion of the Chinese loan, an ICA loan for a highway from Rangoon to Mandalay, a World Bank loan for locomotives and spare parts, and Japanese reparations totaling $80 million over the next four years.

The original reparations agreement will end in 1965. But since the Japanese have agreed to pay the Philippines $550 million (plus $250 million in private loans) and Indonesia $223 million (after canceling trade debts of nearly that much), the Burmese have resorted to their "equality clause" and for more than a year have been demanding additional reparations. Lacking capital of their own for investment, they have suggested that Japan put up $200 million more in straight reparations and then induce private Japanese firms to match that with capital goods and technical assistance. The foreign investment law has been changed to reassure those who fear nationalization, and the government has indicated that foreign firms may be allowed a 50 per cent share in joint ventures.

For their part, the Japanese are still interested in Burmese iron, antimony, and other resources. As the Bank of Tokyo representative put it, "The situation in Burma often seems hopeless but never collapses entirely, and we have to stay here because the country is rich in raw materials." But the Japanese have made no progress whatever toward private investment and many of them are growing tired of Burmese demands and delays. When still another Burmese mission visited Tokyo in October the Japanese dutifully laid on the entertainment routines at Atami, but the only visible result of the negotiations was a photograph of Burmese delegates enjoying themselves at a geisha party. The photograph was harmless enough, but when it appeared on page one of an opposition daily in Rangoon, Burmese officials charged that the Japanese had deliberately planted it to embarrass the U Nu government. Last week, while I was in Rangoon, Prime Minister Ikeda arrived on a "good-will" visit with a large group of Diet members, a Foreign Office negotiating team, and enough newspapermen to make even the Strand Hotel seem lively. But after a week of haggling no progress was reported. The Burmese still wanted $200 million more; the Japanese still offered about $75 million. Both sides claimed they wanted joint ventures, but talks were broken off without result.

*   *   *

I arrived in Burma from India believing that Japanese reparations payments might fit into an over-all scheme of economic development. This was naïve. Reparations and other foreign assistance have been scattered at random to support changeable policies. This might have been expected, for in Burma at its present stage consequences do not necessarily follow in logical fashion. On paper plans have an irresistible symmetry; practice often is nothing but a succession of expedients to shore up weaknesses.

The idea that Japan might be used deliberately as a counterweight to Chinese Communist influence in Burma had no appeal to those

Burmese whom I met. At the same time, not everybody is happy about the Chinese loan or about the "settlement" of the border question with China. Admiration for the Chinese desire to reassert China's "greatness" in the hearts of their own people is mixed with fear of encroachment from the north and a measure of resignation about the future. One intellectual who had just returned from a month in China declared that Burma was "neutral because China permits us to be neutral." Peking, he said, will remain friendly for the time being because it suits its purposes to be so, but "this is merely the honeymoon. In a few years, maybe five, maybe 25, the notion of China as a peaceful nation will be built up in the Burmese mind, and the people will be lulled into the sleep of peaceful coexistence; Burma will then find itself isolated and the Chinese can take us over whenever they please. Our policy of giving China the benefit of every doubt is ideally correct, even irreproachable. But the illusion of a peaceful China is still an illusion."

During the last war more than a hundred promising young Burmese were sent to Japan for education as future leaders of the "new Asia." Some spent years in Japanese universities and became fluent in the language. Today these people are sprinkled through Burmese society, some in fairly high-ranking military posts, others in government or politics. One, a government engineer, combined studies at Kyoto University with a degree from the University of Iowa. Another, a planning official, attended universities in Hiroshima and Kyoto and later graduated from the London School of Economics. In conversation several of these men put great stress on Japanese reparations in their country's economic life, but all denied that an increase in private Japanese business activities could influence the government in any way to change its foreign policy. Like the Indians, the Burmese will take what they can get from every source, but in theory, at least, there must be "no strings attached."

Some Burmese who studied in Japan during the war also criticized the Japanese for supposedly abandoning their Asian cultural heritage. As one of them remarked: "The Japanese not only taught us nationalism, but they also taught us pan-Asianism. Of all Oriental peoples they seemed to us the most Oriental. Yet after the war they turned around and embraced Western culture. I cannot quarrel with their alliances with the West; these may be necessary for their survival. But I do not like their taking in all those Western cultural influences. Of course, when we go to Tokyo we like to visit Ginza night clubs, like every-body else. But that sort of thing won't do for Burma. We do not go to extremes of acceptance and rejection as the Japanese do. We are more stable. You may call it stagnancy, but anyway, to us it is stability."

Burma's foreign policies may not change simply because of increased contact with Japanese business. But the Japanese in Burma today clearly regard China as their main competitor. Over and over through their conversations runs the theme that Japan must "do something" in Burma and in all of Southeast Asia to counter what the Chinese are doing there. Japan's textile exports to Burma are running neck and neck with China's. Through reparations, agricultural projects, and other means, the Japanese have to some extent returned to the Burmese scene. Should negotiations with Burma eventually produce agreements for joint ventures, and should even a few of these agreements be carried through, the results might be encouraging to all those who are not resigned, as some Burmese apparently are, to Burma's eventual control by the Chinese Communists.

APPENDIX I

Japan's Trade with Burma
(excluding reparations)

(in US$000)

Year	Export	Import	Balance
1955	39,709	42,704	−2,995
1956	31,247	33,999	−2,752
1957	50,289	22,772	27,517
1958	20,558	10,416	10,142
1959	36,564	8,233	28,331
1960	46,858	10,464	36,394
1961 *	25,139	5,078	20,061

* Jan.–June
Source: Foreign Exchange Control Department, Bank of Japan.

APPENDIX II

Structure of Japanese Reparations to Burma, 1955–1960

ITEM	4/55–3/56 %	4/56–9/57 %	10/57–9/58 %	10/58–9/59 %	10/59–9/60 %	Total %
Food products		1.4	2.0	1.6	2.9	1.8
Pharmaceuticals		0.2	1.6	1.0	1.9	1.0
Basic materials (including G.I. sheets)		16.5	21.4	18.8	36.4	21.1
Machinery (including electrical machinery and transport equipment)	20.4	49.3	53.0	44.5	41.9	47.6
Balu Chaung hydro-electric project	79.6	28.3	17.4	26.2	2.8	22.1
Miscellaneous plant exports		3.5	0.5	1.5	6.8	2.9
Miscellaneous other goods		0.5	3.0	4.3	1.7	1.8
Services		0.3	1.1	2.1	5.6	1.7
	100.0	100.0	100.0	100.0	100.0	100.0

Source: Baishō Jisshi no Genkyō (Present Progress of Reparations), published by the Reparations Problems Research Association, Tokyo, March 1961.

CHAPTER *25*   ❀

THE POLITICS OF
FLOWER ARRANGEMENT

Manila
December 26, 1961

Last week in Manila a Japanese lady teacher of flower arrangement, arriving from Australia at a late hour, was met at planeside by a member of the staff of the Japanese Embassy, who insisted that she accompany him at once to the home of a leading member of the Liberal party, to which incoming President Macapagal belongs, for a demonstration of her skill. When she protested that she was exhausted and had no proper flowers or other materials, he ignored her complaints and drove her to the American Cemetery, of all places, to collect what she needed. At seven-thirty the next morning she was awakened to go to the Presidential Palace, where she performed for friends of outgoing President Garcia and his wife. Later she held a press conference and was taken by another embassy official to participate in a television show. An American family who had known the teacher years before in Japan invited her to their home for the night, but the Japanese Embassy refused to allow her to go and insisted that she use the hotel room that had been officially reserved for her. By this time the teacher was beside herself, and practically breaking down in the lobby of the hotel, she complained that all foreign-service officials were stupid, thought of nothing but "face," and furthermore had given her too many half-dead flowers. "Either dead or alive is all right, but in-between ones are absolutely unmanageable."

The teacher's visit was the most recent gambit in the odd game of improving cultural relations that goes on all the time between Japanese and Filipinos, two peoples who like each other probably as little as any two on earth and whose relations in most spheres are marked by distaste and calculated self-seeking. This is not to say that cultural relations need intrinsically to be regarded with cynicism; but in this case, at least, they persist in a sort of airy vacuum—if such were possible—that bears little or no relation to other factors of political and economic diplomacy. The goal of these efforts may be entirely salutary—to demonstrate sincerity, decency, or the elegance of traditional arts—but stubborn differences of national interest show few signs of being removed by cultural exchanges alone. Thus last week the "great Kinoshita circus" was playing to capacity crowds on Manila's Luneta, an elderly scholar from Tokyo was making a romantic speech about Rizal's meeting with a Japanese girl, and a Japanese youth team was paying a good-will visit to Filipino schools. Conversely, a Filipino folk-dancing troupe had recently been a great success in Tokyo. But 16 years after World War II Japanese businessmen still were unable to get visas to stay long enough in the Philippines to carry on normal business; a foreign investment law had not been passed and the Central Bank was disallowing dollar allocations for joint ventures with Japanese; a Treaty of Amity, Commerce, and Navigation had been signed but was not yet ratified by the Philippine Senate; and many Japanese firms were not even listed in the Manila telephone directory and their representatives sat in offices behind doors bearing such noncommittal legends as "Air-Conditioned. Come In Without Knocking."

Twenty years after Pearl Harbor and Bataan much of the open and violent hatred of Japan felt by Filipinos has disappeared. Manila hotels are filled with Japanese visitors, who may walk in the city, at least, without greater fear for personal safety than any other foreign traveler might feel. A smaller number have ventured into provincial towns and even into rural areas without published injury. A young Japanese acquaintance of mine, who is an economic geographer, spent two years studying at the University of the Philippines between 1958 and late 1960. At first his professor warned him not to leave the Manila area; but after a few months he went on a trip to Sorsogon and Albay in southern Luzon, where he was one of the first Japanese to appear since 1945. When he took a bus into the hills near Legaspi his fellow passengers at once spotted him and asked politely but, he thought, ominously whether his father or any of his brothers had been in the country during the war. He said no; and when it was learned that he was a student at the University of the Philippines, one Filipino passenger invited him to stay the night at his home. From then on he was out of danger, and he found the people warmhearted and their country beautiful, though he also realized that "they have not forgotten what happened to them and their families at Japanese hands during the war."

Such extended residence and confrontation without intermediaries can often give understanding and even, perhaps, some affection. This is not inevitable, however: another acquaintance who also lived for years in the Philippines described the people as "English-speaking Koreans" —a peculiarly hateful phrase—and the ordinary Japanese stereotype of the Filipino is a lazy, pleasure-loving person, mesmerized by shiny consumer goods, whose culture has been dangerously thinned out by too much Americanization.

A few Filipinos, too, have stayed in Japan longer than is required to transit the Ginza department stores and night clubs and have taken away some of the pieces of the puzzle of understanding. In a novel entitled *The Bamboo Dancers*,[1] N. V. M. Gonzales, one of the best-known contemporary Filipino writers, devotes a long section to the hero's travels in Japan. Obviously modeled on the author's own experiences, the book describes with grave perceptiveness a Filipino artist's reactions to Japanese people and places. He felt all the petty frustrations other foreigners feel, especially at the difficulty of communicating: his interpreter seemed "more amused over us than interested in helping us out." Such small resentments led back to ugly memories of the war: "The temples and old castles began to appear [on a train journey] and I felt somewhat uneasy. I couldn't forget that there was this interpreter who could tell us all about them but didn't even try. My mind went back to feed on old notions about the country—the overpopulation, the value of night soil to agriculture, and all that. It was as a boy of thirteen that I had seen these people overrun the Philippines . . . and I remembered how they had tried to transform all of Sipolog [a fictional] province, traditionally a coconut-producing area, into one Japanese Army-owned cotton plantation. Father had

[1] Published by The Diliman Review, Quezon City, Philippines, 1959. Quoted by permission of the author.

refused to turn his farm over, which earned him a visit from the Kempeitai. It was in 1942 when, as they say, he was 'taken' for questioning and nearly three months later came back to us half-dead. . . . If the interpreter had been only half helpful, I would not have begun thinking of those things."

After a few days, however, the hero became absorbed in the Japanese scene and began to have other thoughts. Soon he could "find no relation between the horror of the Occupation that I remember from my boyhood and the scenes and sights in this country. It is a queer feeling, as if Fuji inoculates you against hate. I met a group of Filipinos at the hotel in Tokyo, tradespeople who seemed to have been doing business with the Reparations Mission, and even they had forgotten. I couldn't stand their talk about the chorus girls at the Nichigeki and the public baths . . . so eventually I drifted into the PEN Club headquarters. . . ."

In Hiroshima, where the opportunities for compassion and bathos are both very great, the hero of the book fell in with a group of Japanese who had to recite their personal miseries. He felt deep sympathy with them, but the story is saved from sentimentality by the author's powers of observation. After one long account of the symptoms of radiation disease, the hero concludes that, "We were getting too solemn about it. . . . I had thought it would be interesting to get Mrs. Ishikawa's story, too. But this is really getting too solemn, I told myself. It was particularly difficult because of Dr. Mori. He had buckteeth and such large, expressive eyes. I began to feel he would burst into tears any moment. The way he flecked his eyelids was enough to make me feel uncomfortable." At another point a Japanese woman stops in the midst of telling her personal history to observe: "There's no day that passes without great unhappiness for me. And what I would really like to tell you about is my unhappiness." Later, reflecting on his meeting with these people, the hero feels the same perplexity that many other foreigners have felt: "I could practically hear Mrs. Kumagai saying again, 'All I really want is to be able to tell you about my unhappiness.' I wondered whether there was any resignation and acceptance there. Maybe there was, or maybe there was none. Somehow I had to learn the language that the Kumagais used."

These passages are quoted to show that the quality of this Filipino's experiences was not unlike that of other sensitive observers of Japan.

But the quality of Japanese-Philippine relations as a whole is a very different matter from the net product of a talented writer's feelings or the skill in a flower arranger's hand or eye. It is not they who set the main tone of relations between the two countries, but the Filipino businessmen talking about sex at the Nichigeki Music Hall and grabbing war-damage reparations, and their Japanese counterparts doing business in Manila behind unmarked doors or facilitating the debauchery of their Filipino associates at Atami hotels.

Wherever one goes in Tokyo or Manila the reparations story is treated as an open joke, until one feels finally that any straightforward account of the subject, complete with statistics, would on its face be almost meaningless. Since 1956 nearly $150 million in goods and services has been sent to the Philippines, and over the next 15 years more will continue to be sent until the total value reaches $550 million. In addition, $250 million in loans from private Japanese sources has not yet been touched. Lists of reparations goods and their recipients are available from several different sources, which match each other very well. They show that about one-third of the total has been turned over to the Philippine government, where agencies ranging from the Manila Railroad to the University of the Philippines have received some amount of goods: cargo ships, rolling stock, a pleasure yacht for the President, cannery ships, machines for weaving fish nets or for making rattan and bamboo articles, dredger boats, tugs and barges, rails, trucks, fire engines (300 of them), steel rods, cement, and a host of other things. Nearly 50 private firms have received the remainder: cement and paper plants, sawmills, ceramic-making machinery, textile plants, glass-bottle and food-processing plants, auto repair shops, refrigeration equipment, ocean-going vessels and fishing boats, plywood-making machinery, and much other equipment.

What the lists of goods and the other statistics do not show, and what has nowhere been shown with any completeness or accuracy, is the manner in which these things were acquired, their value to the Philippines, and the uses to which they have been or may be put. No evaluation of reparations is yet available in anything like complete form; rather the subject has been immersed in rumors of corruption and obscured by the denials and evasions of officials. On the Japanese side the official attitude has been negative: reparations had to be paid as an unpleasant duty, but what might become of them was none of

Japan's business, and no study of their effectiveness was made. Rather they were viewed merely as a form of export promotion.

The Philippine side issued some impressive reports through the Reparations Mission in Tokyo, but these were immediately attacked by the press and the opposition party in Manila. From the first reparations, like everything else in the Philippines from Church to customs house, were embroiled in politics and turned into a means of paying political debts or earning patronage. According to the Philippine Reparations Law, all goods received were supposed to fit into development plans of the National Economic Council, which sent its priorities to the Reparations Commission, which in turn forwarded them to the Philippine Reparations Mission in Tokyo. However, the Reparations Commission was within the President' office, not the Foreign Ministry, and success in obtaining reparations goods was linked in the public mind with political influence. Filipino businessmen were allowed to seek goods directly from Japanese manufacturers, arrange prices and terms very largely to suit their convenience, and secure allocations which might have only accidental relevance to government planning. A crowd of Filipino profit seekers descended upon Tokyo, many of them armed with special passports to which they had dubious right. With the single motive of making private fortunes they put pressure on the Reparations Mission for contracts of all sorts, many for overpriced goods, which led to accusations of graft on both sides. Private recipient were obliged to repay the Philippine government for goods received; but they had the advantage of low interest rates and a two-year moratorium on repayment. Thus it was more profitable to apply for reparations goods than to borrow from Japanese private sources. Reparations contracts could also be used for speculation; allocations could be sold before goods reached Manila or goods left unpacked in warehouses because the profit on them had already been made or the first "end user" was trying to find another "end user" to whom to transfer ownership.

The use or abuse of reparations brought out some of the worst qualities of Philippine public life. Floating canneries were stripped of their expensive equipment and converted to interisland transport vessels. At the National Steamship and Steel Corporation transformers, motors, cranes, switchboards, pumps, and other equipment were reported to be rusting in the rain. Machines which were supposed to be used by the Bureau of Public Schools to stimulate the growth of small industries were unused for lack of trained personnel or allowed to pass into private hands in some provinces. Elaborately equipped fishing boats stood at anchor with their gear unused. Of the 50-odd private companies receiving reparations, the Securities and Exchange Commission in Manila recently could report data on only about 30. Most had very small paid-in capital and were incorporated after the reparations program began in 1956. Only four claimed more than 20 employees; many were unlisted in the Manila phone directory.

Up to now reparations have contributed little to the productivity of agriculture and fishing, which must be improved if the Philippines is to have a sound foundation for industry. Nor have reparations created anything that might be pointed out as a monument to Japanese aid or a permanent reminder of the possibility of friendship and trust. The masses of people in the *barrios* have had almost no contact with the program, while the "politicalization" of reparations has reinforced the easy belief of most Japanese that Filipinos are a shiftless people who put their own selfish ends above progress as a nation.

There is more to the Japanese view than this, however. Exports to the Philippines have expanded steadily in the past ten years; like Burma, the Philippines has grown as a normal market as well as a reparations market. Conversely, Japan has become the second largest purchaser of Philippine goods. While the United States' share of Philippine exports declined to less than half of the total, Japan's share rose from 10 per cent to 25 per cent in the decade since 1952. Filipinos know that their country's preferential position in the American market is declining and by 1974 will have disappeared. Many members of the new Filipino entrepreneurial class admit that, whether they like it or not, closer ties with Japan are probably inevitable. For their part the Japanese see the Philippines as a country with rich resources, which are, however, scattered and not inexhaustible. The population is small, but it is growing rapidly, and per-capita income is higher than in most Asian countries. Urbanization and industrial development are moving ahead, and the Philippines is an excellent potential market for Japanese refrigerators, air conditioners, automobiles, and other durable consumer goods as well as capital equipment. Even today plans are being made to assemble Japanese passenger cars, possibly first in the Visayas where chrome-covered American limousines are not quite so numerous as they are in Manila.

By the late 1950's the governments of both countries realized that a new legal basis for commercial relations was essential if normal business was to flourish. Negotiations for a Treaty of Amity, Commerce, and Navigation were begun early in 1960, and in December the treaty was signed in Tokyo.

The treaty resembles others of the same general type. Those few people in the Philippines who have read it with care take exception to one or two of its provisions. Old fears of Japanese immigration and settlement have by no means disappeared; guarantees of most-favored-nation treatment with respect to travel and residence of Japanese are considered too liberal by some Filipinos, although "all matters relating to permission for permanent residence" are specifically excluded from the treaty. Some other sections are criticized more or less justifiably for their vague wording, especially the sentence stating, "Neither party shall hamper the introduction into its territories of capital or technology of the other party which will contribute to the sound and balanced development of its national economy on a self-sustaining basis." Of this one critic wrote: "The word *hamper* is especially woolly and wanting in clearness of meaning. Almost any kind of regulatory measure adopted as to foreign capital admission could be construed to be 'hampering'. . . . And what is meant by 'development of the economy on a self-sustaining basis?'" These criticisms reflect the fear in even the best-informed minds that the Philippines might somehow again be thrown open to Japanese commercial exploitation.

Quite aside from responsible criticisms, the treaty became a political issue even before it was signed; afterward it could not be submitted to the Philippine Senate for ratification because of the Presidential elections of November 1961. President Garcia and his Nacionalista party had made much of "Filipino-First" policies and promoted a nationalism that often sought to discriminate against aliens for economic gain. Now Garcia's opponents accused him of selling their country into another black era of foreign economic control. In 15 years of independence the Philippines had not signed an FCN Treaty with any country, and the idea of beginning with Japan seemed especially repugnant. Some accused the negotiating team of putting personal gain ahead of patriotism. The pro-treaty group countered, rather implausibly, that *Amity* was a weaker word than *Friendship*; they argued with more logic that it was best to sign the first such treaty with Japan, because no Filipino was likely to be very generous to the Japanese, and therefore the standard of "most-favored-nation" treatment established by the treaty would do the Philippines less harm than if it were signed with a really friendly country like the United States. (The rights of American citizens in the Philippines were specifically reserved by the treaty.) But the attackers were not satisfied by these arguments. They worried about Japanese penetration of coastal waters, even though the government insisted that Philippine waters extended out nearly 100 miles from all coasts. They argued that although investment rights were supposed to be reciprocal, Japan would have all the advantages: "How can we invest in Japan," wrote one columnist, "when we haven't even enough capital to develop the Philippine economy?" To which the *Japan Times* in Tokyo smugly replied: "That is a sad revelation, but all we can say is that we hope this condition of affairs is only temporary . . . If political maneuvers and ultranationalist ideas are to be allowed to embarrass the Philippines' economic development, that country's advance is likely to be retarded indefinitely. There is a certain amount of feeling in Tokyo . . . that the outlook in Manila is too parochial."

Such pious comments merely inflamed further the opponents of the treaty and led to some more vivid language. In a speech to the Manila Jaycees in the summer of 1961 Arsenio Lacson, the redoubtable mayor of Manila, accused the Japanese of seeking to control Philippine natural resources and wondered how Filipinos could possibly do likewise in Japan: "The only natural resource Japan has is its women," he exclaimed, "and they are not virgin." (The mayor was proud enough of this speech to play it back for a small audience in Manila recently.) Such vulgarity could scarcely be expected to improve the tone of Japanese-Philippine relations, no matter how many flower arrangers, collectors of Rizaliana, or other cultural missions made their way patiently back and forth.

The Philippines' old ties with America are weakening and many Filipinos feel insecure and isolated. Some of them argue that Japan is allied with the West and is a non-Communist country with whom they should seek closer ties. But no matter how "inevitable" closer relations may be, Filipino leaders in both parties are skeptical of Tokyo's present alignment and suspicious of ultimate Japanese intentions. As a present military threat Japan has disappeared from their minds, but hatred has been replaced by apprehension. One of the key men in the new administration remarked that his son spent a year studying in Tokyo and came away with the strong feeling that the Japanese had not lost their belief in their own uniqueness or superiority. This person admitted the advantages of broader economic contact but he was not at all sure that the Philippines should seek Japan's closer company.

The new administration in Manila has indicated that it will support a foreign investment law and otherwise encourage the entry of capital from abroad. But the incoming Vice-President and Foreign Minister, Emmanuel Pelaez, insists that the treaty with Japan will be carefully restudied before it is submitted to the Senate; new laws may have to be passed to protect local interests, and there is a possibility that the whole treaty may have to be renegotiated. Once a treaty is ratified and goes into effect, Philippine fears may be quieted. This could be true especially if the new government gives a more disciplined lead and pursues programs that will hold the imagination of all the people, not just a small elite. Japan and the Philippines (and the United States, for that matter) could co-operate imaginatively in Philippine development. However, the two countries have a poor past to build on, and reparations have accomplished little that is constructive so far. Instead, contact proceeds on two disconnected levels, one cultural, the other economic and political. The latter governs, and its theme on both sides is selfish gain. The politics of flower arrangement is a game with pretty pieces, but in the more visceral world of trade treaties and reparations deals differences are expressed in rawer language and emotions manipulated in rougher and more thoughtless style. Profit, not the triangulation of blossoms, is what each side finds really absorbing about the other.

CHAPTER *26*

"IN TEN YEARS, IN FIFTY YEARS": COMMENTS ON CHINA TRADE

October 30, 1958

On May 12 of this year the Chinese Communist government canceled a trade agreement with Japan, the fourth since 1952, which had just been signed in Peiping after months of negotiations. The Japanese government had refused earlier to approve the agreement reached by unofficial Japanese delegates, since it would have given flag-flying rights and virtual diplomatic recognition to the proposed Chinese trade mission to Tokyo. The Japanese were influenced by strong protests from the Chinese Nationalist regime in Taipei, which Japan recognizes as the legal government of China. Behind Tokyo's action lay a reluctance to disturb relations with the United States by moving too hastily toward recognition of Peiping. At about the same time a young Japanese in Nagasaki tore down a Communist flag at an exhibition of Chinese postage stamps in a department store; he told police he "found the atmosphere of the exhibition insufferable." These events increased Peiping's already sharp distaste for Prime Minister Kishi and his administration and led to a breakdown of all commercial and cultural ties between the two countries. Kishi's policy was, and is, trade but no recognition. Peiping responded, in effect, no trade without recognition.

In the intervening months the Japanese government has followed what it calls a "wait-and-see" policy toward China. Since 1952 Tokyo has conducted barter dealings with Peiping, but figures have not been large; in 1956, the best postwar year, Japanese exports exceeded $67 million, while imports reached nearly $84 million, about 2.5 per cent of Japan's trade in each direction. Organizations of small-scale manufacturers, cotton spinners, and traders in miscellaneous goods continue their long-term lobby for more business with China; makers of steel, chemical fertilizers, and synthetic fibers also have been affected by the trade shutdown. However, pressure from economic circles has not yet been sufficient to force a change of government policy, nor is there much evidence that it will be sufficient. While it desires to trade with China, the government maintains, officially, that nothing it has done is grounds for offense in Peiping, a government with which Japan still is legally at war.

Apart from official pronouncements, opinion in this country on trade with China is very far from uniform. But in terms of Japan's long-range trading needs, as well as in many other respects, mainland China holds a vital significance in Japanese thinking about the future. What are some of the main positions taken by Japanese on this question?

I

Many Japanese-language newspapers and magazines give the impression that all Japanese deeply yearn for closer ties with China (which is largely true) and that such ties should be established posthaste, at whatever cost to relations with the United States (a much more dubious conclusion). Since the breakoff of trade last spring, intellectual magazines like *Sekai* (on the left, circulation about 100,000), *Chūō Kōron* (nearer to center, circulation about 300,000), as well as magazines with larger circulations like *Bungei Shunju* (well to center, circulation about 650,000) and the weekly tabloids (which reflect the line of the newspapers that publish them), have carried whole clutches of articles by economists, professors of literature, "social critics," and other "men of culture" deploring the unnatural state of Japanese-Chinese relations. Some of these writers, like Dr. Shigeru Nambara, former president of Tokyo University, have introduced themes of guilt: the Japanese people have a "moral obligation" to be friendly with China because of past crimes committed against the Chinese people. Others, who have visited China recently, are most impressed with Chinese economic growth and the "new atmosphere" that has supplanted the corruption of the Chiang Kai-shek era. Some, even within the government party, frankly conceive Japan's choice to be between Dulles and peaceful coexistence and choose the latter. Still others distrust the condescension and pride that are evident in the attitudes of many intellectuals who clamor for more Japanese solidarity with the "Asian bloc."

Academic economists, many of them influenced by Marxian thought, and other "China trade expansionists" are deeply disturbed by Japan's isolation from China at just this time, when the COCOM [1] restrictions on trade with the Communists have been relaxed and China is engaged in five-year plans for economic development. They naturally wish to shift their dependence for such imports as coking coal from the United States to cheaper, closer sources. Beyond this, they regard China as a stable, automatically expanding market for Japan's exports of plant and technology, and they fear that Japan is losing out to Western rivals in its efforts to sell China what it needs and integrate more closely with the Chinese economy.

In none of these articles have I found any apprehensiveness about the kind of society that Japan will be dealing with in China in the future. In none of them is any real fear for Japan's future safety as a nation expressed. These writers apparently are not concerned over the fact that 75 per cent of China's present trade is carried on with the Communist countries. Indeed, most of the trade arguments are presented without reference to political differences, which, one might suppose from reading them, do not exist.

One of these economists, whose articles appear often in *Sekai* and other intellectual magazines, gave the following estimate of Japan-China trade prospects: [As sometimes happens, his views seem more measured in conversation than in print, where a writer must often follow an editorial policy.]

"Japan's trade with China last year totaled $150 million both ways. According to my careful estimates, total possible trade with China ten years from now will be $600 million both ways. This would mean not more than ten per cent of Japan's imports and ten per cent of her exports. I regard this trade as essential, because we must have access to our natural sources of raw materials in China. But there can be no

---

[1] Co-ordinating Committee, an informal international consultative group, composed of representatives from Canada, the United States, Belgium, Denmark, France, Italy, Luxembourg, the Netherlands, Norway, Portugal, the United Kingdom, Greece, Turkey, West Germany, and Japan, which co-ordinates policy on trade with the Soviet bloc by the member countries.

possibility of return to the prewar position. The main problem is imports; China has little to exchange for large imports from us. Difficulties are involved even in importing one thing the Chinese have plenty of, soybeans. Two-thirds of the soybeans imported by Japan are for processing into oil; the other third is for human consumption as *miso*, *tōfu*, etc. For oil purposes American beans are far superior, and our oil processors don't want to switch back to Chinese sources of supply; since the war they have grown accustomed to the American product and like it. Our main hope for switching imports is cotton, which used to be grown in large quantities in north China.

"Of course, there is a great deal of talk about resolving the impasse in our relations with China. As a Japanese, I sympathize with this and am myself involved in this campaign. But there are all sorts of problems that don't appear in print. Politically, the key issue is Taiwan, but the Japanese can't agree among themselves on the best disposition of Taiwan. Personally, I see no solution, except that Chiang will probably die in a few years. Neither can the Japanese agree on who is to be in control of the national front for restoration of relations with China that is now being organized. The Communists are in it, but the Socialists want to run it, and they oppose letting some of the anti-nuclear test organization people into the movement. Personal differences are involved in this, as in everything else touching Japanese politics. Socialist policy is incoherent half of the time. A few years ago we had the Association for Promotion of Restoration of Relations with Russia and China (*Nisso Nitchū Kokkō Kaifuku Sokushin Kyōgikai*), but they dropped the "Russia" after Japan restored relations with the Soviet Union. A good many people dropped off the bandwagon at the same time because they were scared of offending the United States by seeming too eager toward China. The eagerness is there underneath, but it is hard for the Japanese themselves to get together.

"Inside the government party there are obvious differences of opinion. Kishi lacks the political ambition of Hatoyama [Prime Minister, 1954–56], who staked his reputation on bringing the state of war with Russia to an end. So he drifts, and he is not going to break openly with the United States. [Minister of International Trade and Industry] Takasaki has known Chou En-lai for a long time; he saw him at the Bandung Conference and talked then about economic development of Manchuria with Japanese help. Takasaki is being used by [Ichirō]

Kōno [Chairman of the Executive Board of the conservative party], who is ambitious to capitalize on restoration of relations with China to propel himself into the Premiership. But nothing will be done for the time being. Some of us tried to get [Shintarō] Ryū [editor-in-chief, *Asahi Shimbun*] to go to China last summer to sound out Mao Tse-tung, but the *Asahi* refused to send him.

"I am not pessimistic about the future. Things are at a standstill now, but fifty years from now Japan and China will be on friendly terms, co-operating with each other. Japan will certainly not be a Communist country, but, like the United States, will have to coexist with China. Seen in the long view, the disposition of Taiwan, American bases in Japan, Okinawa, and so on, are all nuts that we have to crack. Some of them are difficult, but none is impossible, and in the end they will all be solved. We are living in the period of transition, moving slowly toward accommodation and independence."

II

Intellectuals are not the only partisans of China trade. A Tokyo merchant, formerly a trading-company executive and director of one of the many organizations for promotion of trade with the Communist countries, estimates that about 25 per cent of the Japanese business world wants to trade with China very badly indeed. This figure may not be accurate, but the "China lobby" in Japan includes many who feel the pinch of the trade cutoff most severely: the small makers and the depressed textile operators with quick, vociferous views, who are anxious to collar anybody who will listen to their real or imaginary woes. Here is the way Shōnai Morii, the president of a talc manufacturing firm in Osaka and a leader in agitation for China trade, put it:

"My best raw materials are now cut off from me in China, and the United States won't buy what I can manufacture from the stone I get in Hong Kong unless I can furnish a certificate of origin. So I am forced to use domestic materials of inferior quality and sell mostly in this country (of course, we are protected from foreign imports of talc). Southeast Asia is an unpredictable market; the people there have no ambition or entrepreneurship, and their purchasing power is low. The balance of United States-Japan trade is most unnatural, and the whole relationship must be readjusted. Once we are on a new footing with the United States we can begin to do business with China. I think our relations with China should be just as important as our relations with the United States. Each should influence the other, but we should not be bound entirely to either side, as we are now.

"China is a planned economy undergoing vast growth. We can integrate China's needs with our own. In doing this Japan should not attempt to rearm or revise the no-war Constitution but should try to stand between China and the United States. The best resistance is non-resistance. It might take ten to twenty years to solve the impasse with China, but eventually it will be solved. I am not joining in the national front but am working from the inside to influence conservative politicians like Takeo Miki, Kenzō Matsumura, and others."

It is not difficult to perceive the self-interest behind this man's views, no matter how ignorant he may seem of Chinese realities. Others repeat hollow cliches about the "natural unsuitability" of communism for the Chinese. For example, the president of a large spinning company, who was educated in Shanghai, had this to offer:

"The Chinese people are not Communists. For the time being, living standards are rising and the government is secure. But later communism will fail. The Chinese are free and independent by nature. I reject the American argument that United States recognition of China would cause unrest among the overseas Chinese; they will continue to do business regardless of politics. The United States should recognize China at once; it should have done so long ago. When I say this I am not in the least supporting the Socialists or advocating radical ideas. I fully support Kishi's 'wait-and-see' policy toward China. But the United States could, by acting now, help to prevent the conversion of millions of Chinese youth to communism. It may not be too late to act, but I also know that the United States is not likely to change its policy. I wrote Dulles in 1951 that he was wrong about China, and I have written others. Trade with China has been negligible since the war, but the future possibilities are unlimited. Cotton spinners may not get much business, because the Chinese are developing their own textile industry, but there is still a great field for synthetics in China."

And the owner of a small machine-tool shop near Osaka:

"Before the trade cutoff last May, I had sold a few machines to China through C. Itō and Co. Right now I am selling only ten per cent of my production overseas, and I have had to cut back drastically because of the business recession. My main overseas market is India, but I have great hopes for the China market in the future. Why? For two reasons: you can trust the Chinese more than you can trust the Indians and the other people in Southeast Asia; and the Chinese are more accustomed to our machines. Their economic development is moving much faster than Southeast Asia's. They can use what I have to sell them and not let it rust on the dock."

III

Most businessmen, however, take a very different line:

"Tokyo is always blaming Osaka for its mistakes. It said we got them into the war, we wanted expansion, now we want to trade with China. But how can we trade with China today except with political strings attached?"

An Osaka merchant, the third generation of his family to head his large trading company, and a good representative of the upper levels of the *Kansai* business class, with its celebrated condescension toward Tokyo, was speaking. He went on about China:

"Some of our young fellows here in Osaka, who recently got out of college and are in the best companies, large and small, are active in the movement to trade with China. There are about fifty of them from good families in the local branch of the *Keizai Dōyūkai* [a management organization], and recently they lined up a fellow named Morii [mentioned previously, a leader in the pro-China trade agitation] to get a bus and parade to Tokyo with placards advertising the China trade." He twisted in his chair and smiled down his long nose at me: "I call myself a nineteenth-century liberal, but some of my contemporaries were Communists in the twenties and now are pro-China. Some others are coarse people who will do anything for money. You know the saying, 'In Osaka, if you have no money, you are nothing.'

"The China problem can't be solved for the present. I like Kishi's policy of 'wait-and-see.' Of course, Kishi is a time-serving politician, and I have no use for politicians generally, but personally he is capable. He represents a fusion of businessman and bureaucrat, the elite of the society. What else is there for us to do but wait? Just before you came in I was talking with a left-wing Socialist politician from the upper house of the Diet—an awful person, really, with a peasant background. Our ideas are poles apart. He was trying to tell me how important it is to trade with China. But it is no good at present. I have many Chinese experts in my company, people who have lived in China and speak Chinese. But we don't feel that anything can be done until there are some big changes in the international situation.

"No, Japan should strengthen its trade and other relationships with the United States. For the time being, that is our only wise course, and we need wise men if we are to avoid being taken over by the Socialists. The Indians are no good; the Chinese can't be dealt with profitably, they are unpredictable; and the other countries of Asia are not really of first importance to Japan, at least not yet.

"China's harsh policy of cutting off trade has been resented, but this hasn't served to make the Japanese feel any closer to the United States. We are very different from you, and there should be no doubts or sentimentality about that. You are a well-intentioned people, nice individually, but I don't quite 'fix' you, if you know what I mean. But you are very powerful, you have the world at your feet; and Japan needs the wisdom to wait, to remain strongly allied with you. What we really need now is more propaganda for Japanese goods in America, better marketing practices. The people as a whole want to renew trade with China, but my top estimate of future trade volume with China is only half a billion dollars both ways, whereas our trade with the United States is two billion now and must grow larger.

"A war between the two worlds is inevitable, and I have a hunch that if Japan can sit still, remain wise and wait, in the new formulation of world forces her position may be stronger. The real key to diplomacy is not trade but military power. The biggest danger now is implication in Communist Asia. I have no hope of Japan drawing closer to the rest of Asia. Southeast Asia is going backward, not forward, and the kind of state socialism that those governments represent is vastly different from Japan. In this country private capitalism is immensely strong; it is we who have the drive to move the economy along, although, of course, we cannot avoid a certain amount of state intervention and control.

"The secret is to be able to wait. I admire the British. They may have grown gradually weaker, but they haven't made any really serious blunders. Japan is like Germany—we have had a great development, but we have also made great blunders. The war, of course, was a vast blunder. If we had waited instead of acting we might be in a much better position today. Even so, look at us: we are prospering, really.

And we did fight you. We did that. In the beginning we were ahead.

"The people I associate with, the top businessmen in *Keidanren* [the largest and most powerful management organization], all are aware of the futility of trying to trade with China now. In the Chamber of Commerce are some small-industry groups who want to trade and some textile people who want to because they have been hurt by the depression. Also some steel people who want to get rid of surplus stocks. But the Chinese are really interested in war and violence, not in trade. We must wait. The new formulation of power may not come in my lifetime, but it is worth waiting for anyhow."

IV

Back in Tokyo, Takeo Miki saw me in his office between dashes to the Diet to attend committee sessions and meetings with delegations of his constituents. Director of the Economic Planning Agency, the Science and Technology Agency, and the Atomic Energy Committee, Miki has held cabinet posts and top party posts since the war. Since 1937 he has been a Diet member and for some years has been regarded as the white hope of the younger, more moderate conservatives; he represents the party careerist as opposed to the ex-bureaucrats who even before the Occupation ended had begun to enter the conservative ranks and fight for control over them.

Miki looks younger than his fifty-one years; his dapper, rather passive manner does not jibe with his record of sharp political infighting for more than two decades. Well-dressed and prosperous-looking (his wife is the daughter of a prominent businessman), he had taken care to tuck his long winter underwear neatly into his sock tops in the best approved fashion, even though the weather outside was a mild October afternoon. He spoke in the clear, well-modulated voice that has made him famous as a platform performer:

"Everybody in Japan wants to trade with China. Nobody is against it, but matters are now in Peiping's hands. We can do nothing more here."

I asked: "What about differences of opinion on this issue within the conservative party? Aren't you yourself more eager to trade with China than some others?"

"No big policy change on China is possible," he replied, "while the conservatives are in power. But, of course, among the party leaders there are many different personalities and backgrounds, and ways of thinking about China are not necessarily identical. The Chinese might change their own views, depending on who is in control here."

"In other words, if Kishi were removed, then China might soften its attitude?"

"I think so, yes. The trouble with the party is that there are too many bureaucrats in it. Even the head of the *Seichōkai* [Political Affairs Research Board, a policy-forming organ of the conservative party] is an ex-bureaucrat. You see, all the top ministerial posts now are party posts, and if a man is ambitious to get beyond vice-minister he has to get into the party and get himself elected to the Diet. So we are loaded down with ex-officials, who have close ties in the Ministries. I saw this problem when I was head of the *Seichōkai* last year. The party men simply have got to study and learn more about how to carry on the business of the Diet. But, to come back to the China problem, I repeat that there can be no really basic solution until many other things have changed first. A settlement of the Taiwan question obviously is a prerequisite to recognition of Communist China. I see three possible solutions for Taiwan. First is direct negotiation between Peiping and Taipei. This seems unlikely while Chiang lives. Second is Communist recognition of Taiwan's independence—in other words, two Chinas. But I think it improbable that either Chiang or Mao would accept that. The third solution is a plebiscite. Of course"—he smiled broadly— "if most of the people voted to join the mainland, the problem would be settled. In any case, I believe several years must pass before Japan recognizes Peiping. Japan's recognition will accompany America's; there will be no great time lag between the two. Nothing is likely to happen until the Democrats take over in the United States, and nothing is certain even then, but at least there would be a possibility." [He repeated *possibility* in English to make sure I had understood.]

"Last week in Osaka a businessman told me that another war was inevitable and Japan might pick up some of the pieces afterward."

"No major war will come, because both sides are afraid of atomic destruction. But there will be little wars, like those in Korea and Viet-Nam."

"How serious are the reports of Communist Chinese competition with Japanese exports in Southeast Asia?"

"Not too serious or significant yet. We are not very worried now. But ten years from now the picture will be very different. Then China and Japan will be fighting it out for economic supremacy in Asia. India will be running along behind, a poor third. The Indians haven't got what it takes to catch up with us. Our major problem is to change the structure of our exports. This year textiles still amount to around 40 per cent of our total exports. In ten years we must bring that down to between 10 per cent and 20 per cent. This will take some doing, but it can be done."

* * *

Although it is impossible here to reproduce the opinions of more than a few Japanese, short-term attitudes toward China evidently are very diverse, ranging from emotional calls for confessions of Japanese guilt and friendship with the Communist regime (and abandonment of Chiang Kai-shek) among intellectuals to deep skepticism about early trade or other relationships with Peiping among conservative business and political circles.

The long-range view, however, is more unified and serene. Small-scale business operators and others who are perennially at a disadvantage as marginal suppliers of the world's needs may still talk about "poor Japan's" lot; but the volume of such talk, loud in bad times, clearly has diminished in the last few years. Moreover, while interest in "economic co-operation" with Southeast Asia is widespread, there is a noticeable tendency to contrast the slow rate of progress in that part of Asia with the dynamism of Chinese economic growth.

Friendship with China does not imply subordination to China, nor does it imply aggression under the prewar guise of "co-prosperity." Most Japanese with whom I have spoken about China (including some not reported here) cherish an image of an autonomous Japan of the future, somehow free of binding ties with either the Communist or non-Communist worlds, but trading vigorously with both. They seem unperturbed by the spectacle of Chinese totalitarianism so near at hand; rather, they appear confident that Japan will participate significantly in the Asian future and that this country, though it must loosen its unequal ties with America, will not be absorbed by the Communist sphere. This Japanese judgment of their own future may seem a naïve dream, especially when one considers Japan's relatively small population, its scarcity of natural resources, and its worsened position in the postwar balance of power in Asia. But Japan is its own ally and no one else's; and I believe that most Japanese who think at all about China trade cling to a progressivist ideal in which Japan's latent greatness is taken for granted.

CHAPTER 27

JAPAN AND KOREA:
THE BITTER LEGACY

June 10, 1961

Sixteen years after World War II Japan remains cut off from Korea, hardly able to influence, much less to control, events in a country that was for 35 years a Japanese colony. To Tokyo residents what happens in Washington, D.C., is more read about and better known than happenings in Seoul, a few hours away across the straits of Tsushima. A vague weight oppresses the Japanese consciousness when Korea is thought of; there the armies face each other; there the fearful destruction may again break out. But aside from this general uneasiness, Korea is meaningful mainly to those who have, or hope to have, special interests there: to a few scholars digging in the past, a few bureaucrats who must talk with Koreans and make or implement policy, and a few businessmen who expect to profit from dealings with their Korean counterparts. Whatever the politics or the private interests of these Japanese, nearly all of them, from the Tokyo intellectual to the fisherman on the Nagasaki docks, look down on the Korean people and share a common prejudice against them.

This prejudice sometimes is expressed in very specific terms, e.g., "Koreans eat too much garlic,"[1] or it may be more generalized: "Korean thinking is distorted; Koreans need to have something to

---

[1] One Korean in Tokyo retorted to this complaint: "Negotiating with a Japanese is like peeling a green onion. You never know what's there until it's all gone."

347

protest against; they are too excitable; they need to feel inferior because they have been inferior for so long," and so on. Japanese writers on Asian affairs often show nostalgia for China and occasionally express regret for past deeds of their countrymen there, but no such feelings of yearning or guilt are shown toward Korea. On the contrary, one finds a stubborn refusal to make amends or to admit the slightest regret for the colonial past. Japanese insist that they developed Korea. They took over a decayed, expiring monarchy that was no more prepared to live in the modern world than some African tribal kingdoms are today; there they built railroads, harbors, and industries, raised agricultural productivity, created schools and public-health systems, and enforced orderly administration on a people with a thin, inferior culture who could not have done these things for themselves. The thought that Koreans might not be grateful for what was, in fact, done in Japan's own interest is offensive to them. Rather than offering apologies that the Koreans have demanded ever since the war, and that Japan has offered to the countries of Southeast Asia that she overran, the Japanese still seem to expect a show of gratitude for the exploitation of Korea and the calculated repression of whatever capacities for self-government the Koreans possessed.

Those who cherish the notion that Asia is somehow inscrutably One may find all this very disturbing. But this is only a part of the richly complex problem of how industrialized Japan, the only ex-colonial Asian power, is to relate itself to the transformed Asian world of today. The impasse in Japan's relations with Korea is the product of causes, part psychological, part political, that affect its relations with every country of Asia.

BACKGROUND OF THE JAPAN-KOREA IMPASSE

The Japanese Empire was not turned back voluntarily by its proprietors to the rightful owners, territory by territory. Neither was it lost piecemeal in bitter, rear-guard actions against nationalist guerrilla forces. It was dismantled quickly and totally as a consequence of total defeat. In the process one of the most extensive population movements of modern times was carried out. Between 1945 and 1948, when the Republic of Korea was created below the 38th parallel, nearly 900,000 Japanese were repatriated from the Korean peninsula to Japan. (About a third of these came from Soviet-occupied northern Korea.) Most repatriates were civilians uprooted from their colonial holdings and forced to return to the home islands with what they could carry on their backs. Their property, and all Japanese government property in the American-occupied zone on or after August 9, 1945, was confiscated and later disposed of to the South Korean government or to private Korean citizens. In one blow the Japanese lost the strategic and economic position they had built up since the late nineteenth century in the Korean peninsula. Soviet Russian influence was established over a large part of the "dagger pointed at the heart of Japan" from which Tsarist Russia had been excluded by Japanese arms 40 years before.

While these Japanese were being returned, more than a million Koreans were repatriated from Japan, where they had gone or had been taken against their will during the war to work in factories or to fight in the Japanese armed forces. Not all returned, however; Japan was left after defeat with about 700,000 Koreans, a far larger number than had lived there before the war. These Koreans formed the only significant racial minority in the country, and from the start they were a source of trouble for the Japanese authorities. Discriminated against socially and economically, most of them were able to find only low occupations or none at all. Some drifted into the big city underworld. As the lines of political division hardened in their own country at the 38th parallel, Koreans in Japan clustered around rival political organizations; a majority were affiliated with, or under the influence of, the pro-North Korean *Chōsen Sōren*, while a smaller number supported the pro-South Korean *Mindan*. These two rival associations waged propaganda warfare on Japanese soil.

As long as the Occupation lasted it allowed the Koreans rights of residence and treated them as Japanese citizens. However, Japan no longer possessed a Korean colony, and once full independence was recovered Japan would automatically regard them as aliens. They could scarcely be treated just as other aliens were treated; but what was to be their precise status? Unless they were to be sent back en masse to a Korea now split in two, some special effort would have to be made to clarify their rights and duties in Japan. In short, the Korean minority was another of the numerous displaced groups washed up in the wake of World War II. Solution of the problem they represented would have been difficult in the most peaceful of worlds, among men of the best will.

Negotiations between the Japanese government and the government of South Korea commenced in late 1951, after the San Francisco Peace Treaty had been signed but before it took legal effect in April 1952. These negotiations have continued ever since, and although some trade and other relationships between the two countries have been possible under agreements made during Occupation days, official diplomatic relations have not yet been established. Instead of addressing themselves in a constructive spirit to the problem of the Korean residents, Japanese and Koreans both allowed the contempt and resentment they felt for each other to spill out in a flood of claims and counterclaims, all of them heavily charged with emotion. During most of the nine years of sporadic talks the Japanese were confronted by the irreconcilable figure of Syngman Rhee, incarnation of exiled Korean nationalism. President Rhee continually inflamed anti-Japanese sentiment and sought to link hostility to Japan with anticommunism to keep his own position strong at home through the frightful back-and-forth struggles going on there. The Japanese hated him, and their representatives at the talks, especially in the early years, were a pretty arrogant, hard-bitten lot, who expected no forgiveness from Rhee or his representatives and were reluctant to seek any.

The main positions on both sides were staked out in the first clutch of talks that extended, off and on, from February 1952 until October 1953. The Korean side presented a long list of claims, many of them indefinite but all of them high. Rhee demanded that all Koreans in Japan, regardless of place of origin, become citizens of the Republic of Korea, that they be given special rights denied to other aliens, and that some of these rights be extended to their descendants. Korean negotiators presented claims totaling many hundreds of millions of dollars for unpaid wages of Korean workers and soldiers, pensions, postal savings deposits, unpaid insurance claims, gold and silver stocks removed from Korea during the colonial period, and many other categories of monetary claims. Korea demanded title to all Japanese ships which had been caught in Korean harbors on August 9, 1945. The Korean side also called for return of an extensive list of cultural properties, including art objects, contents of excavated tombs, paintings, books, etc., which had been removed to Japan by the Japanese government or purchased in Korea by Japanese citizens. The suggestion was made from time to time that Japan owed Korea war reparations, although the Japanese side pointed out that Korea had not been a belligerent at war with Japan. As if to give these claims an added sting, President Rhee in early 1952 announced the establishment of the "Peace Line," an arbitrary sea boundary around the southern half of the Korean peninsula, at some points more than 60 miles offshore. Japanese fishermen would cross this line at their peril; actual seizure of fishing boats by Korean patrols began in September 1953.[2]

Countering these claims, Japan demanded restitution of vast Japanese properties in Korea. By the terms of the San Francisco Peace Treaty Japan had abandoned all claim to such properties; but the Japanese delegate to the talks now challenged the legality of the Allied disposition of private Japanese assets in Korea, as opposed to government assets. This claim rested on a legal technicality and was put up to some extent as a gambit in the early stages of bargaining, but it infuriated the Koreans.

Negotiations broke down in late 1953 on a note of mutual intransigence. From then until his departure from the Korean scene in April 1960, Rhee kept anti-Japanese feeling hot and frequently accused the Japanese of being "soft on communism." In due time he held several hundred Japanese fishermen in Korean jails. He interfered with trade with Japan or banned it altogether, refusing at times to allow purchases of United States aid supplies in Japan, even though this country was the logical supplier. He made it difficult or impossible for Japanese to visit Korea and forced those who did to leave after short periods.

On its side, the Japanese government persisted in its unreconstructed attitudes and refused to take any very active initiative to break through the impasse. In 1957, after the United States Department of State had given its view that Japan had no right to confiscated properties in Korea and that Japanese-Korean claims in effect canceled out each other, the Japanese apparently abandoned their blanket demand for compensation. But as long as Rhee remained in power there was a disposition to let the Koreans make all the first moves. The long series

[2] For a more detailed account of this problem, see The "Rhee Line": A Japanese View (LO-8-'55), an AUFS publication.

of "preliminary talks" wore on without result except for rumors, intrigue, and press propaganda on both sides. Japan felt little need for Korea, with its meager resources, most of them in the Communist-held north. On the contrary, Japanese negotiators believed that South Korea would be forced sooner or later to turn to industrialized Japan for all kinds of economic assistance. In the middle of 1959, after Rhee had refused to accept Korean repatriates from Japan unless accompanied by a substantial cash payment for their resettlement, the Japanese government sanctioned voluntary repatriation to North Korea for all Koreans, regardless of their place of origin, under the supervision of the International Red Cross. President Rhee fumed and threatened naval intervention; in the end he broke off all trade with Japan but took no more violent action. As of the end of May 1961, 60,000 Koreans had left for the Communist People's Republic, and another 16,000 were signed up to go. Repatriates were being ferried in Soviet vessels from Niigata on the Japan Sea to Chongjin at the rate of approximately 1,000 a week.

JAPANESE INTEREST IN KOREA

Last January an official of one of Japan's largest banks visited Korea briefly as an observer with a group of businessmen inspecting certain export products and facilities. On his return to Tokyo he circulated a report in Japanese to the bank's branches, giving his general impressions and reactions. Written shortly before the army *coup d'état* of May 16, this report contains some useful insights into the Korean situation as seen by a conservative, responsible Japanese businessman:

The Korean economy is riddled with all kinds of problems. To begin with, the economic structure was originally built up during the Japanese period with the whole peninsula as a unit. North Korea has the industry and mining; South Korea exists by agriculture. But with the peninsula artificially bisected at the 38th parallel, South Korea by itself can have no self-supporting industrial structure. Agriculture still is predominant in its economy, which would be fine if secondary industry were also developed, but unfortunately no base or backbone has been created for such industry. On the other hand, tertiary industries have proliferated in a very odd manner; one has the feeling that this growth of service industries is related to the problem of finding jobs for excess population, but it is also connected with the stationing of American troops in the country. Primary and tertiary each account for 40 per cent of the national income, while manufacturing is very weak and accounts for only 20 per cent.

The country was torn to pieces by the Korean War a decade ago. Since then it has been necessary to maintain a huge standing army of 600,000 men as the front line of defense in the cold war between East and West. Electric power is extremely inadequate, and factories must make up for the scarcity by generating what power they can for themselves. Electricity is shut off for household users all night, and temporary shutoffs also occur during the day. Two million persons out of a working population of eight million are said to be unemployed. Along with this situation, consumer goods flow out of American Army PX's or are smuggled into the country by way of Tsushima [a Japanese island between Japan and Korea] and flood the retail markets of the cities. The shops are loaded not only with American-made consumer goods but also Japanese transistor radios, cosmetics, and even Japanese magazines like *The Housewife's Friend*.

The balance of payments shows a colossal deficit, and the gap is filled mainly by the American ICA Aid Fund. In the last ten years this ICA Fund has totaled around three billion dollars. If this money had been used in an organized fashion to encourage a productive manufacturing base, it could have been the key to creation of a self-supporting economy. What has in fact happened is that the money has been paid out for fertilizer, raw cotton, and wheat; moreover, a corrupt environment has grown up around the Aid Fund. The Korean economy must continue to rely on ICA for the time being; and it is absolutely essential that a backbone for the economy be created while this aid is still available. The problem is not merely that the economy is in trouble today, but that there is no prospect for a productive backbone in the future. What is more, Korea is our nearest neighbor, not a distant country. Here is the problem for Japan.

The dictatorship of Syngman Rhee has been destroyed, the old Liberal Party and those who prospered by connections with it have fallen out of sight, and power has gone over to the opposition Democrats; but that party is split into two factions over personal, not policy differences, so that there are two parties, the Democrats and the New Democrats, opposing each other. Freedom of speech, which did not exist in the Rhee period, has been recognized, and the newspapers print whatever they like. But despite the fact that the government party has a majority, it is quite needlessly shaken up by the utterances of the opposition. In addition, labor unions have been organizing since the new regime came in; all the city banks except the Bank of Korea now have unions, and a Socialist party has been born. Then there are the university students who, though they are not leftists, take the lead in public demonstrations. All these phenomena have been released in reaction to the oppression of the Rhee government, and the times are unstable.

Korea is not the only country where one finds such economic and political conditions: in Southeast Asia, Laos, Indonesia, and Viet-Nam are much the same. But what is different about Korea is that it is next door to us. If things are left as they are now, there is no assurance that a nation identical with the present North Korea will not extend all the way to Pusan. For this reason I felt very keenly while I was there that we Japanese must pay more attention to Korea.

KOREAN SENTIMENT TOWARD JAPAN

This has two aspects. One is shown by the cancellation of a Japanese economic mission last January 23 when it was on the point of enplaning for Seoul, and by the "#2 Hagerty Incident" when Foreign Minister Kosaka visited Seoul last September. Anti-Japanese elements fall into two categories:

(a) The older generation cherishes resentment at the oppression and exploitation of long years of Japanese rule;

(b) The young people know nothing of Japan but were brought up under a decade of Rhee's rule and followed the anti-Japanese lead of his regime.

However, active anti-Japanese elements are not very numerous; they mostly remain submerged and drag the issue out from time to time. . . . For instance, the 500 Koreans who demonstrated against the economic mission before it was to arrive in Seoul were reportedly paid money for their pains.

On the other hand, Koreans over 28 or so, who received their education during the Japanese period, all speak Japanese; their feelings about life and their customs are similar to Japan. On my recent trip all my business was conducted in Japanese, and I had no feeling of being in a foreign country and no unpleasant thoughts whatever. In this sense a common foundation exists between Japan and Korea. Side by side with many who feel antipathy and revulsion are many others who feel that Japan is their neighbor, and since this country shows the effects of a marvelous economic growth, they believe it is desirable that we co-operate. In any case, the feeling is general in Korea that current negotiations should liquidate past differences and make a new start. . . .

Some Koreans, of course, argue that Japan's economic growth was greatly benefited by the Korean War; they say that Japan goes forward and prospers without having to have any direct contact with the Communist world, precisely because Korea is holding the line at the 38th parallel. And they ask whether it would not be well for Japan to think a bit more about Korea. This is a very natural reaction, I believe. The hope was also expressed to me that both sides would give in a little in the negotiations: for example, if the legal status of Koreans in Japan could only be solved, then the Korean side would like to restore diplomatic relations. It is essential to wipe away past differences and make some progress now toward a settlement.

Political differences have so far made economic co-operation and aid impossible. Even today, this boils down to a Korean insistence that Japan buy more Korean goods. The problem is that Korea has little or nothing to sell; nevertheless, the Japanese side should be ready to buy more Korean products, even if they are not needed. For example, edible seaweed and rice should be bought in greater quantities, even though the Agriculture Ministry fights against it. Suppose Korea sold us 100 to 150 million sheets of seaweed, what would that amount to compared with domestic production of three billion sheets? . . .

Nothing in this study will be news to a reader familiar with contemporary Korea; however, it very clearly shows a Japanese concern for a danger near at hand. Laos may be taken over by Communist guerrillas without producing much sense of urgency in the banker's mind; but Korea is a different matter, and something should be done about it, in his opinion, before it is too late. Thus the ancient Japanese strategic interest in Korea is repeated in the present context of emotional and political stalemate between the two countries. Likewise, the overgeneralized indictment of American aid policies reflects feelings that are common in the conservative government, which is fond of expressing pious horror at the corruption that is supposed to radiate like an evil sun wherever American consumer goods are gathered together.

The banker's final point needs to be repeated: South Korea has very little that Japan wants to buy. Korean exports to Japan in the period 1955–60 averaged 47 per cent of its total exports; but this was only 0.3 per cent of Japan's total imports. Imports from Korea are almost entirely primary commodities—fish, seaweed, mineral ores. Japan has been selling around 40 million dollars a year worth of chemical fertilizer, machinery, steel sheets, and other aid goods to Korea in recent years. Fertilizer sales have amounted to a substantial part of total exports of this commodity; but apart from United States aid materials, ordinary Japanese exports have come to only about $14 million annually, and even this small amount is larger than ordinary imports, so that by last winter Korea had accumulated a trade debt of over $45 million, causing Tokyo to suspend open account trading temporarily. The point of all this is that Korea can manufacture almost nothing to sell abroad, while Japan is turned to the West for its most important economic relationships.

The most obvious role for Japan would be investment in the Korean economy. Up to now this has been blocked on both the private and governmental levels by the stalemate in political negotiations and by the more general uncertainty about Korea's future. However, some interest in investment exists, both as an end in itself and mixed with Japanese political interests in a more diffuse way.

Some of the largest, most responsible trading companies (as well as some less responsible ones) have conducted surveys and written reports on investment possibilities. A representative of one of these companies recently visited Korea for two months and recommended investment in several power plants, to cost a total of $50 million, a $30 million urea fertilizer plant, a cement plant, and a rayon yarn factory. All such plans depend upon government guarantees which cannot be given until political problems are solved. There are also other difficulties. On both sides commercial dealings have not always been above suspicion: a Japanese company recently was involved in a scandal concerning alleged private payments to the manager of a Korean government-operated tungsten firm. This affair was used by the Korean opposition to attack the Seoul government, and the Japanese authorities were not happy about it.

Aside from the activities of trading firms, what might be called a "Korea lobby" has operated for some years in an informal way. This group includes a number of right-wing politicians, some of them, like former Deputy Prime Minister Mitsujirō Ishii, with close business and industrial connections. A "committee for the study of Korean problems" was set up not long ago inside the Liberal-Democratic party, with Ishii as its chairman. Other members of the group include former Defense Agency Chief Naka Funada and former Finance Minister Keizō Shibusawa. Some of these men are concerned primarily with the security aspect of the Korean problem; the Communist threat to Japan is what they see first there. Others have money primarily in mind. They are tied to Japanese firms, like Yawata Steel, which have connections with a few wealthy Korean businessmen in Japan or otherwise engage in commerce with South Korea (and probably also with North Korea, though there is very little Japanese trade with the north). Some are opportunists or adventurers with a flair for intrigue.

Some representative views of the "Korea lobby" are expressed in the monthly magazine of the Nikkan Shinwa Kai (Japan-South Korea Friendship Society), which publishes articles on the negotiations, cultural subjects, folk songs, poems, and the like. Contributions to this magazine have a very nationalistic tone. They criticize American policy in Korea in far stronger terms than the Tokyo banker used in his report. The United States gave China to the Communists, and American aid to Korea has been deplorably ineffective. Japan knows Korea better and is really friendlier to her than any other nation. Prewar Japanese industrialists, who may have exploited Korean resources, have passed from the scene, and today's more "modern" industrialists have little interest in the country. This will be especially true as long as the Korean government stalls on a political settlement and discriminates against Japanese businessmen. Japan should be included in Korean-American economic planning from the outset, rather than merely being used as a source of aid goods or consulted after plans are made. The United States and South Korea both should understand Japan better. They should not distrust Japanese intentions. Japan has no desire to recolonize Korea, but it could help train Koreans to rebuild their country. The Japanese only want to work for world peace in the United Nations side by side with Korea as an Asian colleague, and so on.[3]

Some of these arguments sound like echoes from the dim past, when China was weak and Japan could back up its "special interest" on the Asian mainland with armies and aggressive policies. But although some leaders of Japan's conservative party feel a strong strategic concern for Korea, they have not been well united up to now on a definite policy toward that country. Militarily weak and harassed by a Socialist opposition that stands for unarmed coexistence and calls American militarism the main cause of tension in Asia, Japanese initiative has been hesitant and diffuse, and Japan remains without any real control over developments in Korea until today. This has been dramatically illustrated in the most recent events.

After the student uprising in South Korea and Rhee's departure for Hawaiian exile in April 1960, Japanese-Korean relations entered a new and somewhat improved phase. The same old psychological barriers existed as before; but the government of Premier Chang Myun, buried under economic crisis from the start, showed more interest in getting Japanese help. The Japanese responded grudgingly and without much enthusiasm, but at least they attempted to respond. The United States, which had long desired better relations between Korea and Japan, urged both sides to reach a settlement; in fact, one reason

[3] The above is a paraphrase of an article entitled "Promoting South Korean Economic Construction," in *Shinwa*, #83, September 15, 1960.

for renewed Japanese interest was their irritation at being asked interminably by foreign reporters and diplomats why they could not get along with South Korea.

Early last September Foreign Minister Kosaka visited Seoul on the invitation of the Chang government. He got a cool reception, and one carload of his party was mobbed by angry Koreans (this was the "# 2 Hagerty incident" to which the banker referred in his report). But Kosaka's visit resulted in new Japanese offers of economic aid, in return for cancellation of Korean claims; a new series of "preliminary talks" began in Tokyo, and for the first time since 1952 a political solution appeared possible. Last month, when a delegation of conservative Diet members and government officials spent a week of talk, travel, and entertainment in South Korea, they were delighted to find Japanese novels in Korean translations outselling anything else in the bookstores and customers in Korean coffee shops listening to the Japanese popular tune, "Let's Meet at Yūrakuchō." On their return on May 13 the delegation declared that diplomatic relations would soon be restored.

Three days later, before dawn on May 16, elements of the Korean military overthrew the Chang government and established rule by revolutionary committee. Japanese leaders were completely baffled by the Korean *coup*. Economic conditions there were obviously serious, with massive unemployment and famine in some areas. One Tokyo newspaper had speculated as recently as May 14 that "the only conceivable force that could save the situation would be the army." But except in Communist propaganda there was no suggestion that the Japanese had known in advance about the *coup*. The leader of the recent delegation to Korea was taken entirely by surprise. He had just brought home a glowing picture of the Japanese-Korean future; now, in his own words, the young generals had "killed a chicken with a knife big enough to slaughter an ox." He showed no dismay at the eclipse of elected government in Korea; but he was disappointed by the fall from power of Koreans who had been willing to countenance new relationships with Japan, and he reflected the government's concern (this was less than 48 hours after the *coup*) over the effect of events in Seoul on Japan's security.

Today, three weeks later, the Korean military junta has indicated its wish to continue negotiations with Japan and its interest in Japanese aid. But it has also strengthened patrols against Japanese fishing boats, and Tokyo authorities still are in the dark concerning the true meaning of events in Korea. Apprehension has replaced the optimistic view of Korean-Japanese problems that was evident just before the *coup*. The young generals are regarded as more excitable and less experienced than military men who have taken over in Pakistan and elsewhere in recent years. Japanese government leaders, themselves primarily technicians and economic managers, are not sanguine about the ability of young officers to develop the dirt-poor economy of South Korea, and they wonder what might come if the army fails.

* * *

If either side had been more eager to solve the impasse between Japan and Korea, it might have been solved long ago. But the Koreans went on arresting Japanese fishermen in waters far from the Korean coast, thus keeping the atmosphere tense and making their other claims seem even more unreasonable than they already were to the Japanese. For their part, the Japanese refused to make amends for the past, when a simple expression of regret and apology might have gone a long way toward achieving reconciliation. Leaders on both sides used deep-seated cultural prejudices as an excuse not to reach understanding. As one high official in the Japanese Foreign Ministry explained, "Public opinion will not allow us to take the initiative toward Korea." But the government did little or nothing to re-educate public opinion and reduce its ingrown prejudices, because these prejudices were shared by the leaders themselves.

Japanese international attitudes, like their personal attitudes, tend to fall into vertical rather than horizontal patterns. A country is either to be looked up to or it is to be treated with condescension. Korea has been in the latter category for many, many years. But, apart from the condescension felt by a former imperial power toward its long-time colony, on the level of economic interest Japan after 1952 was preoccupied with building up its ties with North America and Europe. With exports to the United States running to over $1 billion in 1959, ICA purchases of around $40 million for Korea were not of decisive importance in the Japanese balance of payments. Aside from some tungsten, a little coal, and a few agricultural products,

Korea had little that Japan needed. Before the war, Korean rice had been imported in large quantities, but by the late 1950's Japan was virtually self-sufficient in this staple food. On the other hand, Korea badly needed Japanese know-how, capital goods, and equipment. The economic dependence was all on one side.

Emotionally and economically, then, Japan remains isolated from Korea. Politically, too, there is a certain alienation, as I have already suggested. Rhee's old charge that the Japanese conservatives are "soft on communism" is assuredly not true. But the desire to play a more detached, independent role in Asia and the world exists as an underlying political reality, no matter how timidly it may be expressed at the present time. Japan is allied with the West and supports the UN position in Korea. But the ruling Liberal-Democratic party is a collection of cliques and factions, and within it there is some disposition, if not to embrace "neutralism," at least to look on both sides while remaining conscious of the dangers from the other side. This tendency, added to the habit of regarding Koreans as contemptible, naturally gets in the way of warm relations. Meanwhile, the government continues to advertise itself rather implausibly as a "bridge" between East and West, to do business where it can and cleave to the United States.

CHAPTER *28*

OKINAWAN PERSPECTIVES

May 25, 1959

I

Before World War II the Ryukyu Islands were a backward agricultural prefecture of Japan, regularly swept by devastating typhoons but otherwise unnoticed by the world. Few Americans had ever heard of Okinawa, the largest island and capital of the group. Okinawa prefecture had the lowest per capita income in Japan. Farmers grubbed out a living by growing sweet potatoes on the hard clay hillsides, feeding the potato tops to hogs, and eating pork, a habit born of ancient Chinese influence. On the pocket-sized plains near the sea they planted two crops of rice a year, but the Ryukyus are too small to have streams useful for irrigation; depending entirely upon rainfall, the rice crop was frequently lost.

Sixty per cent of the prefectural income came from agriculture, but the islands were a food import area and showed trade deficits in every year from 1923 until World War II. In 1934–36, the standard prewar index period, exports were 69.2 per cent of imports. Deficits were made up by government subsidies and remittances from Okinawans abroad. Japan took out some agricultural produce, about three-fourths of it black sugar and centrifugal sugar, plus some rice brandy, Panama hats, handicraft textiles, and lacquer ware. Imports included rice from Siam, Japanese factory textiles and processed foods, fertilizer, lumber, and miscellaneous commodities. The Japanese provided schools modeled on the central system and a bureaucratic administration in

361

which all the key positions were reserved for Japanese dispatched from Tokyo. Few Okinawan leaders emerged; Okinawans were Japanese citizens, racially akin to Japanese and speaking the language, but they suffered social discrimination, and those who were able to secure a good university education in Tokyo stayed there, entered the government or private business, and merged with the Japanese generality.

In May and June of 1945 Okinawa was swept by an unprecedented typhoon of lead and high explosives. After a campaign of historic ferocity, in which more than 12,500 Americans, 100,000 Japanese, and many thousands of Okinawan civilians were killed, U.S. forces occupied Okinawa island and the rest of the Ryukyu chain. The already sparse landscape was left utterly desolate by the battles; in the southern half of the island all trees were destroyed and almost all buildings were leveled. Today about all the Okinawans can point to as prewar relics are a few massive stone walls belonging to former temples; the temple buildings themselves are gone.

The American arrival in Okinawa was an episode in a hot war; its continued presence there is a consequence of the Cold War. The record of U.S. occupation is a record of improvisation, uncertainty, political insensitivity, and gradual admission of the necessity of a constructive civil policy. But at whatever stage of its evolution, from first to last the American interest there has been strategic, and civil policies continue today to serve essentially military ends.

For several years after the war economic life in Okinawa was at a standstill. Military government organized local administrative units and distributed relief goods. Grants in aid began to pour in. From the outset Okinawa was detached from the four Japanese home islands, and most of the social and economic reforms instituted by the Occupation in Japan did not apply there. Government was direct and military, first under the U.S. Navy, and later under the Army, where it remains today. In the immediate postwar years it was supposed that American forces would soon withdraw; consequently few constructive plans were made. Okinawa came to be regarded as a kind of Siberia to which mediocre or undesirable personnel in the Occupation of Japan were exiled.

However, Okinawa was not to remain a backwater for long. With the deterioration of American-Russian relations in the late 1940's, the emergence of Communist China in 1949, and the outbreak of the

Korean War in June 1950, the strategic significance of the Ryukyus became apparent. Okinawa is an unsinkable air base some 30 minutes from Shanghai, jet flying time.

Changes in the U.S. administrative structure reflected a new determination to remain in the area indefinitely and in force. In December 1950 the U.S. Civil Administration of the Ryukyu Islands (USCAR) was set up under military control. The San Francisco Peace Treaty in September 1951 left the ultimate fate of Okinawa deliberately vague but assigned complete jurisdiction over its affairs to the United States until such time as the latter might wish to propose that the area become a UN trust territory. In 1953 the American government announced that the U.S. would remain in Okinawa "for the foreseeable future" and would not withdraw while a "state of tension" existed in the Far East. However, the U.S. noted that Japan retained "residual sovereignty" over the territory. America thus undertook a commitment to return Okinawa to Japan, but the date of reversion was left obscure.

From 1950 the American Occupation of the Ryukyus entered its second phase, characterized by a rapid expansion of bases, airfields, housing areas, and all other military facilities, which were primarily concentrated in the southern half of Okinawa island. Direct economic aid fell from $49 million in 1950 to $1.6 million in 1955 and less than $1 million in 1958. But military spending shot up rapidly, and thousands of Ryukyuans found jobs on bases or were absorbed in one way or another into the base economy. By 1958 at least 60,000 of them out of a total population of 800,000 were directly employed by U.S. forces, and thousands more depended indirectly on U.S. support.

When this large military build-up began, there was little time or inclination to look at what it implied for the Ryukyus' economy. However, the expansion of bases required land, and land-acquisition policies for the first time involved the U.S. in serious problems. In an overcrowded, infertile, land-short territory, with a total land area of only 542,000 acres, and a people tenaciously attached to their land plots, the U.S. by January 1959 had acquired about 67,000 acres, 40,000 of them on Okinawa island. Of this land 16,500 acres were described as arable and constituted 10.8 per cent of total arable land in the Ryukyus. However, on Okinawa, by far the most heavily populated island, around 20 per cent of all arable land was utilized by U.S.

forces, and in the southern end of the island the percentage was much higher.

Rents paid by U.S. authorities for much of this land were too little for the displaced families to buy or lease substitute land in the free market. Moreover, in 1956 the U.S. proposed a new method of land acquisition which, while leaving titles in Okinawan hands, would have granted full use of the land to the U.S. for an indefinite period in return for one lump-sum payment made in advance. Okinawan leaders vociferously opposed the lump-sum payments for land acquired and demanded increased rents and regular, periodic payments. This led to the most serious crisis in Okinawa since the war.

Whatever the needs for more land may have been, the land policies of the United States were so clumsy and high-handed that they alienated a people noted for their docility and provided a classic opportunity for political opponents of America to gain influence. These policies were characteristic of a period when the U.S. military command in Okinawa regarded as Communists all but the most conservative and co-operative political elements, and when the command seemed totally unaware of the repercussions of their policies on America's relations with Japan.

By early 1957 the Occupation of Japan had been over for five years, and large-scale retention of American bases on Japanese soil was becoming politically difficult. By the time of Prime Minister Kishi's visit to Washington in the summer of 1957, the State Department was prepared to offer withdrawal of U.S. ground forces from Japan; but there was also the probability that Kishi would bring up the Okinawan land question and make representations for the reversion of Okinawa to Japanese administration. The uproar over land policies was playing directly into the hands of the opposition Socialists who, though most of them knew little about Okinawa (and many cared less), cried emotionally for reunion with their "blood brothers" there.

To forestall Japanese demands and cool off the situation, the U.S. on June 5, 1957 issued Executive Order 10713, calling for America to develop "responsible local government, democratic principles, a viable economy, and higher living standards"—all high-sounding objectives that had been the admitted goal in Japan a decade earlier but had never received similar organized attention in Okinawa. All powers of jurisdiction over Okinawa were confirmed in the Secretary of Defense, but a new office of High Commissioner of the Ryukyu Islands was set up, to be occupied by the commanding general of the Ryukyus Command. Assisting the High Commissoner was a Civil Administrator, also an army general, and beneath him was placed the American civilian bureaucracy which, in turn, would supervise the Okinawan-staffed government of the Ryukyu Islands. Power remained firmly in U.S. military hands, but the role of civil administration was hereafter to be given new prominence. The initial phase of base construction was over, and a new period of consolidation was in order.

After negotiations by a joint American-Ryukyuan group set up for the purpose, the United States in 1958 agreed to suspend lump-sum payments for land and instead adopted a system of annual or five-year term payments with rentals substantially larger than those formerly paid. The U.S. thus, in effect, recognized Okinawan demands, but not before its land policies had helped to bring to power a pro-Communist mayor of Naha, who had to be ousted from office by a U.S.-ordered change in the election laws—"Operation Heave Ho," as the Americans in Okinawa called it, a symptom of the futility of the position in which the U.S. had lodged itself over the land question.

II

Today the political situation in Okinawa is quiet. The "land problem" has been solved, at least for the time being. Twelve million dollars in land rent payments for 1958 and 1959 are beginning to filter into the economy. An additional estimated $6 million a year may also become available if a bill now before Congress to return U.S. income-tax collections in Okinawa to the territory is passed. The Okinawan legislature, cockpit of political struggles in the past, seems reasonably orderly. There is the usual merging and dividing of political factions, with the conservative "party" now in a minority and seeking to overturn its moderate "Socialist Masses Party" rivals. Issues seem in short supply for the moment, though there are indications of trouble ahead over demands that a civilian Civil Administrator be appointed to replace the present military incumbent. The new mayor of Naha, though elected as an opposition candidate, is "co-operative," and his more extreme predecessor, momentarily discredited, is sucking his wounds and engaging in "self-criticism." The new American line is softer. The High Commissioner appears to be aware that not all Okinawans who disagree with him are Communists, and persons formerly considered "dangerous" are invited with their wives to social gatherings. As one observer wrote recently, the Americans seem to be taking a firm grip on their bouquets and setting out to woo the Okinawans.

The hard point is that America has got to give the Okinawans a break roughly as good as, or better than, they would get under Japanese jurisdiction. Japan as an ally is more important to America than Okinawa as a military base. Should the clamor for reversion to Japan grow sufficiently strong, Okinawa might have to be given up, if the pro-Western orientation of Japan were at stake.

Thus it is no accident that American officials in Okinawa emphasize that the per capita income of Ryukyuans is now higher than that in seven out of 43 Japanese prefectures; and it is not surprising that they recommend to Washington that more aid be granted to Okinawan education, because Japanese prefectures get half or more of their education budget from Tokyo. As Americans in Okinawa now point out, it is futile for the U.S. to suppose that it can gain the wholehearted support of the population for its continued administrative control and the use of much of the arable land for military bases merely by citing the Okinawan contribution to Free World defense. To Okinawans this contribution could be made equally well as a part of Japan. Okinawan schoolteachers get no pensions, and few Okinawan workers are protected by social security. But Japanese teachers get pensions of a sort, and social security of a sort is available to millions of Japanese workers. A failure to attend to human needs and desires in Okinawa as well as they are attended to in Japan will only intensify the demand for reversion.

If the Japanese were to get Okinawa back tomorrow they would inherit an unproductive economy packed to the bursting point with people who are temporarily better off because of American bases but whose per capita annual income was still only $173 in 1958, compared with the Japanese average of $245. The dislocation of the Ryukyus economy by war and its later redirection have had some spectacular effects. Today only 16 per cent of the area's income derives from agriculture, as against 60 per cent before the war. More than 200,000 Ryukyuans were repatriated from other Japanese islands in the

Pacific after the war, but only 52 per cent of the working force today is engaged in agriculture, as compared with 75 per cent in pre-war days. American bases provide more than half of the national income. In 1957 Ryukyus exports totaled $15.7 million, of which 44.3 per cent was scrap metal left over from the war, and 44.7 per cent was processed agricultural products, mainly sugar and a little pine-apple. Nearly all of these exports went to Japan. Imports in 1957 totaled $94.1 million, of which 60 per cent was consumer goods and the rest mainly building and construction materials. Over 70 per cent of these imports came from Japan. The deficit of about $80 million was made up largely by yen payments of various kinds—for base construction, wages and services, sales to American servicemen, and land rentals and other base-connected receipts. Okinawa has obviously become a base-dependent economy.

Now that the need for a more positive policy has been felt, some effort is being made, several years too late, to improve the productivity of the Okinawan economy and make it more nearly self-sufficient. But responsible American officials have few illusions about their task. Okinawa is a small island with almost no resources to work with. One high civilian official expressed the prevailing opinion: "Okinawa would be the worst possible place to try to build a 'show-window' of democracy. What we have to do is to leave the place better off than we found it, so that when we finally turn it over to the Japanese we will have reason to be proud, and nobody can accuse us truthfully of using the Okinawans and squeezing them dry." Another seconded this and added, "If Americans, with all their power and know-how, can't leave 800,000 Okinawans better off than they found them, there will be no excuse for our failure in the minds of Asians of whatever political persuasion."

A recent government report summed up the difficulties of the Oki-nawan economy in ponderous, muffled prose: "A variety of problems tend to contravene the maintenance of political and economic sta-bility—the lack of natural resources and productive capacity, over-population, lack of a tradition of self-administration, native mistrust of the U.S., a desire to 'belong' and its concomitant manifestations, pro-reversion sentiment, all compounded by those who would ex-ploit these problems. Yet at stake is the ability of this military base to play its assigned role among the global complex of strategic bases necessarily maintained by the U.S. and other free nations." Progress so far has been limited because it is difficult for USCAR to get much money for economic development purposes. The Budget Bureau still tends to think of Okinawa in purely military terms and will not release funds unless projects can be justified as military-connected. A TB hospital may be urgently desirable but goes unprovided for on these grounds. (In 1959 U.S. aid to the government of the Ryukyu Islands will be less than 13 per cent of the GRI's budget.) It is also difficult to urge tax reforms, new agricultural practices, programs of training in public administration, and the thousand other things that Americans normally advocate for "underdeveloped" countries, when it is obvious to everyone that the strategic interest is really paramount. Okinawa is fundamentally a military operation. Moreover, the American interest may be short-lived, and most Okinawans want to return to Japan. Any program of economic development must try to promote Okinawan skills and resources, increase domestic capital accumulation, and encourage foreign investment in productive enterprises; in short, it must try to make Okinawa more nearly self-sufficient. But self-sufficient for whom? It is hard to work enthusiastically for a people who have no separate integrity of their own, who do not want independence separately but derive their satisfaction from feeling that they are a part of Japan and resent their separation from Japan. Under the circumstances the temptation is to provide them with the minimum to keep them quiet and let the Japanese look out for them in the future.

Within these limitations steps are being taken to put the economy on a more productive permanent footing. In the summer of 1958 Okinawan B-Yen currency was withdrawn and U.S. dollars were introduced as legal tender. This move was denounced by the opposition in Japan and Okinawa as "American imperialism," but since the currency conversion deposits in Ryukyu banks have substantially increased, Japanese banks have made deposits in Ryukyu banks, and the capital supply appears to be slowly increasing. (Prices also have risen slightly since the conversion.) One main goal of conversion was to attract foreign investment by allowing relatively unrestricted repatriation of dollar capital and remittance of dollar profits in enterprises contributing to the long-range development of Okinawan skills and resources. It is too soon to know what the ultimate effect of the move will be, but before Americans will invest in the Ryukyus, the local government must do more than it has done to create a favorable climate for investment. It is unwilling to do this because it distrusts Americans' motives and unable to do it because nobody really knows how long America will be in the Ryukyus. USCAR maintains rather careful supervision over American business operations and has not hesitated to refuse or withdraw licenses or even to eject businessmen in order to avoid obvious charges of exploitation. However, most American money continues to be put into commercial or service-type ventures like garages, car agencies, import-export, insurance, and the like.

There also are plans to develop the pineapple-canning industry and plans for a free port area near Naha, where goods might be imported and processed for re-export without payment of the usual customs tolls. Light industries and other subsidiary services might grow up around such a zone, but this idea is in its early stages and has met with some resistance and skepticism among Okinawans. Most of the foreign capital in the Ryukyus is Japanese; Japanese are active in the sugar industry and elsewhere, but the U.S. has remained officially cool to Japanese offers to set up a "Southwest Islands Economic Development Corporation" for exploitation of Okinawan resources. The U.S. has also refused Japanese suggestions that Tokyo give grants in aid to the Okinawa school system and assist emigration to South America through its Liaison Office in Naha. The American authorities apparently wish to avoid anything that would lead to resumption of Japanese civil authority or anything resembling it. Elements in Okinawa and Japan have long called for the U.S. to surrender civil administration to the Japanese while keeping control of military bases. But the U.S. continues to regard this "compromise" as impossible. However, each time the U.S. refuses Japanese offers of "economic co-operation" it is put in an embarrassing position unless it can make some counteroffer of assistance to the Okinawans.

III

During my brief visit to Okinawa I met a few Americans who apparently believe that if the United States stays there long enough, many of its people, perhaps most of them, would prefer not to return to Japan. According to this view, the U.S. might eventually pick up its option under the Peace Treaty to make Okinawa a UN trust territory; and they dream of the day when Okinawa might become a kind of cultural and economic entrepôt in Asia, filled with agricultural experiment stations, public-health demonstration centers, and the like. This would enormously multiply its international usefulness by changing its role. Or, they say, Okinawa might acquire commonwealth status, à la Puerto Rico, and despite being virtually without resources, somehow undergo a miraculous economic growth. One enterprising Okinawan businessman, a graduate of Waseda University in Tokyo and the president of a local oil company, expressed a somewhat similar vision. Since it may not be possible to recover for agricultural purposes much of the land that is now covered by concrete, and since most of the permanent-type construction is concentrated in the southern end of Okinawa island, Okinawa might become the ready-made capital of some future federation of Asian nations—a kind of international Canberra.

I do not believe that most thoughtful, responsible Americans in Okinawa envisage any other fate for the place than eventual reversion to Japan. Unquestionably some Okinawan businessmen—heads of construction companies, distributors of electric power, and others—who have grown fat on the Americans and who fear the return of Japanese financial control would like to put off reversion as long as possible. That they should want to take advantage of the Americans while they are there is only human. But nearly all of these, too, expect reversion to come eventually, and each is making his plans for that day. Rather than the deserted American facilities becoming another Canberra, it is more likely that Japanese military units will take them over some day, though they may have some difficulty adjusting to their lavishness. As one American-educated bank official observed, "I was in the Japanese Army during the war, and afterward I went to the U.S. to see how you beat us and find out why you are so strong. I am here using what I learned in America while the Americans are here, but the day they leave I expect to be on my way to a better job in Tokyo."

One final problem needs mentioning. The Japanese left is fond of crying out over the "Americanization" of Okinawa; but while American influence is obviously present in a variety of ways, I found very little evidence of deep "Americanization" of ideas or ways of life during my visit. True, a four-lane paved highway leads from Naha City up through the vast bases at Sukiran, Kadena, and beyond to Koza, the "city that sin built." On this highway American-sized traffic is thickly packed; alongside it are displayed advertisements of American cars, gasoline to burn in them, and garages to repair them. The wide, glary sky, bluer than Japan's, the burnished cars, and the dusty-oily smell of the highway reminded me a little of East Texas around Orange or Port Arthur. Acres of dependent housing areas flank the highway, filled with flat-topped, boxy bungalows and "ramblers" in tropical, landscaped grounds enclosed by high steel fences. Far too much land has been wasted for lawns that nobody uses and sidewalks on which nobody walks. Each base has its clubs, PX's, theaters, gymnasiums, libraries, etc., etc.

Blonde girls in bright red slacks drink American soft drinks on billboards; but the Okinawan countryside is a drier, more destitute version of Japan's, and Naha, the capital, looks like a Japanese town. Its modern evidences reflect not "Americanization" but Japanese modernism at one remove from Tokyo: the concrete banks, insurance companies, and newspaper offices look like those of Hamamatsu or Sendai, and the men working inside them have received their ideas of the modern world largely through Japanese-type schools and, in many cases, in universities in Japan.

The point is worth repeating: Okinawan nationalism hardly exists apart from Japanese nationalism. No doubt the Japanese had some difficulty in getting the Okinawans worked up over State Shintō, Emperor worship, and the rest of the prewar paraphernalia. Nevertheless, Okinawans served faithfully in the Japanese Army, the language of the islands is Japanese, and Japanese models of social and political behavior have had a decisive influence there. It is as a part of Japan that Okinawans have realized their political autonomy and felt their cultural identity in modern times. Small wonder that one young Okinawan intellectual should have exclaimed, "Our only choice is to co-operate with the Americans, who control us, or revert to Japan. There is no third course. We will co-operate because we must, but the only way to real freedom is reversion." Or, as another slightly older, more experienced Okinawan teacher put it, "Our sense of identity requires us to return to Japan. Otherwise we will be nothing in the outside world. Japan is a nation with its own autonomy, but we can never have real autonomy under the United States." As I have indicated, feelings concerning reversion are not as simple and clear-cut as these opinions suggest, but differences relate primarily to timing. Some Okinawans say, "Yes, and now"; others, "Yes, but not now"; still others, "Yes, much later"; and a few say, "Never." But nearly all agree that some day Okinawa must return to the "residual sovereignty" that America has said Japan still retains.

CHAPTER 29

BERLIN FROM JAPAN

August 1961

Those who believe that Japan has more than export merchandise, Zen Buddhism, and cherry blossoms to contribute to the improvement of human difficulties have a right to feel misgivings at the Japanese reaction to the Berlin crisis in midsummer 1961. They will hardly be surprised by the tendency to wish away trouble; but they will be discouraged by the failure of those in authority to explain to the people the real significance of the crisis or to show that they believe Japan can be in any way instrumental in its solution.

Foreign observers who were here during the Hungarian Revolution or the Chinese invasion of Tibet learned then, if they did not already know, that there is something unreal to the Japanese about crises they cannot see or emergencies half a world away. And in this summer's stifling heat, the worst in a decade, problems much nearer than Berlin are being ignored if they possibly can be. What engages most people is not the Cold War but escape to a cooler Japanese climate. Tokyo's frantic railway stations, Ueno, Shinjuku, and the rest, have never been so full of people, better dressed than they have been since World War II, off to the mountains or the seashore encumbered by a large assortment of amusement gear. The desire to deny that the Cold War concerns them or that they are part of it is strong; this feeling is sometimes called "neutralism" or "pacifism," but "noninvolvement" is perhaps closer to its essence. The press has long nourished this negative mood and fed upon it, and the government has been aware of it but has not done much to change it up to now.

On the level of national policy and national interest the conservative government has responded promptly and predictably to the tightening crisis. The alliance with the United States has been reaffirmed. Government and conservative party leaders were gratified by the important treatment given Prime Minister Ikeda during his American visit in June; since his return, and especially since President Kennedy's Berlin speech of July 25, the government has declared itself behind the Western position.

Even more prompt has been the reaction of Japanese officials and commentators to the statements of Soviet Deputy Premier Anastas Mikoyan during his visit to this country, which ended yesterday. Since the war Russians have competed with Koreans and Australians for the title of the people least esteemed by the Japanese, and Mikoyan did not raise their stock any by his visit. His performance was crude and heavy-handed. Ostensibly in Tokyo to open a Soviet trade fair, he was not here two hours before he had accused Japanese officials of aggressive intentions and threatened them with destruction unless American bases were removed and the Security Treaty with the United States abrogated. Foreign Minister Kosaka and others replied politely that Japan's ties with America were entirely defensive and quite unavoidable, given the present state of the world. They reminded Mikoyan that he said nothing about Russia's 1950 treaty with Communist China or the treaty of last month with North Korea. Nor did he mention Russia's entry into the war against Japan in 1945 in violation of a nonaggression treaty. The press accused Mikoyan of interfering in Japan's internal affairs—the worst of all offenses—and otherwise criticized his behavior. In a front-page story the *Tokyo Shimbun* on August 19 declared that by believing public opinion could again be inflamed through attacks on the Security Treaty, Mikoyan had fundamentally misunderstood the Japanese temper and misjudged the complex nature of last year's riots. The paper speculated that Russian diplomatic reporting from Tokyo must be very poor, indeed.

The government handled Mikoyan's ill-mannered threats with skill, but it continues to do little or nothing to interpret the distant Berlin crisis to the Japanese people or to increase their sense of involvement in a struggle between freedom and totalitarianism. At the Bank of Japan one official remarked that "the Japanese have grown accustomed to the idea that there can never be another war"; he had no thoughts about how the unaccustomed might be prevented from happening. Public education in foreign affairs is very weak, and the need for it is recognized only by a small group. On his return from America Prime Minister Ikeda was described as deeply disturbed by the seriousness of the crisis; however, he has given the people little indication that he thinks Japan might help to reduce it. Interference such as Mikoyan was guilty of brings a swift response, but there is little sense of common cause with other peoples. Two powerful members of the latest cabinet, Eisaku Satō and Ichirō Kōno, spoke out most capably when Mikoyan attacked the Security Treaty. In the pungent idiom of Japanese politics Kōno told Mikoyan that Japan, like it or not, was a member of America's "stable of wrestlers." On the other hand, these same politicians agreed in a press interview that it would not be wise to tell the people any more about Berlin than they already know.

The press, too, though quick to take issue with Mikoyan, has on the whole treated Berlin in a very oversimplified manner. It has seen the crisis there as an all-or-nothing affair. The burden of most editorials is that war cannot, must not come, but that it may very well come unless both sides throw down their arms in an attitude of sweet reasonableness. A few editors have found it hard to stomach the building of a concrete wall through the center of Berlin to choke off the flow of refugees from the East: the *Asahi* printed a deeply felt editorial deriding this evil action. Most papers, however, have seen the crisis primarily as a matter of American and Russian "face."

For example, *Tensei Jingo,* an anonymous column in the morning *Asahi* which is probably read by more people than any other column in the daily press, recently chided both sides for getting into a position from which neither could afford to retreat. Rather than attempting to explore the root causes of the crisis or to suggest possible avenues of compromise, the writer exclaimed that "there is no reason at all why peoples throughout the world, who are now living in peace, should be forced to commit suicide in a war over Berlin, a mere pinpoint on the map of the world." (At least one Japanese reader wrote, taking the columnist to task for calling Berlin a pinpoint and asking whether he would call Tokyo a pinpoint in similar circumstances. His letter was printed; but very few Japanese will admit that anything similar could happen to them.)

There are a number of reasons why the Japanese government has not gone beyond affirming its necessary ties with the United States. Conservative politicians and businessmen fear the effect of their statements on politics at home and on the position of Japan in Asia. Berlin is in Europe, and the government frequently asserts that it cannot influence European politics. It clearly wants and expects to influence Asian politics, but it is still weak militarily and apprehensive of the vast military forces and potential nuclear weapons of its continental Communist neighbor. So far it has shown little interest in joining in a treaty organization of non-Communist Asian states, though it aspires to leadership among such states. Nor is it prepared to launch an anti-Communist crusade in Asia, although it certainly is not pro-Communist.

At home the government is keenly aware of the mood of noninvolvement. Nuclear war is rejected with a sort of mind-click of revulsion by a people who have already experienced atomic death among themselves. A year ago the prestige of parliamentary institutions was damaged by violence arising from a foreign-policy issue and the clumsy way it was handled. Since then the government has diverted the people's attention to domestic economic concerns, but the basic lines of political division are drawn much as they were last summer. Not long ago, when I tried to discuss the Berlin crisis with a Socialist, I found myself facing the usual opposition arguments: the only proper foreign policy for Japan is neutralism, nonaggression pacts "guaranteed" by the major powers, and peaceful coexistence. My Socialist acquaintance held no brief for Mikoyan; but almost before I could get the words "freedom" and "justice" and "obligations to two million West Berliners" out of my mouth, he was throwing his soft reproaches back at me: "What do you mean by principles? What about Franco? What about Chiang Kai-shek? What about American support of the French in Indochina and Algeria? What about discrimination against African UN delegates in New York restaurants and hotels?" And we were off on what Albert Camus once called the process of "outrageous outbidding," from which little profit could be derived.

Among the Socialists there will have to be less willingness to resort to "people's movements" and demonstrations on foreign-policy issues, while the government will have to do more to educate the Japanese people in foreign problems before their full potential in the world can be felt. As it is, the tendency merely to turn away from the Berlin crisis or to see it in all-or-nothing terms, like the tendency to reduce the legislative process to fist fights and police riots, suggests the vein of extremism that lies under the mock-placid surface of Japanese life. It is this sense of living in a world of extremes, of Armageddon or the millennium tomorrow, instead of a world in which more people are searching for ways to improve the human mess, that is particularly discouraging to me in Japan today. The Japanese might not be able to do much about Berlin, but if they are doing anything it is not apparent to me. Instead, one is left with a feeling of being not at the operative center of things but far out on a hedonistic periphery, where the golf bags and the knapsacks clutter up the railway stations, the politicians posture and glower at one another, the press talks piously about "face," and most people are certain either that war is impossible or that it is inevitable, but at any rate certain.

September 12, 1961

In the first part of this Report, dated August 1961, on Japan's response to the Berlin crisis I noted that the government had reaffirmed its official support of the Western position but that most people here were disposed to ignore distant events and those in authority were not doing much to educate the public about the crisis or about foreign affairs generally.

In the few weeks since then Soviet renewal of nuclear testing has shocked the Japanese far more than Berlin itself, and fear of imminent war has rapidly increased. This has been evident in formal protests from the government and nongovernmental groups to both East and West. It has also been evident in one's personal encounters with Japanese: with the women who have come to the door holding up anti-bomb-test petitions to be signed, the first I have seen for several years, or the taxi drivers, those faulty but often garrulous sources of hearsay, who have complained that both sides are endangering humanity. As one of them shouted menacingly over his shoulder at me the other day, while we careened through Shimbashi, "Jesus Christ didn't stand for either right or left, did He?"

Beyond such chance encounters, since the Soviet and American announcements on testing, the big city press has been almost wholly diverted from its usual domestic concerns and preoccupied with the crisis outside. Much of its writing shows an awareness that Russia is responsible for provoking the present crisis; American good intentions in trying to avoid war are widely accepted, but this acceptance is overshadowed by an increasingly anxious call for both sides to talk to prevent catastrophe. Where assigning responsibility is concerned the major papers are not "neutral"; but in the more frightening matter of consequences they demand that the United States and Russia answer equally for the security of humanity. In the fulfillment of this imperative they do not see that America has any special claim to moral superiority over the Soviet Union. Facing Armageddon without significant arms, the Japanese editorial imagination can only join in appeals for a retreat from power politics.

For example, in recent days more than half of the *Asahi Shimbun*'s editorials have been given to the Berlin issue. On August 26 the paper criticized the latest Soviet move threatening interference with the Berlin air corridors and warned that "the East should think about American national feeling and realize that it is flirting with an extremely great danger. . . . We urge the East to consider that the measures it is taking are destroying the chances, one by one, for the mutual East-West talks, which the West is trying hard to find. . . ." On September 2 the *Asahi* recognized the American wish for peaceful solutions: "Just when the West was seeking a chance to hold talks, because of its fears over the heightening tension, the Soviet Union announced that the transfer to the reserve of noncommissioned servicemen whose term of service would end this year would be deferred . . . and when the chances for talks had thus been diverted the Soviet Union announced that it had decided to resume nuclear tests unilaterally." On September 5 the paper applauded the Kennedy-Macmillan appeal for suspension of atmospheric tests and concluded that "if the Soviet Union is sincerely interested in the welfare of mankind, we believe it should study this proposal in a constructive attitude and co-operate for the realization of a better agreement."

Nevertheless, while assigning the origin of the crisis to a deliberate Russian power play, the *Asahi*, like most other papers, deplored the American decision to resume testing and on September 8 endorsed the appeal of the Belgrade Conference of neutral nations for immediate East-West talks. The paper spoke for the Japanese people as a whole when it declared, "Every line of this appeal is marked by a deep fear and hate of the dangers of war which would lead the world to destruction."

I quote the *Asahi* because it is one of Japan's most distinguished newspapers and certainly its most literate one. Its editorial line has sometimes been the despair of those who value consistency—the only real consistency in modern Japanese journalism has been in constant attacks on the regime in power—but many of its editors are highly respected in Japan, where senior journalists have considerable intellectual standing. What these men say in print has a good deal to do with what the informed public of this literate nation thinks; their writings tend to mirror the public's prejudices. In the past what the *Asahi* has been pleased to print has not always been pleasing to the United States. Last year, before the Tokyo riots startled responsible editors and brought them to issue warnings against mass violence, the paper opposed the new Security Treaty with the United States and often carped at American policies. Since then its editorial line and some of its staff have changed; it now accepts the treaty, and its editorials have become much more moderate in tone.

Recently I had a private talk with one of the senior members of the *Asahi*'s editorial board, a man with over 25 years on the paper, whose writings are widely known and respected and who in many ways represents a sensitive register of educated Japanese opinion. This person, who wrote some, if not all, of the above editorials, expanded upon the views there expressed in a frank and earnest manner:

"Khrushchev doesn't want war, but he is trying to get all he can short of war. After that comes his peaceful coexistence. He is merely continuing the Russian expansionist nationalism that motivated Stalin, in later life at least, a reversal of the idea of 'socialism in one country.' Facing him is Kennedy, a young man but very cool. I like him, and his advisers also are coolheaded despite their youth. But I deplore two things: the awful ineptitude of American propaganda, and the chance of another uproar over American military bases in Japan. You still seem to think that all you need to do is to tell people that you are right and they will immediately agree with you. Your previous ambassador used to gather us newspapermen together at your embassy and lecture to us. 'Communism is bad, democracy is good,' he would say. 'Why do you criticize American bomb tests in the Pacific?' But does this sort of lecture make news? We sit in offices where the news pours in, and we have to take what is newsworthy and print it. Platitudes are not news.

"Many Japanese know that the Russians speak lies. Why don't you learn to refute these lies in ways that will get into the newspapers and be read by more people? Instead you keep repeating over and over your true, simple feelings, that you believe to be right but that finally sound rather flat, or else you issue inflammatory statements that match those of the Russians and agitate the Japanese people further. What you should do is keep quiet, build up your strength, and refute lies promptly and skillfully. For instance, most people know that it is not you who are threatening the Russians, but quite the reverse. But you don't refute this lie effectively enough. You know you are right, and you get propaganda mixed up with moral principles."

He went on to complain that American foreign aid was based on the notion that one could "buy democrats for dollars," and he urged more "realistic" aid polices and less moral righteousness: "If some country has a practical need for aid and comes to you for it, you ought to consider giving it to them; but this indiscriminate spending in the hope of converting people to your point of view is naïve in the extreme."

I told him I thought there were signs the new administration was trying to frame new policies that would offer American resources without requiring a complete identity of political views. I further said I thought he was criticizing certain American qualities and values that were very old and deep-rooted and that expressed themselves also in the realm of foreign affairs. I referred to the custom of American politicians of holding press conferences at which they issued pronouncements on many subjects, including foreign relations; and we agreed that in Japan such behavior by ordinary members of the Diet might bring reprimands or more severe disciplinary measures by party leaders.

In all this my editor revealed that, though he was distressed at the clumsiness of American actions, he still was friendly to America and its basic intentions. But when he began to talk about military bases, stronger emotions of fear and alarm were at once evident. I mentioned that the political situation in Japan seemed very quiet, and he agreed, but warned: "I have great anxiety over the future. The United States still has bases all over Japan, and if you try to bring missiles into this country in the next year or two, as I am afraid you will, then there will be another uproar. In case of war these bases will inevitably draw Communist attack, and they have already lost much of their strategic value. What the people want is for all bases to be withdrawn from the main islands of Japan and concentrated in Okinawa and the Bonins, which are really American-run territories."

I told him I believed this was a poor time to expect a pull-out of bases, though the Kennedy administration had promised an over-all study of the problem. The rest of our conversation rang the changes on this old theme, which grows and fades in the public's attention but never disappears from it entirely. Whether the introduction of missiles would provoke an uproar is debatable and would depend upon the circumstances of the moment. But for my editor, as for large numbers of Japanese, emotions generated from fear of nuclear war clearly made any life more important than what kind of life, and bases appeared to heighten the risk to all life. In this he was not being "anti-American," but he regarded himself as pro-Japanese (he seemed to care less what happened to Okinawa), and his remarks demonstrated again that while most Japanese prefer American intentions to Russian ones, they do not allow that Japan should, in their view, court nuclear annihilation for any reason whatever.

PART FOUR   ❁   ❁   ❁

THE NEW JAPAN

CHAPTER 30

A NOTE ON JAPAN

April 1962

Not far from my house in Tokyo the Meguro Automobile Driving School operates a training ground resembling a miniature golf course with asphalt fairways just wide enough for cars, where Japanese prepare for driver's license examinations. All day six days a week throughout the year applicants, some of them women and most of them young, thread their way round the tiny streets, stopping, starting, backing at model turns and intersections, repeating a kind of slow-motion mechanical ballet that contrasts sharply with the trucks, buses, and other vehicles roaring by at full throttle in the street outside. After a certain number of lessons they are allowed to venture into the maelstrom beyond the fence, accompanied by an instructor and equipped with a learner's license plate, and in due time they are graduated and released permanently into the traffic.

The driving course consists of 20 to 30 lessons of an hour each and is not cheap: each lesson costs 900 yen (US $2.50), but a course in such a school is normally required before would-be drivers can qualify for a license, and some applicants travel for long distances on packed city trains or subways to keep their appointments. The driving schools are not merely a big-city phenomenon but are found on the edges of nearly every town of any size throughout the country. After graduation many of the new drivers drive company cars, the little black Toyopets or Nissans with white cloth seat covers in which businessmen or officials ride; others drive delivery trucks, taxis, or miscellaneous smaller craft that dart through Tokyo's byways, dodging school children, telephone poles, potholes, and the enormous city buses that roll around like lumbering bears. Some own their own cars. For although the era of private car ownership has not fully arrived in Japan, it is on the way, and the learner-driver, paying for the privilege of a license so that he can add his exhaust fumes and parking problems to the rest, is a symbol, like the first used-car lots, of the stage urban life has reached in this country.

The three "sacred treasures" of traditional Japan were the mirror, the jewel, and the sword. In the 1950's these were replaced in the popular imagination by the television set, the washing machine, and the refrigerator. Today nearly 65 per cent of urban households owns a television set (30 per cent of rural households); 50 per cent has an electric washing machine (15 per cent of rural households). Relatively few possess refrigerators, but already there is a new trio of popular "treasures": the hi-fi set, the room cooler, and the family car. These dreams are advertised daily in millions of newspapers and magazines; for the vast majority they remain only wishes, and there are some Japanese who feel that in a country as crowded as this one the automobile might better have been prevented entirely. But more and more people are dreaming of owning one. If the roads are abominable, they will have to be improved somehow, along with all the other evils of industrial living. (If possible this should be done before 1964, when the Olympic Games will be held in Tokyo.) But in the meantime they have to be borne, for to do without the car or any of the other artifacts of industrialism is unimaginable. In this Japanese aspirations are not greatly different from those of millions of other Asians and Africans. What sets them apart is the stage they have achieved: try to imagine driving schools in India or China today, and the point becomes clear.

Economic progress in Japan since 1945 has hardly been matched anywhere. A whole people have picked themselves off the floor of defeat, rebuilt their cities, modernized their heavy industries (if not the relations between human beings in them), raised their agricultural output to far above prewar levels, and impressed a new generation of visitors with their exhausting but inexhaustible vitality.

For the first decade after surrender this recovery could be called postwar rebuilding. That period is now over, but even more spectacular growth has occurred since 1955. In part this was due to fortunate circumstances outside Japan. As world trade expanded the Japanese could secure abundant raw materials for processing and re-export. Foreign technology also was available to bring industrial know-how up to date after years of wartime isolation: of the more than 1,400 technical licensing agreements completed between Japanese and foreign firms since the war, nearly 1,000 were with Americans. Unusually bountiful rice crops reduced food import requirements to the lowest levels in many years. Equally important, however, were government policies encouraging high rates of savings and investment. Conservative leaders were determined that Japan should "catch up with the West" in the quickest possible time. One of the most characteristic sights in towns and cities today is the long banners hanging from banks and other public buildings urging people to save for a "stable future" and a "bright life." The people have responded to these calls; in 1960 Japanese saved over ten per cent of their disposable income, and instead of putting their money under mattresses or in low-yield savings deposits, more and more people bought securities; one in ten now owns stocks, and investment trusts are growing in popularity.

Backed by these savings and other financial resources, the government in the late 1950's and early 1960's encouraged basic private industries to invest heavily in new plant and equipment. While roads, schools, and public facilities generally remained inadequate, the major steel companies undertook ambitious modernization programs with the government's blessing; from less than 10 million tons in 1955, steel production rose to 28.5 million tons last year, fifth largest in the world. In 1961 oil refining capacity passed a million barrels a day, the world's third largest; and the petrochemical industry, which hardly existed five years ago, began to turn out many new products. Japan has paced the world's shipbuilding industry for a number of years; Japanese electronic equipment has gained and held a high reputation in world markets. The goals of Japan's leaders were evident from almost any reading of economic statistics. In the six years from 1955 to 1961 over-all manufacturing production tripled, but machinery manufacturing multiplied seven times, and certain other types of manufacturing, such as electrical appliances and vehicles rose even more rapidly. Electricity generation doubled. Investment begat investment; manufacturers not only expanded existing plants but built new ones, and economists adopted the Russian word *kombinat* to describe new clusters of interrelated industries built near each other on the same site. In 1960 private equipment investments were up nearly 30 per cent over the previous year, and officials responsible for the government's "double the national income" program were astonished to discover that investment targets for 1970 already approached completion in some fields.

By late 1960 this dynamic expansion had begun to slow down somewhat, though the rate of growth was still astonishingly high. Heavy import surpluses developed and the government was forced to take deflationary measures. A similar cycle had occurred in 1953 and 1957, but this time growth was so rapid that it could not be slowed at once merely by manipulating the money rate. New phenomena appeared which, like the driving schools, reflected a higher stage of economic development. For instance, some industries, such as electrical and chemical manufacturing, reported shortages of trained workers. Employment agencies which a few years before were not regarded with much favor by companies seeking new employees now had many more attractive openings; "help wanted" signs were as common in some places as "position wanted" ones; personnel sections of large firms began to bid against each other to secure new people, and managements of small companies found it harder to keep their workers. Fewer young men fresh from the provinces were willing to stay on as delivery boys for vegetable stalls or apprentice hands in tiny machine shops when they could earn more in larger modern plants. Many employers were forced to raise wages, although low wages had traditionally been the only way they could break even. The shortage of girls for menial tasks, the tea-pourers and water-sprinklers of Japanese offices, was especially noticeable. (The tea girls' new work often was no less monotonous than the old had been; the plight of the new tribe of business-machine key punchers has been taken up in the newspapers, and two months ago one such girl jumped off a Tokyo building in protest against her unchanging routine.) The labor shortage is not yet general, and the total work force will rise more rapidly in the next year or two when children born during the "baby boom" of 1947–48 become old enough for legal employment; but a trend toward higher wages is quite evident today— industrial wages have risen nearly 50 per cent in the last seven years— and is accompanied by a gradual decline in rural reservoirs of labor.

The combination of higher wages and labor scarcities in some fields has meant higher prices. Japanese who have traveled abroad for more than a brief period invariably complain of price rises on their return. For example, the supply of meat and dairy products cannot keep up with big-city demand in this era of changing food tastes. Haircuts that used to cost fifty cents now cost sixty; public baths have gone up from five to seven cents, streetcar fares from four cents to a nickel. Here again one can see only the beginning of a trend. Total productivity still is running well ahead of wage and consumption increases, and inflation is not an imminent threat. But the government, as always in this narrow, overcrowded land, must once again impress on its people the necessity for raising exports and otherwise try to reduce demand and control the rate of economic expansion.

These observations relate to cities, and although around 30 per cent of the work force still is engaged in agriculture, the urbanization process continues at a rapid pace. More than one Japanese in ten live in Tokyo, and a third of the population is concentrated in the four great industrial nodes on the Pacific shore from Tokyo south to Kyushu. Large numbers of these "city" residents are recent migrants from the countryside—on an average day between 400 and 500 arrive in Tokyo —and the cities to which they move resemble small towns infinitely extended and with their garishness magnified. Urban consciousness in the classical sense is very weak; "public-spiritedness" hardly exists, and although its absence is often deplored by Western-oriented Japanese, most people are less concerned with "civic" or national duties than with fulfilling their obligations within the local hierarchies that make up the living tissue of Japanese society: the family, the workplace, the school, and so on.

In the cities, and in the villages, too, birth, death, and infant-mortality rates are low and life expectancies Western. In 1960 tuberculosis accounted for less than five per cent of all Japanese deaths; the main causes were cerebral hemorrhage, cancer, and heart disease, in that order. Literacy is universal or nearly so, and a web of mass communications covers the entire country. Everyone from six to fifteen is in school or is supposed to be; truancy is almost unheard of, because to study hard is an axiom of society and the reach of a man's career is largely determined by the level of education he achieves. The school entrance examination system imposes a heavy burden on young men and increases their nervousness and rigidity; however, it is at least based on the idea of merit and is not notably corrupt. The sons of the well-to-do tend to get into good universities, but some fail; conversely, the poor but bright boy has some chance to rise if he applies himself. Performance counts, though it is usually performance to match the conventional criteria of the herd that is desired, not the flowering of individual talents that might help raise the level of all. "Egoism" is regarded, at least in theory, as a vice, order and harmony as primary ideals.

Japanese city dwellers have their characteristically modern diversions along with traditional ones. This year the "leisure boom" is in full swing; four million people went skiing last winter, large numbers of them taking planes as far as Hokkaidō to indulge in this popular sport. Millions more made for the golf courses, watched *sumo* on TV, played *go*, or listened to jazz in coffeehouses. Wherever they sought amusement they were faced with some somber problems. When I hear the phrase "the Japanese people," I think not of farmers in their fields, or country crowds gathered for local occasions, but of the dark blue-black waves of commuters surging through the catacomblike railway stations of Tokyo and these same "salary-men" and their wives or sweethearts milling around the Ginza and other shopping areas on weekends. If a great many of these people achieve automobiles, where can they possibly put them? The newspapers already predict complete traffic paralysis in a few years, and the city fathers pass law after law, none of which they enforce, to bring order to the streets. One Japanese writer not long ago suggested half-seriously that the Japanese as a race are unfit to drive cars; their driving habits are, he thought, merely another symptom of mass hysteria.

If my description has a certain shrillness, this is not surprising, for these dark cities are marred by ugliness and life in them has some nightmarish strains for Japanese and foreigners alike. One can only plunge in, but this entails penalties; e.g., guards on the Chūō Line, which bisects Tokyo on the west, each day collect boxes full of buttons and the broken and torn apparel of commuters. For a long time "pushers" have been hired to shove people into coaches so that the automatic doors can close. Now there is talk of "pullers" to extract those whom the "pushers" are unable to wedge in more than part way. Streets are wildernesses full of holes, blocked by interminable construction of sewers, subways, and other evidences of progress. Long stretches of roadway have been dug up and replaced by temporary wooden platforms over which cars must be driven. Sidewalks hardly exist, and pedestrians who pick their way through the streets are likely to be run down for their pains; hit-and-run accidents are common, and victims often can expect nothing but token compensation for their injuries.

Among the new urban phenomena are the *danchi* dwellers, families who live in public apartment "developments," some consisting of a dozen or more buildings. Like the driving schools, these are not found only in Tokyo, but they have had their greatest growth here. Living space in the *danchi* is miniature; a family of four may pay $20 a month for three tiny rooms (e.g., 9′ x 12′, 9′ x 9′, 9′ x 9′) plus a kitchen alcove, toilet, and small bath. Smaller families have less space. Friends of mine moved not long ago to such an apartment, where they live with their two small boys. The husband is a newspaperman who translates on the side—he put Pasternak's autobiography into Japanese. He commutes long distances to work while his wife, a women's college graduate, stays at home and peers through a peephole in the door at neighbors who call or delivery boys who come to take orders for food. The latter are not as common as they were, however; nowadays she often shops at the "supermarket" which has opened down the street.

When I first met these people several years ago they were living in miserable circumstances in a rented house. Today their material situation has improved, but they live in almost total isolation from their neighbors. Residents of the *danchi* have started various formal organizations, as is their custom—the women's club, the self-government association, and so on—but my friends take no interest in any of them. Their in-laws live elsewhere and they would not have it differently. They have no desire to reject the independence that their style of life gives them; rather they are jealous of it, but they do not feel a part of anything larger than the "nuclear" unit of themselves and their children and so are turned in constantly upon themselves. The husband finds some variety with his colleagues at the office; his wife, groping in her own way for something to belong to, has joined a religious sect called the Sōkagakkai, a militant offshoot of Nichiren Buddhism, very conservative and antilabor, which has become prominent since World War II.

Things have "settled down" for my friends; they are clothed, fed, housed, and gadgeted, but like most of their fellows they are anxious; they worry a good deal about nuclear fall-out and war and are not really comfortable: the tenant in the apartment overhead comes home drunk nearly every night and fights with his wife; the people across the way object to the noise of piano practice. My friends are not members of a disaffected, unemployed intelligentsia; Japan has very few unemployed intellectuals, though it has many underpaid ones. However, like many, many others, they are a rather dispirited pair. They accept government above them but do not know what its goals are and are not fired by its slogans or programs. Politics forms almost no part of their daily conversation; the sense of personal participation, the notion that "I with my vote" can change things for the better, is not really developed at all. They wait and complain rather than organize to throw the rascals out. Although they could not imagine being anything but Japanese, they do not belong to anything larger than their small family.

*　*　*

Those who govern are members of a relatively small elite composed of top businessmen, high officials, and elected politicians. These men do not constitute an aristocracy of birth, but their educational backgrounds and social ideals are remarkably uniform. Most had established careers in the prewar period; men born and educated since the war obviously are not old enough yet to participate in power. However, though the spirit of parliamentarianism is frail and government in Japan still largely "received," party politics has become a habit for rulers and ruled alike, and today's civilian leaders show no signs of wishing to cashier themselves by catering to the ambitions of military careerists or others who may be impatient with elective processes. The longer the careers of the most able men can find fulfillment within a parliamentary framework—albeit one with a strong Japanese flavor—the greater is the chance that these Western-modeled institutions will endure.

Ever since 1945 Japan's conservatives have had to contend with some peculiar difficulties. They represent a tradition of civilian control that failed once before; hence, they are suspect to large numbers of people who regard them and their policies with cynicism. Opposite them stands a Marxist Socialist party whose tactics of obstruction and violence have sorely tried the patience of even the most "liberal" of conservative leaders. Tied to America for their economic and military salvation, constricted by a Constitution that expressly forbids rearmament, and weakened by factional rivalries, the conservative elite has found it difficult to shape a new set of nationalist goals that might replace the shattered symbols of Japan's prewar "greatness" in the popular imagination.

During the administration of Prime Minister Kishi (1958–60) conservative frustration showed itself constantly at the surface of politics. The government could count on the support of the overwhelmingly conservative farmers, the business community, and most of the older generation of middle-class voters in towns and cities. But Kishi himself had figured in Japanese expansion on the continent and held cabinet rank in wartime. His impatience with the niceties of parliamentary procedure was shared by many of his colleagues, and when in 1960 their stiff-necked tactics were met by riots and violence on the left, public confidence in party politics fell to the lowest point since the war.

The present Prime Minister, Hayato Ikeda, though hardly a "new man" in any sense of the term, has had the wit and the luck to turn the attention of the people from political struggles to economic improvement. By slogans and plans for economic growth he and his colleagues have sought to take away the appeals of Socialist programs. Long-range conservative goals have not greatly changed since Kishi's day, but there is a noticeable lull in the atmosphere of reaction against Occupation reforms, the "reverse course" of a few years ago. Ikeda has shown himself to be more flexible and in tune with the times than Kishi was, and he has held to a relatively unbelligerent posture toward the Socialists, even in the face of criticism within his own party. In public, at least, he has repeatedly denied that he seeks to revise the postwar Constitution; in private conservative leaders now stress that public opinion must be carefully "prepared" for such revision, but there is general agreement that this may require a long period of time.

Ikeda has refrained where possible from forcing measures through the Diet on the sheer strength of his party's absolute majority. During his administration a cancerous coal strike has been settled and some progress made in public housing, health, and old-age annuity schemes to give a measure of reality to conservative welfare state slogans. At the same time, of course, the government is confronted with a host of new problems: exploding land prices, inequities of income from area to area and between agriculture and industry, shortages of industrial water, and the like.

The confrontation of conservatives and Socialists is dramatic, but the two parties should be seen as occupying the very broad center of politics, not its edges. The far-left Communist fringe has made some gains since the Security Treaty riots of 1960, yet its influence in politics remains minor. Communism in Japan has against it the liability of open subservience to alien ends, and the party is riven by internal factionalism. The Communists are not likely to come to power from the inside, and it is hard to see how they could prevail from the outside without provoking a world war.

On the far-right fringe there have been some disturbing developments in the last two years, most of them in reaction to leftist violence. Many sorts of rightist organizations exist, feeding on a tradition of elitist violence that goes back a very long way. Some are mere expressions of nostalgia for the supposed good old days; they appeal to ancient notions of racial unity and purity which are still strong. Others are action groups, more or less gangsterish in composition, organized along paramilitary lines. Nearly all such groups are small and fragmented and their goals appear anachronistic to the vast majority of Japanese who, whatever they may lack, do not wish to return to the ugly past to find it. The capacity of these fanatical bands to disrupt politics should not be underestimated; since 1960 Japan has seen attempts on the lives of two Prime Ministers, the assassination of a Socialist chairman, and a wild attack on the home of a prominent magazine publisher who printed a short story describing the decapitation of members of the Imperial Family. It is well known that some conservative businessmen and politicians give financial support to such groups. Ties also exist on a personal basis between right-wing extremists and members of the new Self-Defense Forces; but the military failed completely to respond to calls for support of an abortive *coup* last December, and the Ikeda government, sensitive to the charge of supporting "fascism," has clamped down as promptly on rightist activities as it has on leftist. The government continues to support the new legal guarantees of civilian control over the military. In the broadest sense, as I have indicated, most careers now find their fulfillment within a context of elected institutions; as long as this is true, those at the center of power are not likely to be tempted to turn to the far right, while by itself the right wing can disrupt but lacks the power to overthrow.

In foreign relations Ikeda has held firm to the alliance with the

United States that has been at the base of conservative foreign policy ever since the war. The Japanese may not particularly care for Americans, but they care for Russians even less. Conservative policy reflects Japan's heavy dependence on America as its principal trading partner: a quarter of all exports are sold in the United States and over a third of imports originate there. Alignment with the United States also involves rearmament with American guidance, military treaties and bases, all of which open the conservatives to constant Socialist accusations of pandering to American "imperialist" policies. The Ikeda government is only too keenly aware of this old difficulty and seeks in many ways to mitigate Socialist charges: by taking the lead itself in protests against nuclear tests, by denying permission to bring nuclear weapons into the country, or by pressing for the return of Japanese hegemony over Okinawa, a nationalist symbol of considerable potency however little most Japanese may know or care about the place.

While they cleave to the United States, conservative leaders would, of course, like to think that the Cold War will not last forever; present policy requirements do not necessarily coincide with their long-range hopes for more independence and positive power in international affairs. Today Ikeda is able to say that the United States cannot do without Japan in the Far East. However, from a Japanese point of view, this is an essentially negative assertion, and there is an element of waiting in the attitudes of those charged with foreign policy formulation. Ikeda admits no thought of recognition of Communist China and follows the American lead on the China issue in the United Nations, but he repeats Kishi's statements concerning Japan's willingness to trade with China, while down at his Ōiso villa former Prime Minister Yoshida, the high priest of the Establishment, assures visitors that Japan and China "must" renew relations some day; their differences are "merely political" and will eventually disappear.

Toward the rest of Asia, too, Ikeda and his advisers hold uncertain attitudes. Some agree with Yoshida who, in speaking of Southeast Asia, once said, "You have to trade with rich men; you can't trade with beggars." Others are more conscious, perhaps, that Japan's well-being is linked to that of Asia as a whole; they would like to see more Japanese aid sent to the area to help raise living standards and purchasing power. Nearly all Japanese, leaders or led, are ignorant of actual conditions outside Japan. Like most Americans they believe a unity exists in Asia where there is none. The government is not yet sure of the wisest way for Japan to relate itself to the "underdeveloped" world. So far it has limited itself to bilateral agreements for aid and trade; the official imagination has not ventured far beyond the range of export promotion. Japan participates in the Colombo Plan and in United Nations organizations like the Economic Commission for Asia and the Far East (ECAFE) but hesitates to cast its lot with any regional grouping, either of the anti-Communist or neutralist variety.

Elsewhere in Asia there is evidence of Japanese hesitation. Talks have been going on for years with South Korea, and the United States has urged a settlement of issues between the two countries left over from the war and the era of Japanese colonial rule. But the Ikeda government shows few signs of being prepared to restore relations and recognize South Korea as the legal government in the peninsula. Partly this is because of virulent Socialist opposition to any South Korean regime; partly it is because the government itself has qualms about the military junta in Seoul and does not wish to provoke Peking and Moscow at this time.

The opposition Socialist party continues to be dominated by men who accepted a Marxist interpretation of Japan's modern history in their youth. Like the conservatives they are very much the product of their prewar past; Japanese politics retains a strong flavor of personal factionalism and clique rivalries that go back 40 years. Political forms are Western, but Socialist politicians are as far removed from the masses of the people as the conservatives are.

Some Socialists originally were Communists, but most led movements of workers and peasants that rejected formal Communist party control while espousing a view of society that added up to national communism. In contrast to European Socialists, therefore, their attitude toward communism is very vague; they try to remain theoretically distinct but regard Japanese capitalism as their primary enemy. To them the Communists are merely rivals for the affection and loyalty of the people. They are fascinated by mass movements and continually wonder how they can whip up something that might be big enough to ruin the conservatives and bring on the revolution. In 1960 they were able to bring down Kishi—with Communist help and the help of a public grievance. But the people turned right around and voted for the conservative Ikeda. The revolution is not yet; however, many Socialists believe it cannot be brought to pass solely by parliamentary means, and their view of the Diet's role remains very ambiguous.

The Socialist party is badly split into factions, but nearly all the top leaders spent time in jail for political activities or "dangerous thoughts" before World War II. Although the party has been free to organize since 1945, its paid membership is no more than 60,000, and Socialist representation is weak in local municipal and prefectural elected bodies. Yet the party regularly wins one-third of the votes in national elections and holds, in conjunction with the small right-wing Democratic Socialists, a third of the seats in each house of the national Diet. The Socialist party depends for its voting strength on organized labor (35 per cent of the industrial labor force is organized and the percentage is increasing) and a large but unpredictable floating vote of youth, intellectuals, white-collar workers, and other city dwellers. Socialists are stronger in the cities than in rural areas, and with cities growing their total vote can be expected to increase, as it has gradually in the last four elections. However, eight million votes still separate the two parties, and how to surpass the "wall of one-third" is the Socialists' perennial dilemma.

Up to now the Socialists have preferred to exploit emotional foreign policy issues and cash in on conservative blunders rather than stress any very concrete alternatives to conservative domestic programs. When rationalization and automation cost miners and some others their jobs in the late 1950's, the Socialists and their Sōhyō labor federation supporters accused the government of a capitalist plot and organized "struggles" to fight it. Since the Miike strike in 1959–60 the Sōhyō unions have quieted down somewhat and put more effort into raising wages and reducing working hours. Union evolution may eventually change the party's militant Marxist stand; but Sōhyō leaders themselves are strongly Marxist in orientation and threaten new "struggles" against import liberalization, repayment of Japan's debts for postwar aid from the United States, settlement of diplomatic relations with South Korea, and any other matters on which the left can appeal to nationalist feelings and profess to find American imperialism in league with Japanese monopoly capital. Indeed, the first article of their faith often seems to be *zettai hantai*, absolute opposition. They know that the people yearn unceasingly for peace and noninvolvement, and that American bases are a continual reminder of Japan's vulnerability to nuclear attack. They are aware that many Japanese besides Yoshida think their isolation from China is unnatural and cannot endure forever. It is easy for them to find America responsible for all these abnormal circumstances and the alliance with the United States degrading to Japan's national independence. Appeals to national pride and xenophobia have been a Socialist stock in trade for years.

However, when they bring their Marxist theories into the open and allow theoretical differences to divert them from popular grievances, legitimate or otherwise, which are available for them to exploit, the Socialists go astray. Once they get hold of a good thing they seem unable to avoid running to extremes with it, turning public opinion against them, and losing the trust of many of the people they seek to attract and use. This was true in the 1960 riots, when the action of Socialist leaders in inciting mob violence caused a sudden falling away of their support in the press and public. A more recent instance was the Socialist mission to Peking in January of this year, undertaken after much hesitation by the party.

A 1959 mission to China had resulted in the notorious remark of Socialist Chairman Asanuma to the effect that American imperialism was the "common enemy" of Japan and Communist China. This offended many newspaper editors and others who, however much they may wish to be spared American bases, do not regard America as their enemy. Asanuma's statement was used by the conservatives to show that the Socialists were subservient to Peking. Before another mission was dispatched to discuss Japanese-Chinese relations the Socialists received word from Peking that they would not be expected to reaffirm the Asanuma statement; yet, when the joint communiqué was issued, it was found to contain an explicit endorsement of the view that American imperialism was the prime enemy of both countries, and the Japanese public again received the impression that the Socialists had given in completely to whatever the Chinese wanted to put into their mouths. The Socialists claim that such episodes do them no harm in elections, but neither do they serve to increase confidence in their political acumen or negotiating ability; rather the opinion is reinforced that such an inept, doctrinaire group could not discharge the responsibilities of governing and must remain forever in the political wilderness beyond the "wall of one-third."

The implications of their position are disturbing to some Socialist party members as well as to commentators who wring their hands over the parlous state of democracy in Japan. But the attempts of a few relatively young Socialist politicians to widen their voter appeal and come to power reveal the party predicament very clearly.

Take, for example, the case of Saburō Eda, present Secretary-General of the party, at fifty-five one of the most ambitious politicians of the Japanese left. Eda grew up in simple circumstances in rural Okayama prefecture and just after World War I was sent to live with an older sister in Korea, where he attended school with both Japanese and Korean children and reacted strongly against the oppressive policies of the Japanese colonial administration. In the early 1920's he went to commercial higher school in Kobe; there he read Marxist literature as well as the writings of such "humanists" as Mushakōji and Arishima and heard lectures by early Communists and other pioneers of the "social movement." By 1930 he was a confirmed member of the "Labor-Farmer" (Rōnōha) faction of Japanese Marxism and worked during the depression leading tenant farmers in "struggles" against landlords in his old home territory in Okayama. During this period he spent over three years in jail. When World War II came he worked for a time as a funeral-parlor director—a despised vocation—and later managed an auto-repair shop. In 1943 the Tōjō government sent him to China as an "adviser" on agricultural problems—a euphemism for exile. (Others of his leftist colleagues fared worse: many were sent to Southeast Asia, where they died of disease.) After the war Eda emerged as a member of the left-wing Socialist party and rose through a series of party posts. He came to national prominence in 1960 after the strong figure of Asanuma was blotted from the scene by an assassin.

Eda's career reflects the confused background of many Japanese leftists, but what is remarkable is that in the last two or three years he has shown that he possesses certain assets very valuable to a politician in the new age of mass communications. He is thought to be handsome, with a shock of snow-white hair and big, intellectual-looking eyes behind owlish spectacles. His smooth manner has made a hit on television, and he is known as a "madam-killer" in the popular press. These timely qualities plus his long experience in party organizational work have led some people to see in him the Socialist hope of the future.

Eda knows that up to a point he projects the image of a "new man" and he carefully tends this image, half believing in it himself. He is still as much a Marxist as he ever was, but he is a politician seeking power in an age when parties are powerful, not a professor waging class war from an academic fortress. For several years he has worked to strengthen party organization and membership, setting up party councils in unions where Communist cells had hitherto had no competition and starting discussion groups in unions where no Socialist or Communist organizations were known to exist. He and his group also feel that such organizations as the Council Against Atomic and Hydrogen Bombs (Gensuikyō) have become too openly Communist-dominated, and he has tried to increase Socialist influence in this and other front groups.

In addition to these activities, which have had a very indifferent success, Eda has tried since 1959 to introduce a new line called "structural reform" and make this the party's fundamental strategy. Based to some extent on theories of the Italian Communists, the new line calls for a step-by-step challenge to capitalism and its gradual replacement by socialism through the combined pressure of people's movements and specific programs of Diet action to give the people an alternative to the conservative platform. So far "structural reform" has been little more than a phrase. Theoretical purists like Professor Itsurō Sakisaka have jumped on it and called it revisionism and other vile names. Eda's response to Sakisaka reveals his dilemma, which is the dilemma of any Japanese Socialist who would challenge the authority of the party's prevailing theorists. He calls Sakisaka "a good Marxist emotionally" but claims his Marxism is too rigid: "If Hitoshi Yamakawa [original leader of Rōnōha Marxists] were alive today, he would say that my policies are true and correct." No matter what change he proposes, Eda must claim the sanction of Marxist orthodoxy and make his claim stick. His ability to do this is doubtful; the Central Committee of the party has not yet accepted "structural reform" as basic party strategy.

I have dwelt on these Socialist problems in some detail because they help to illustrate why so little trust exists in Japanese politics today. Extremism waits to show itself in new issues; the conservatives live constantly under pressure to avoid mistakes that could cause new flare-ups, but the Socialist hope of actually coming to power from conservative errors alone is very dim. Meanwhile, the masses of ordinary Japanese are tempted to conclude, like my friends in the *danchi*, that neither party is very attractive or worth believing in.

* * *

The Japanese have abundantly what D. H. Lawrence nearly 40 years ago called the "peace-and-production hope of the world." Lawrence was writing about Germany in the early 1920's, in a dark period of inflation and the failure of democracy, and he felt deeply the danger of what he thought was coming:

Not that the people are actually planning or plotting or preparing. . . . But something has happened to the human soul, beyond all help. The human soul recoiling now from unison, and making itself strong elsewhere. The ancient spirit of prehistoric Germany coming back, at the end of history. . . . These queer gangs of Young Socialists, youths and girls, with their non-materialistic professions, their half-mystic assertions, they strike one as strange. Something primitive, like loose, roving gangs of broken, scattered tribes, so they affect one. And the swarms of people somehow produce an impression of silence, of secrecy, of stealth. . . . The old habits remain. But the bulk of the people have no money. And the whole stream of feeling is reversed.[1]

No serious observer of Japan today would compare this country with Germany in 1924. Unemployment is at its lowest level since the war. In the last few years there has been a clear growth of confidence in the nation's ability to progress in the economic sphere. One still hears talk of "poor Japan," some of it justified. Foreign things are more welcome than foreigners; democracy and individual rights are slogans to which few rally with much fervor. But elected institutions in their Japanese incarnation are not crumbling away and being replaced by primitive racist fascism. The temper of the people is conservative but not reactionary. The base of economic discontent that would create the sort of public sympathy for ultranationalism that existed in the 1930's does not exist today.

Of course, the view is very limited that sees only economic improvement and ignores the weakness of parliamentary institutions and the low threshold of tolerance in this dynamic society. What we have in Japan, I repeat, is a confrontation of entrenched conservatives whose

[1] Lawrence, D. H. "A Letter from Germany." Reprinted in *Selected Essays*. (London: Penguin Books, 1950.)

social outlook tends to be unified but whose methods are *ad hoc* and unsystematic, and Marxian Socialists chronically out of power. Neither side inspires deep trust among the people. In a country with a long tradition of direct action and much unfocused national feeling this makes for insecurity and a sense of impermanence in politics. Certainly there is something frightening about these stony-faced university students screaming against American imperialism and urinating on the gates of the Japanese Diet. Their misconceptions of America are profound and are nourished by professors and other adults, some of whom have been in the West but who regard American life, in particular, as crude and exploitative. Ideological hatred is mixed with pride and feelings of inferiority in their minds. One newspaper recently reported that 80 per cent of university students it questioned thought America imperialistic, as compared with 50 per cent who believed Russia to be the same.

Most of these boys are not Communists; ask them what they want most and they will answer a steady job and a quiet life, and nearly all will get the former, as long as prosperity continues. They cannot be compared with the gangs Lawrence saw; not today, at any rate. But because Japan is definitely aligned with America, it is Americans who must bear the brunt of resentment at Japanese involvement in the Cold War. Russia is distrusted, but Russia has no bases here, no firing ranges, no security treaties. Much of the trouble is ignorance: when the head of the largest Japanese labor federation is quoted in Moscow as saying that Soviet labor is the freest in the world, nobody protests the statement in Tokyo.

At base Japanese leaders are more concerned with national power than public welfare. Public investment lags behind private, and many are the discomforts and inequities of Japanese life. But far more than anywhere else in Asia, Japan has emerged from "Asian" levels of living. Today's leaders leave much to be desired, but they are relatively enlightened; their "progressive conservatism" is not entirely disingenuous. Although the government is rather colorless, it is neither idle nor corrupt. Instead of extremes of left or right, neither of which most people want, it offers economic progress and much better material conditions for the great majority of the people. Meanwhile, it seeks, somewhat more dubiously, to combat apathy and delinquency by shifting from progressive education in the schools to greater emphasis on sober values of order, patriotism, and discipline. It rearms slowly, abjuring military adventures of any sort; in view of the changed balance of power in Asia this is a realistic policy, to say the least; but Japan's civilian leaders show no signs of trying to resurrect the collapsed symbols of Japanese militarism. Rather they hope that a "sound" new generation, purged of the more dangerous "excesses" of the American Occupation period, will continue to restore this non-Communist, conservative country to a position of trust and trade with as wide a world as possible.

A

The AUFS Reports Service, which first published the essays collected in *Dimensions of Japan*, is one of the several program activities of the American Universities Field Staff.

Established as a nonprofit corporation in 1951 by a group of universities and colleges to undertake a new approach to the study of foreign societies, the American Universities Field Staff functions as an academic foreign service. Staff members live in foreign areas with which they are thoroughly familiar to report firsthand on significant developments. Periodically, they return to the United States, where they serve as visiting faculty on campuses of the sponsoring colleges and universities. They lecture to classes, hold seminars, participate in faculty roundtables, advise students, and are available as consultants to teachers and administrators.

The AUFS Reports from abroad were at first distributed only to the academic institutions that sponsor and help to support the Field Staff program. The usefulness of the Reports as authoritative source material on political, economic, and social trends in Asia, Africa, Latin America, and (to a limited extent) Europe brought such favorable comment that the AUFS Reports Service was instituted.

The Reports now go to a steadily growing list of subscribers among colleges outside the AUFS membership, libraries, organizations interested in international affairs, business firms, newspapers, secondary schools, and individuals who have a professional or personal interest in foreign affairs.

For details about the AUFS Reports Service, write to:
American Universities Field Staff, Inc.
366 Madison Avenue, New York 17, N.Y.

DATE DUE

JUL 3 '84			
MY 13 '84			
GAYLORD			PRINTED IN U.S.A.